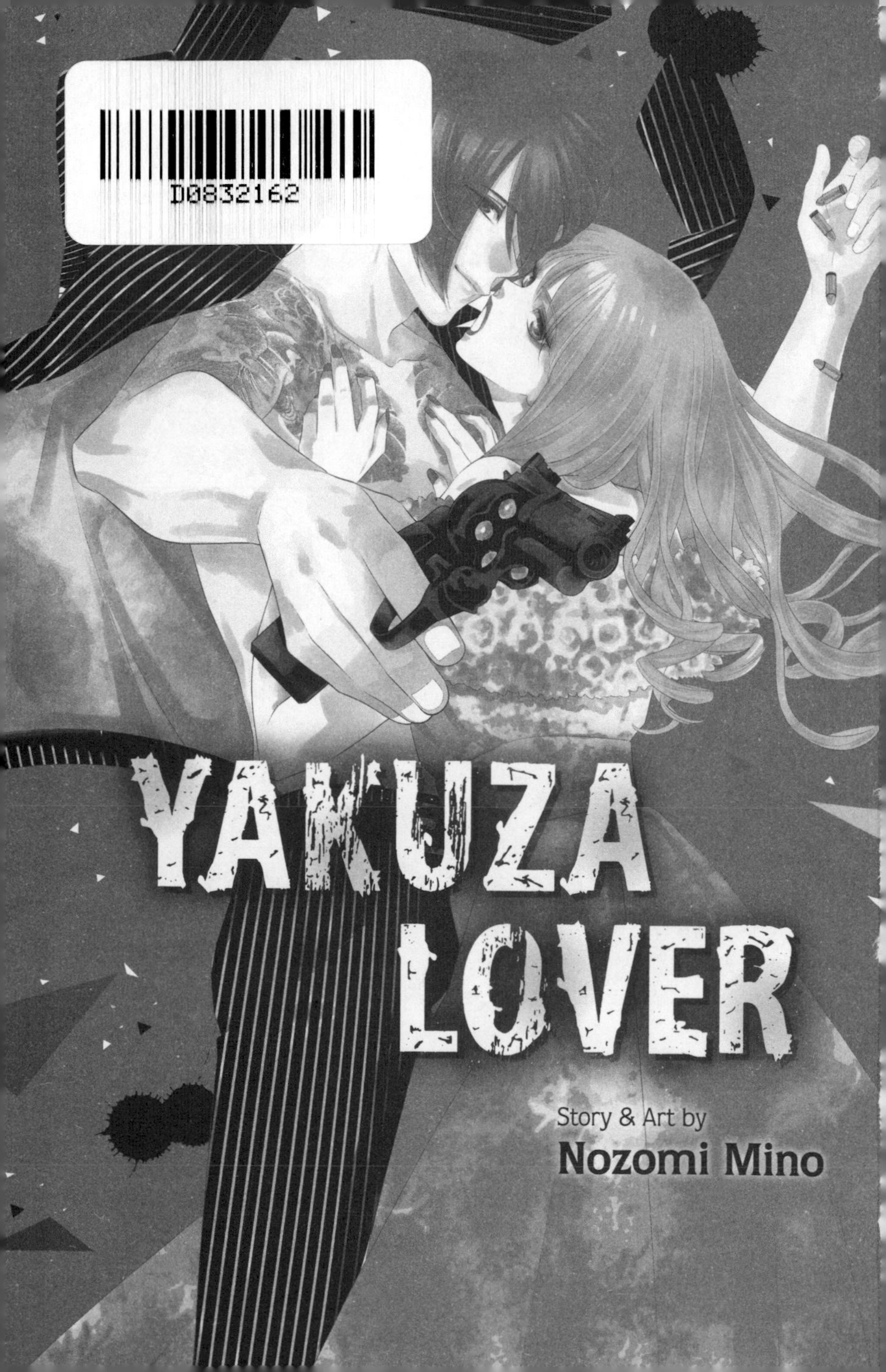
YAKUZA LOVER
Story & Art by
Nozomi Mino

Contents

Characters

Toshiomi Oya
Underboss

Underboss of the Oya yakuza syndicate. He's a gentle man with a heart of gold—yet no mobster would dare defy him. He's drawn to Yuri's inner strength.

Yuri
College Student

A college student with a strong sense of integrity who cares deeply about her friends. After an assassination attempt against Oya, she realizes she's going to need to be stronger to survive as the lover of a yakuza.

Story

Feisty college student Yuri's life is turned upside down when drug dealers attack her at a party and Toshiomi Oya, the underboss of a yakuza syndicate, swoops in to save her.

Toshiomi lives life on the edge with no promise of tomorrow, and Yuri finds herself swept up in their passionate, all-consuming love affair. But after being attacked by Russion mob boss Semilio, Yuri vows to get stronger in order to not cause any more trouble for Oya.

Choko, a hostess obsessed with Oya, sets a cowardly trap for Yuri in her quest to make the underboss hers. But Yuri keeps her wits about her and escapes unscathed. After learning about Choko's plot, Oya mercilessly cuts ties with the hostess, but not before she drugs him with a strong aphrodisiac. Oya is raging with passion and hurries to be with his beloved Yuri...

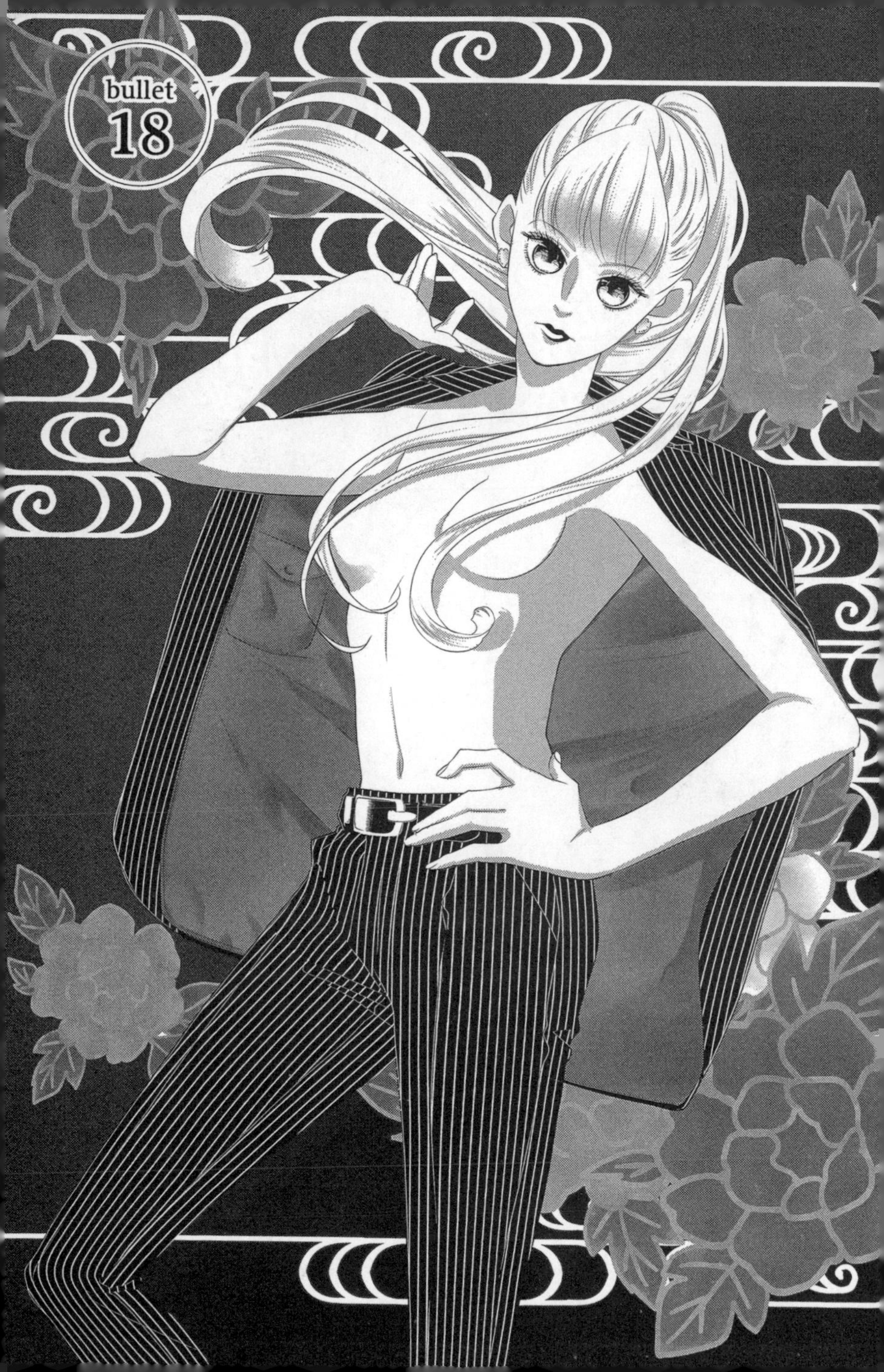
bullet
18

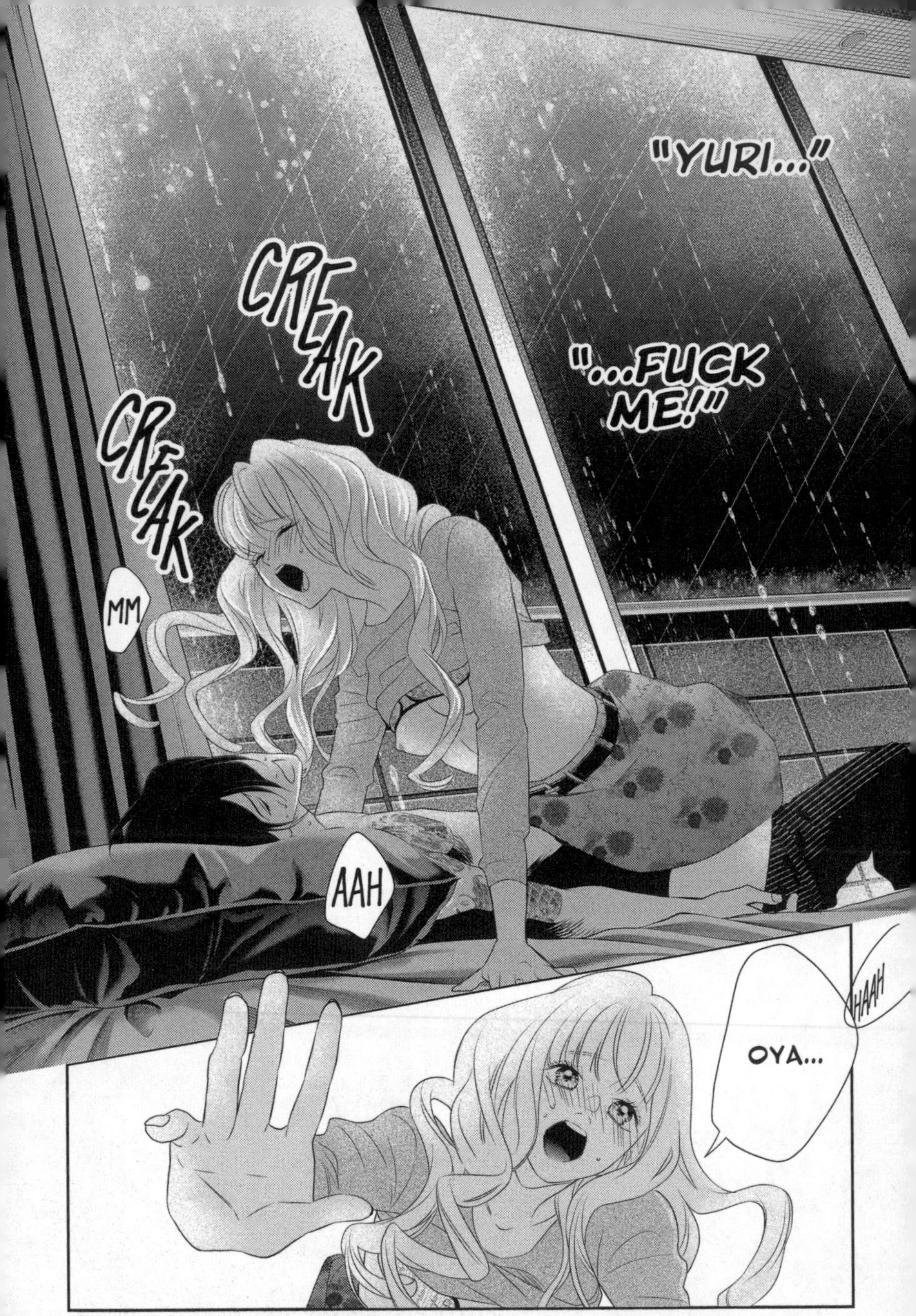
"YURI..."
"...FUCK ME!"
CREAK
CREAK
MM
AAH
HAAAH
OYA...

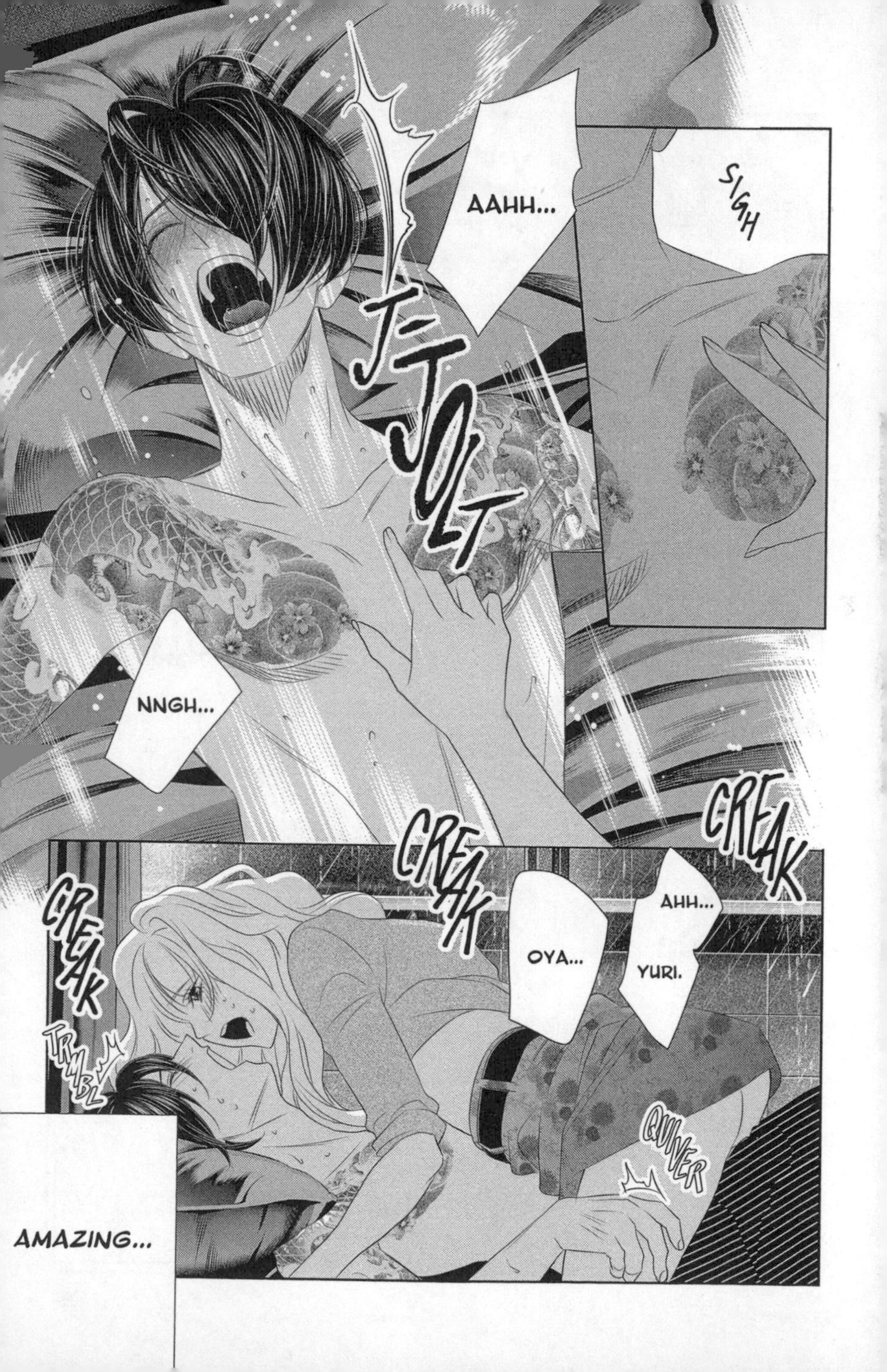
SIGH
AAHH...
J-JOLT
NNGH...
CREAK
AHH... YURI.
OYA...
CREAK
CREAK
QUIVER
TRMBL
AMAZING...

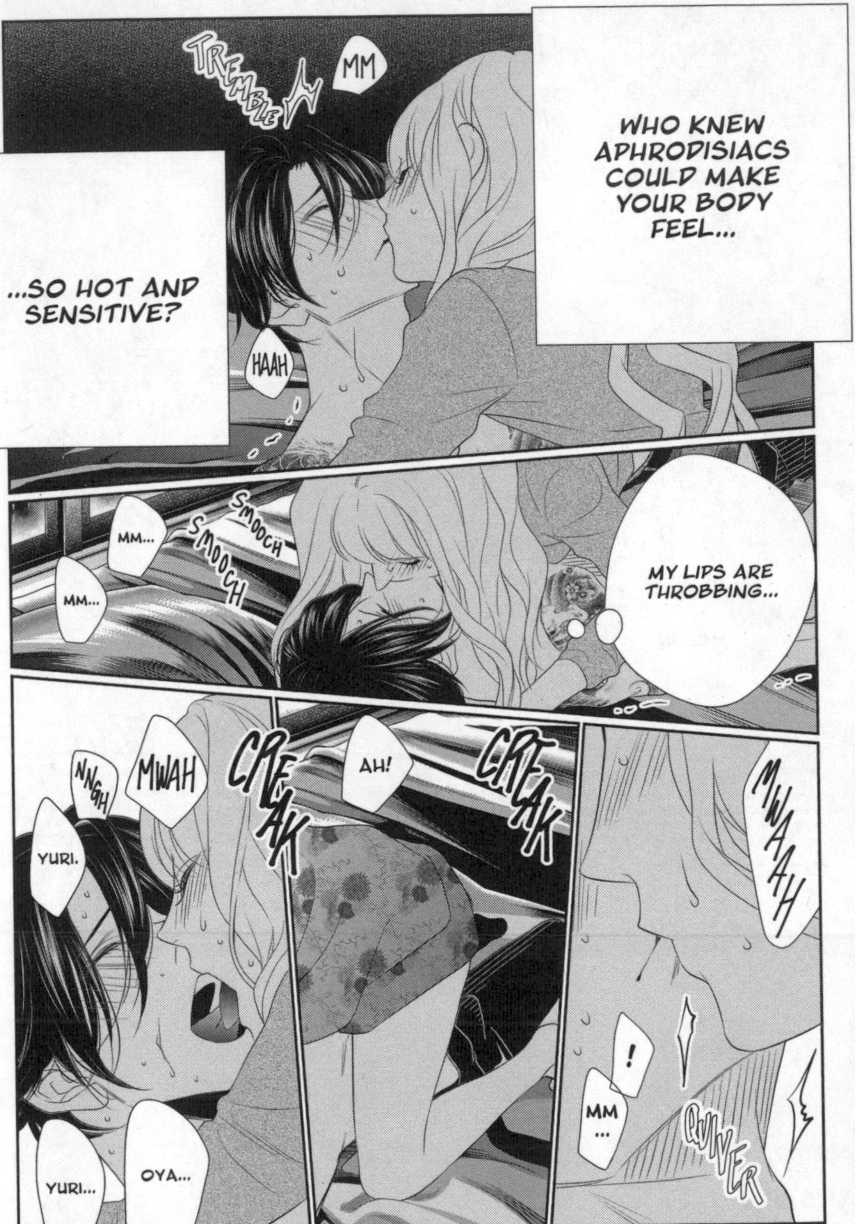

WHO KNEW APHRODISIACS COULD MAKE YOUR BODY FEEL...
MM
TREMBLE
...SO HOT AND SENSITIVE?
HAAH
MY LIPS ARE THROBBING...
SMOOCH
SMOOCH
MM...
MM...
MWAAAH
!
MM ...
QUIVER
CREAK
AH!
CREAK
MWAH
NNGH
YURI.
OYA...
YURI...

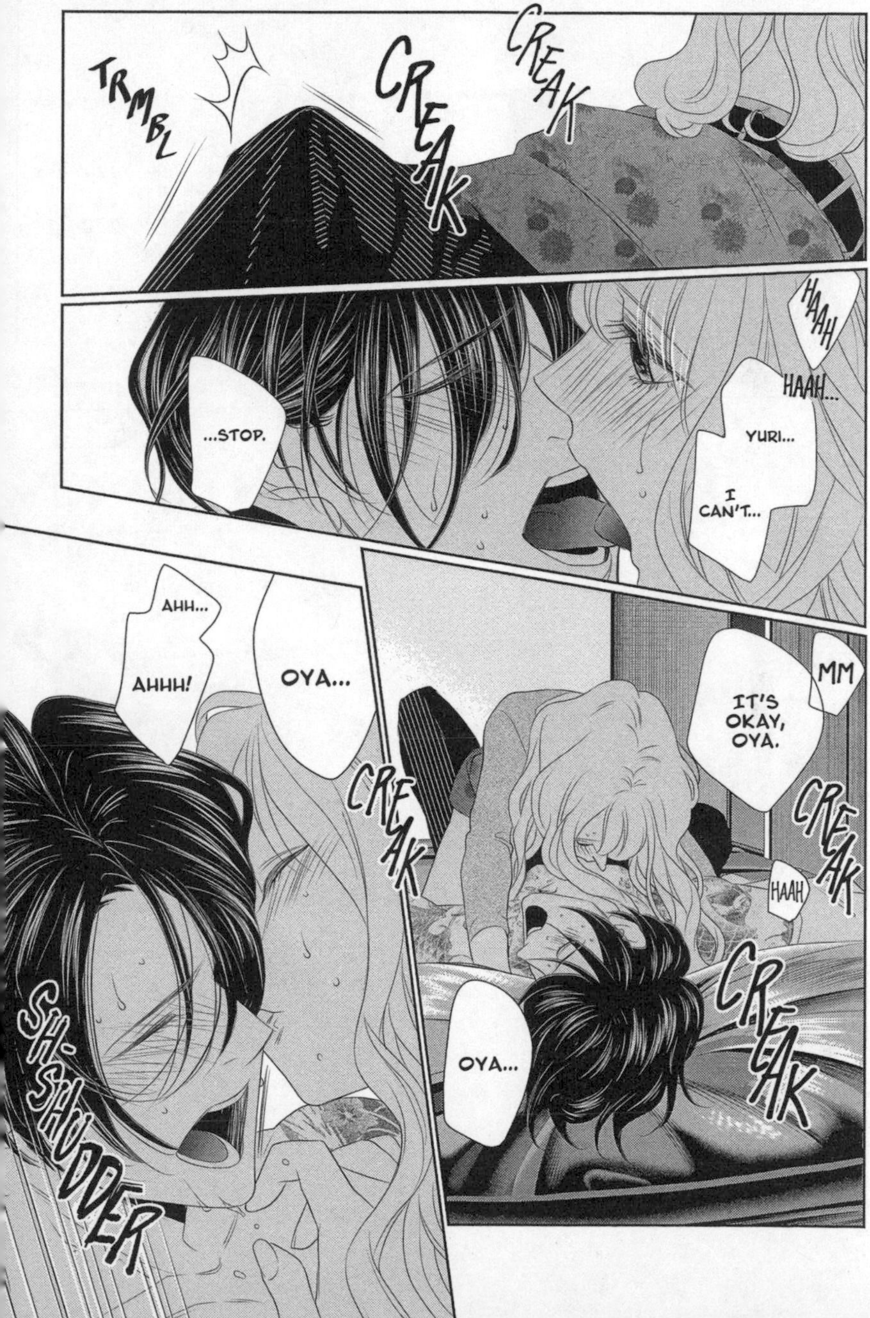
CREAK
CREAK
TRMBL
HAAAH
HAAH...
YURI...
I CAN'T...
...STOP.
MM
IT'S OKAY, OYA.
CREAK
HAAH
CREAK
OYA...
OYA...
AHH...
AHHH!
CREAK
SH-SHUDDER

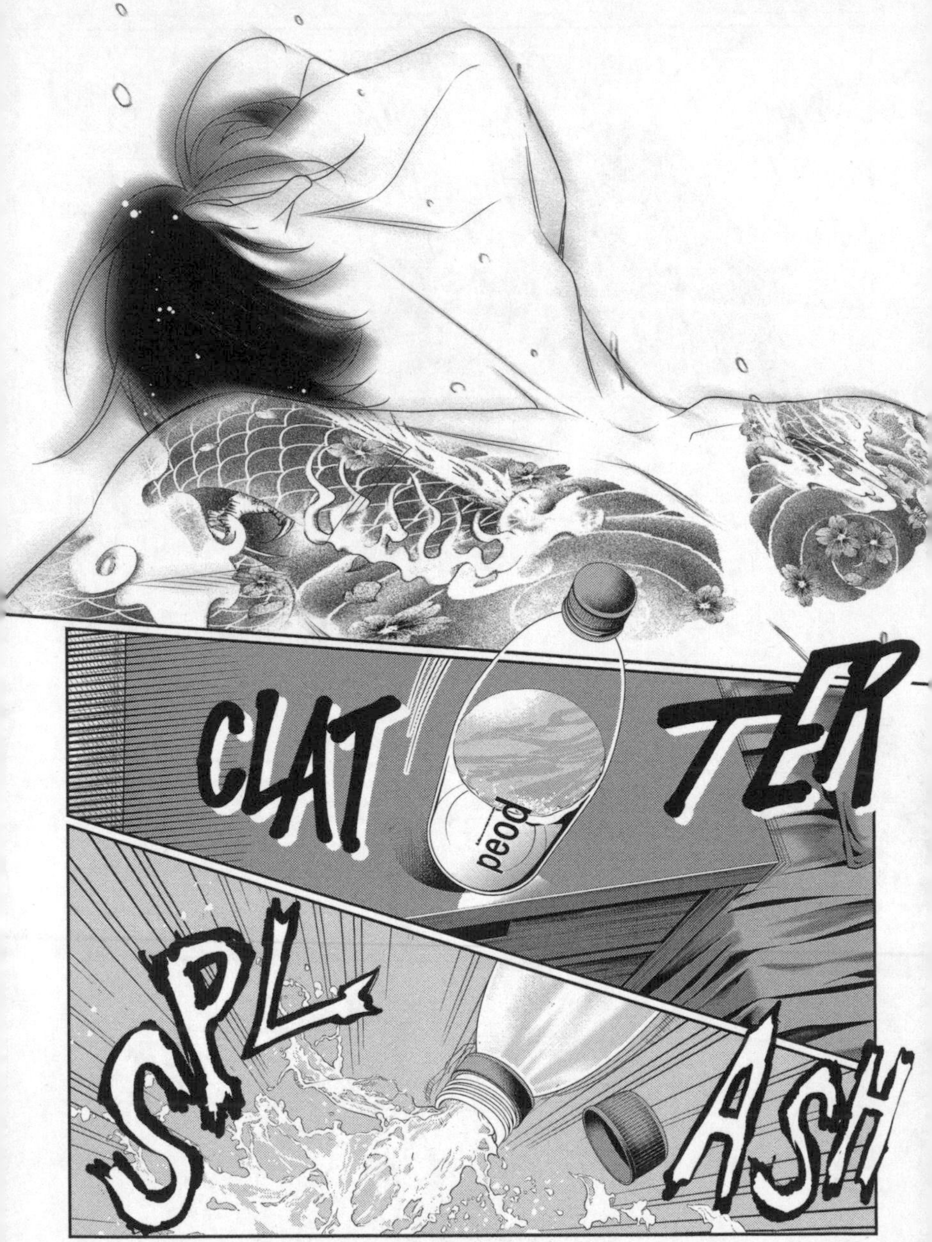
CLATTER
SPLASH

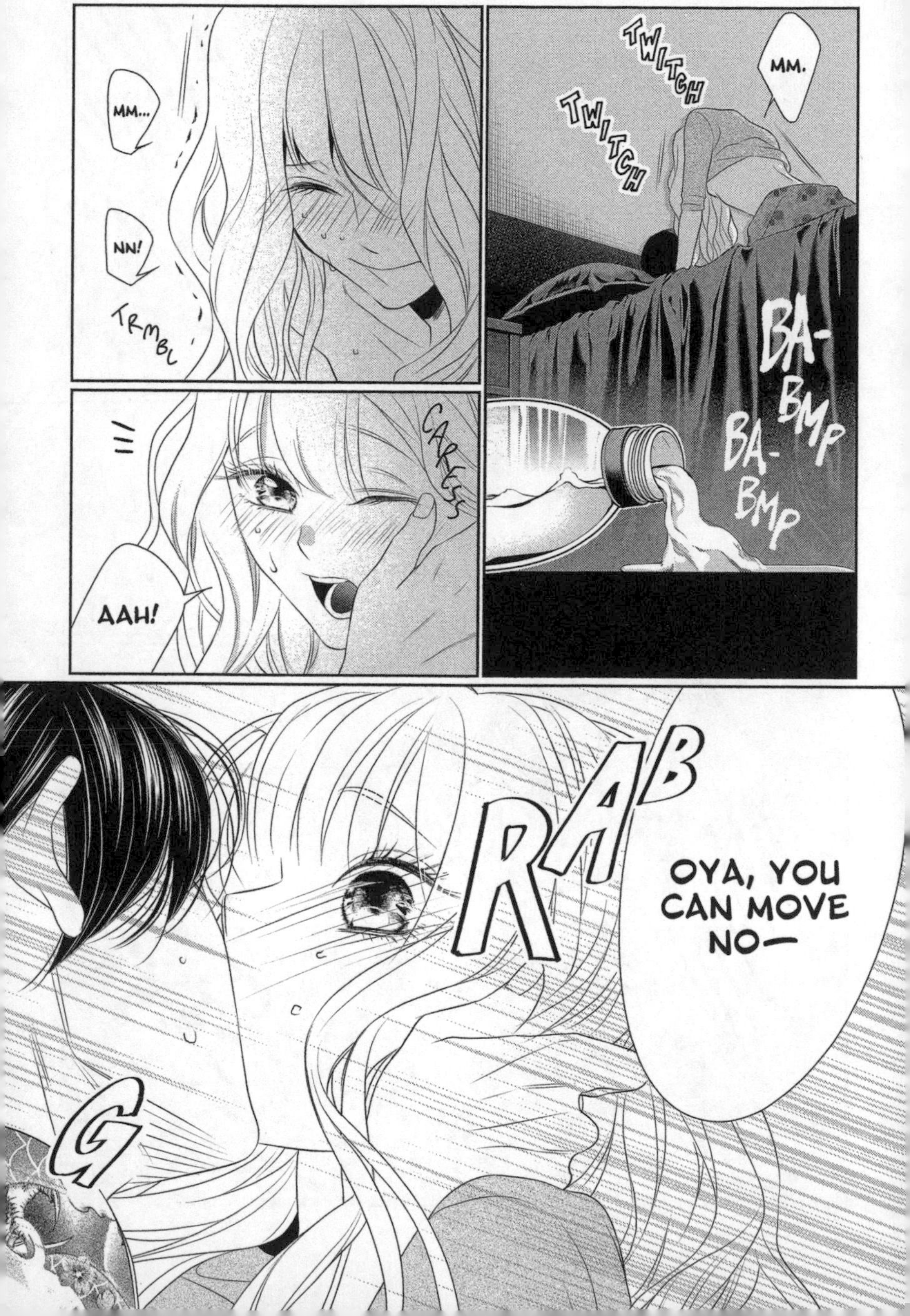
TWITCH
TWITCH
MM.
BA-BMP
BA-BMP
MM...
NN!
TRMBL
CARESS
AAH!
OYA, YOU CAN MOVE NO—
RAB
G

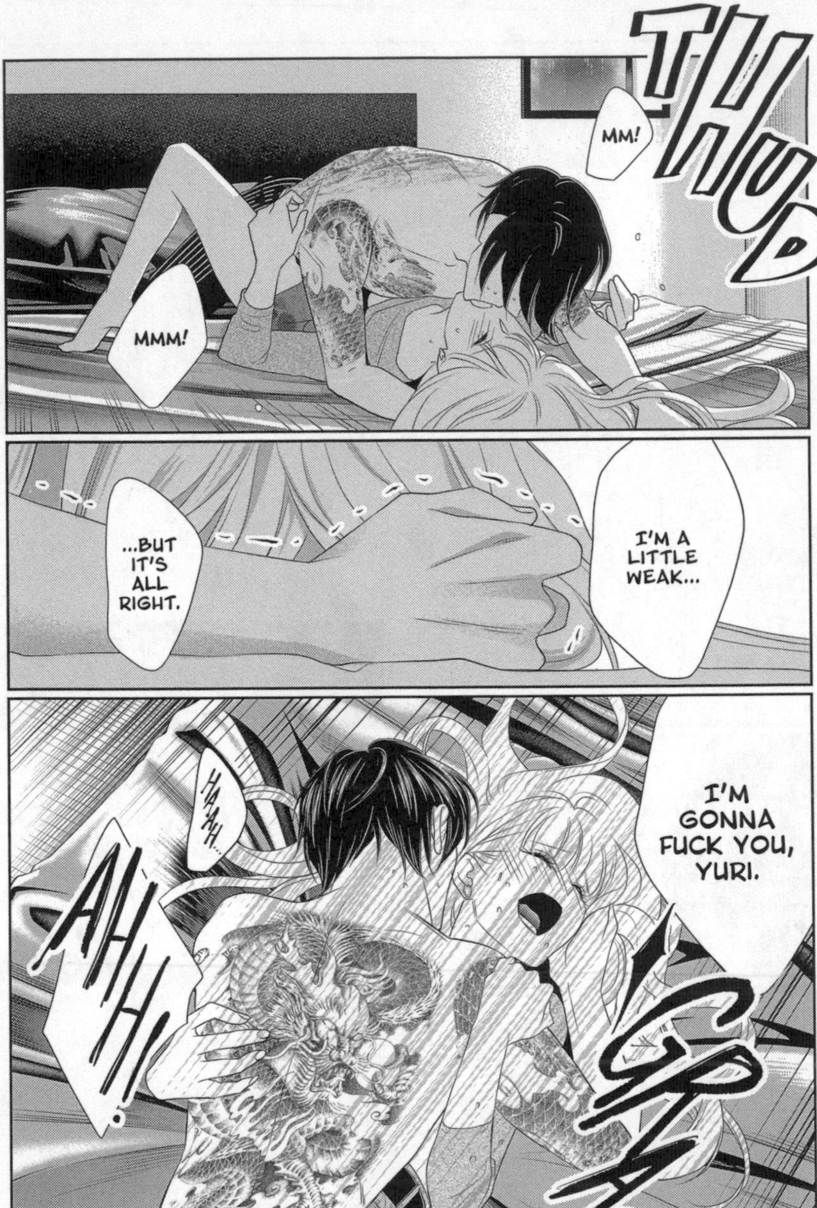
THUD
MM!
MMM!
I'M A LITTLE WEAK...
...BUT IT'S ALL RIGHT.
I'M GONNA FUCK YOU, YURI.
GRAB
HAAAH...
AHH!!

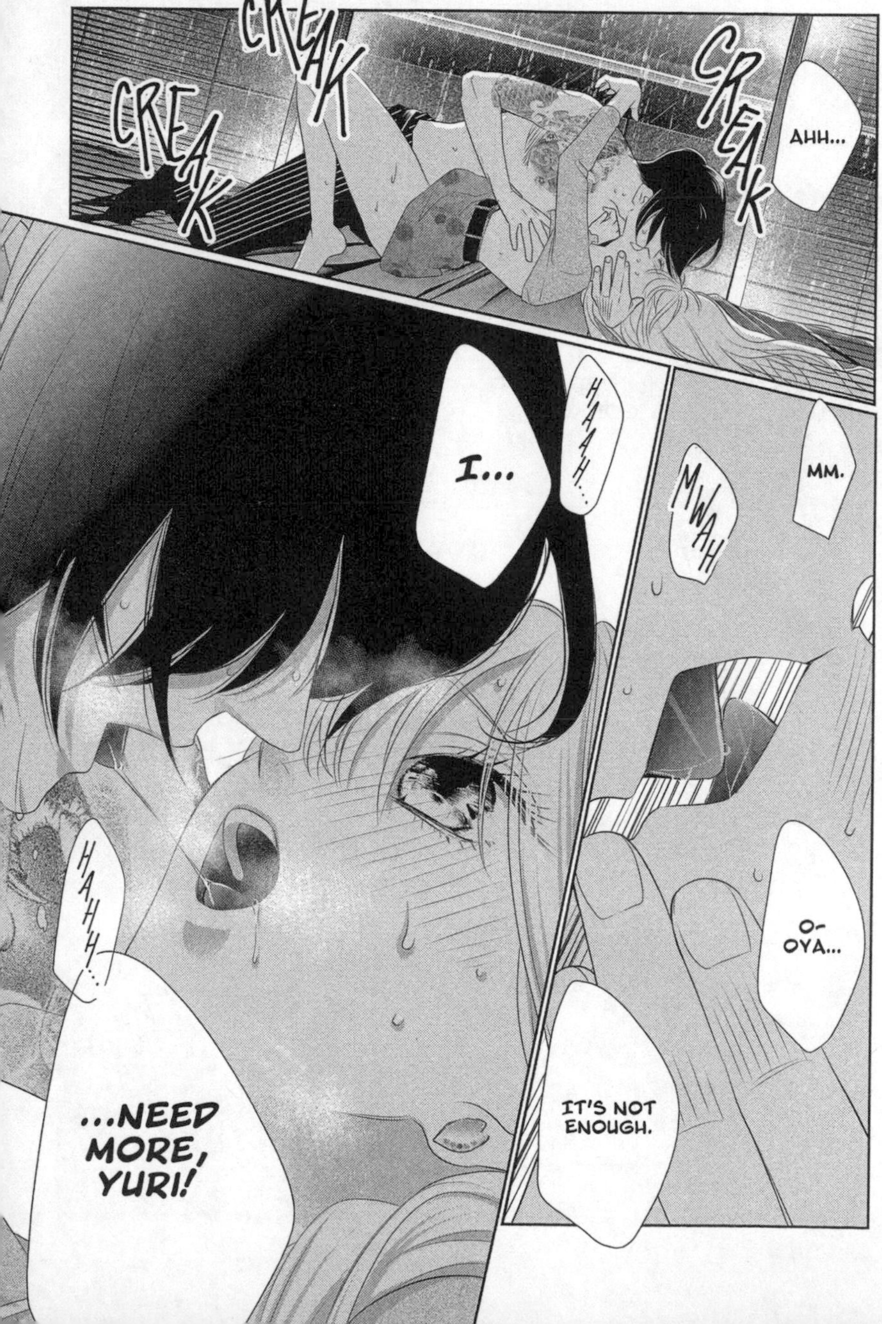
CREAK
AHH...
CREAK
CREAK
MM.
MWAH
O-OYA...
IT'S NOT ENOUGH.
HAAAH...
I...
HAHH...
...NEED MORE, YURI!

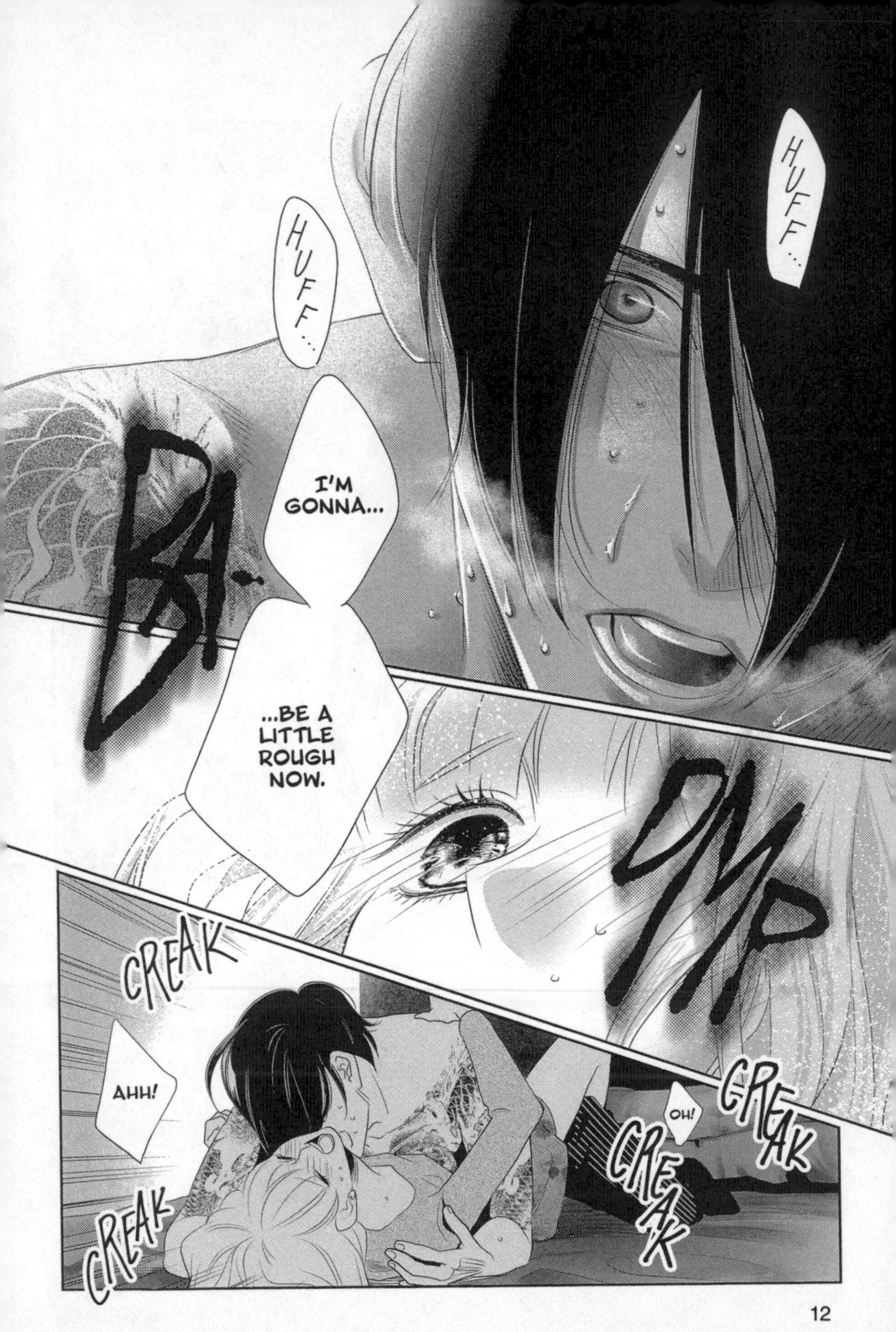
HUFF...
HUFF...
I'M GONNA...
BA-
...BE A LITTLE ROUGH NOW.
DMP
CREAK
OH!
CREAK
CREAK
AHH!
CREAK

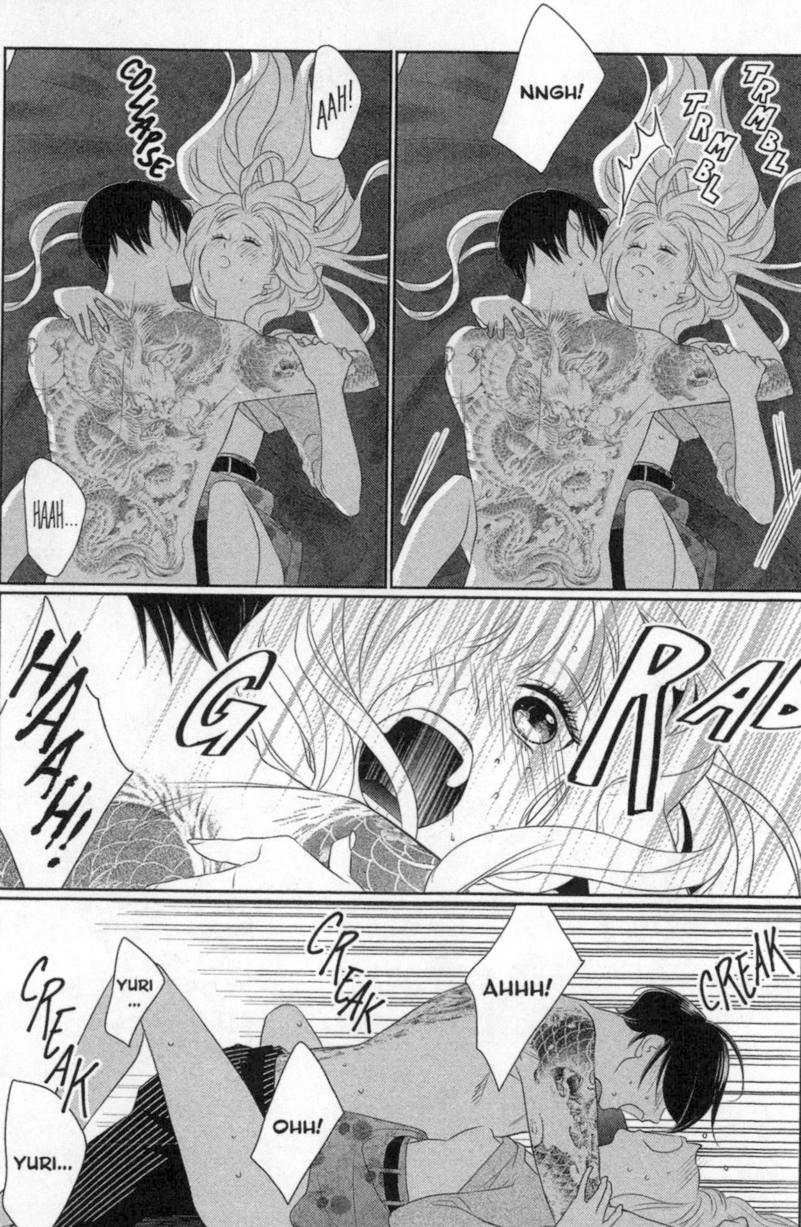
TRMBL
TRMBL
NNGH!
AAH!
COLLAPSE
HAAH...
GRAB
HAAAH!
CREAK
AHHH!
CREAK
OHH!
YURI
...
CREAK
YURI...

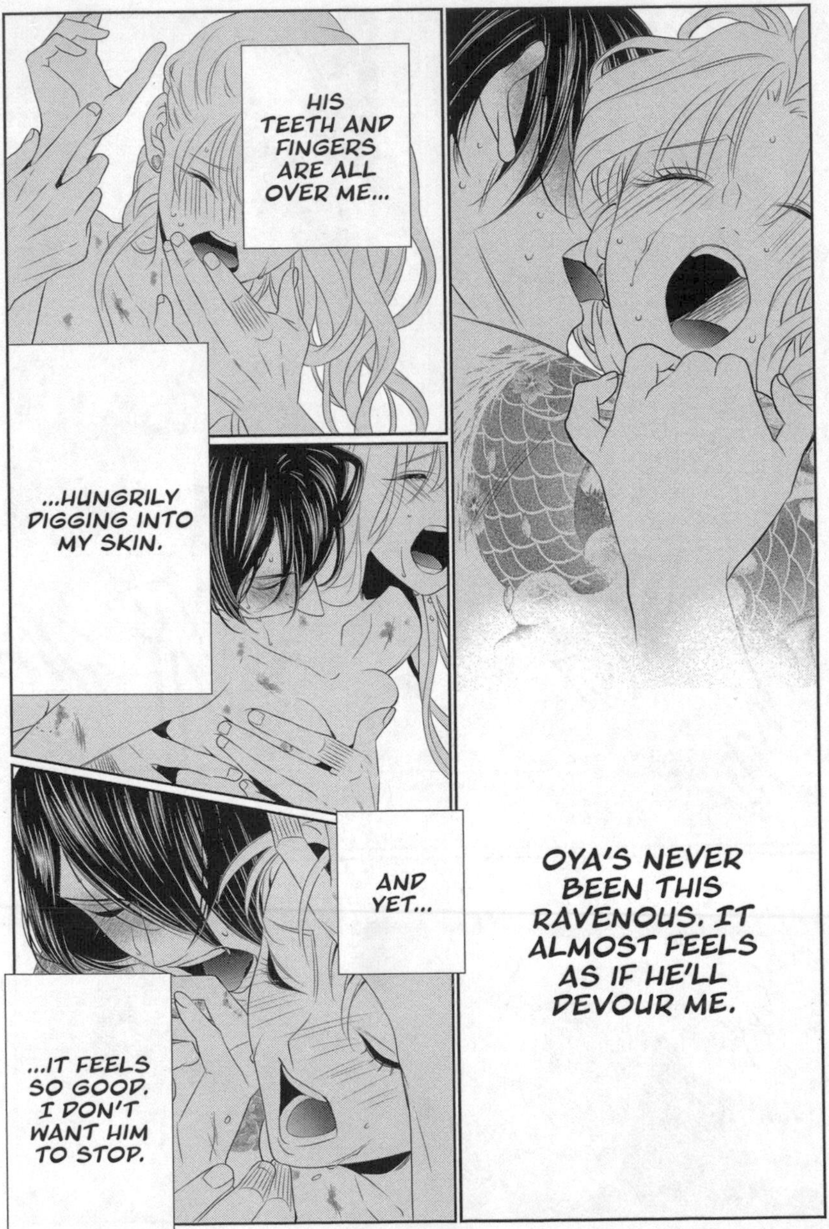
OYA'S NEVER BEEN THIS RAVENOUS. IT ALMOST FEELS AS IF HE'LL DEVOUR ME.
HIS TEETH AND FINGERS ARE ALL OVER ME...
...HUNGRILY DIGGING INTO MY SKIN.
AND YET...
...IT FEELS SO GOOD. I DON'T WANT HIM TO STOP.

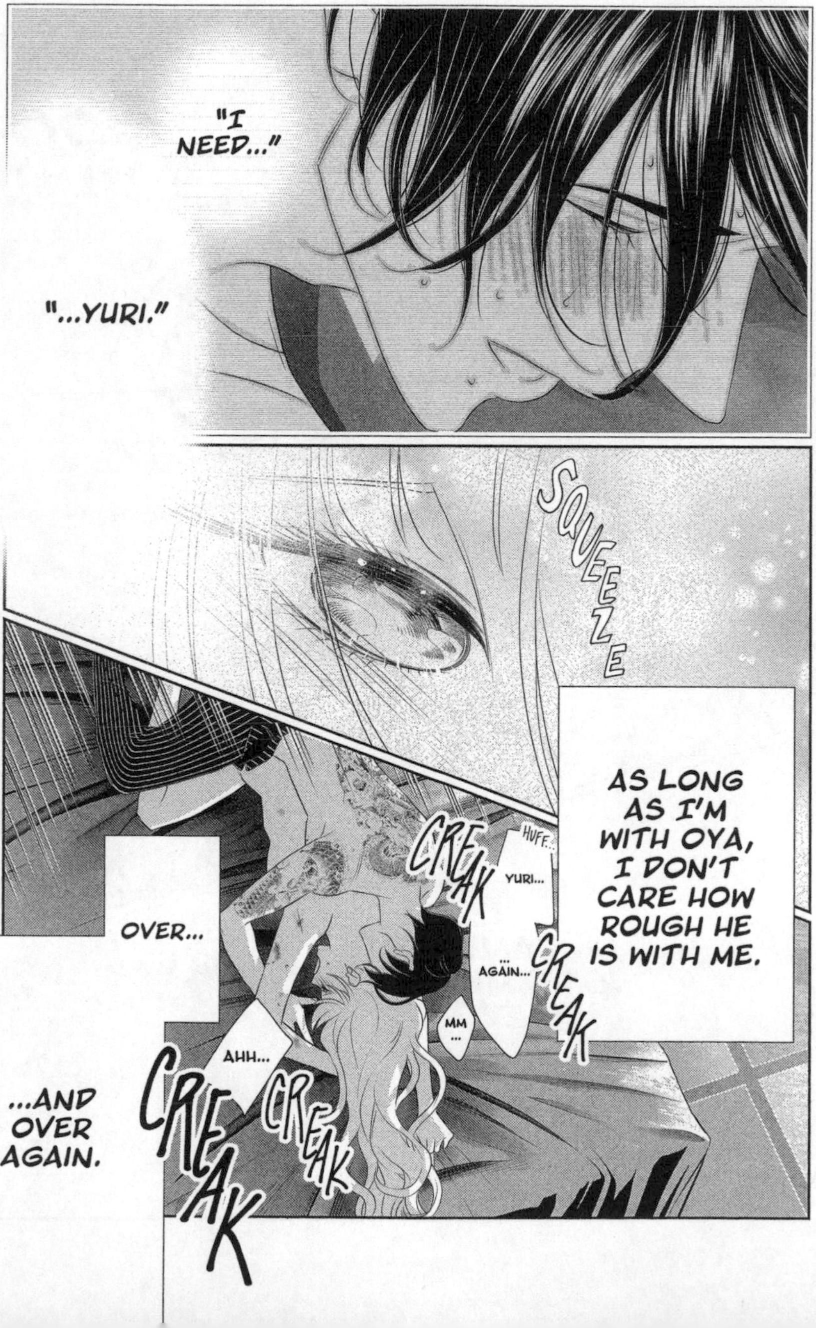
"I NEED..."
"...YURI."
SQUEEZE
AS LONG AS I'M WITH OYA, I DON'T CARE HOW ROUGH HE IS WITH ME.
HUFF...
YURI...
CREAK
... AGAIN...
CREAK
MM ...
OVER...
AHH...
CREAK
CREAK
...AND OVER AGAIN.

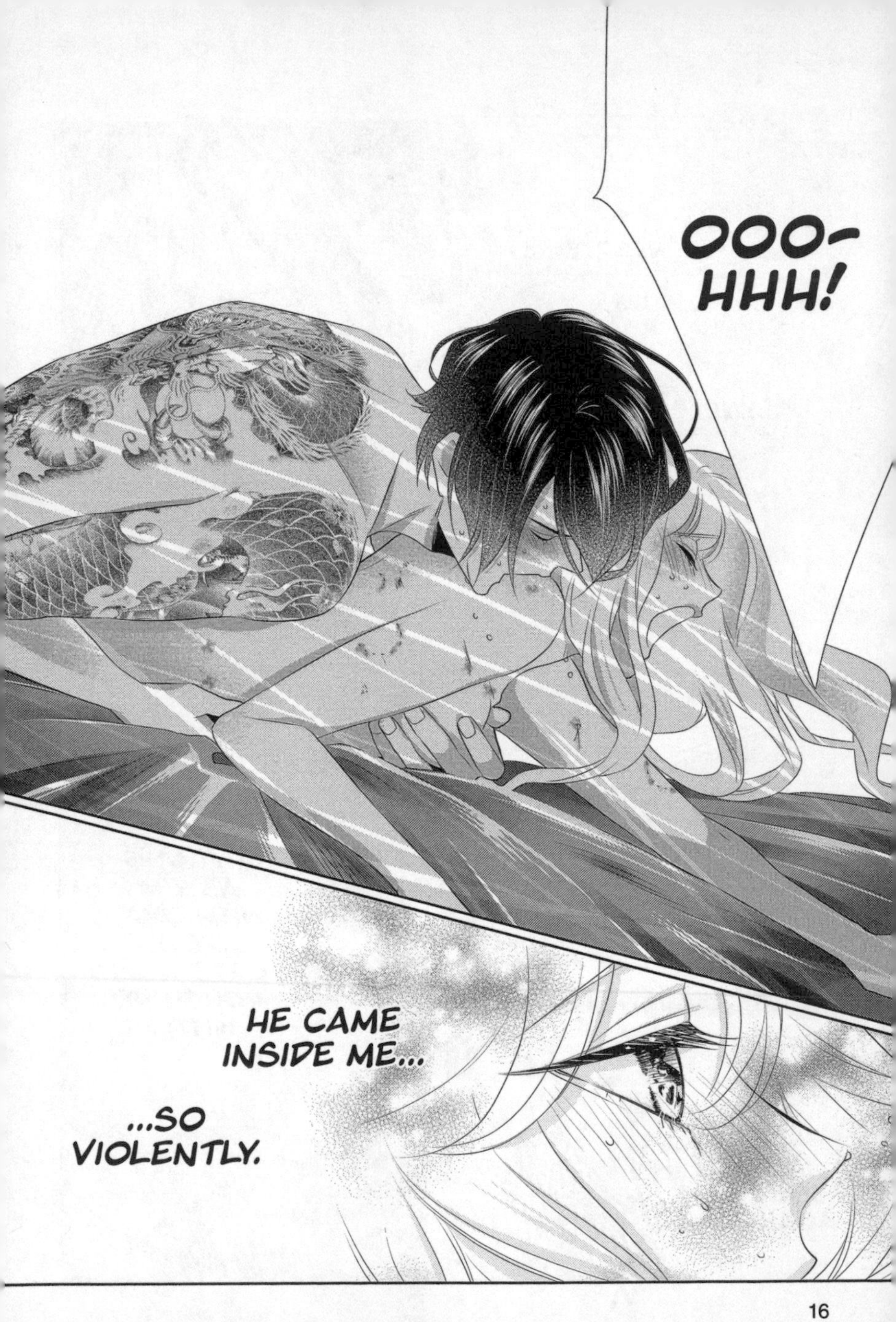
OOO-HHH!
HE CAME INSIDE ME...
...SO VIOLENTLY.

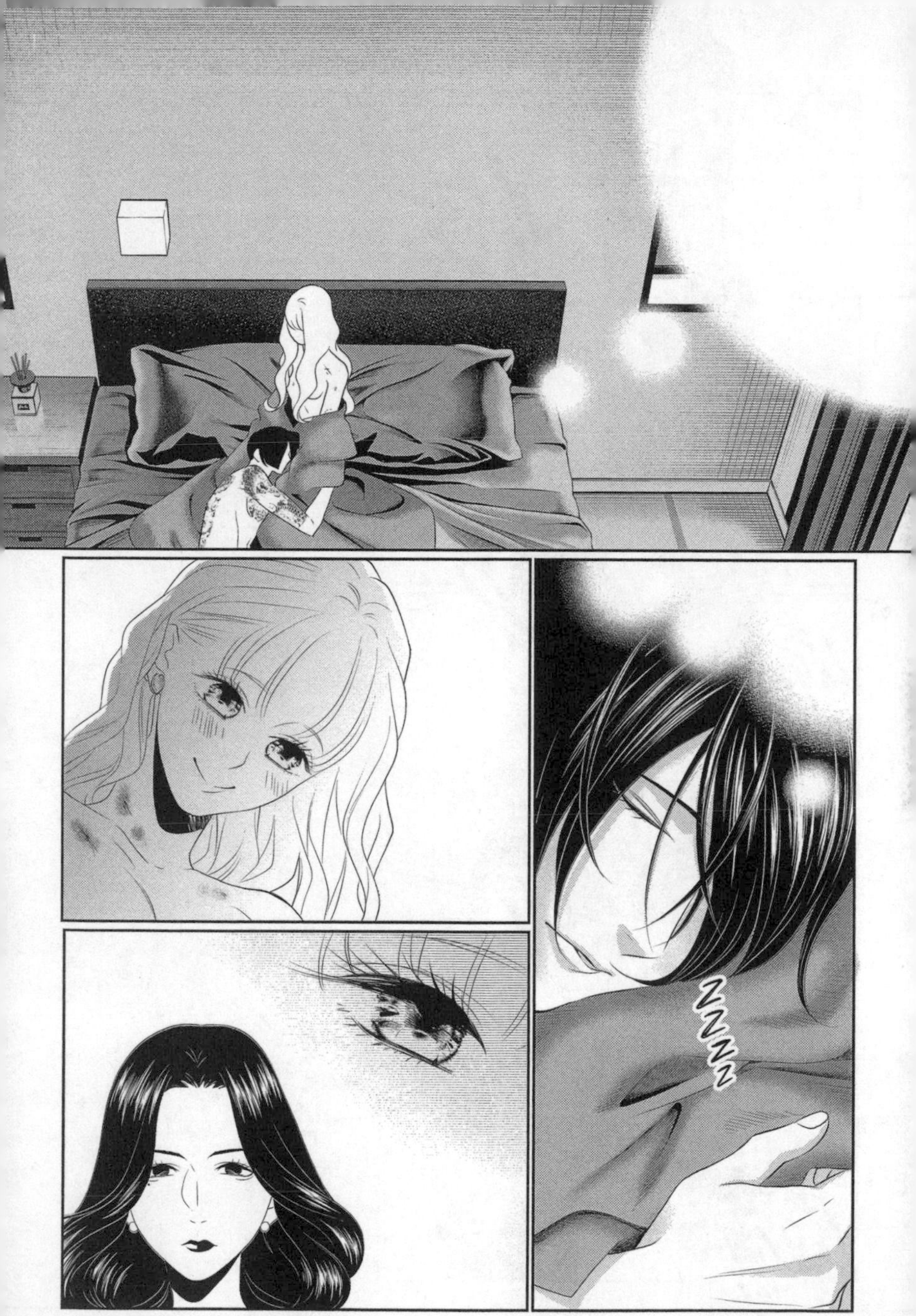
ZZZZ

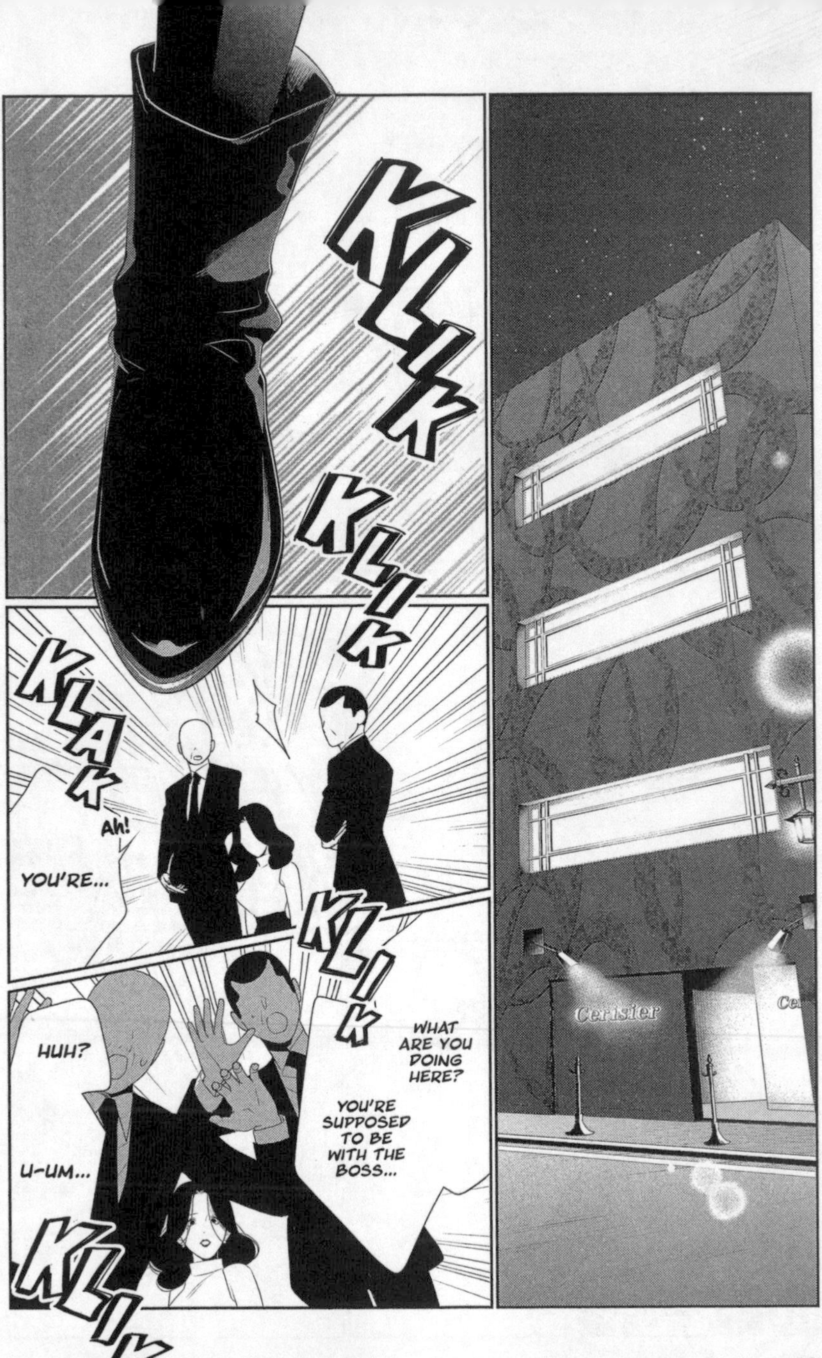
Cerisier
KLIK KLIK
KLIK KLIK
KLAK
AH!
YOU'RE...
KLIK
WHAT ARE YOU DOING HERE?
YOU'RE SUPPOSED TO BE WITH THE BOSS...
HUH?
U-UM...
KLIK

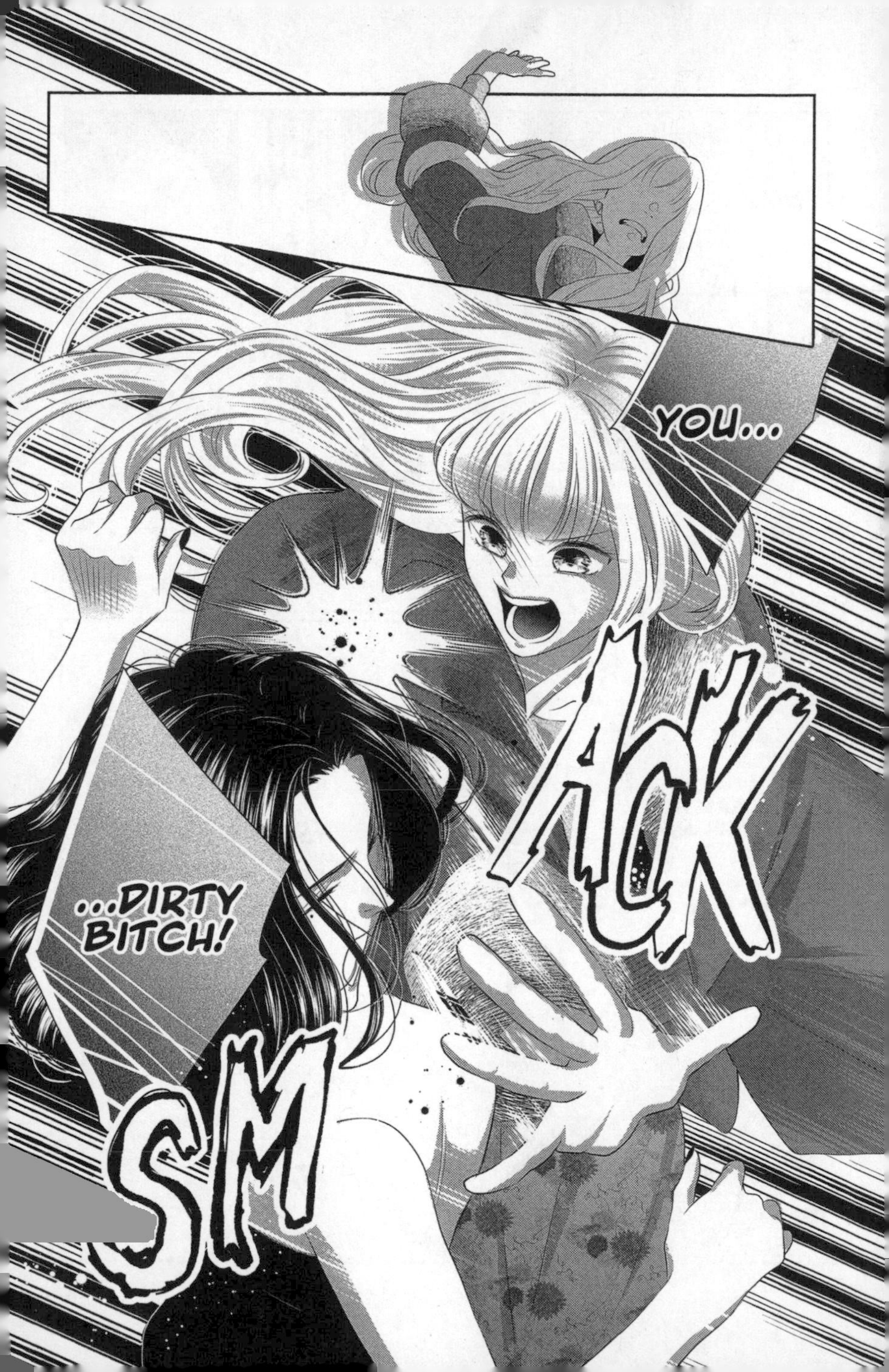
YOU...
ACK
...DIRTY BITCH!
SM

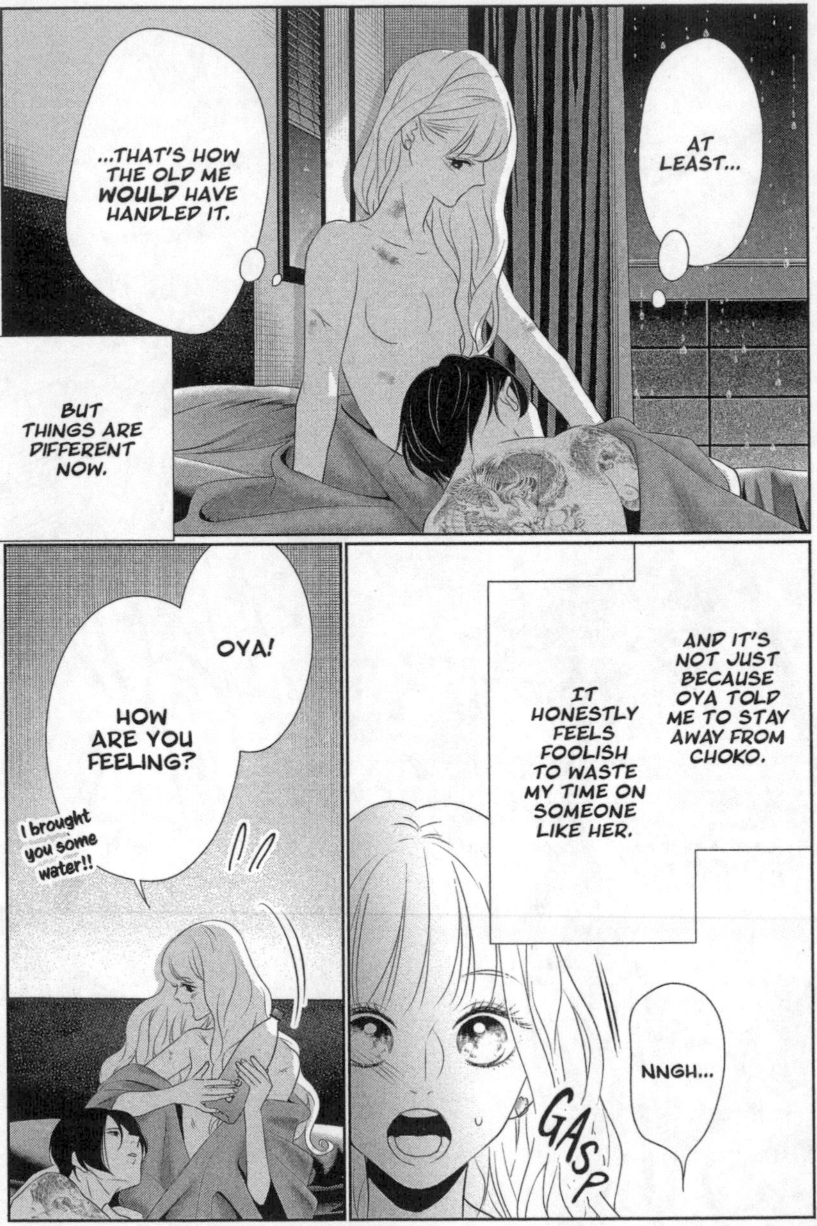
AT LEAST...
...THAT'S HOW THE OLD ME WOULD HAVE HANDLED IT.
BUT THINGS ARE DIFFERENT NOW.
AND IT'S NOT JUST BECAUSE OYA TOLD ME TO STAY AWAY FROM CHOKO.
IT HONESTLY FEELS FOOLISH TO WASTE MY TIME ON SOMEONE LIKE HER.
NNGH...
GASP
OYA!
HOW ARE YOU FEELING?
I brought you some water!!

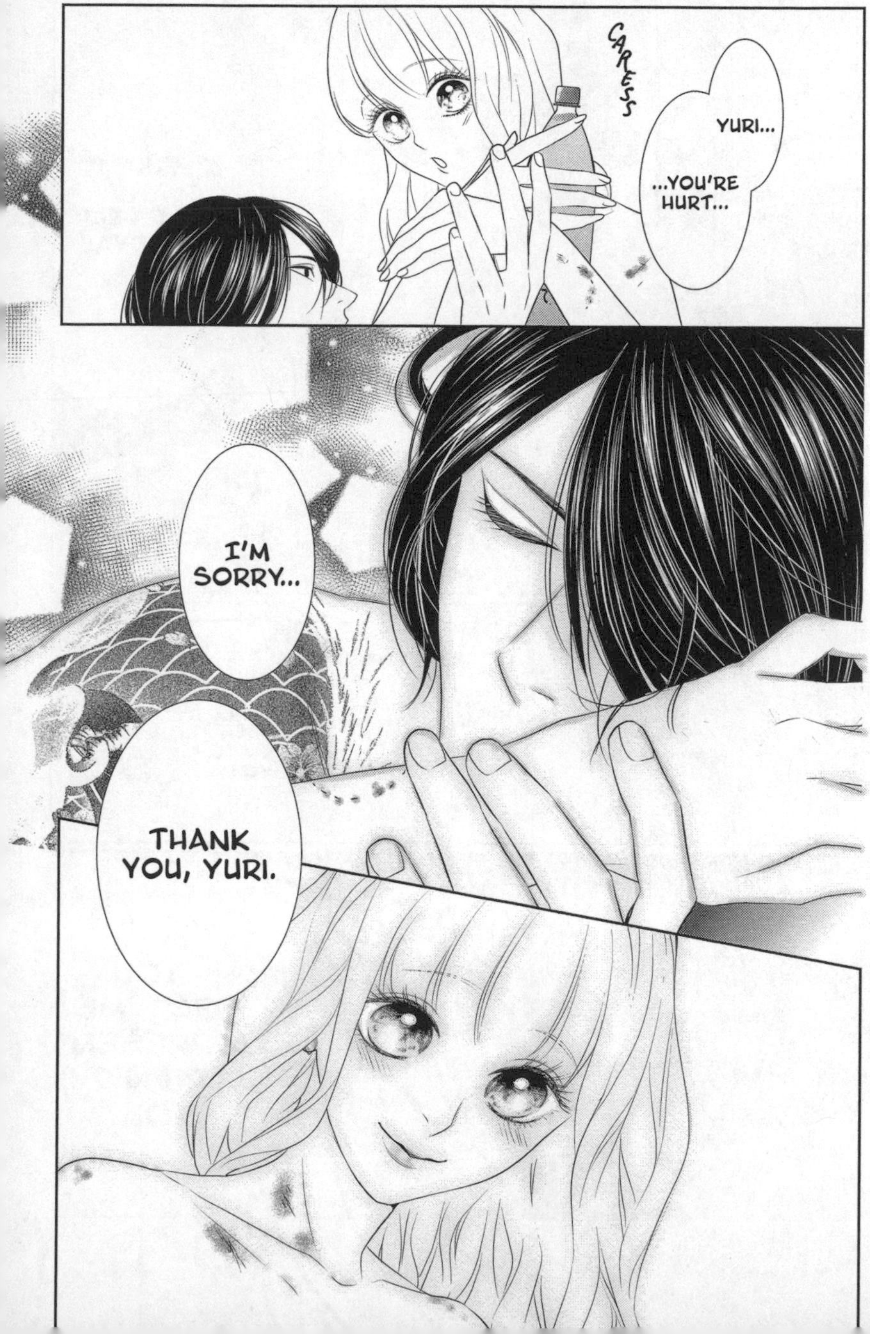
YURI...
...YOU'RE HURT...
CARESS
I'M SORRY...
THANK YOU, YURI.

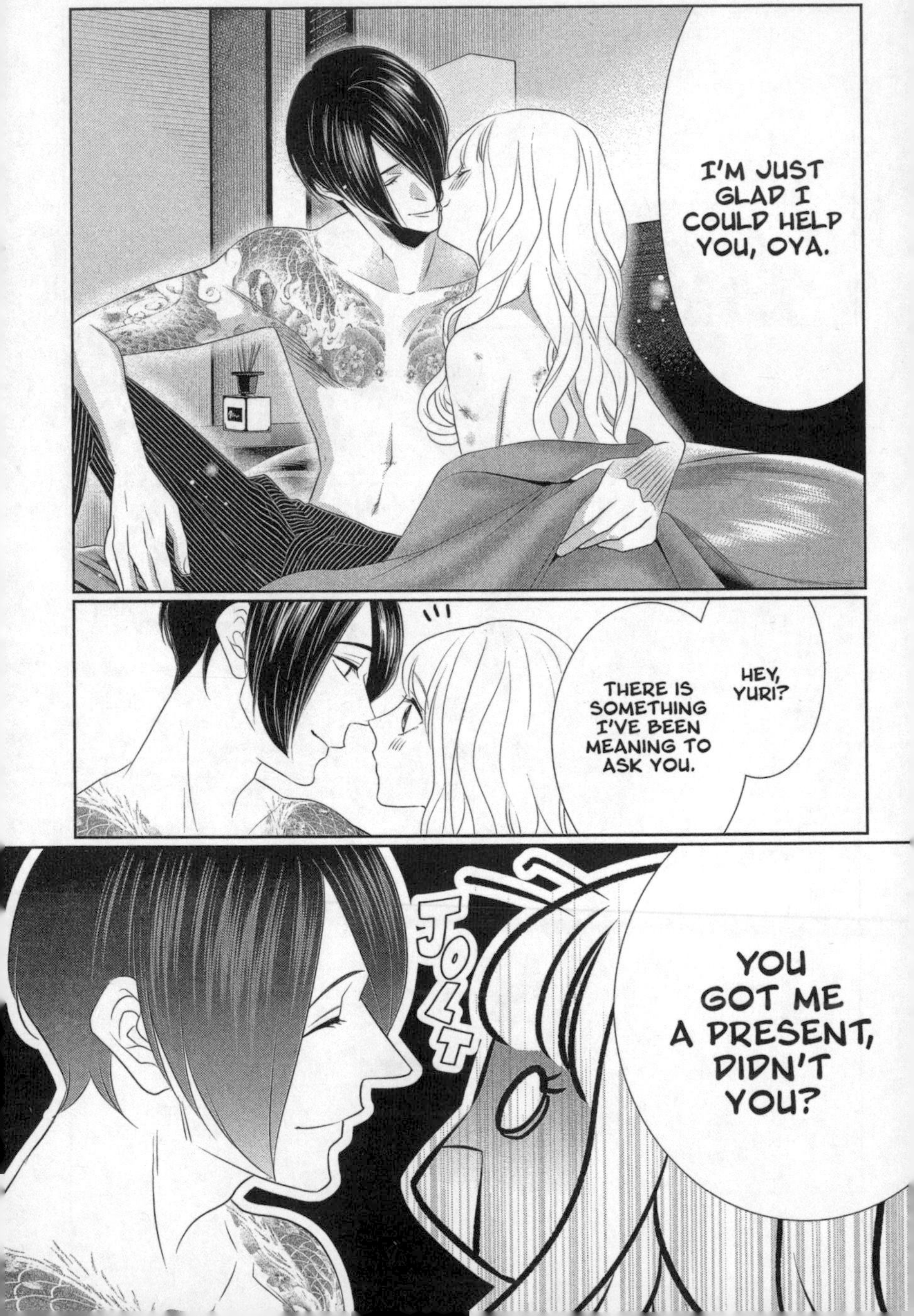
I'M JUST GLAD I COULD HELP YOU, OYA.
HEY, YURI?
THERE IS SOMETHING I'VE BEEN MEANING TO ASK YOU.
YOU GOT ME A PRESENT, DIDN'T YOU?
JOLT

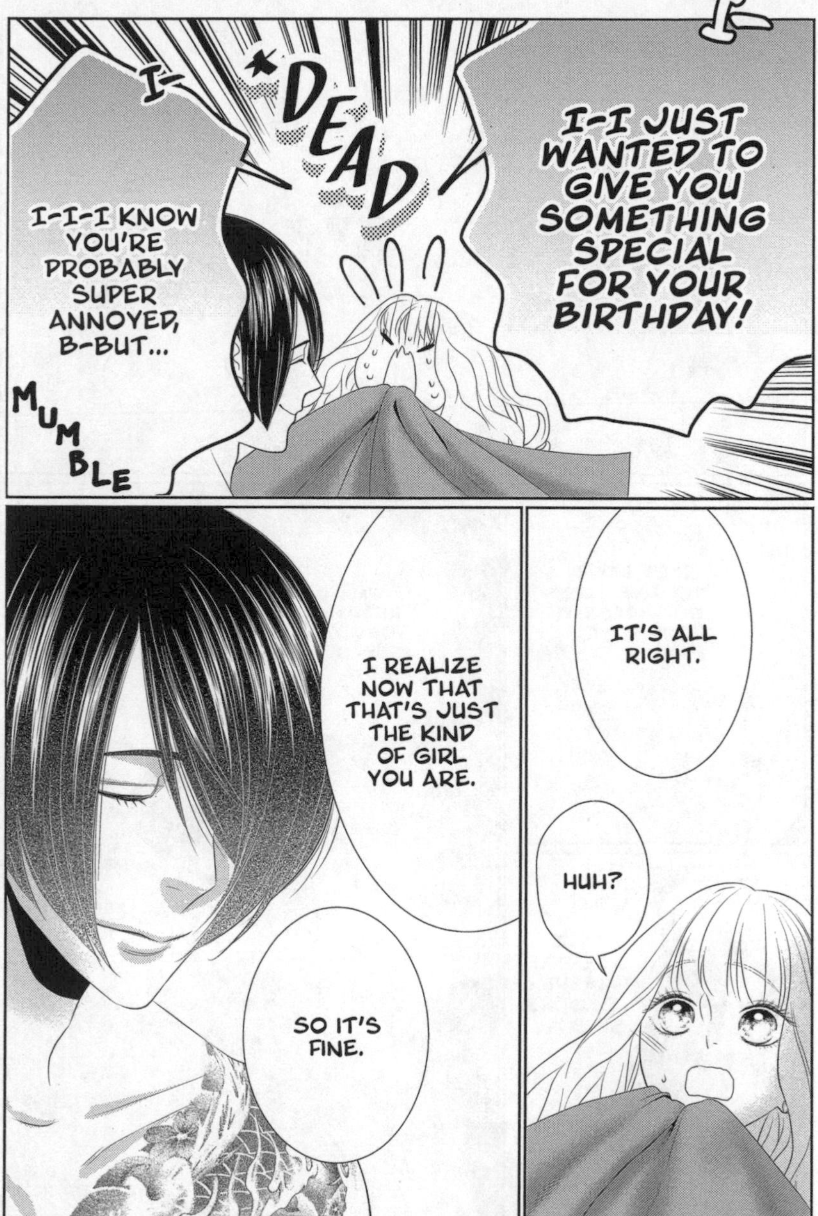
I–
I-I JUST WANTED TO GIVE YOU SOMETHING SPECIAL FOR YOUR BIRTHDAY!
DEAD
I–
I-I-I KNOW YOU'RE PROBABLY SUPER ANNOYED, B-BUT...
MUMBLE
IT'S ALL RIGHT.
HUH?
I REALIZE NOW THAT THAT'S JUST THE KIND OF GIRL YOU ARE.
SO IT'S FINE.

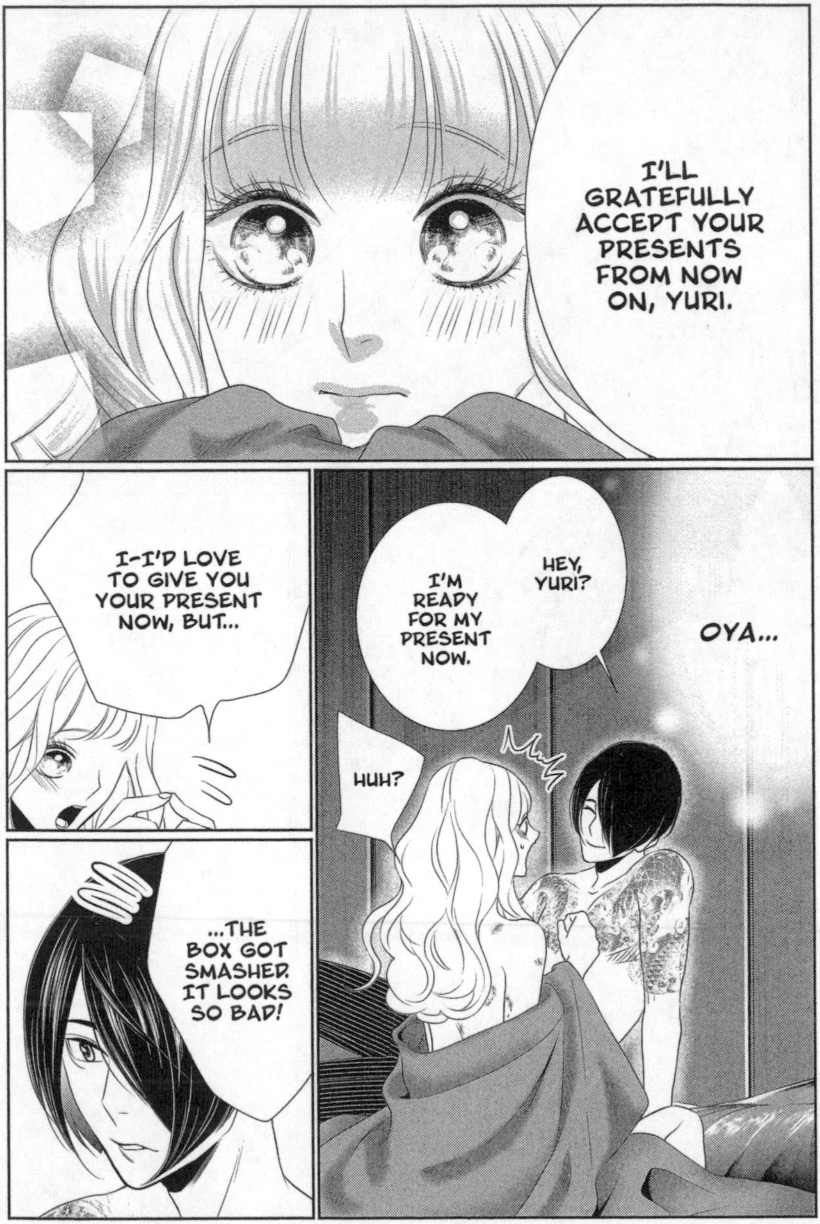
I'LL GRATEFULLY ACCEPT YOUR PRESENTS FROM NOW ON, YURI.
HEY, YURI?
I'M READY FOR MY PRESENT NOW.
OYA...
HUH?
I-I'D LOVE TO GIVE YOU YOUR PRESENT NOW, BUT...
...THE BOX GOT SMASHED. IT LOOKS SO BAD!

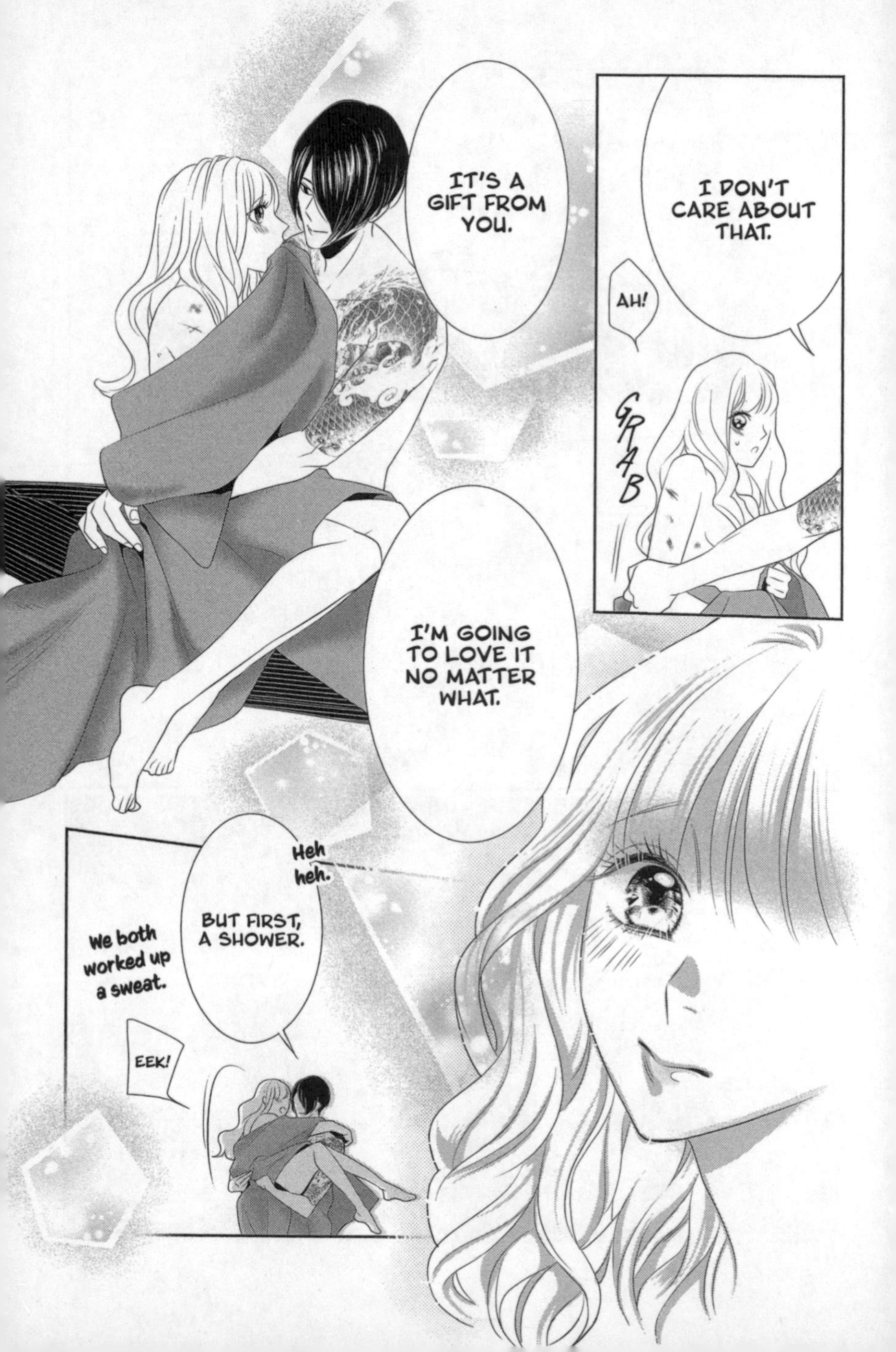
I DON'T CARE ABOUT THAT.
AH!
GRAB
IT'S A GIFT FROM YOU.
I'M GOING TO LOVE IT NO MATTER WHAT.
Heh heh.
BUT FIRST, A SHOWER.
We both worked up a sweat.
EEK!

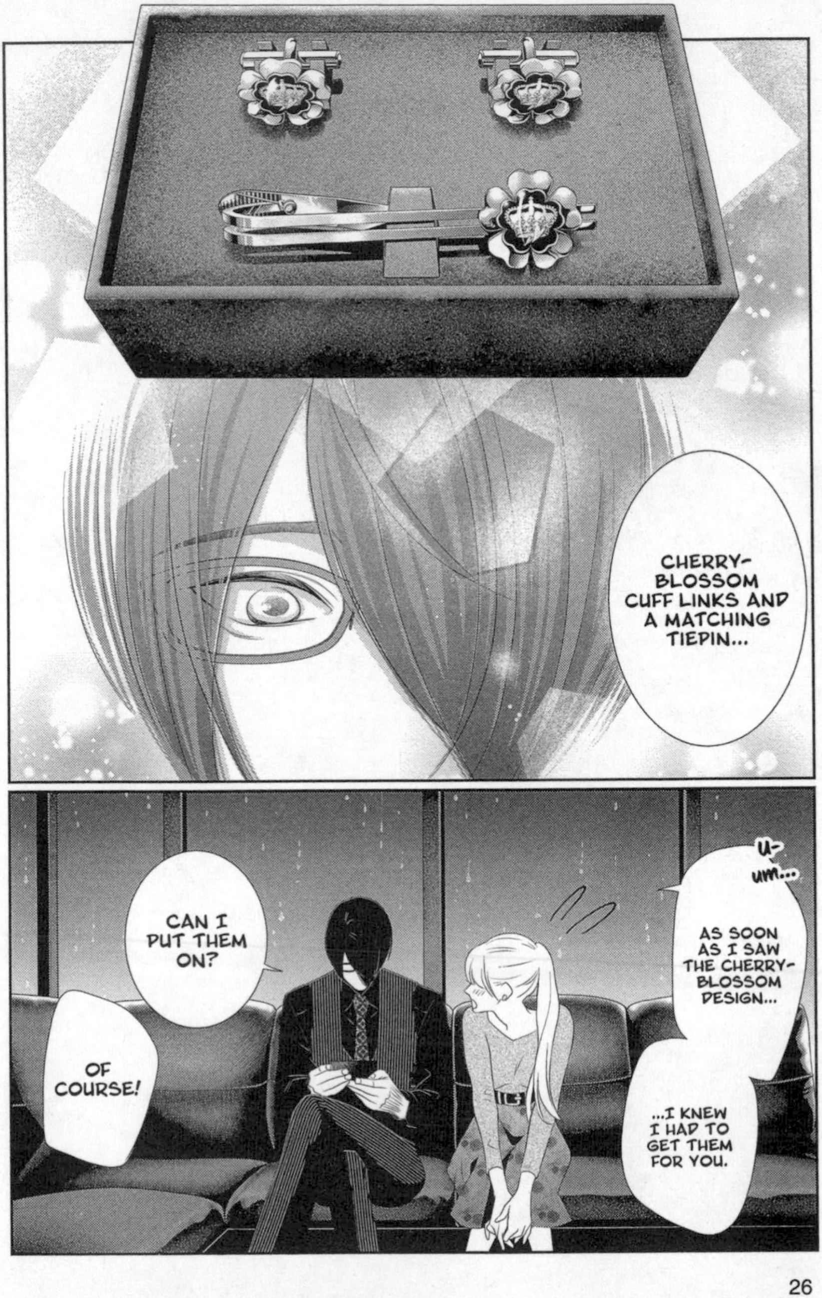
CHERRY-BLOSSOM CUFF LINKS AND A MATCHING TIEPIN...
U-UM...
AS SOON AS I SAW THE CHERRY-BLOSSOM DESIGN...
...I KNEW I HAD TO GET THEM FOR YOU.
CAN I PUT THEM ON?
OF COURSE!

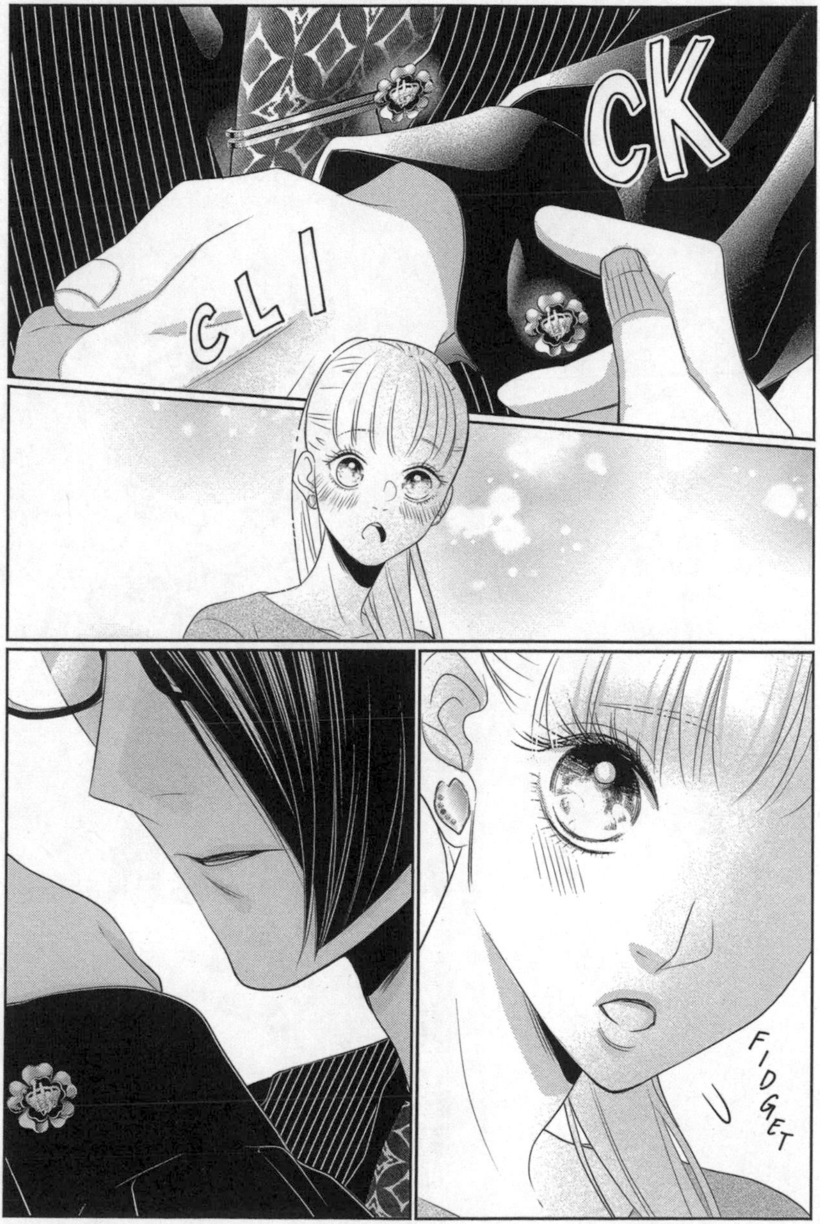
CLI
CK
FIDGET

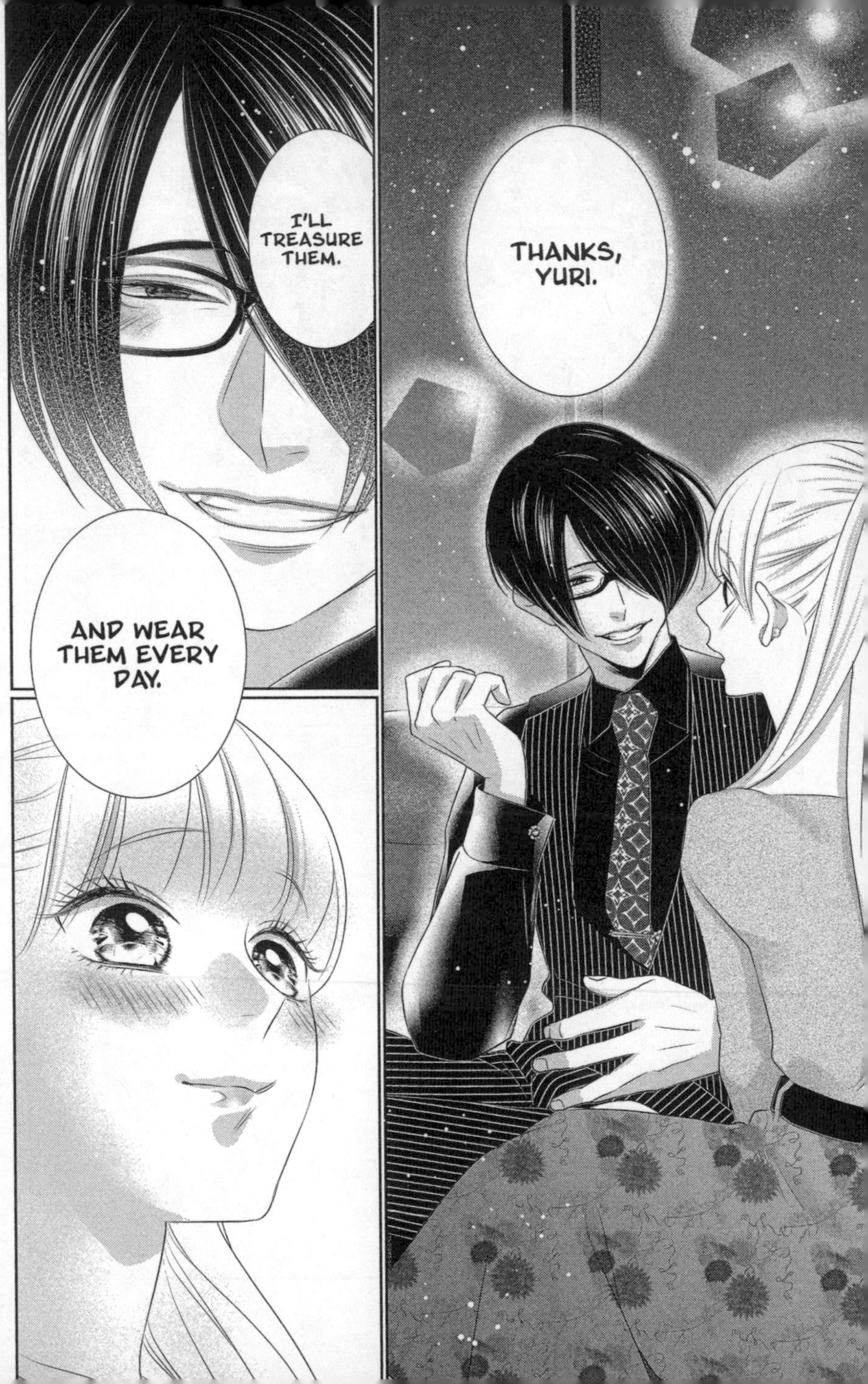
THANKS, YURI.
I'LL TREASURE THEM.
AND WEAR THEM EVERY DAY.

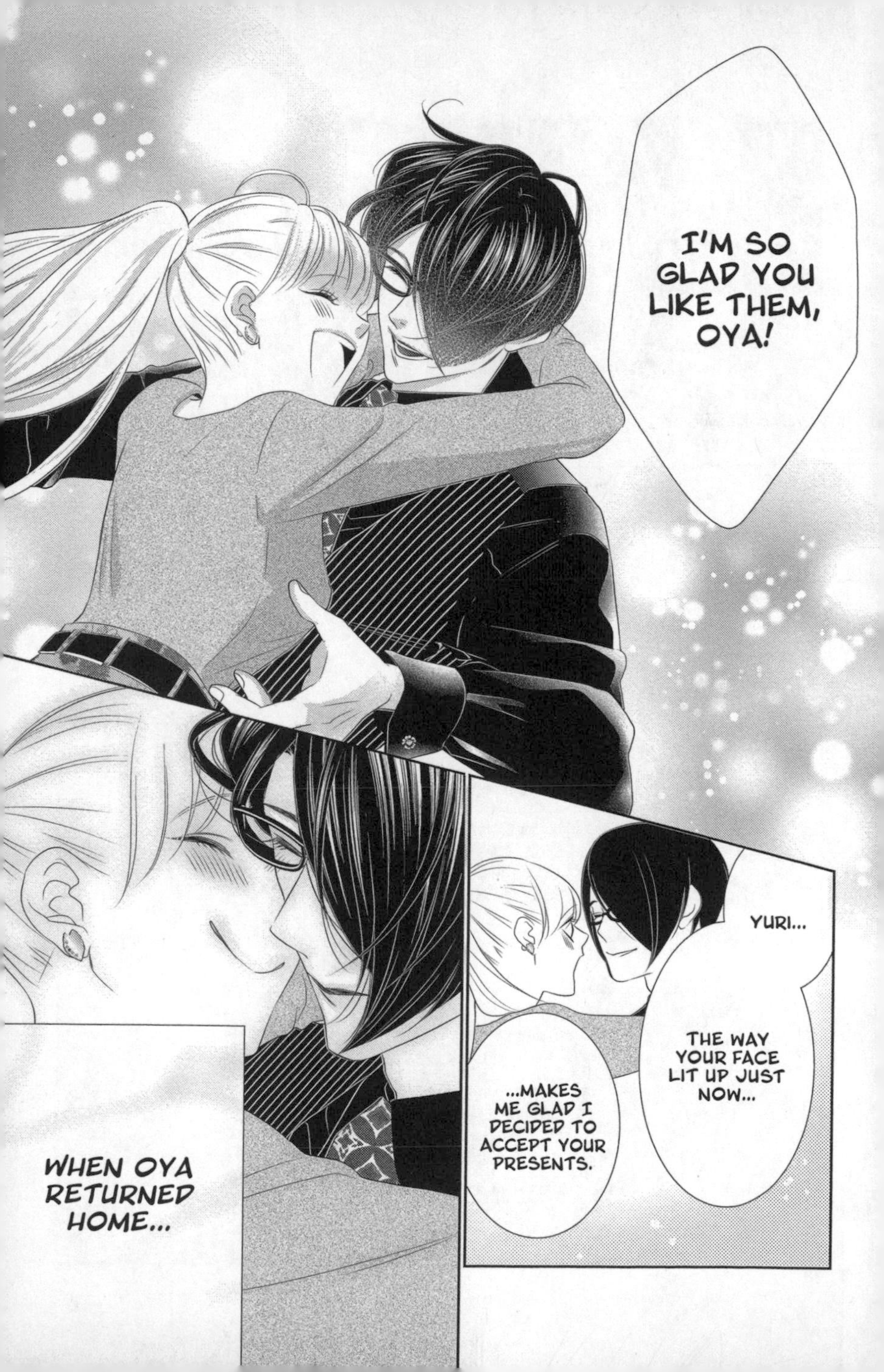
I'M SO GLAD YOU LIKE THEM, OYA!
YURI...
THE WAY YOUR FACE LIT UP JUST NOW...
...MAKES ME GLAD I DECIDED TO ACCEPT YOUR PRESENTS.
WHEN OYA RETURNED HOME...

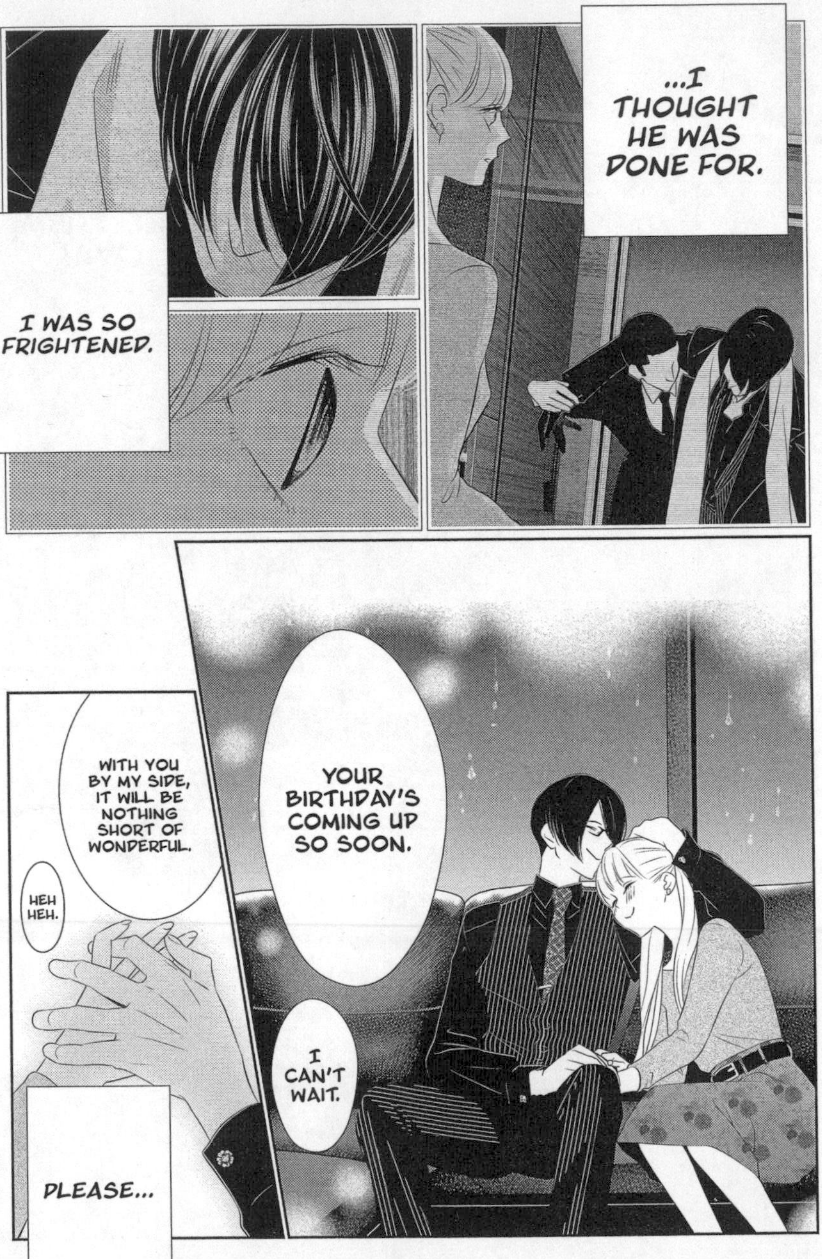
...I THOUGHT HE WAS DONE FOR.
I WAS SO FRIGHTENED.
YOUR BIRTHDAY'S COMING UP SO SOON.
I CAN'T WAIT.
WITH YOU BY MY SIDE, IT WILL BE NOTHING SHORT OF WONDERFUL.
HEH HEH.
PLEASE...

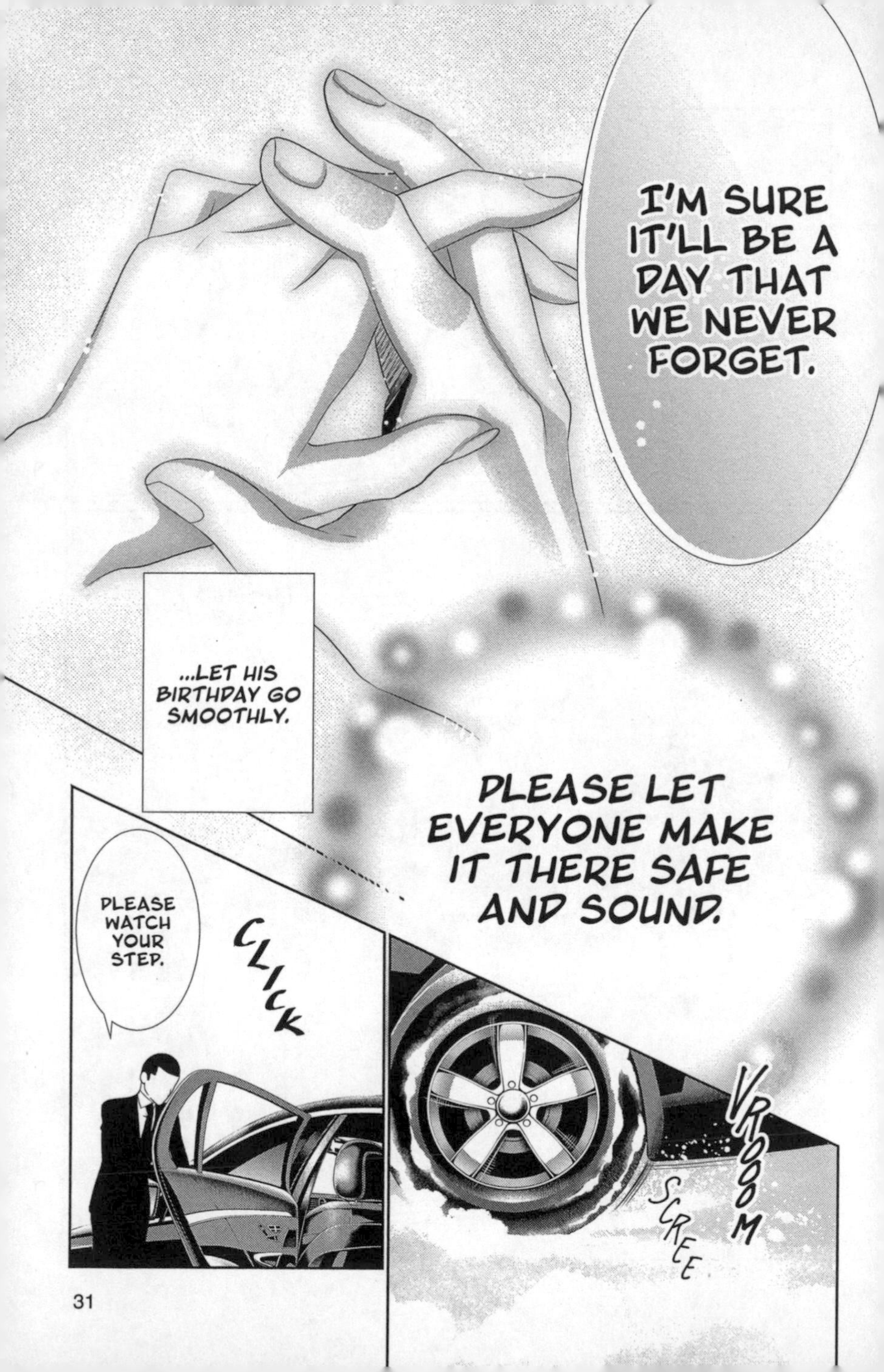
I'M SURE IT'LL BE A DAY THAT WE NEVER FORGET.
PLEASE LET EVERYONE MAKE IT THERE SAFE AND SOUND.
...LET HIS BIRTHDAY GO SMOOTHLY.
VROOOOM
SCREE
PLEASE WATCH YOUR STEP.
CLICK

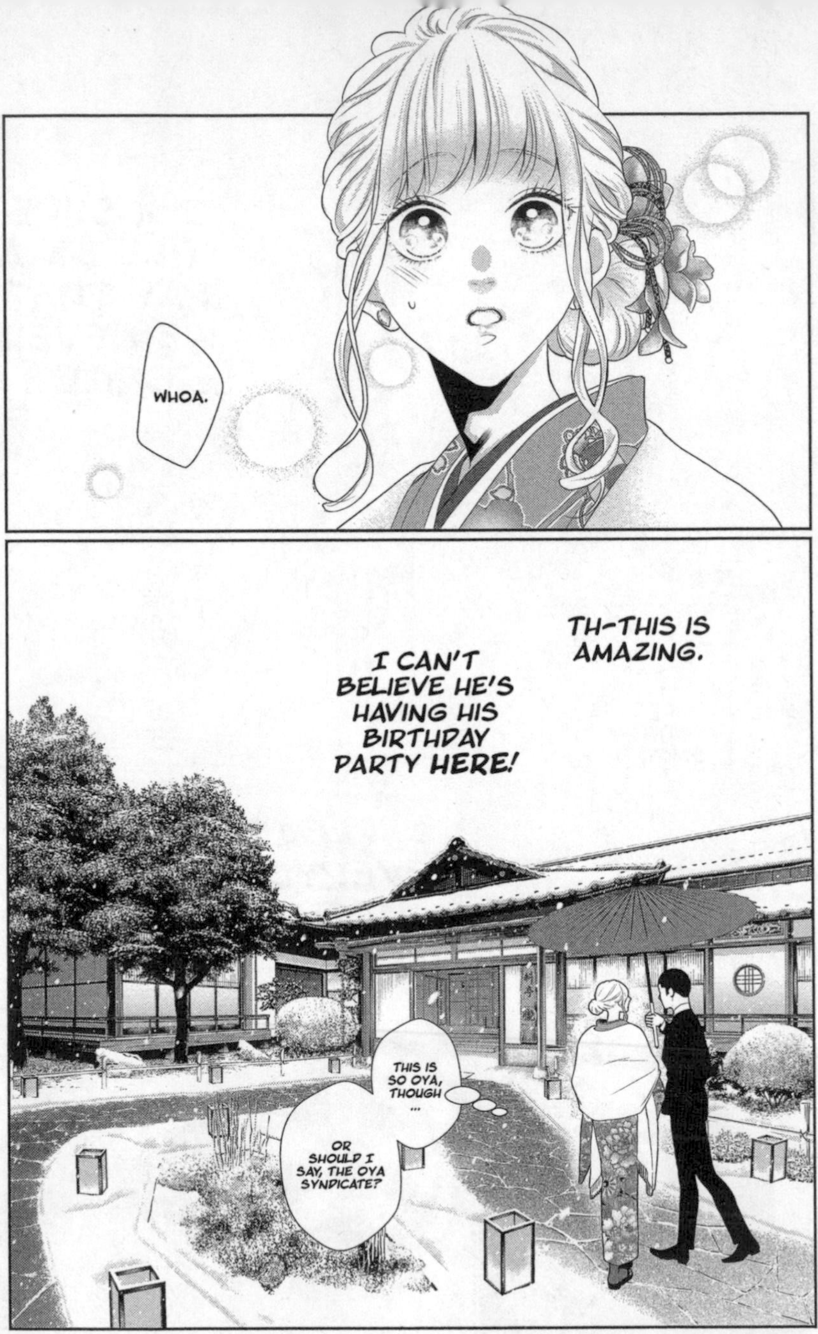
WHOA.
TH-THIS IS AMAZING.
I CAN'T BELIEVE HE'S HAVING HIS BIRTHDAY PARTY HERE!
THIS IS SO OYA, THOUGH ...
OR SHOULD I SAY, THE OYA SYNDICATE?

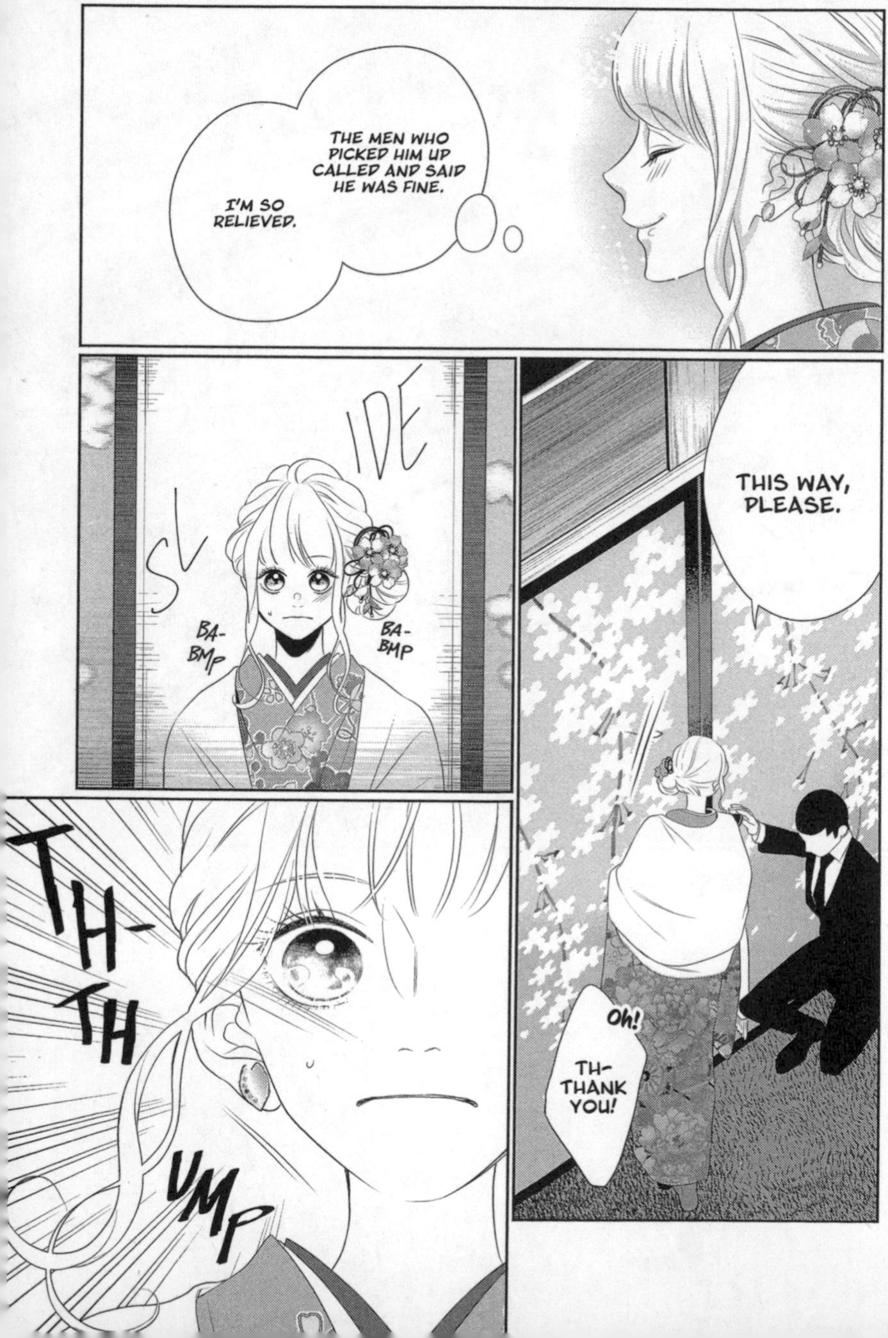
THE MEN WHO PICKED HIM UP CALLED AND SAID HE WAS FINE.
I'M SO RELIEVED.
THIS WAY, PLEASE.
OH!
TH-THANK YOU!
SLIDE
BA-BMP
BA-BMP
TH-THUMP

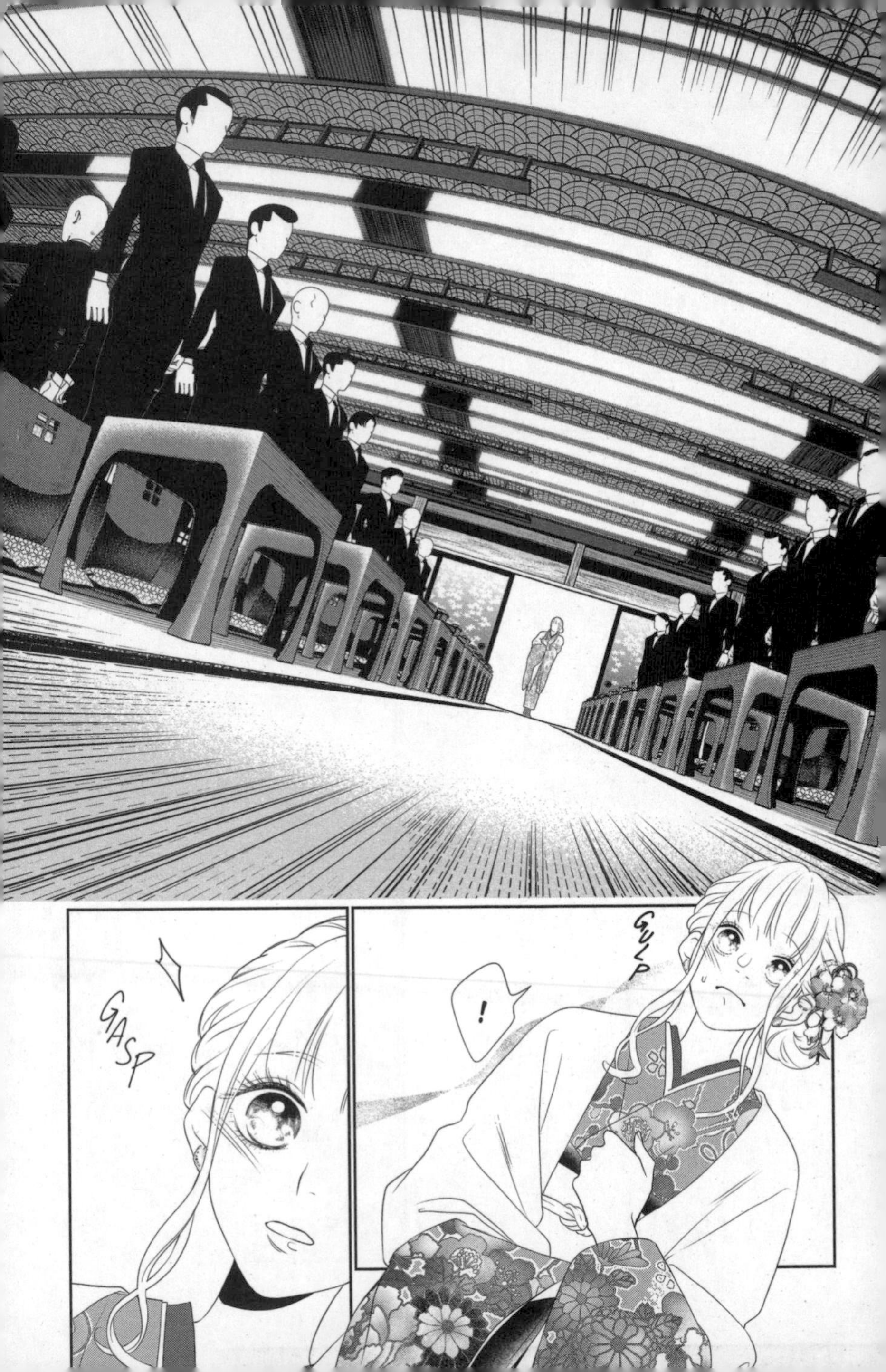
GULP
!
GASP

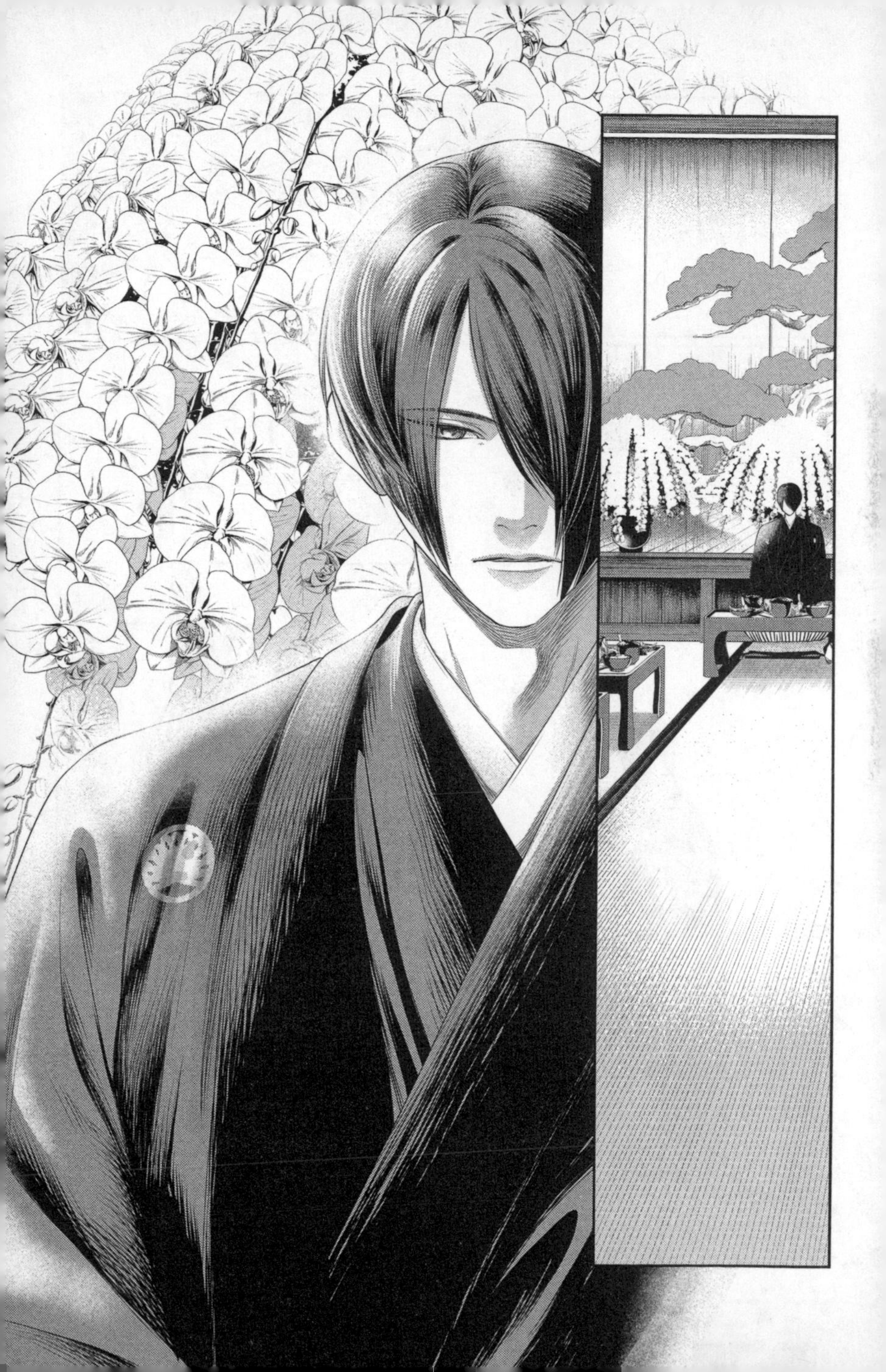

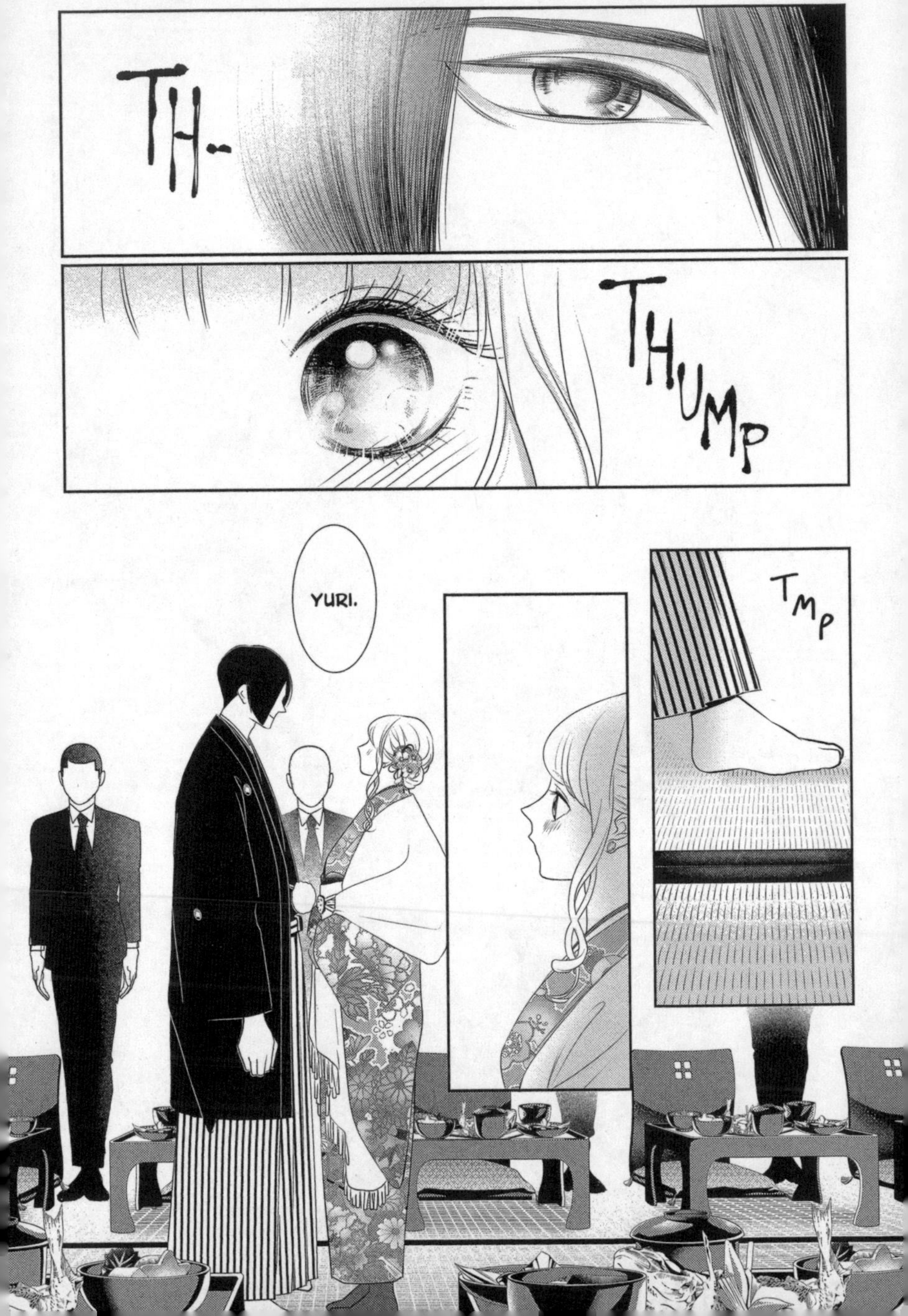
TH-
THUMP
TMP
YURI.

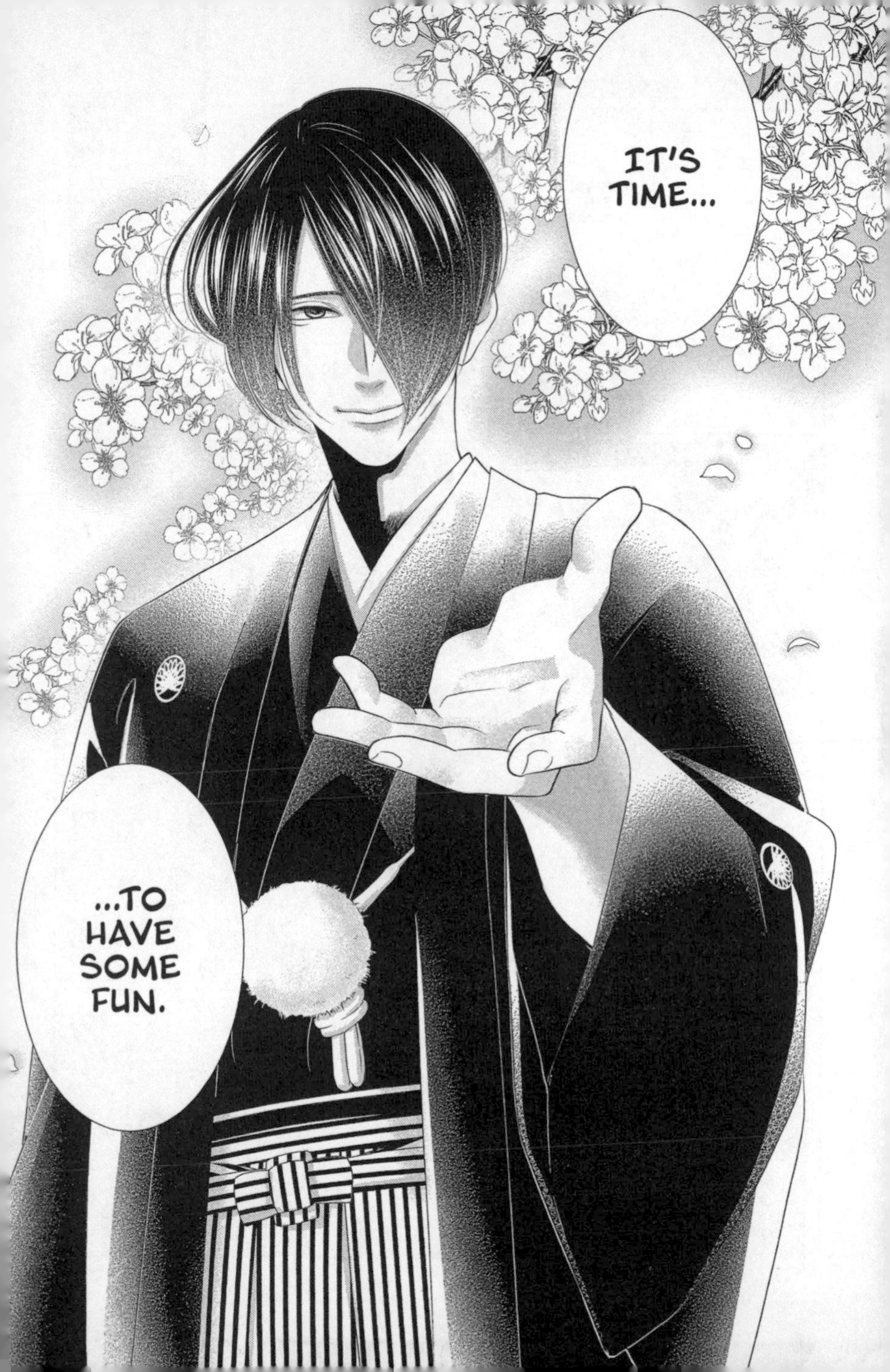
IT'S TIME...
...TO HAVE SOME FUN.

bonus bullet 18 secret scene

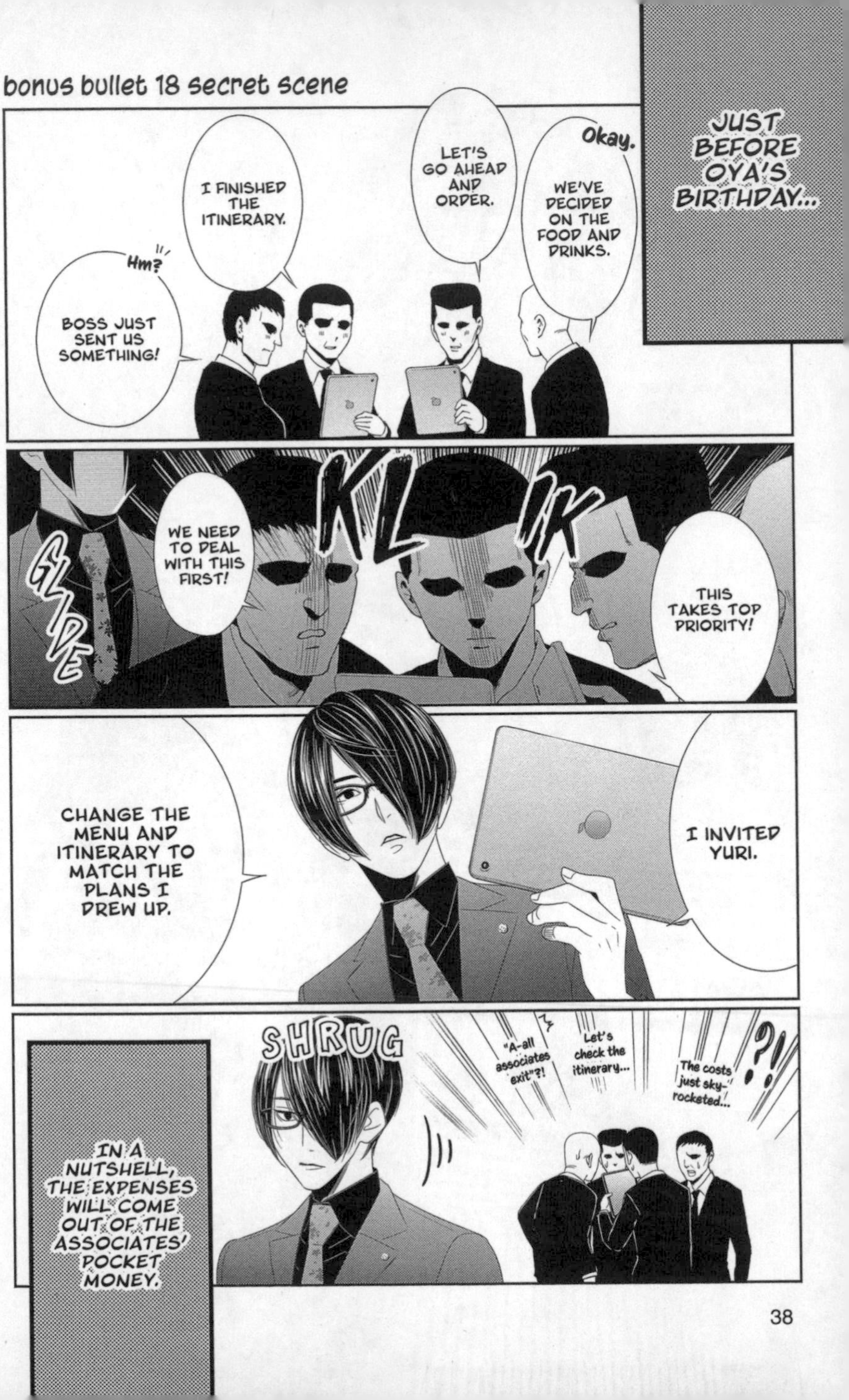
JUST BEFORE OYA'S BIRTHDAY...
Okay.
WE'VE DECIDED ON THE FOOD AND DRINKS.
LET'S GO AHEAD AND ORDER.
I FINISHED THE ITINERARY.
Hm?
BOSS JUST SENT US SOMETHING!
THIS TAKES TOP PRIORITY!
KLIK
WE NEED TO DEAL WITH THIS FIRST!
GLIDE
I INVITED YURI.
CHANGE THE MENU AND ITINERARY TO MATCH THE PLANS I DREW UP.
?!
The costs just sky-rocketed...
Let's check the itinerary...
"A-all associates exit"?!
SHRUG
IN A NUTSHELL, THE EXPENSES WILL COME OUT OF THE ASSOCIATES' POCKET MONEY.

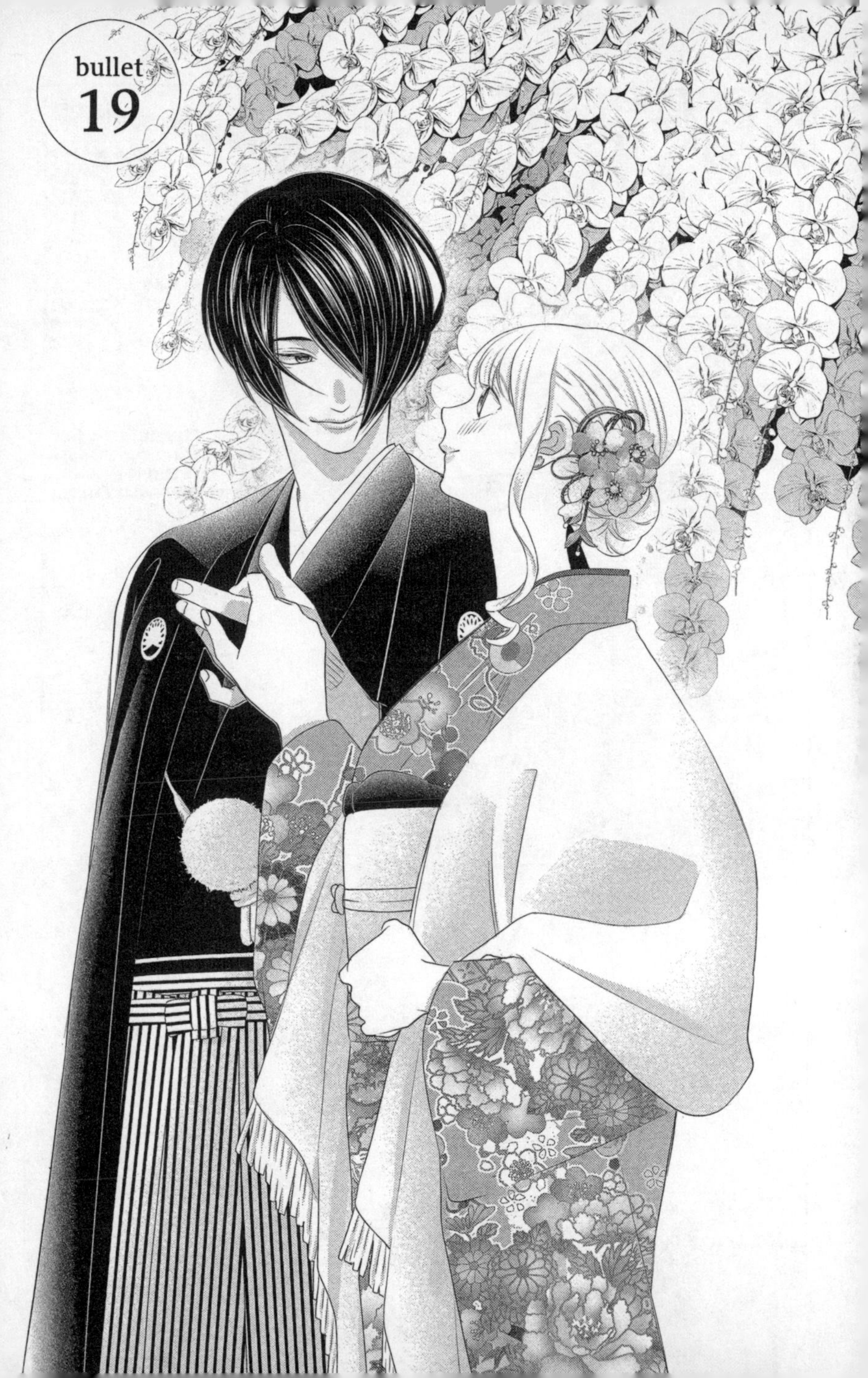
bullet
19

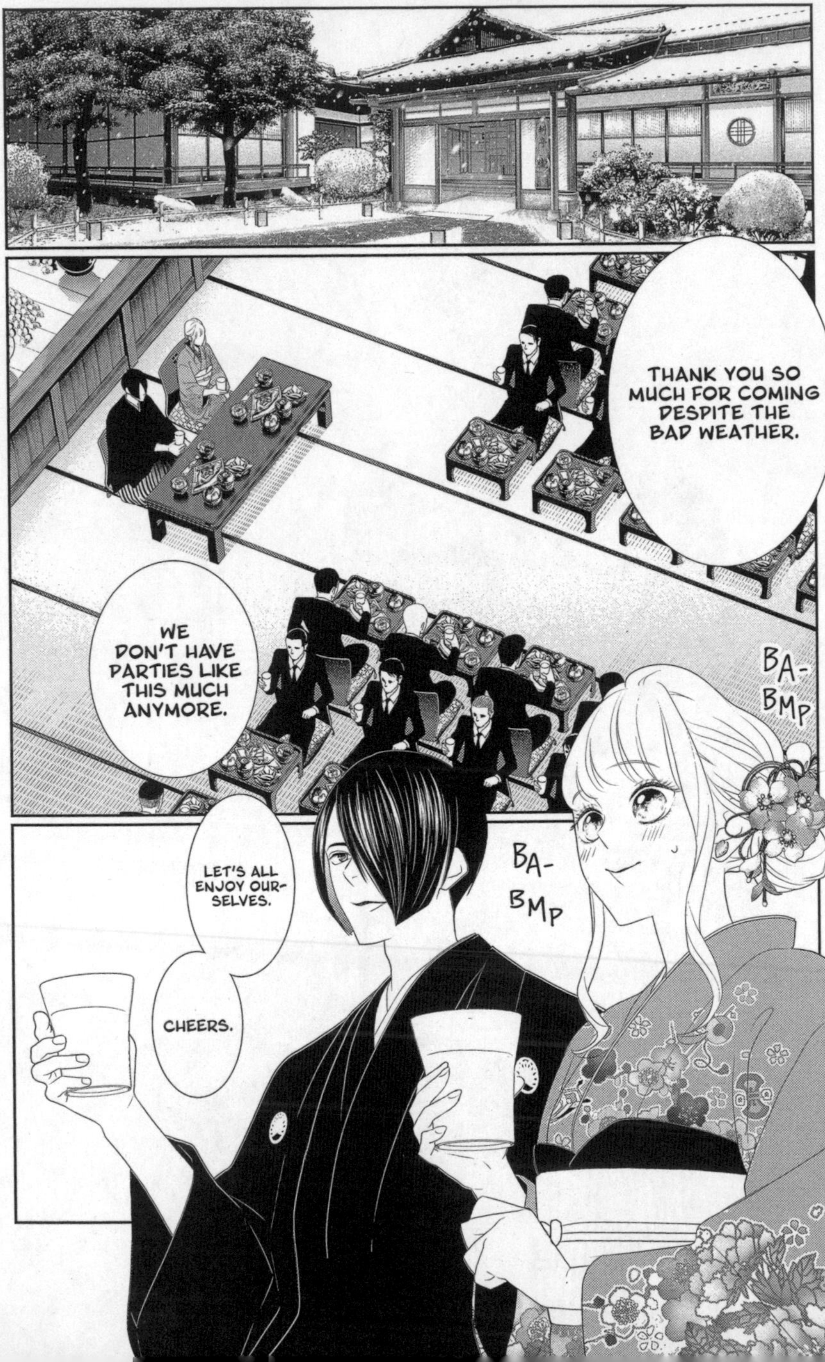
THANK YOU SO MUCH FOR COMING DESPITE THE BAD WEATHER.
WE DON'T HAVE PARTIES LIKE THIS MUCH ANYMORE.
BA-BMP
BA-BMP
LET'S ALL ENJOY OUR-SELVES.
CHEERS.

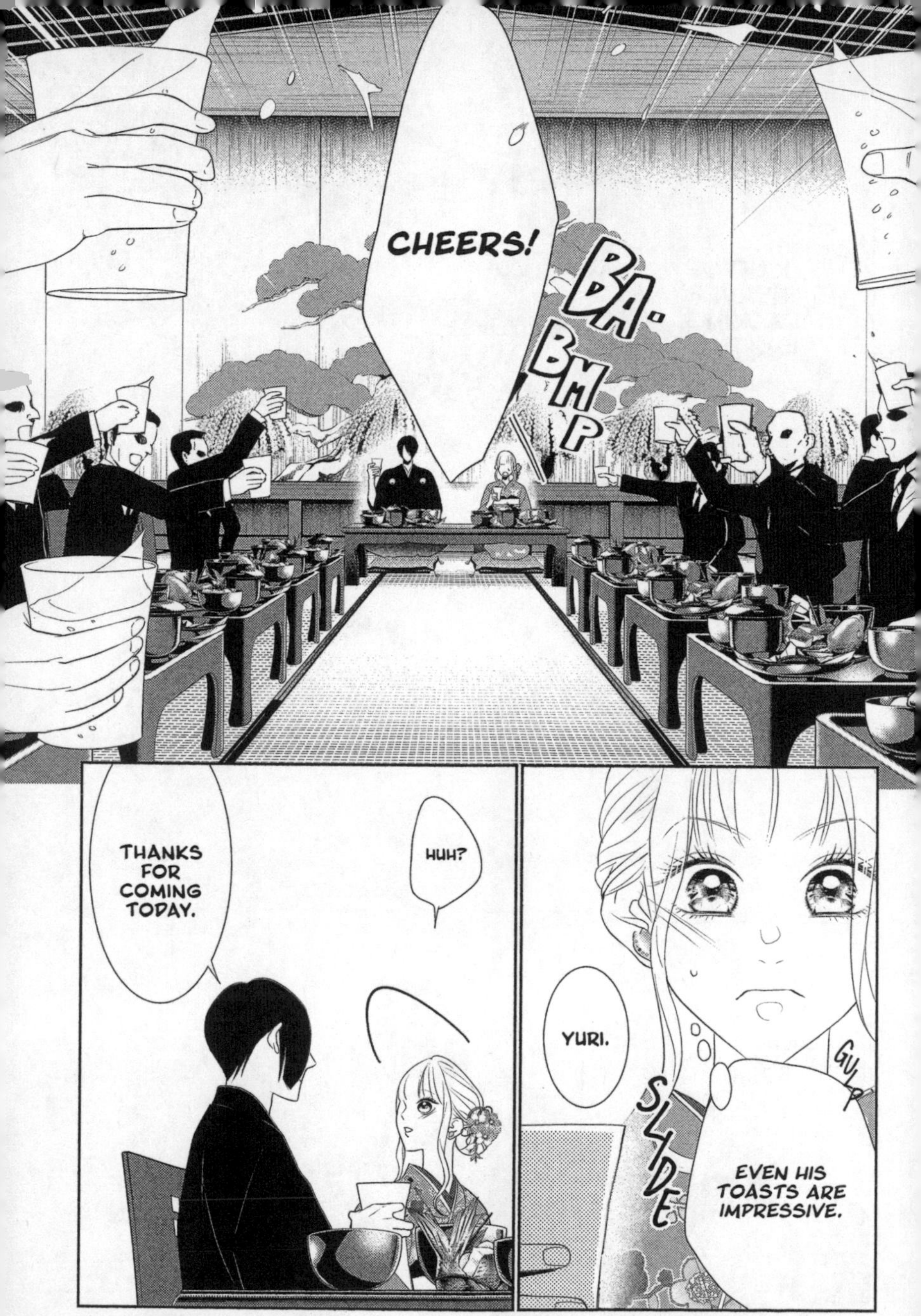
CHEERS!
BA-BMP
YURI.
GULP
SLIDE
EVEN HIS TOASTS ARE IMPRESSIVE.
THANKS FOR COMING TODAY.
HUH?

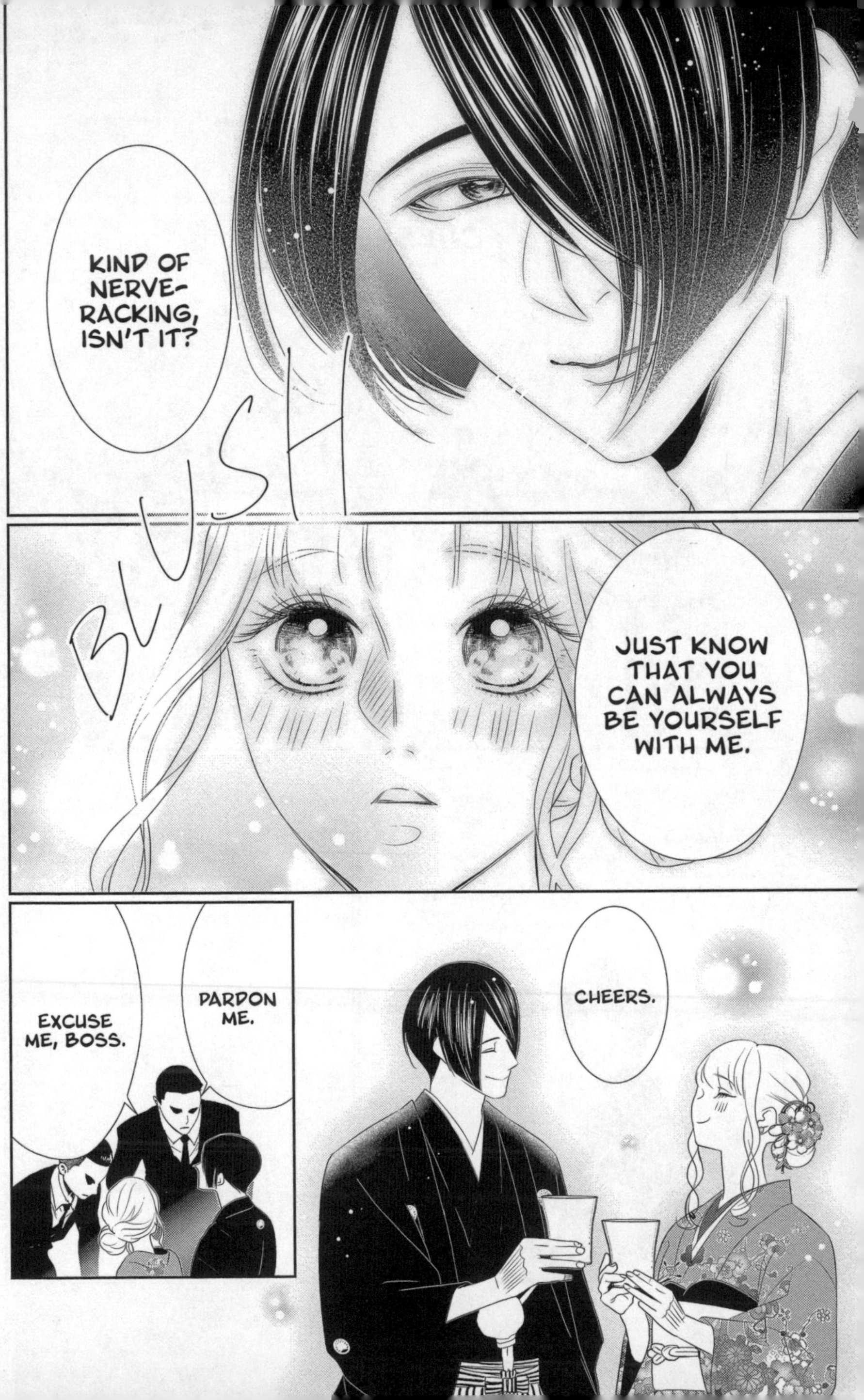
KIND OF NERVE-RACKING, ISN'T IT?
BLUSH
JUST KNOW THAT YOU CAN ALWAYS BE YOURSELF WITH ME.
CHEERS.
PARDON ME.
EXCUSE ME, BOSS.

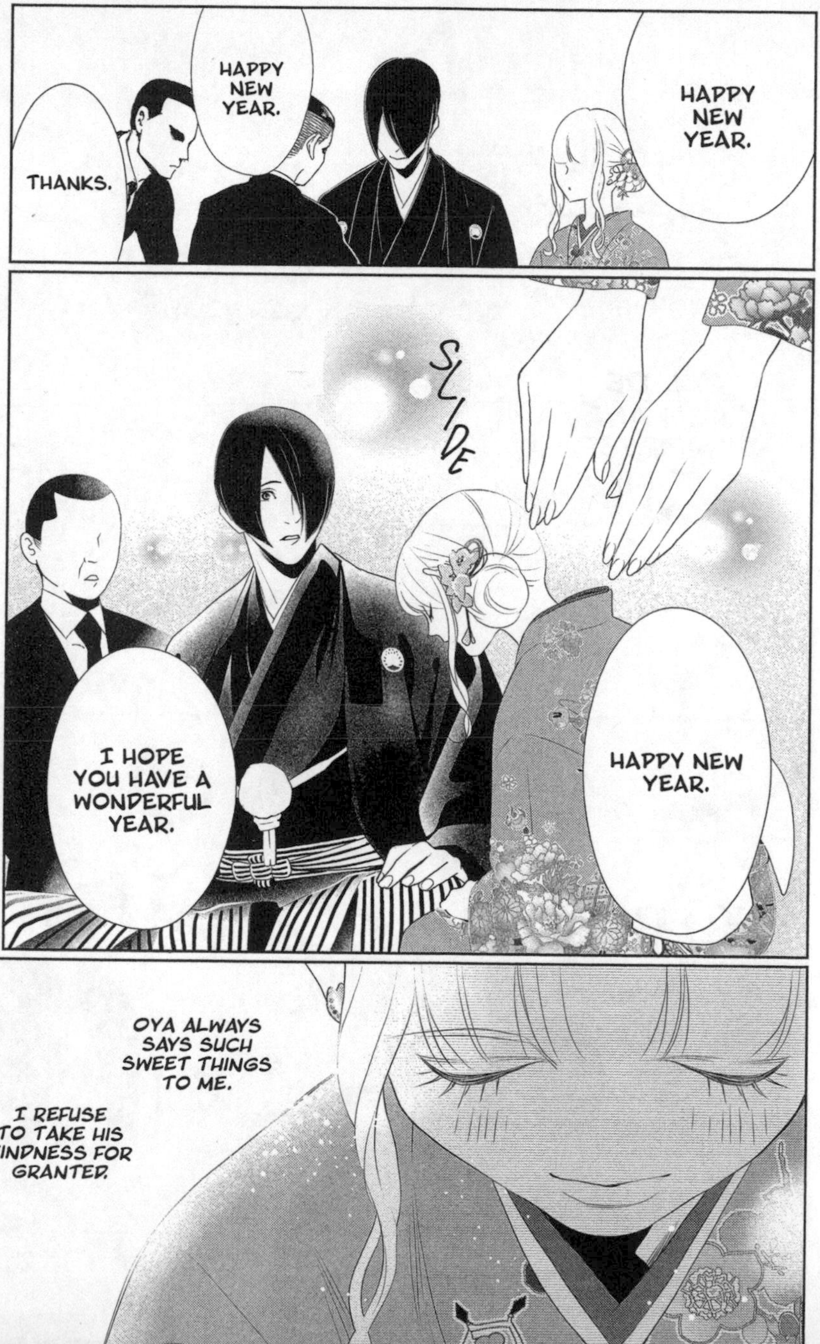
HAPPY NEW YEAR.
HAPPY NEW YEAR.
THANKS.
SLIDE
HAPPY NEW YEAR.
I HOPE YOU HAVE A WONDERFUL YEAR.
OYA ALWAYS SAYS SUCH SWEET THINGS TO ME.
I REFUSE TO TAKE HIS KINDNESS FOR GRANTED.

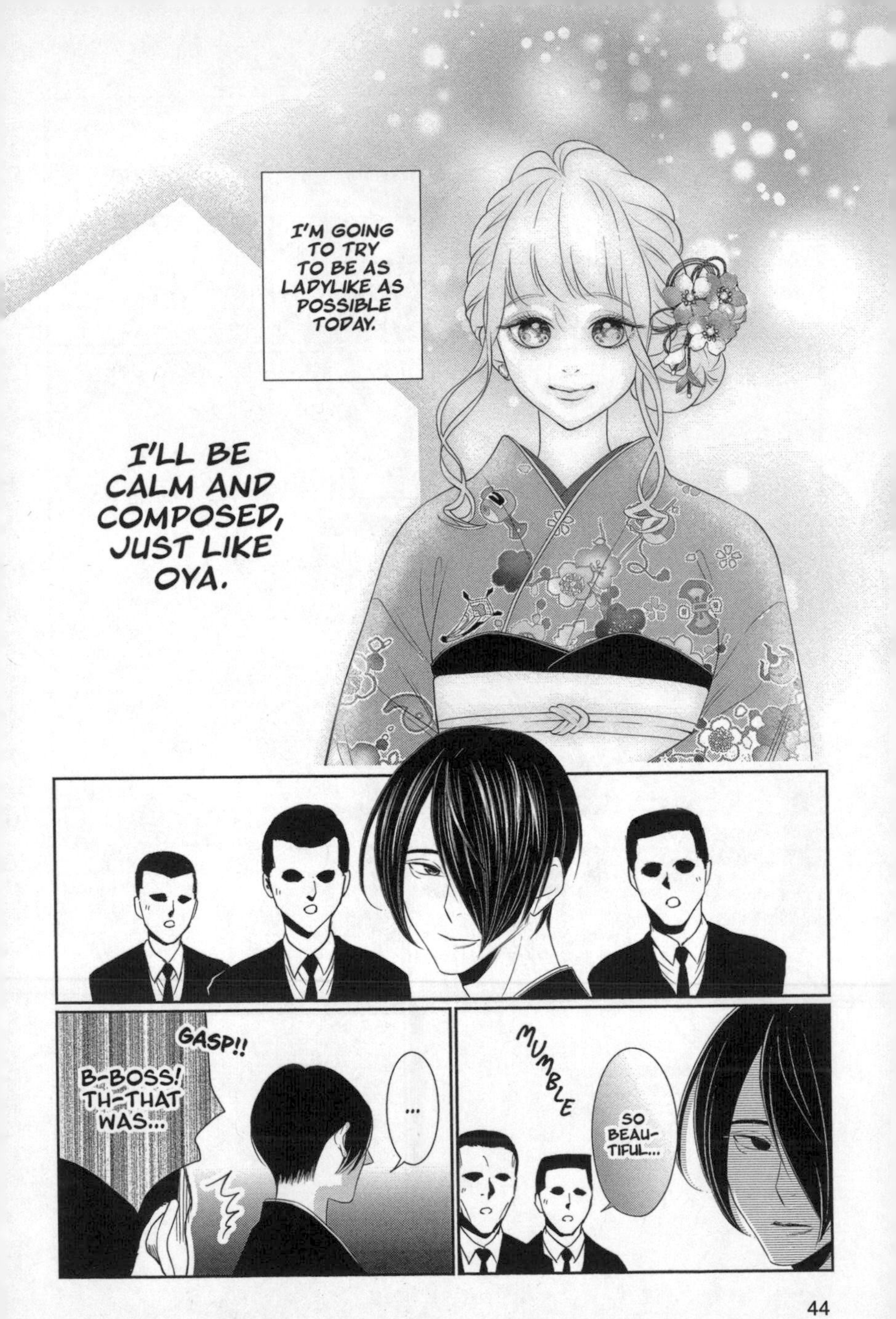
I'M GOING TO TRY TO BE AS LADYLIKE AS POSSIBLE TODAY.
I'LL BE CALM AND COMPOSED, JUST LIKE OYA.
MUMBLE
SO BEAUTIFUL...
GASP!!
B-BOSS! TH-THAT WAS...
...

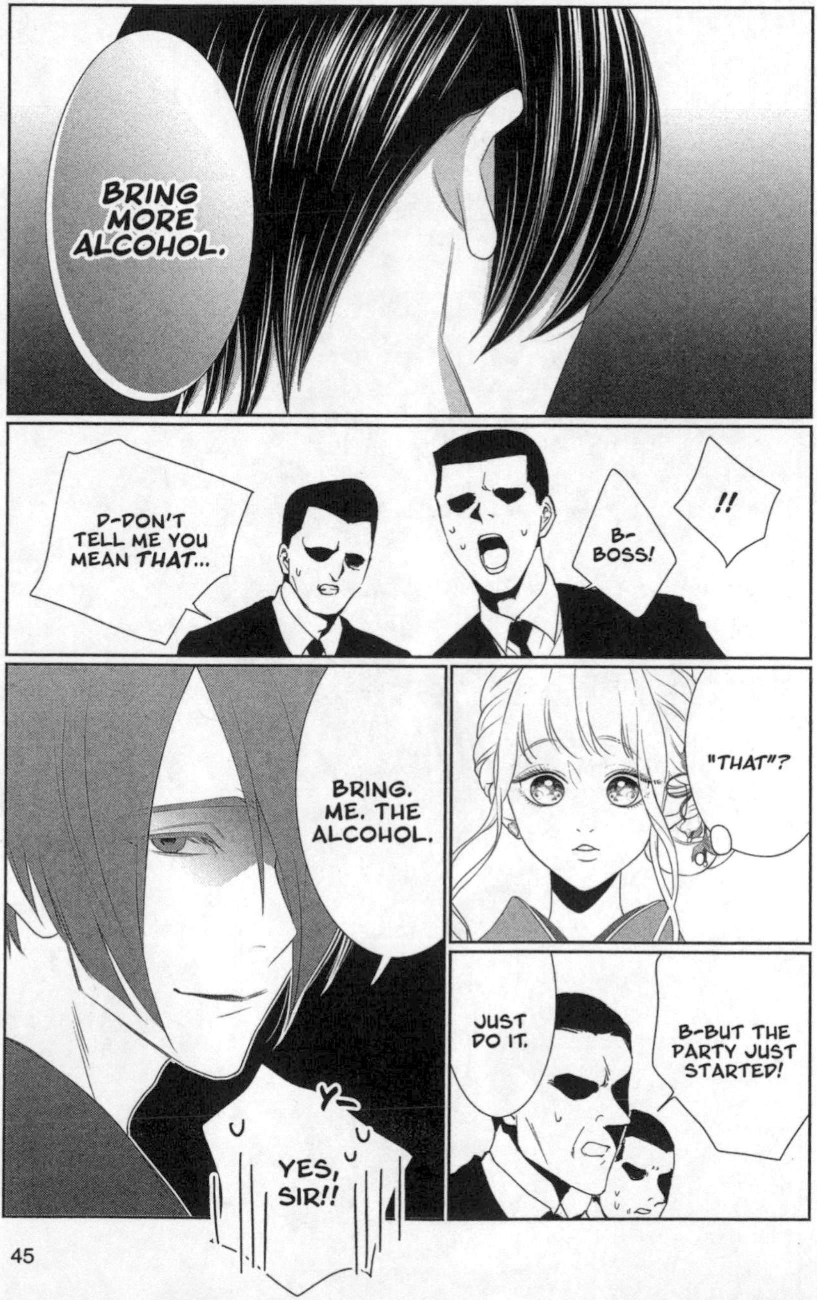
BRING MORE ALCOHOL.
!!
B-BOSS!
D-DON'T TELL ME YOU MEAN THAT...
"THAT"?
B-BUT THE PARTY JUST STARTED!
JUST DO IT.
BRING. ME. THE ALCOHOL.
YES, SIR!!

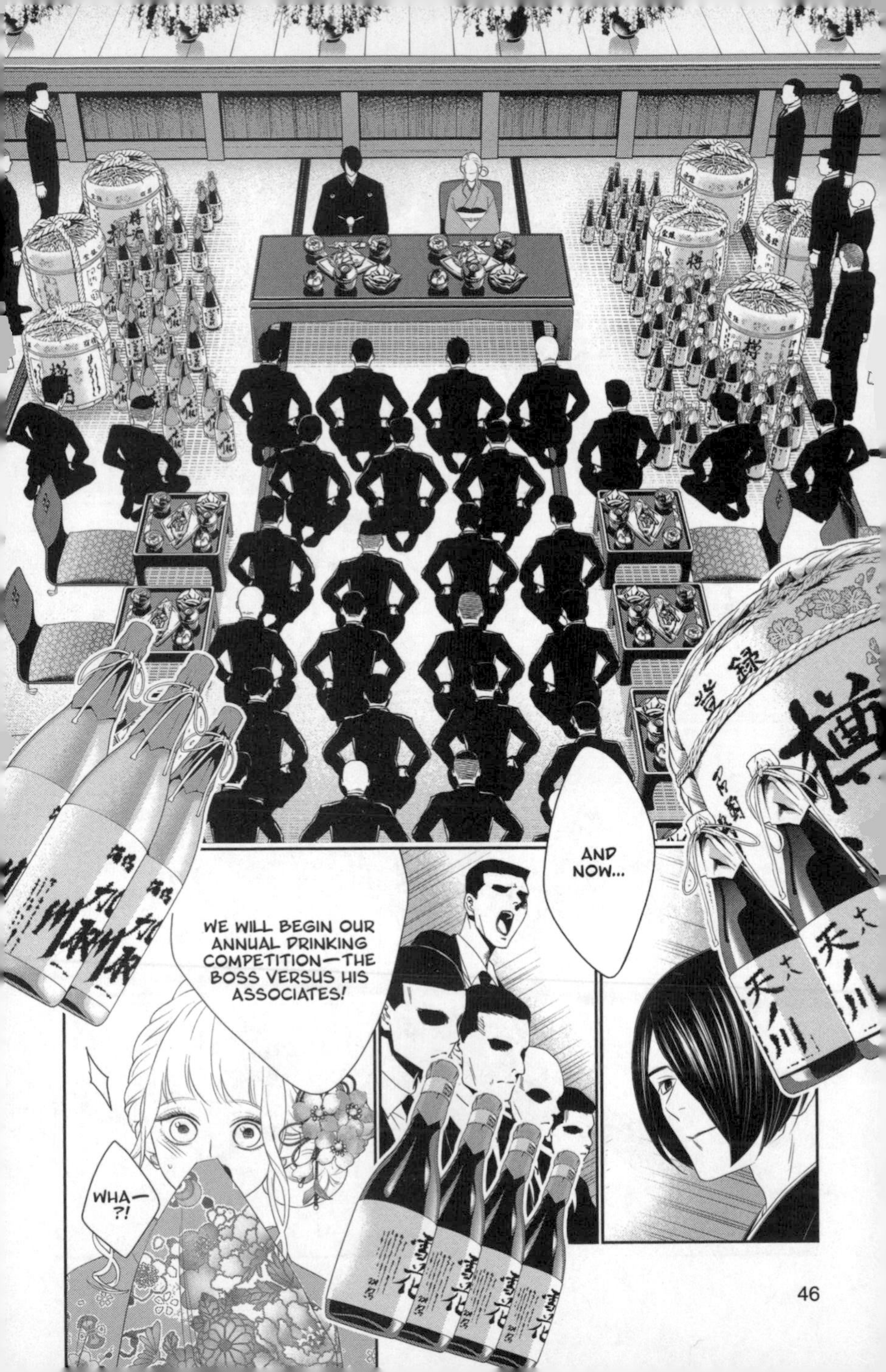
AND NOW...
WE WILL BEGIN OUR ANNUAL DRINKING COMPETITION—THE BOSS VERSUS HIS ASSOCIATES!
WHA— ?!

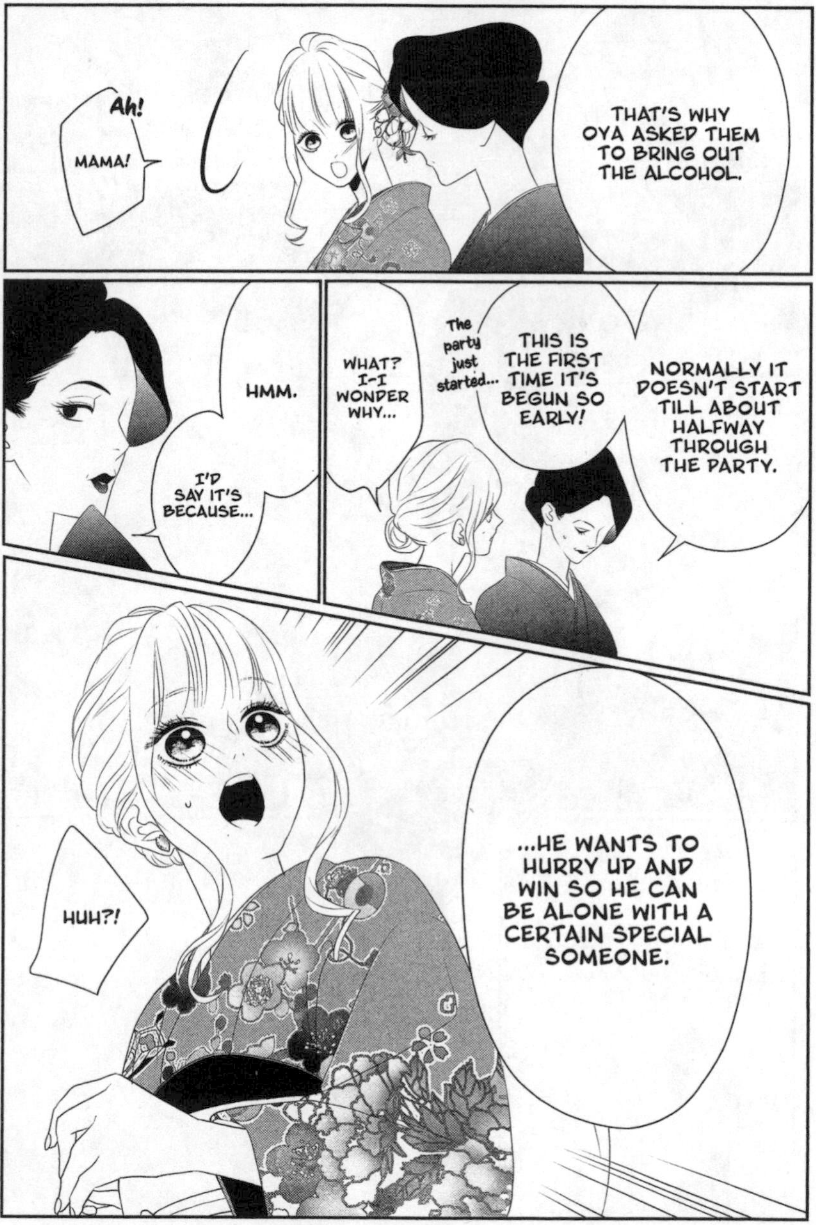
THAT'S WHY OYA ASKED THEM TO BRING OUT THE ALCOHOL.
Ah!
MAMA!
NORMALLY IT DOESN'T START TILL ABOUT HALFWAY THROUGH THE PARTY.
THIS IS THE FIRST TIME IT'S BEGUN SO EARLY!
The party just started...
WHAT? I-I WONDER WHY...
HMM.
I'D SAY IT'S BECAUSE...
...HE WANTS TO HURRY UP AND WIN SO HE CAN BE ALONE WITH A CERTAIN SPECIAL SOMEONE.
HUH?!

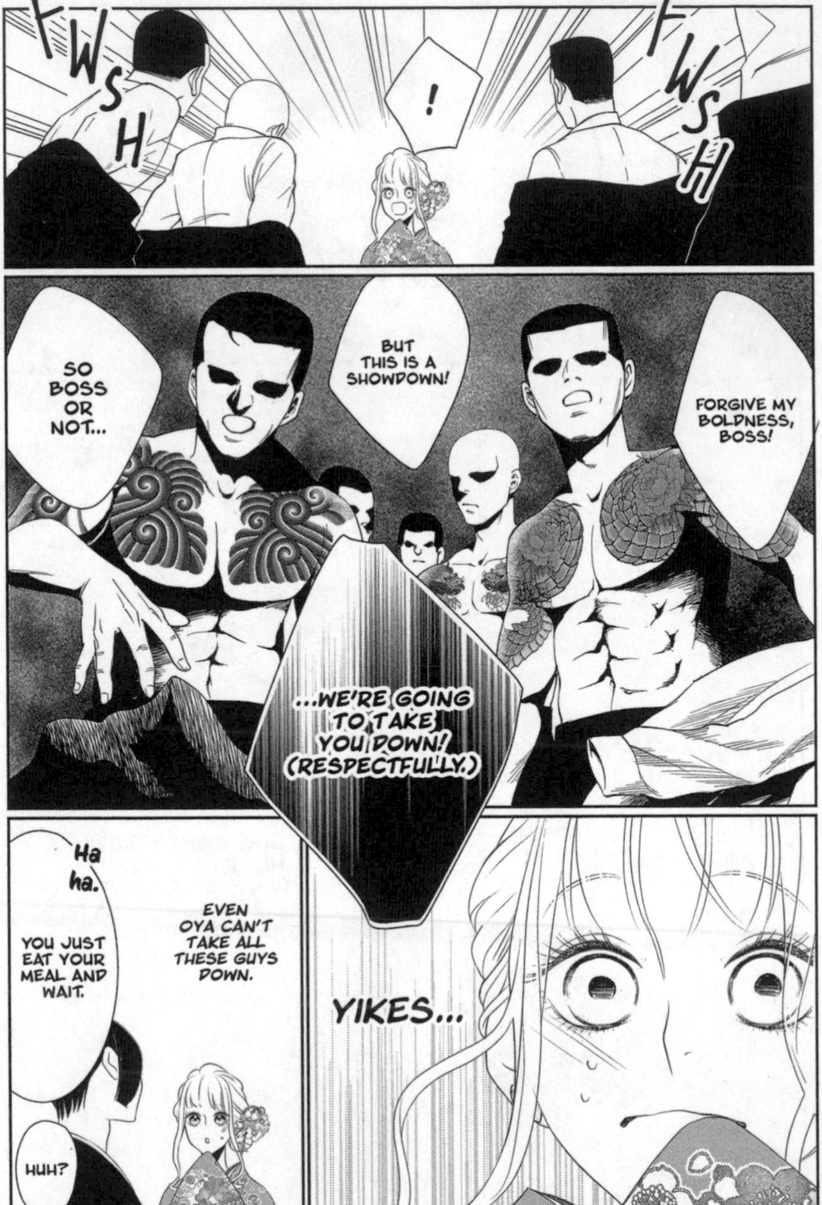
FWSH
!
FWSH
FORGIVE MY BOLDNESS, BOSS!
BUT THIS IS A SHOWDOWN!
SO BOSS OR NOT...
...WE'RE GOING TO TAKE YOU DOWN! (RESPECTFULLY.)
YIKES...
EVEN OYA CAN'T TAKE ALL THESE GUYS DOWN.
Ha ha.
YOU JUST EAT YOUR MEAL AND WAIT.
HUH?

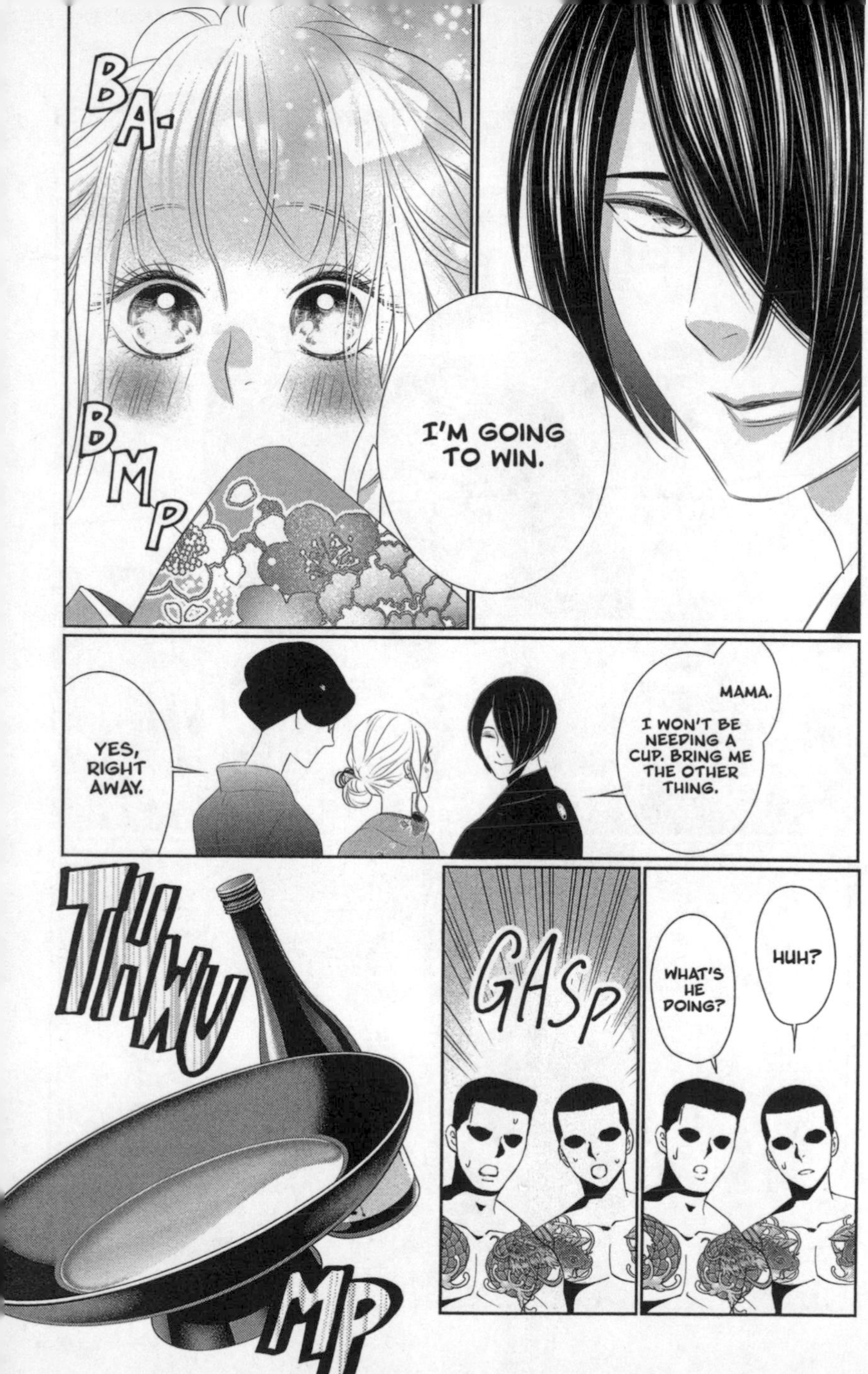
I'M GOING TO WIN.
BA-BMP
MAMA.
I WON'T BE NEEDING A CUP. BRING ME THE OTHER THING.
YES, RIGHT AWAY.
HUH?
WHAT'S HE DOING?
GASP
THWUMP

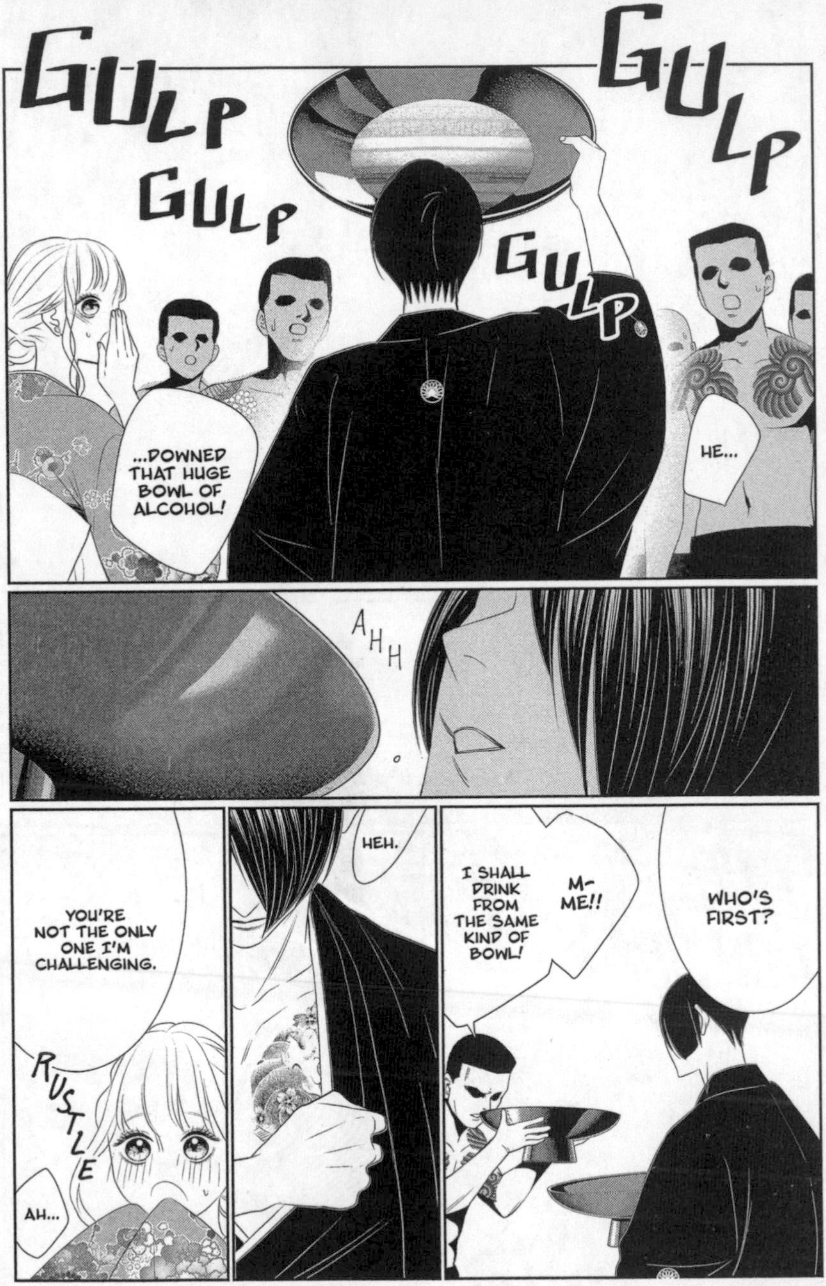
GULP
GULP
GULP
GULP
HE...
...DOWNED THAT HUGE BOWL OF ALCOHOL!
AHH
WHO'S FIRST?
M-ME!!
I SHALL DRINK FROM THE SAME KIND OF BOWL!
HEH.
YOU'RE NOT THE ONLY ONE I'M CHALLENGING.
RUSTLE
AH...

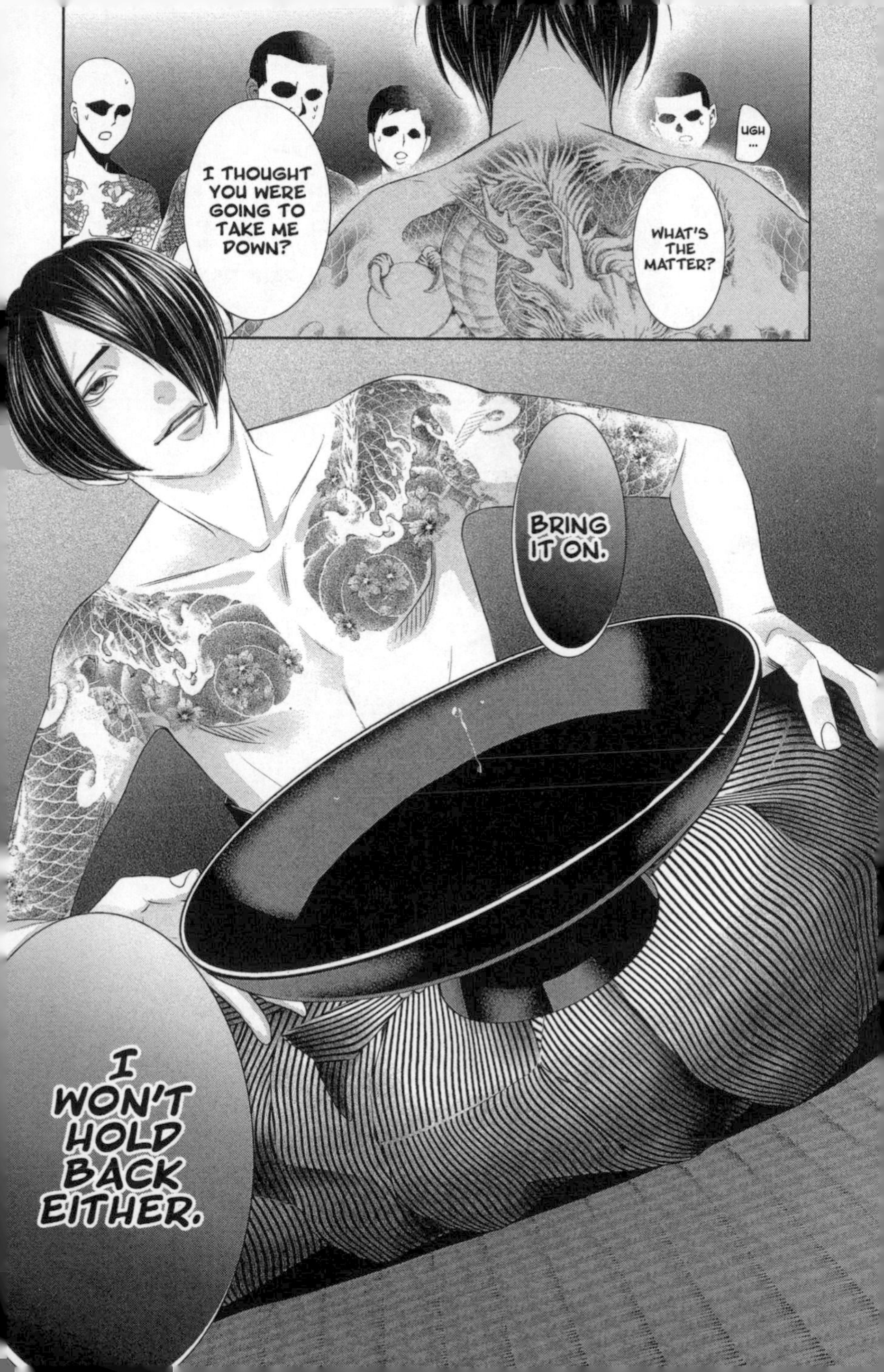
UGH...
WHAT'S THE MATTER?
I THOUGHT YOU WERE GOING TO TAKE ME DOWN?
BRING IT ON.
I WON'T HOLD BACK EITHER.

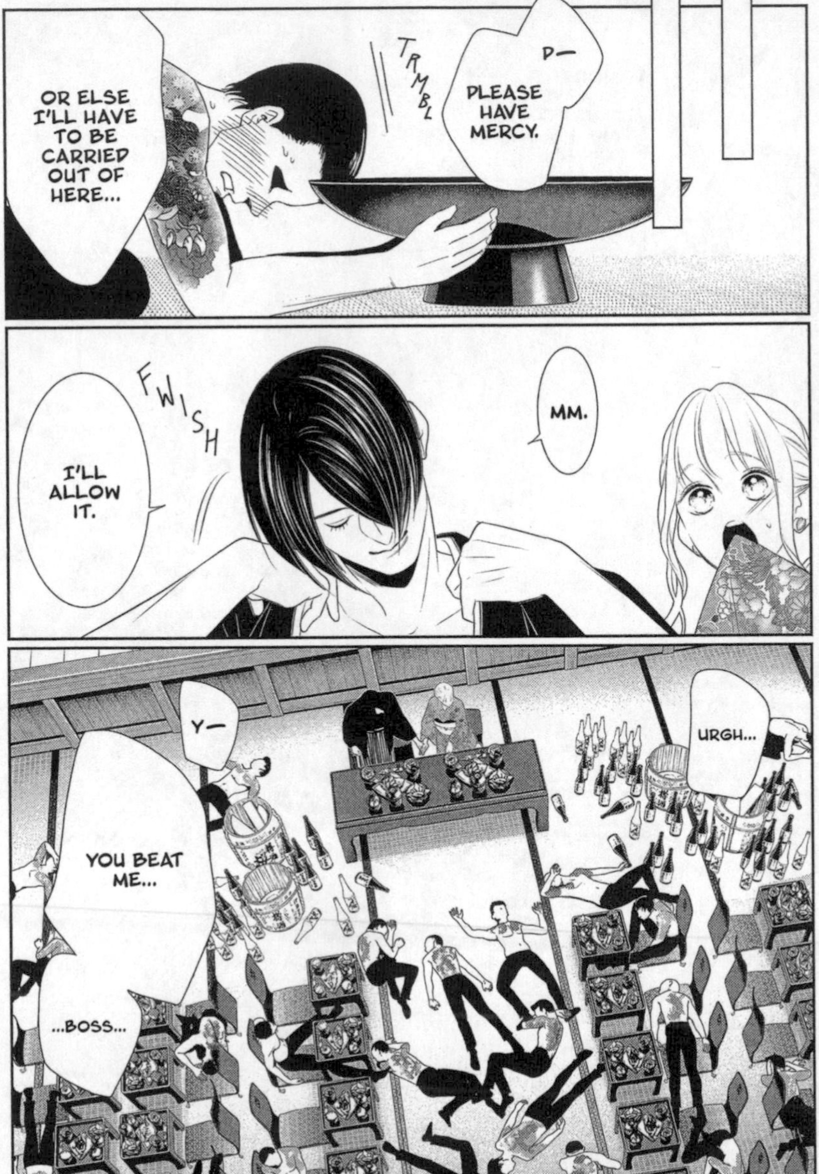
P—
PLEASE HAVE MERCY.
TRMBL
OR ELSE I'LL HAVE TO BE CARRIED OUT OF HERE...
MM.
FWISH
I'LL ALLOW IT.
URGH...
Y—
YOU BEAT ME...
...BOSS...

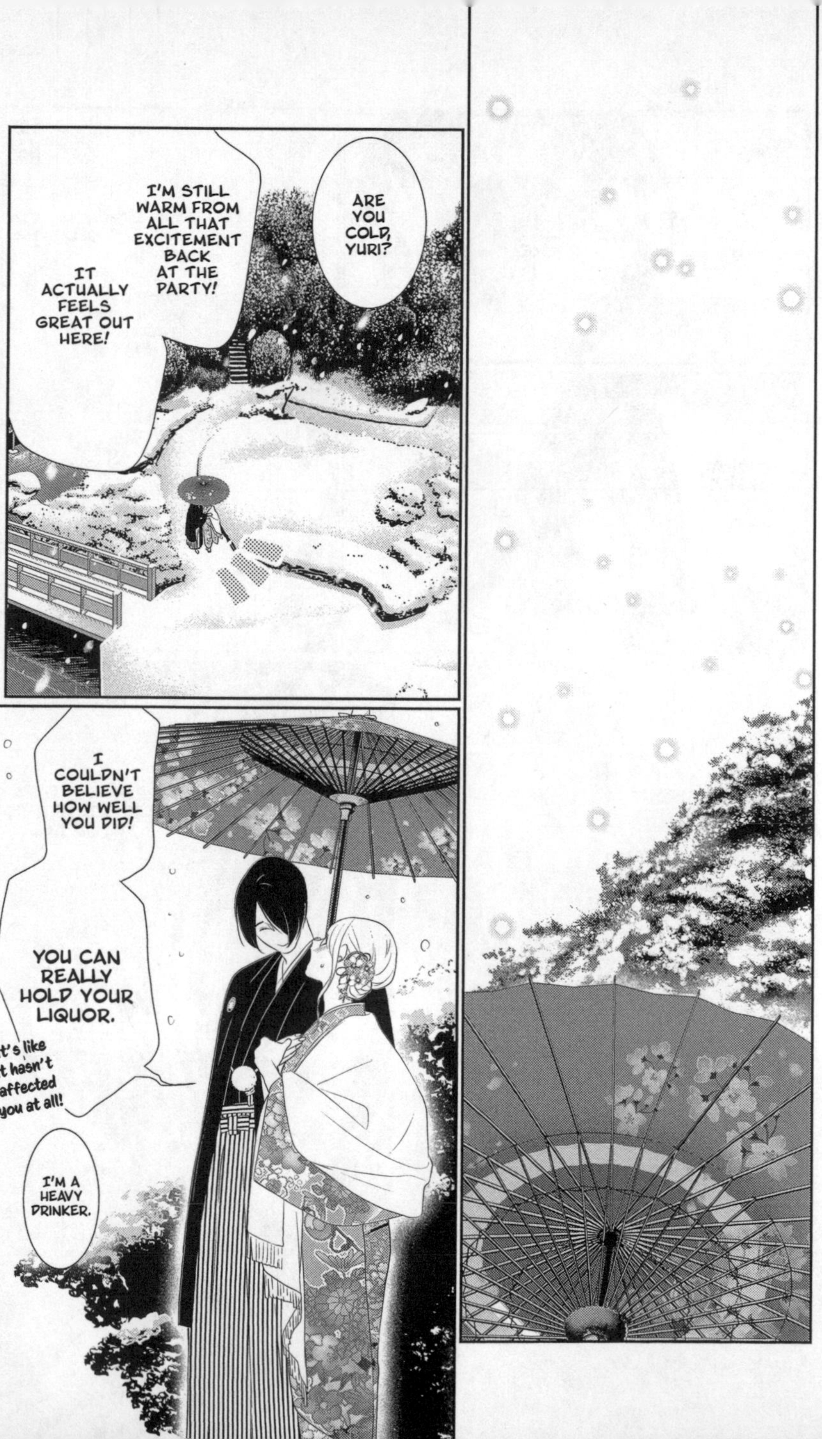
ARE YOU COLD, YURI?
I'M STILL WARM FROM ALL THAT EXCITEMENT BACK AT THE PARTY!
IT ACTUALLY FEELS GREAT OUT HERE!
I COULDN'T BELIEVE HOW WELL YOU DID!
YOU CAN REALLY HOLD YOUR LIQUOR.
It's like it hasn't affected you at all!
I'M A HEAVY DRINKER.

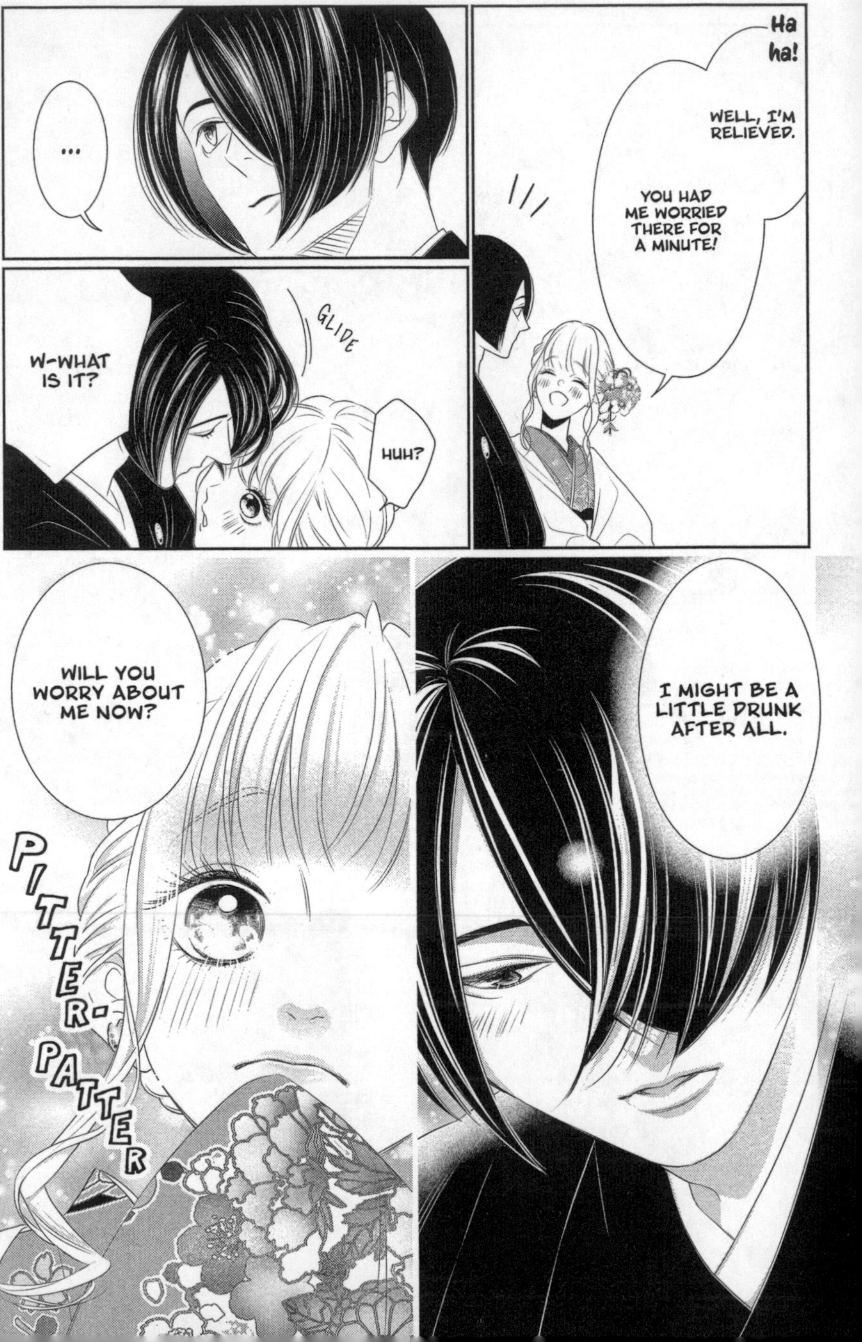
Ha ha!
WELL, I'M RELIEVED.
YOU HAD ME WORRIED THERE FOR A MINUTE!
...
GLIDE
HUH?
W-WHAT IS IT?
I MIGHT BE A LITTLE DRUNK AFTER ALL.
WILL YOU WORRY ABOUT ME NOW?
PITTER-PATTER

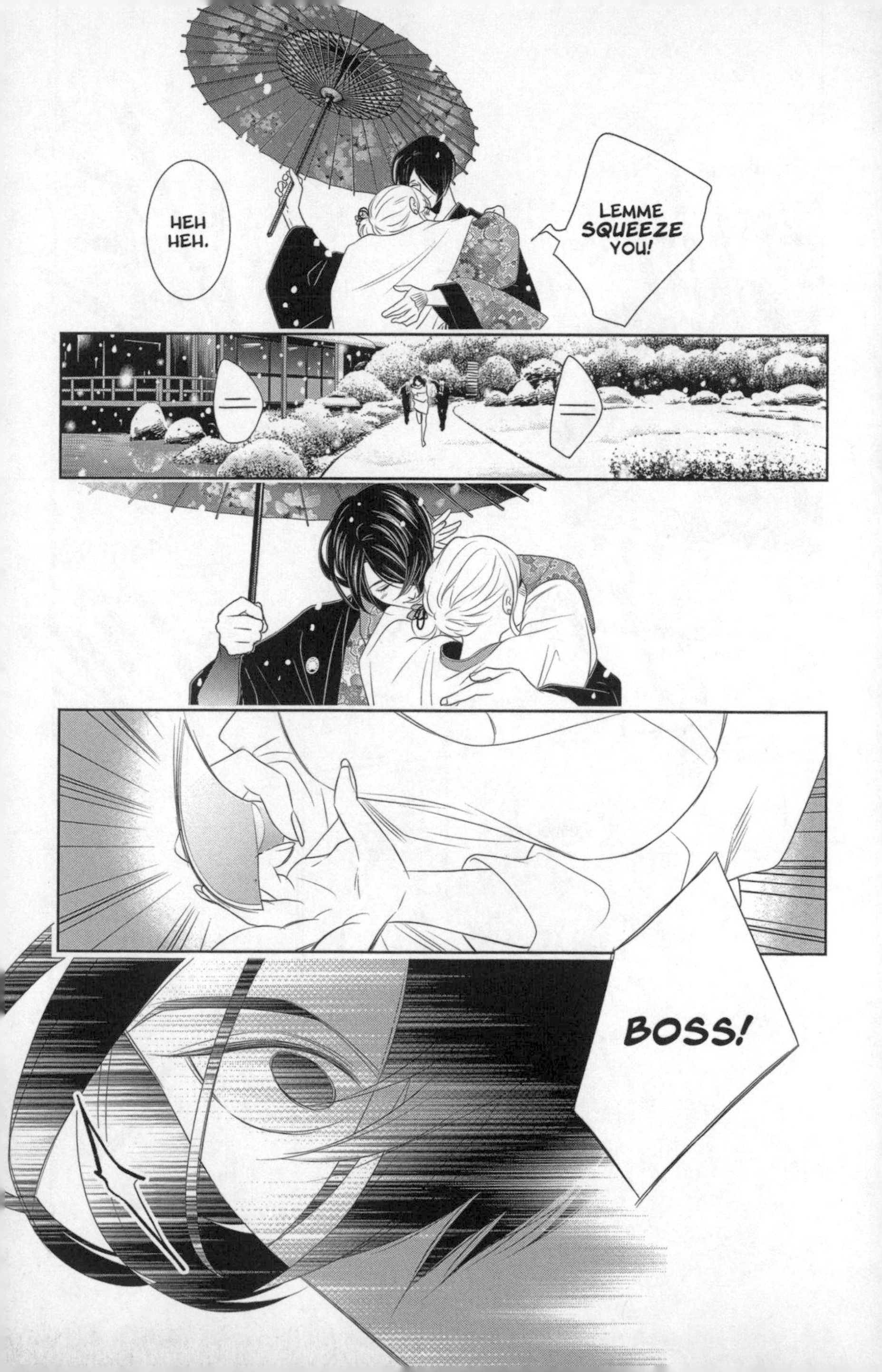
LEMME SQUEEZE YOU!
HEH HEH.
—
—
BOSS!

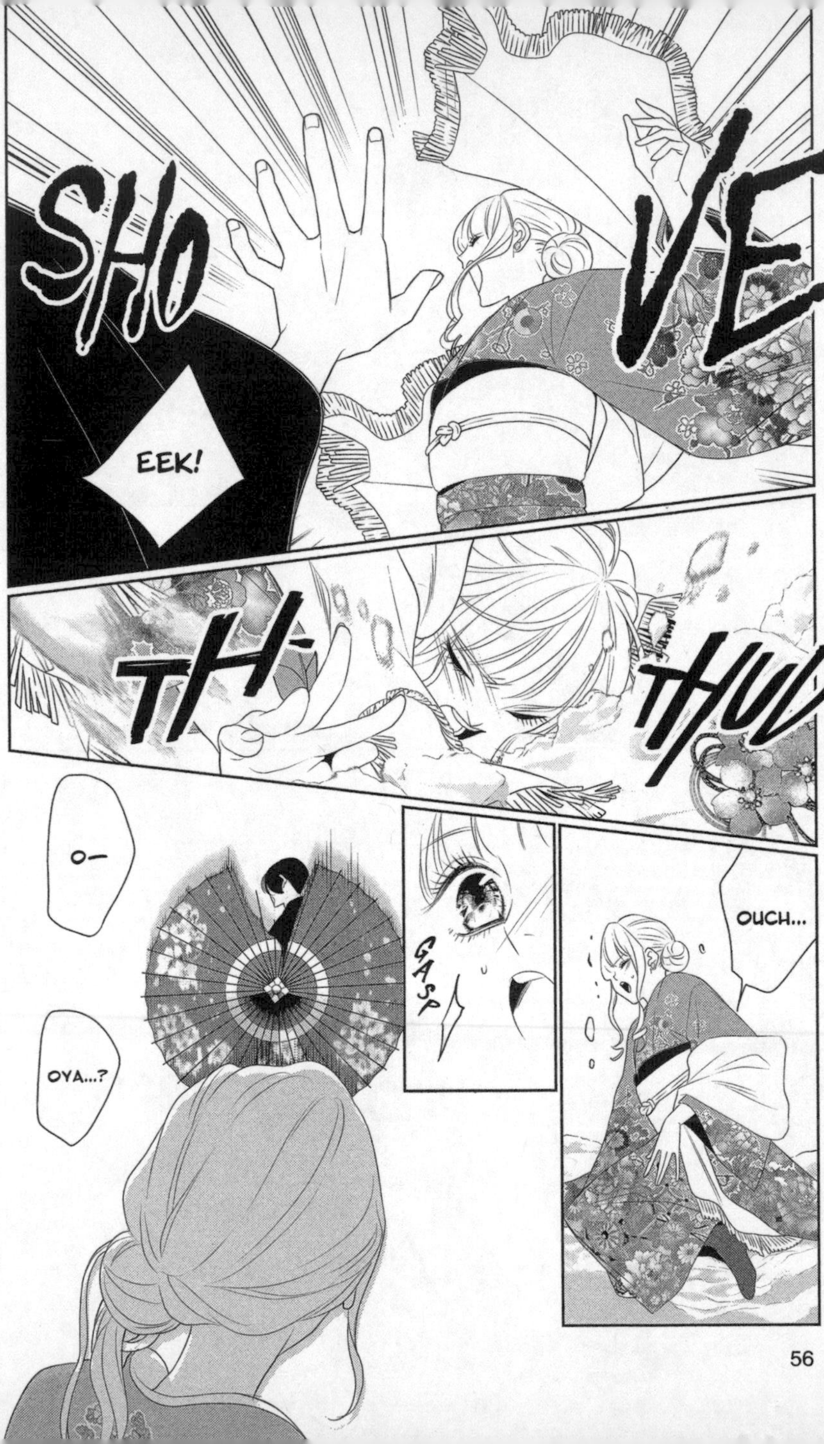
SHOVE
EEK!
TH-
THUD
OUCH...
GASP
O-
OYA...?

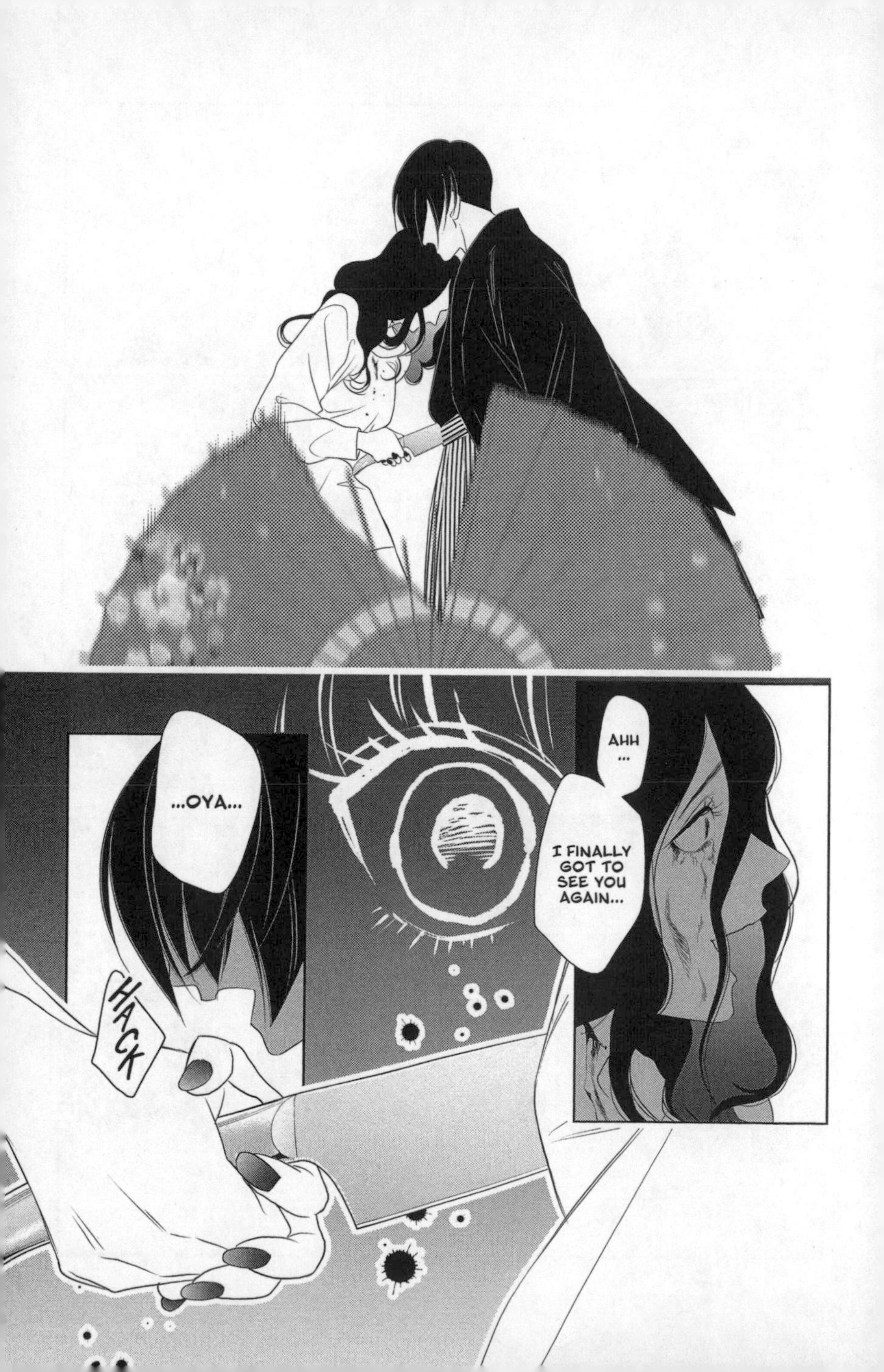
AHH ...
I FINALLY GOT TO SEE YOU AGAIN...
...OYA...
HACK

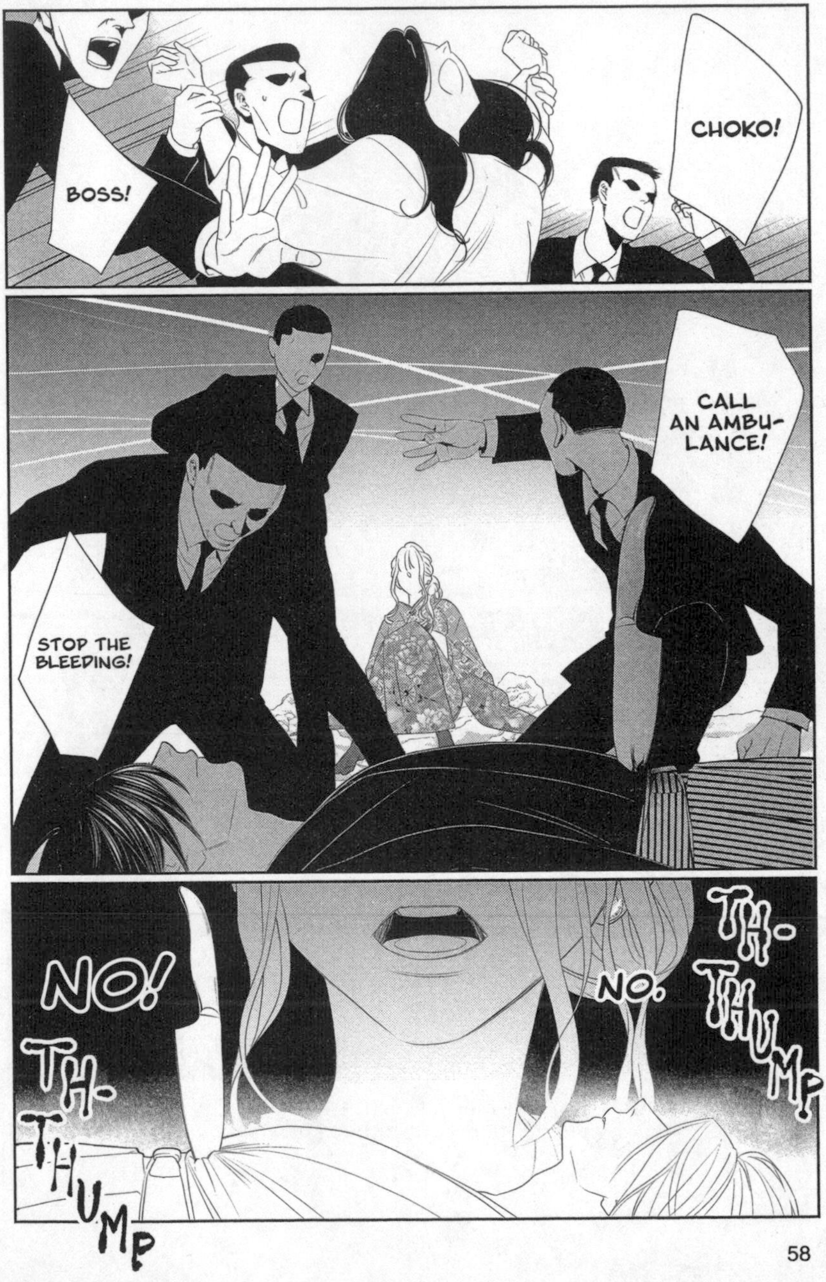

CHOKO!
BOSS!
CALL AN AMBU-LANCE!
STOP THE BLEEDING!
TH-THUMP
NO.
NO!
TH-THUMP

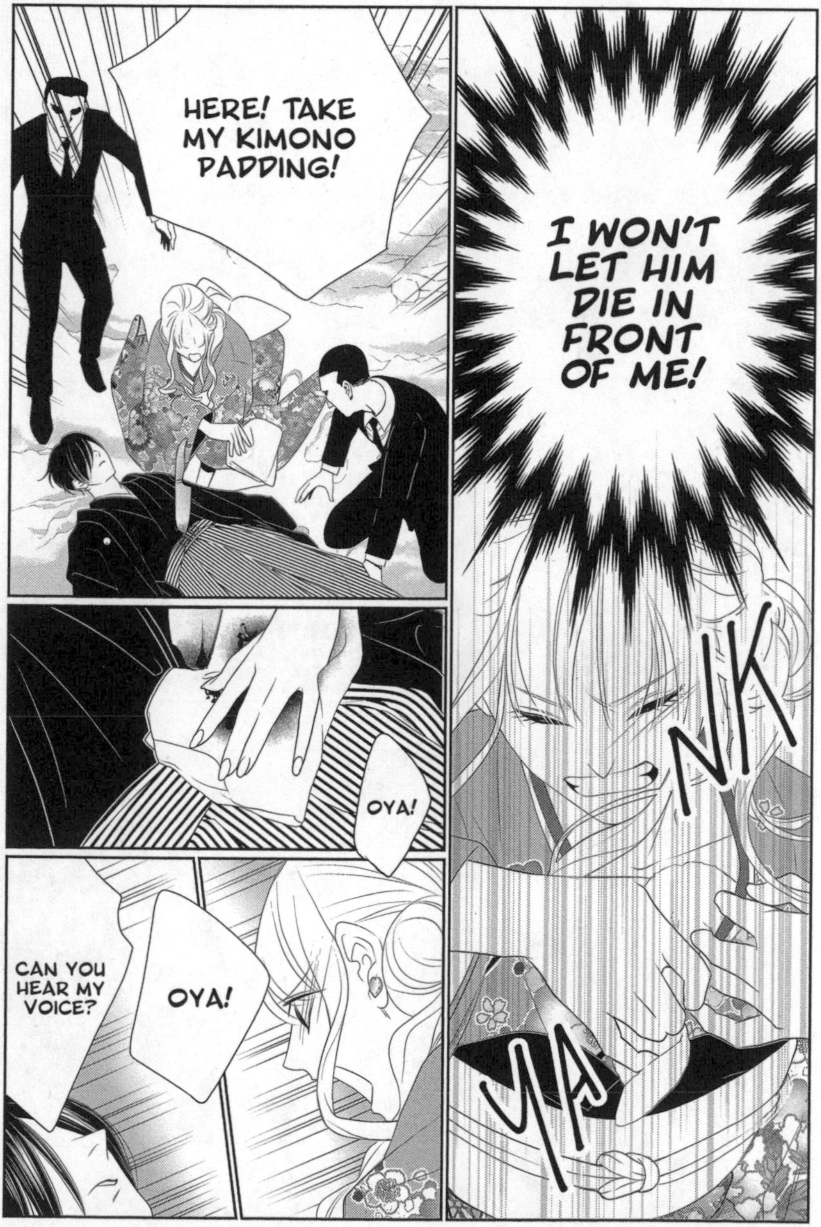
I WON'T LET HIM DIE IN FRONT OF ME!
YANK
HERE! TAKE MY KIMONO PADDING!
OYA!
OYA!
CAN YOU HEAR MY VOICE?

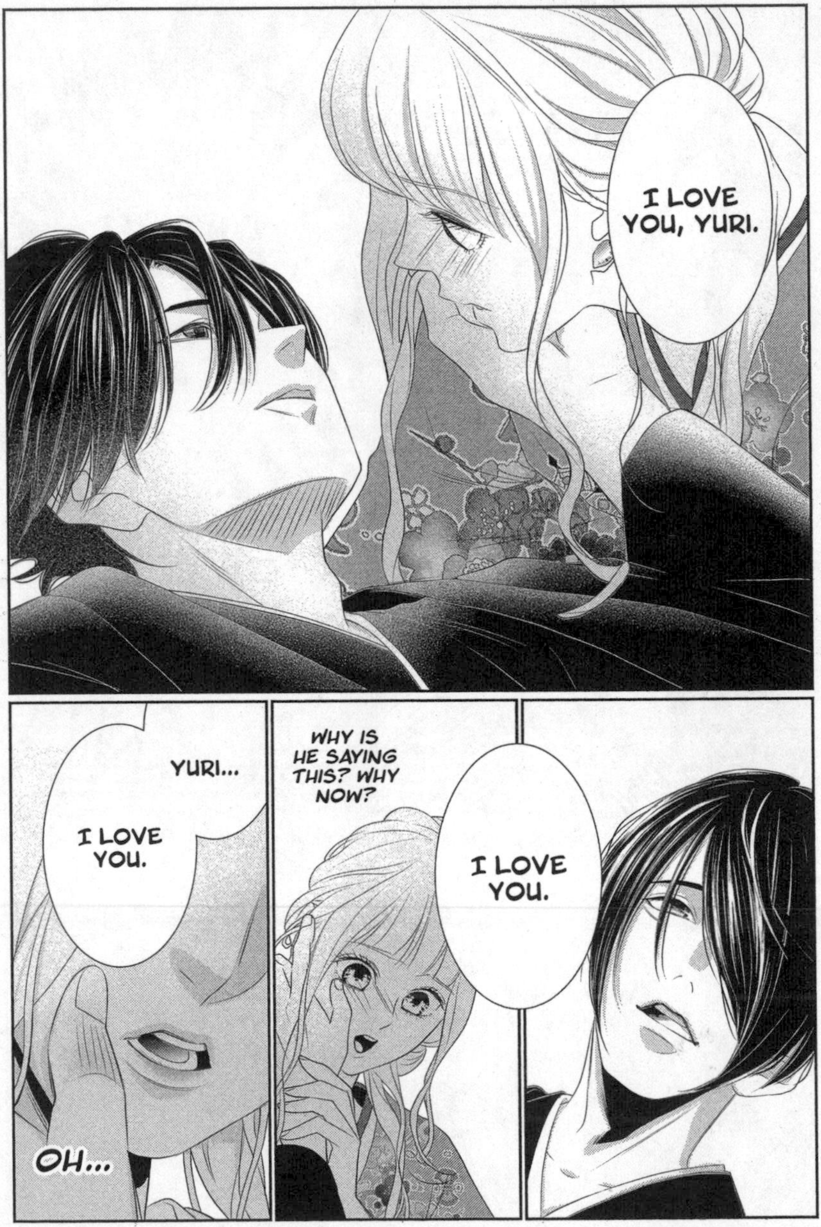
I LOVE YOU, YURI.
I LOVE YOU.
WHY IS HE SAYING THIS? WHY NOW?
YURI... I LOVE YOU.
OH...

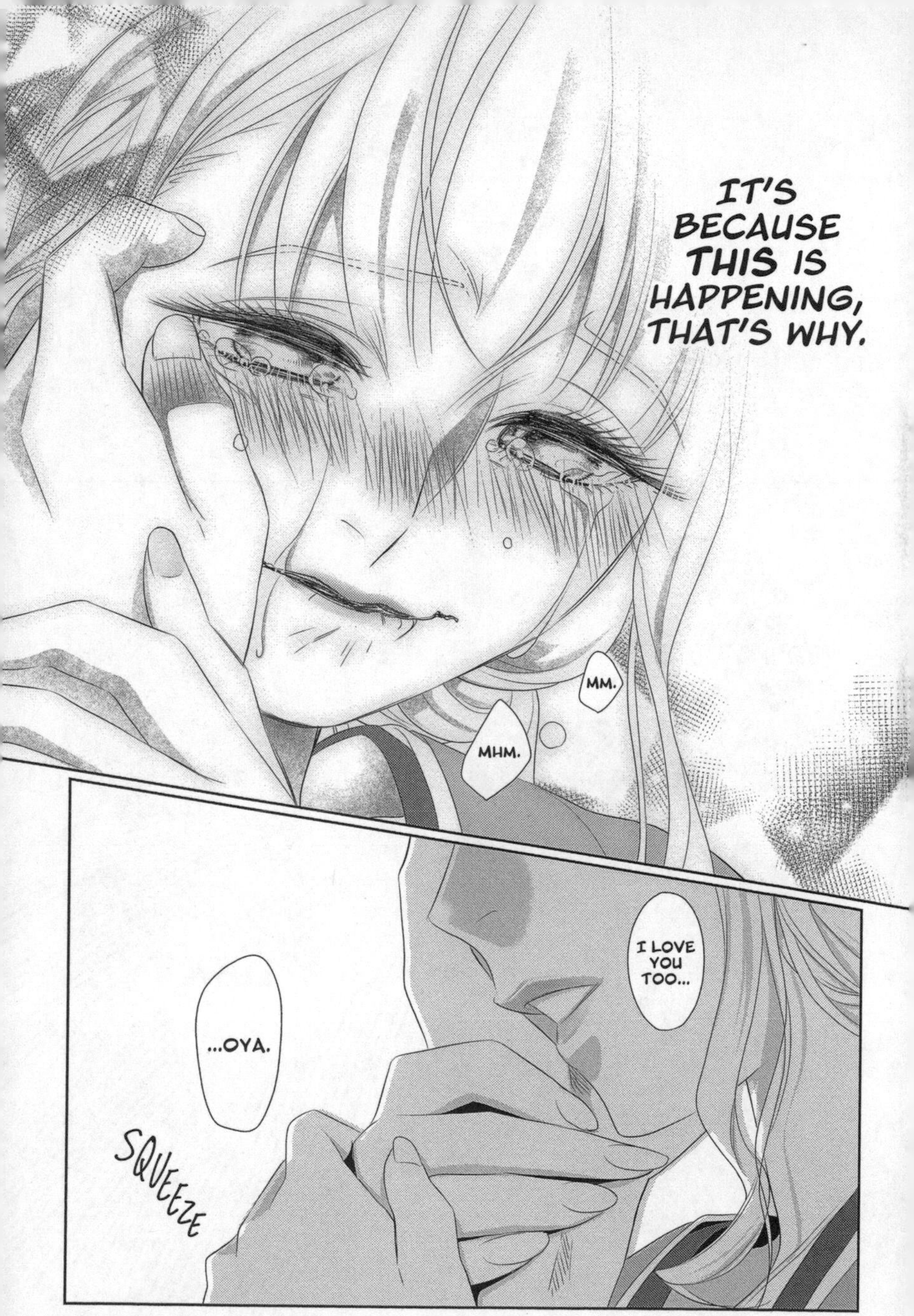
IT'S BECAUSE THIS IS HAPPENING, THAT'S WHY.
MM.
MHM.
I LOVE YOU TOO...
...OYA.
SQUEEZE

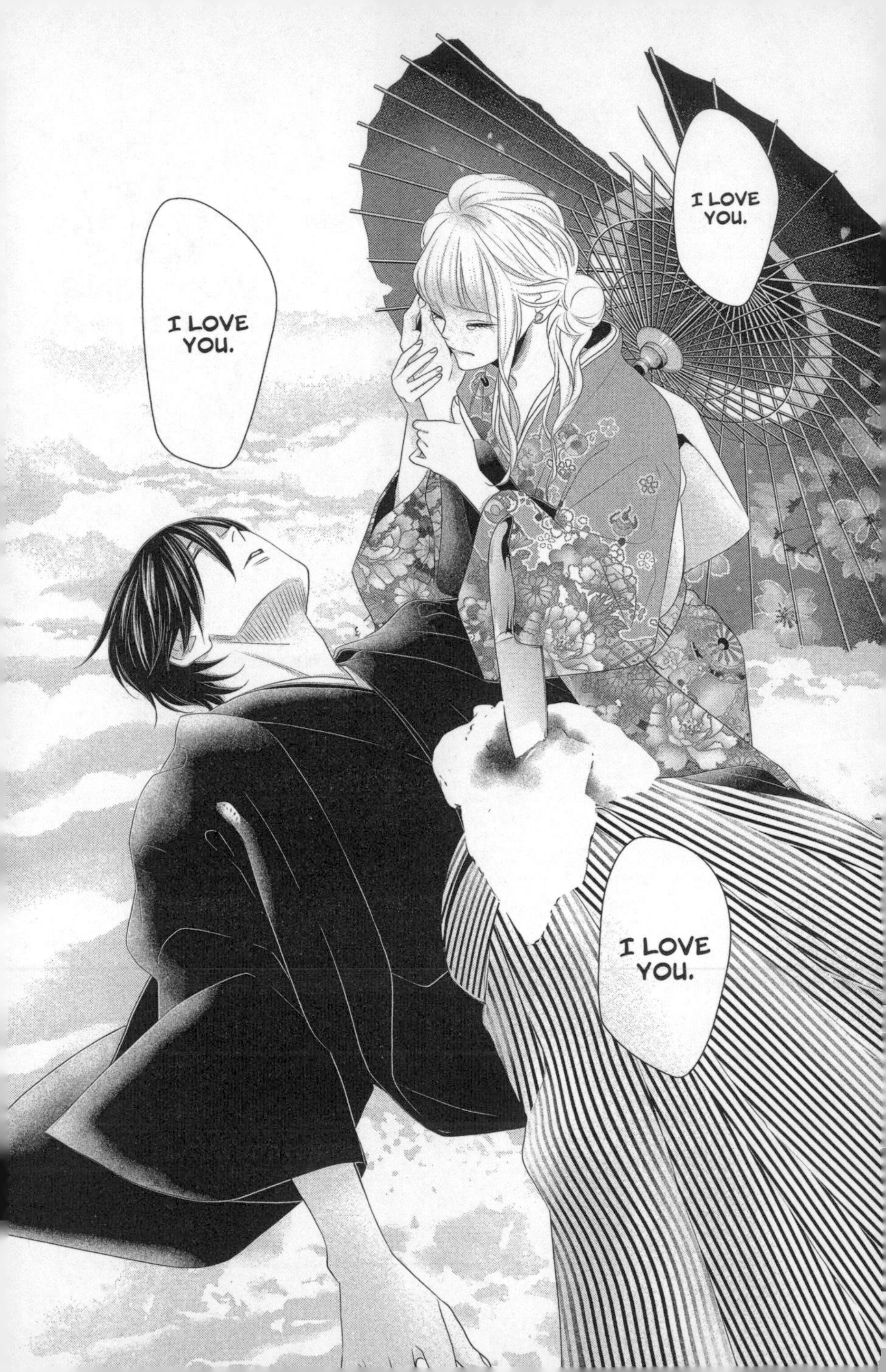
I LOVE YOU.
I LOVE YOU.
I LOVE YOU.

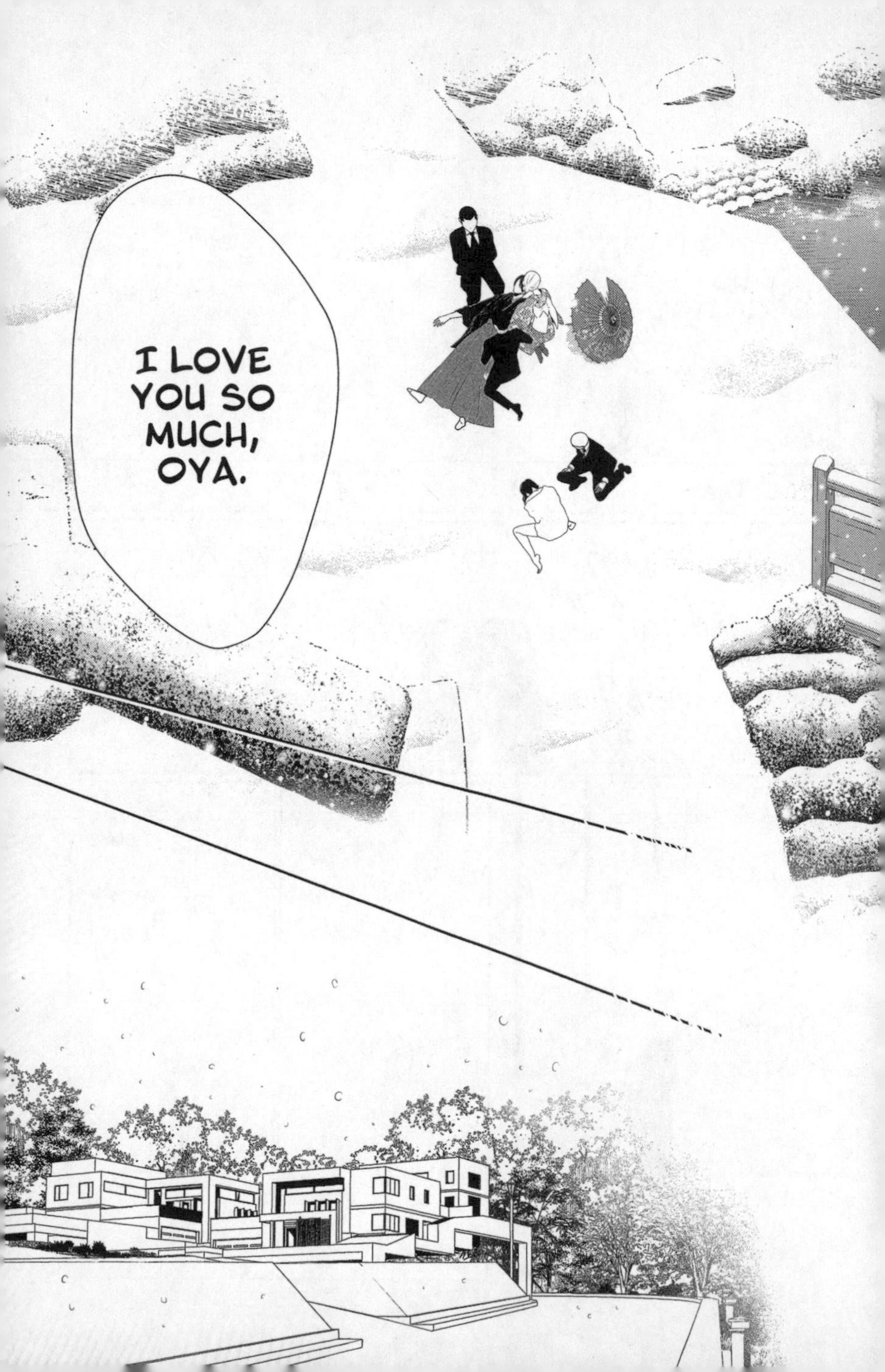
I LOVE YOU SO MUCH, OYA.

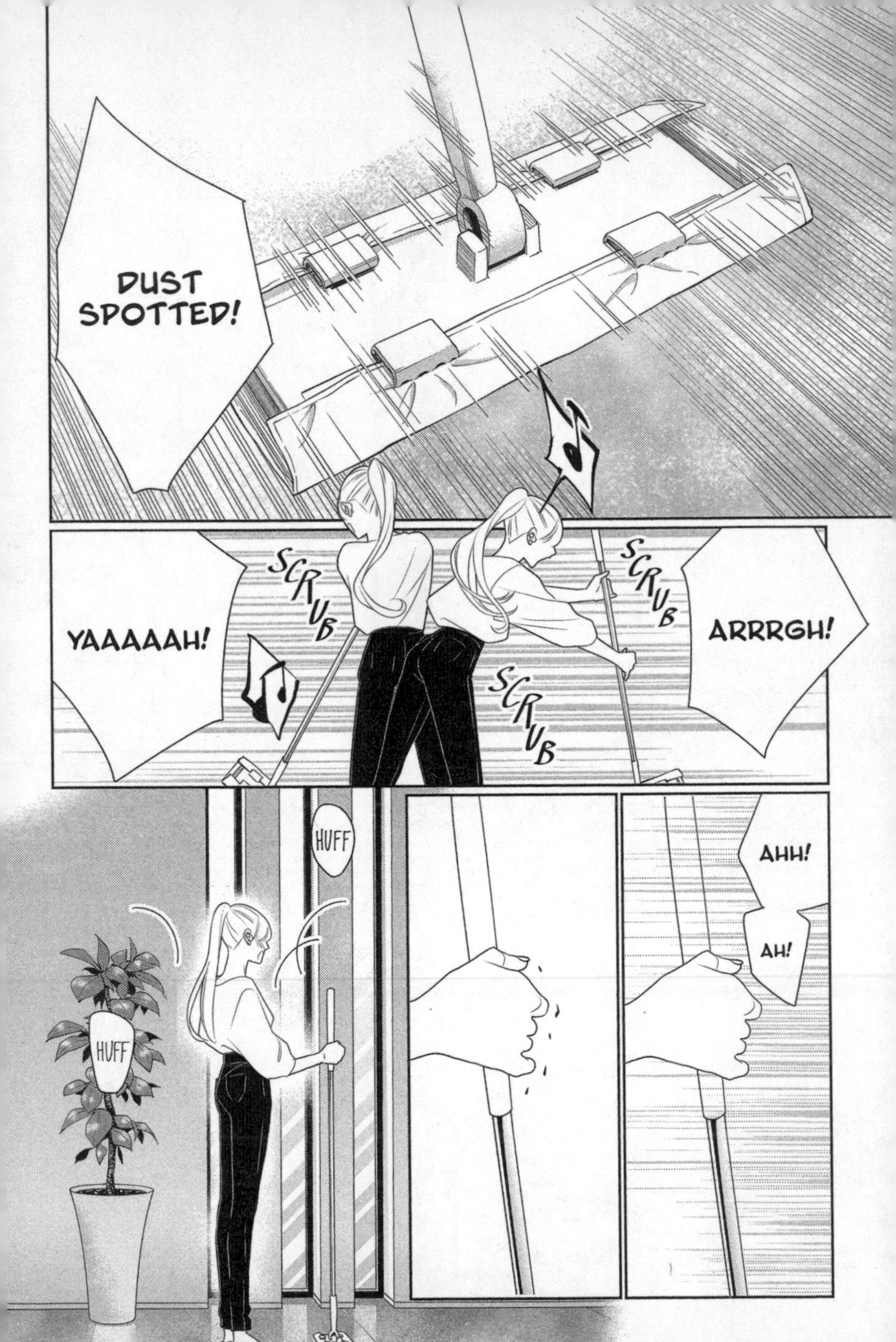
DUST SPOTTED!
ARRRGH!
SCRUB
SCRUB
SCRUB
YAAAAAH!
AHH!
AH!
HUFF
HUFF

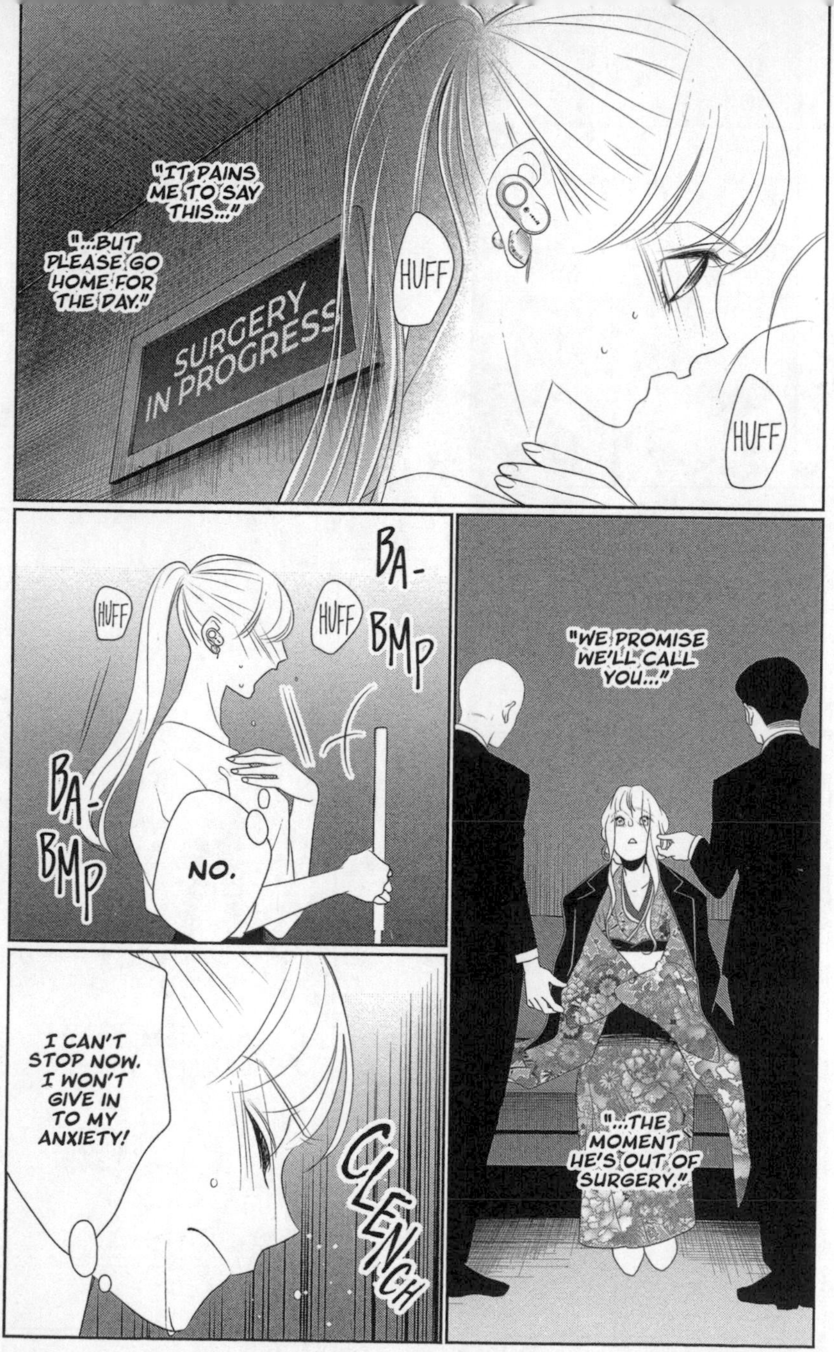
"IT PAINS ME TO SAY THIS..."
"...BUT PLEASE GO HOME FOR THE DAY."
HUFF
SURGERY IN PROGRESS
HUFF
"WE PROMISE WE'LL CALL YOU..."
"...THE MOMENT HE'S OUT OF SURGERY."
BA-BMP
HUFF
HUFF
BA-BMP
NO.
CLENCH
I CAN'T STOP NOW. I WON'T GIVE IN TO MY ANXIETY!

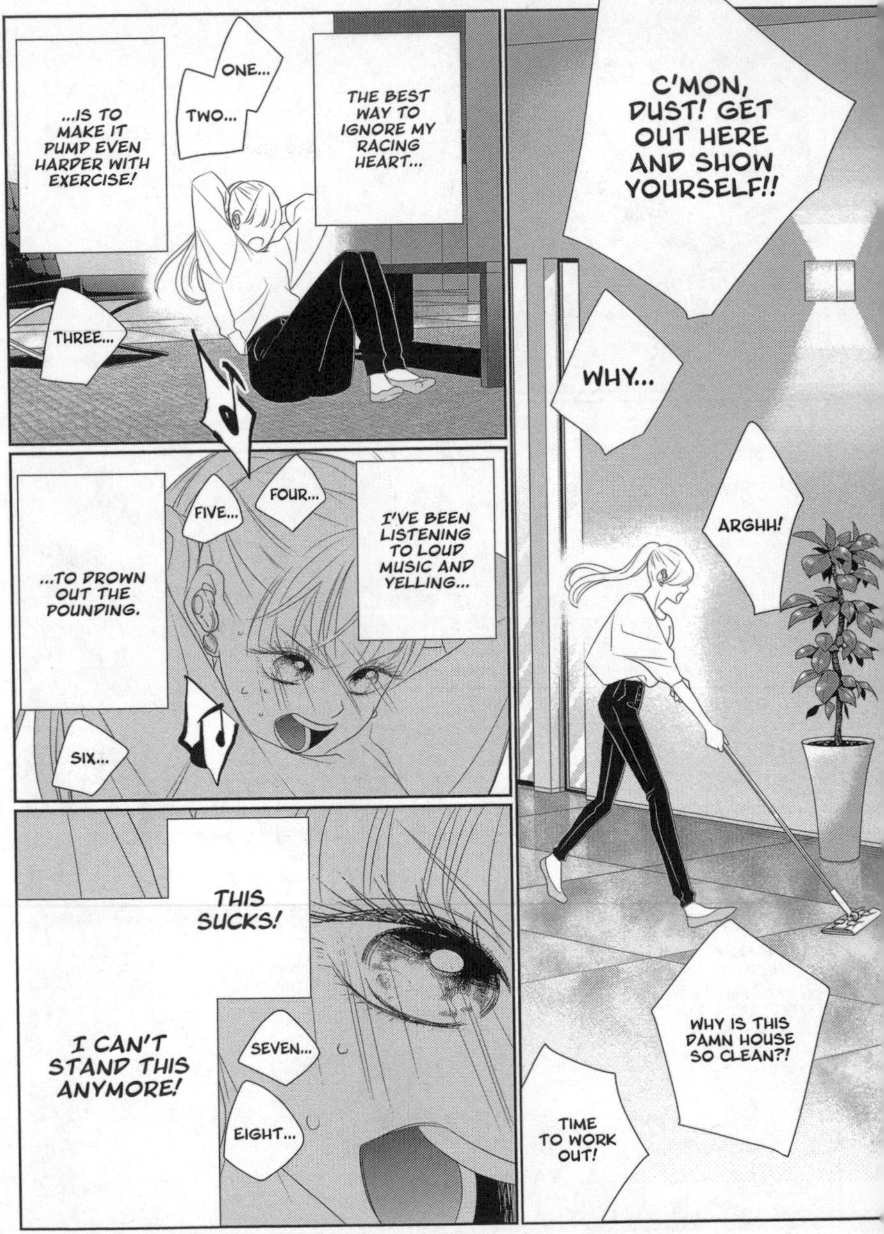

C'MON, DUST! GET OUT HERE AND SHOW YOURSELF!!
WHY...
ARGHH!
WHY IS THIS DAMN HOUSE SO CLEAN?!
TIME TO WORK OUT!
THE BEST WAY TO IGNORE MY RACING HEART...
ONE...
TWO...
...IS TO MAKE IT PUMP EVEN HARDER WITH EXERCISE!
THREE...
I'VE BEEN LISTENING TO LOUD MUSIC AND YELLING...
FOUR...
FIVE...
...TO DROWN OUT THE POUNDING.
SIX...
THIS SUCKS!
SEVEN...
I CAN'T STAND THIS ANYMORE!
EIGHT...

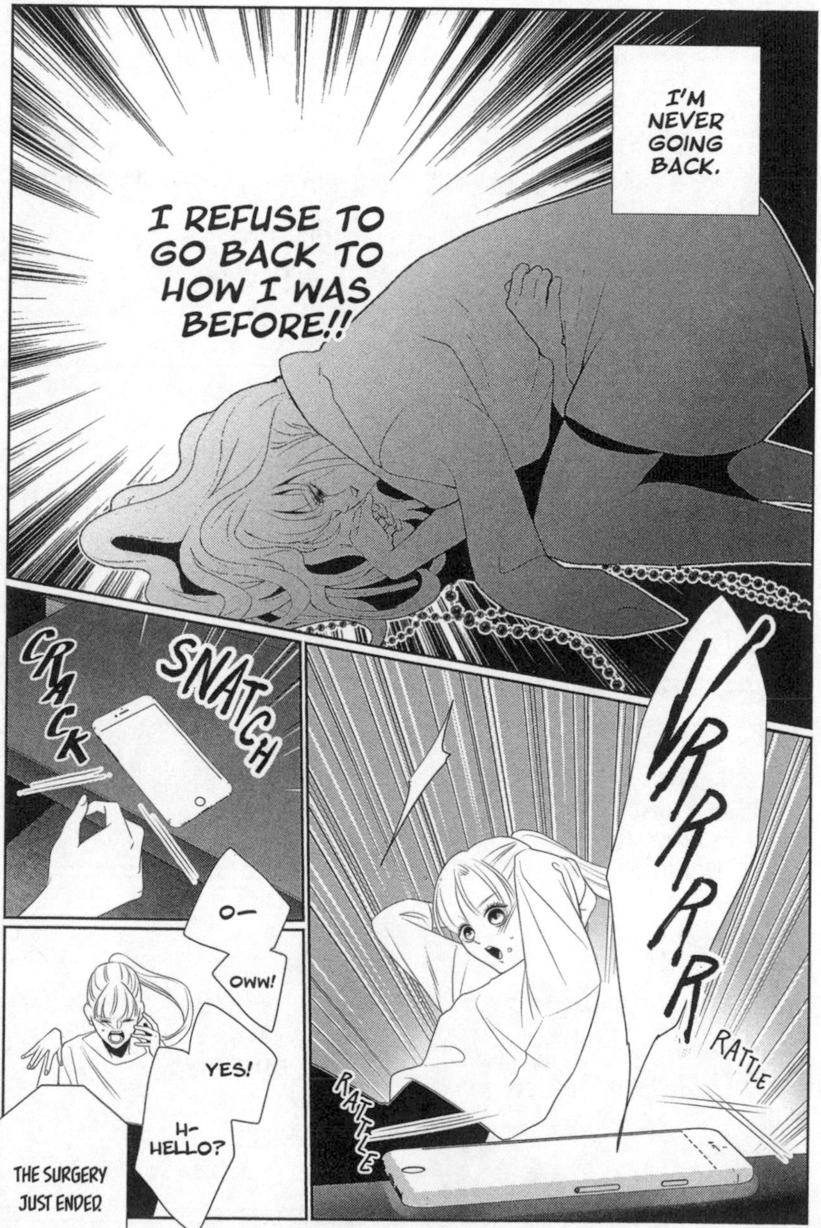
I'M NEVER GOING BACK.
I REFUSE TO GO BACK TO HOW I WAS BEFORE!!
VRRRR
RATTLE
RATTLE
SNATCH
CRACK
O—
OWW!
YES!
H-HELLO?
THE SURGERY JUST ENDED.

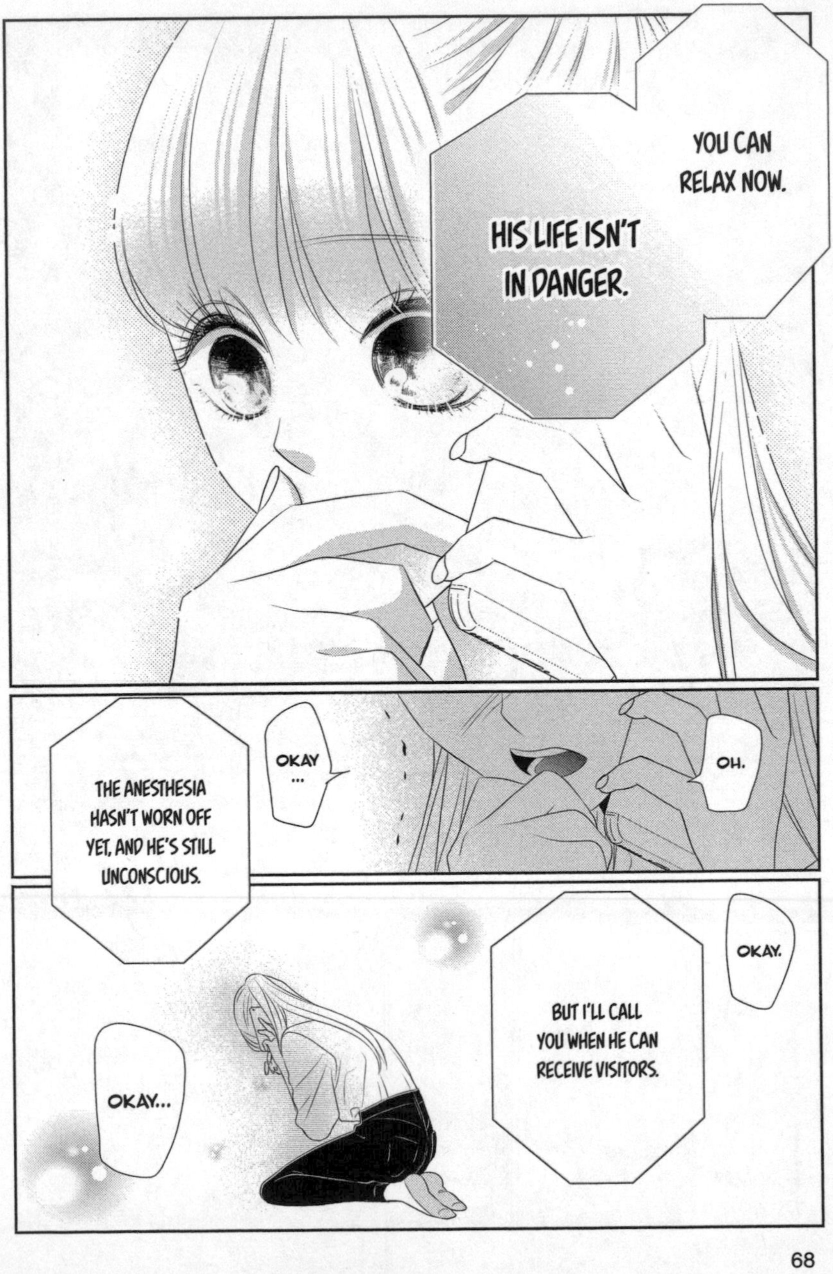
YOU CAN RELAX NOW.
HIS LIFE ISN'T IN DANGER.
OH.
OKAY ...
THE ANESTHESIA HASN'T WORN OFF YET, AND HE'S STILL UNCONSCIOUS.
OKAY.
BUT I'LL CALL YOU WHEN HE CAN RECEIVE VISITORS.
OKAY...

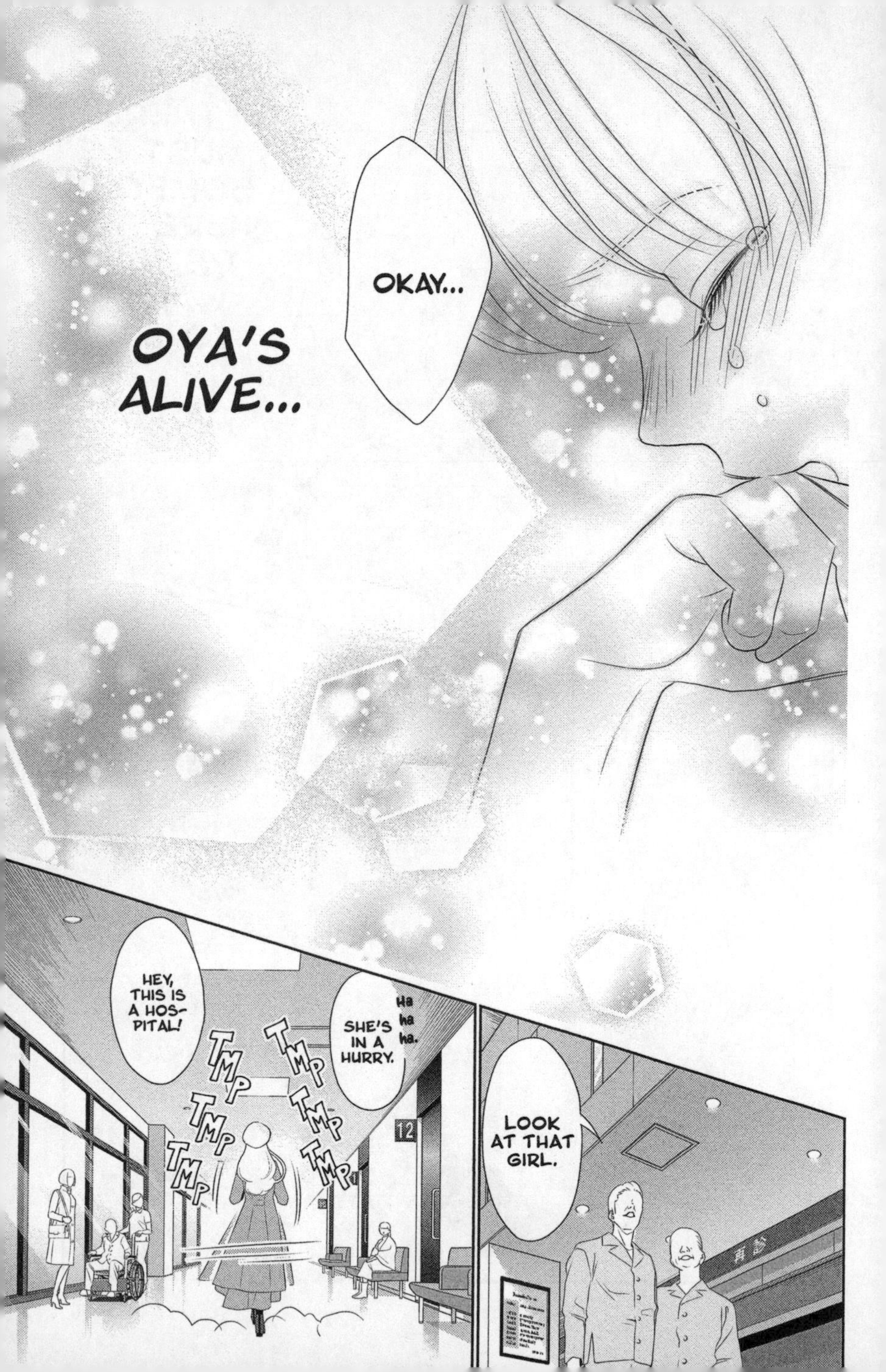
OKAY...
OYA'S ALIVE...
LOOK AT THAT GIRL.
Ha ha ha.
SHE'S IN A HURRY.
HEY, THIS IS A HOS-PITAL!
TMP TMP TMP TMP TMP TMP

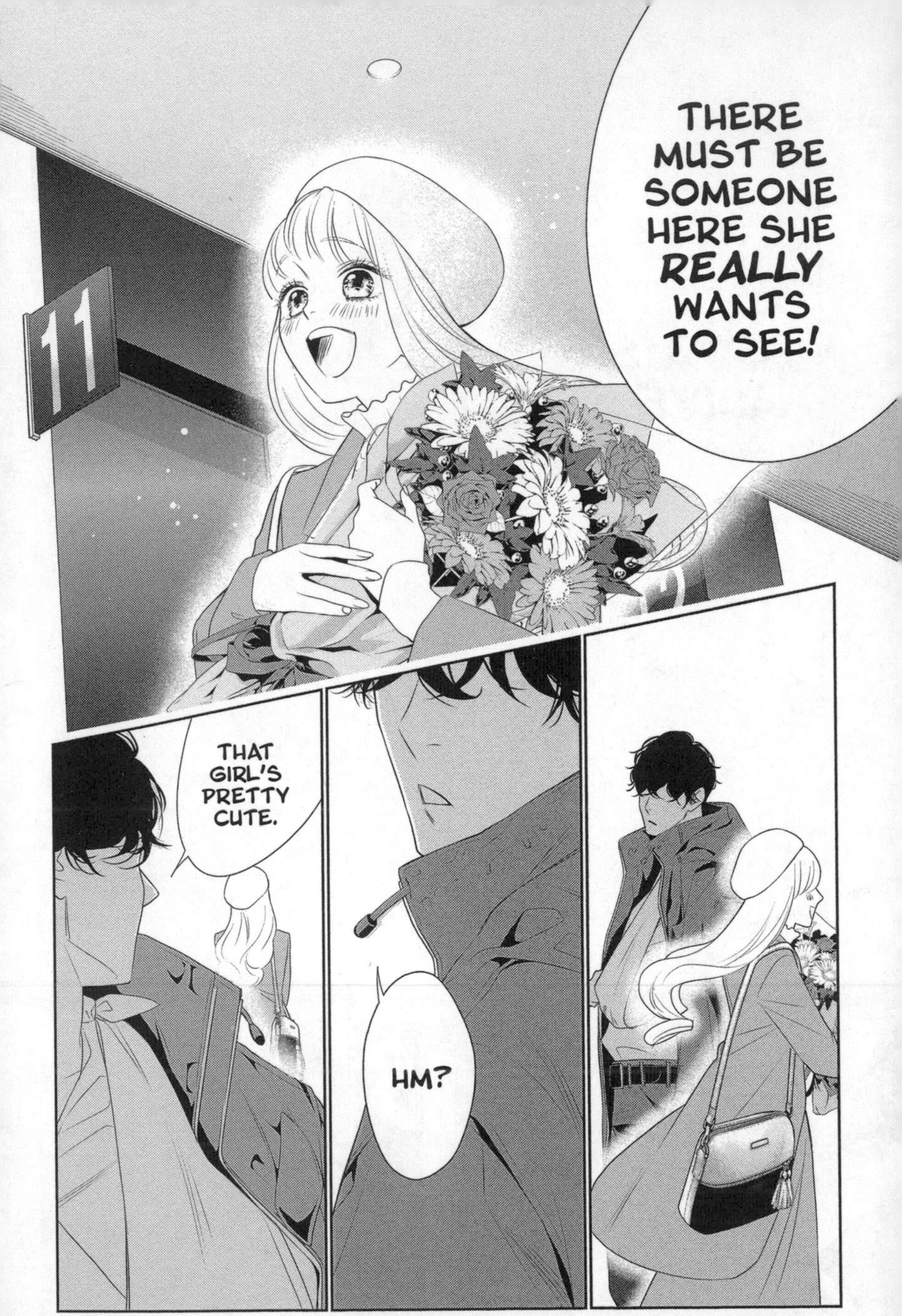
THERE MUST BE SOMEONE HERE SHE REALLY WANTS TO SEE!
HM?
THAT GIRL'S PRETTY CUTE.

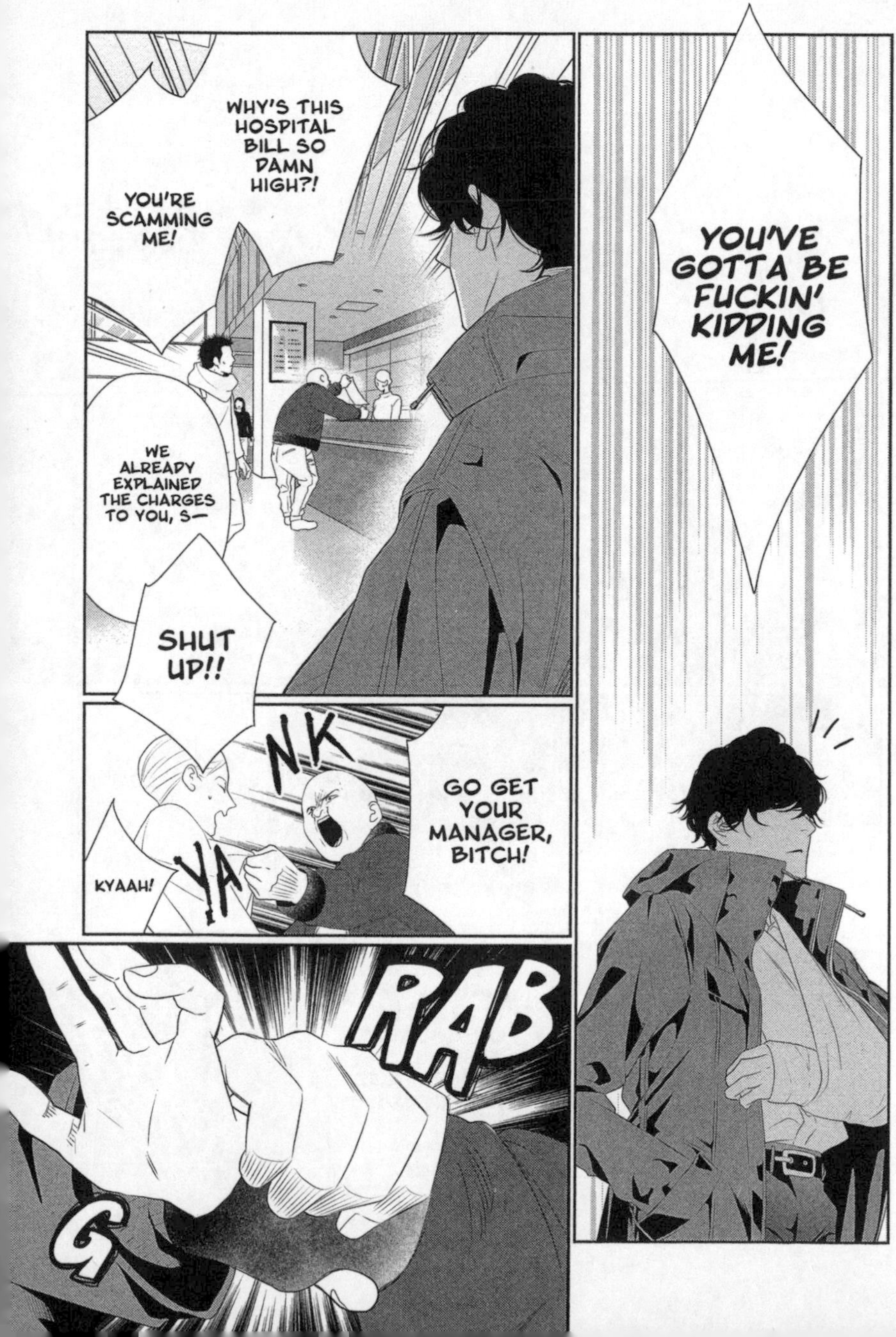
YOU'VE GOTTA BE FUCKIN' KIDDING ME!
WHY'S THIS HOSPITAL BILL SO DAMN HIGH?!
YOU'RE SCAMMING ME!
WE ALREADY EXPLAINED THE CHARGES TO YOU, S—
SHUT UP!!
GO GET YOUR MANAGER, BITCH!
YANK
KYAAH!
GRAB

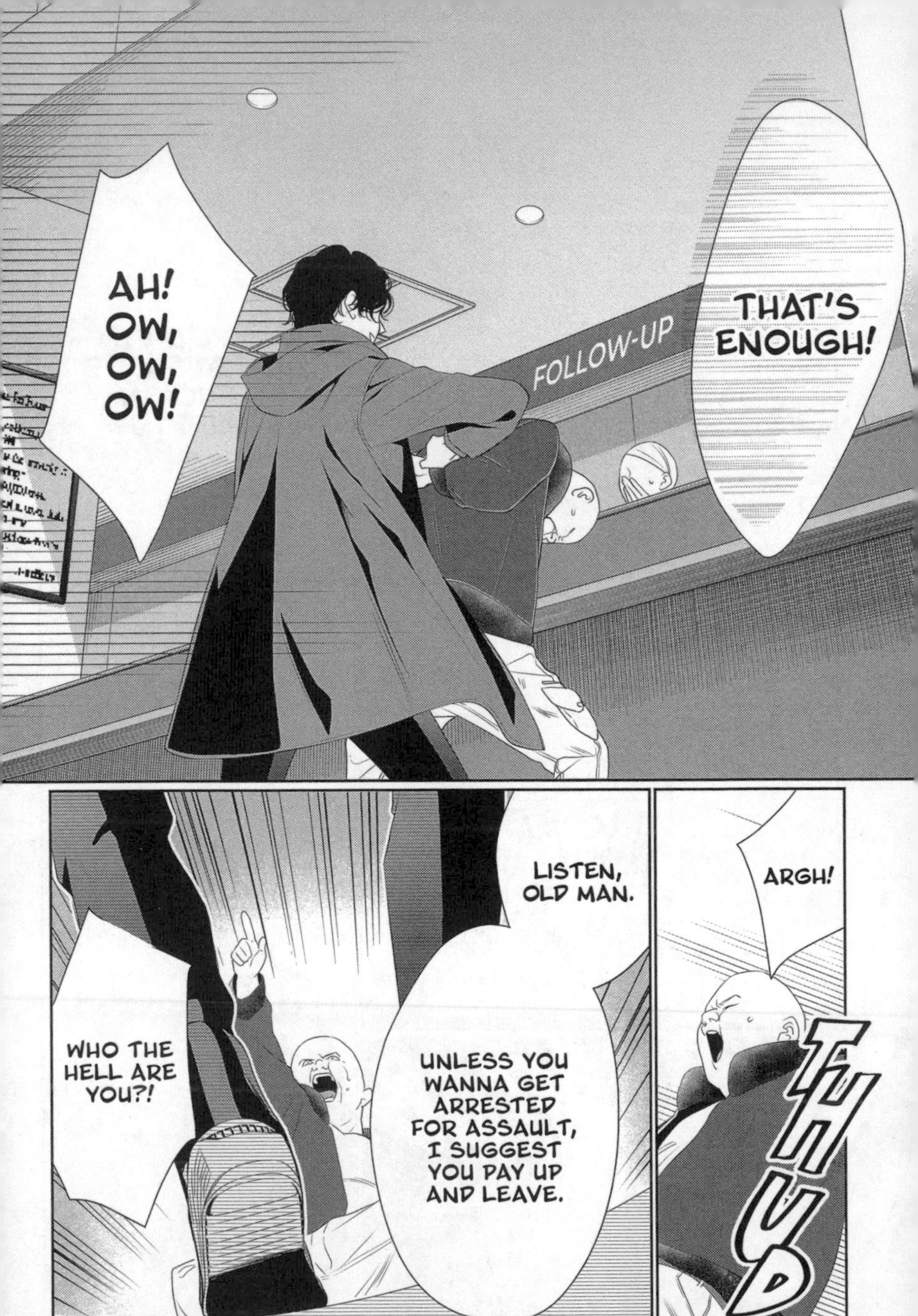
THAT'S ENOUGH!
FOLLOW-UP
AH! OW, OW, OW!
ARGH!
THUD
LISTEN, OLD MAN.
UNLESS YOU WANNA GET ARRESTED FOR ASSAULT, I SUGGEST YOU PAY UP AND LEAVE.
WHO THE HELL ARE YOU?!

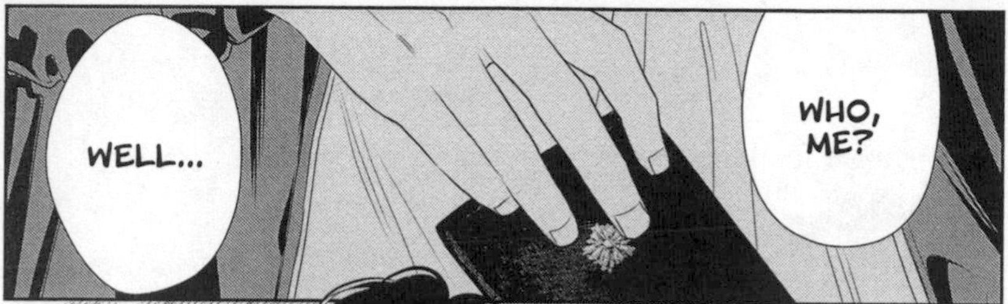
WHO, ME?
WELL...
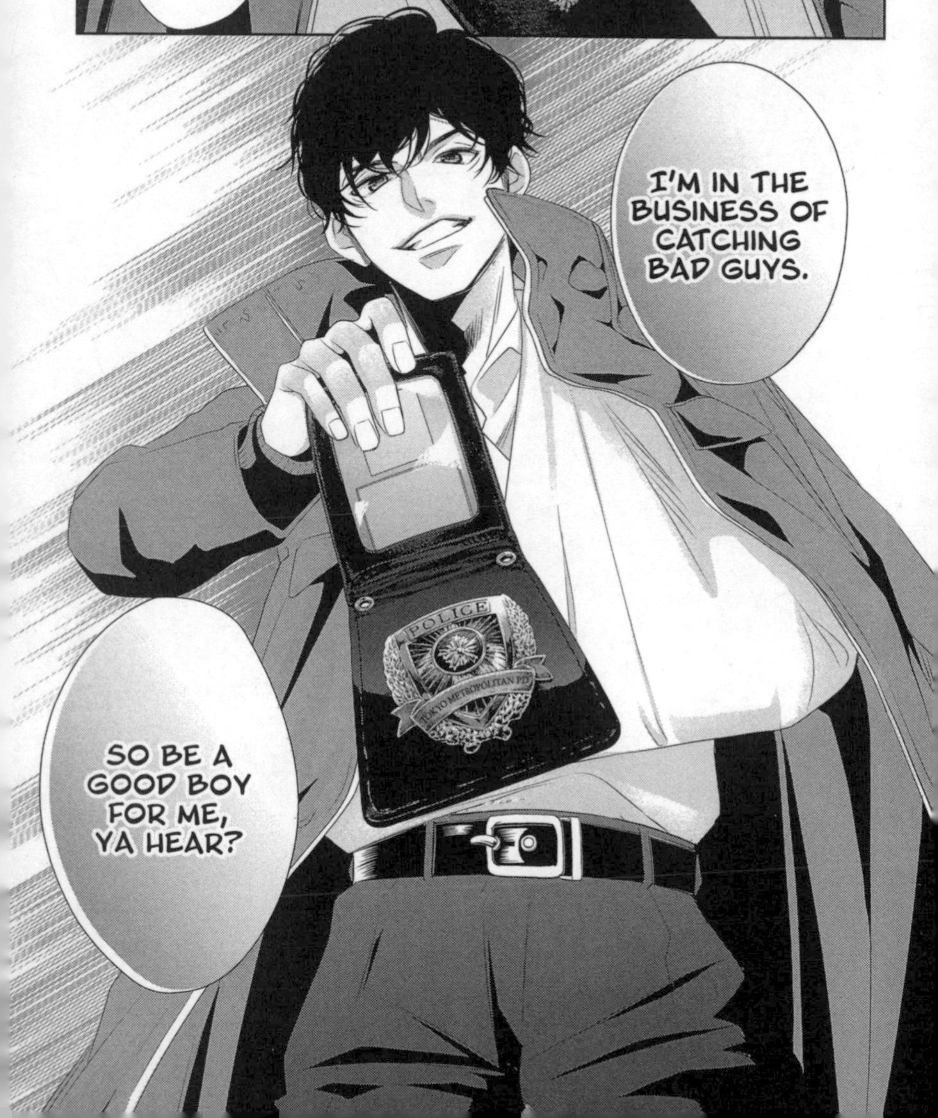
I'M IN THE BUSINESS OF CATCHING BAD GUYS.
POLICE
TOKYO METROPOLITAN PD
SO BE A GOOD BOY FOR ME, YA HEAR?

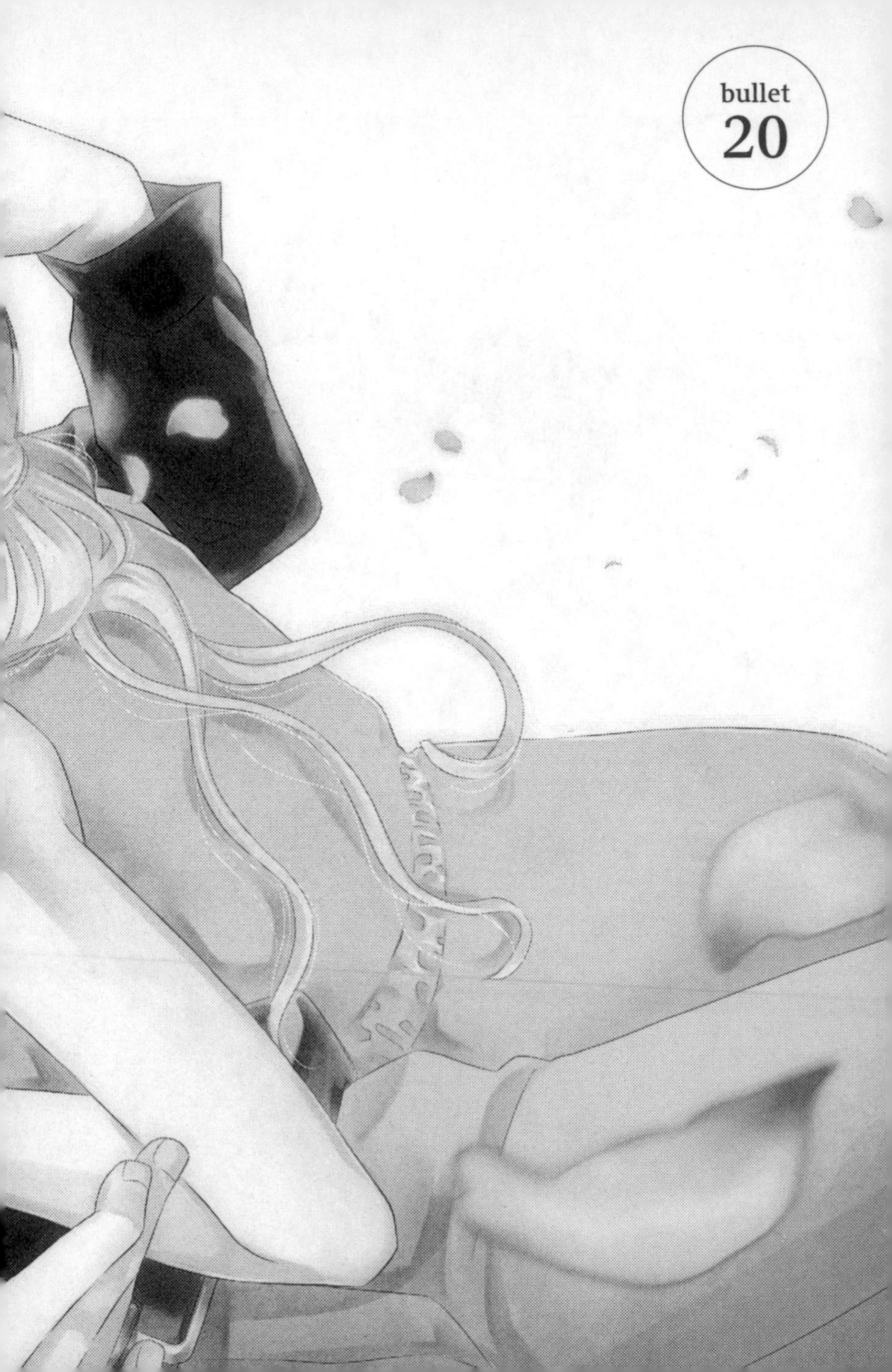
bullet
20

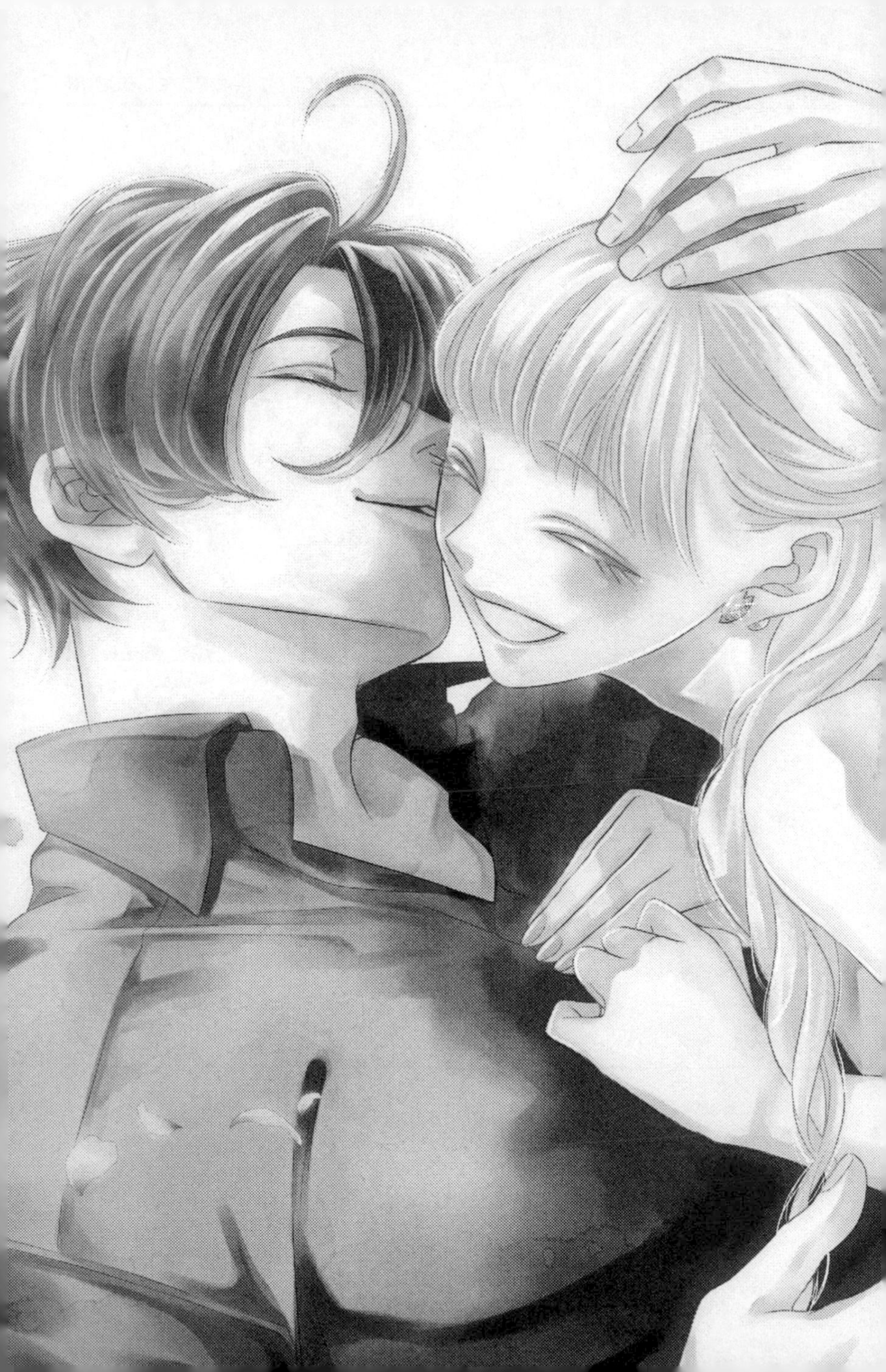

bonus bullet 19 secret scene

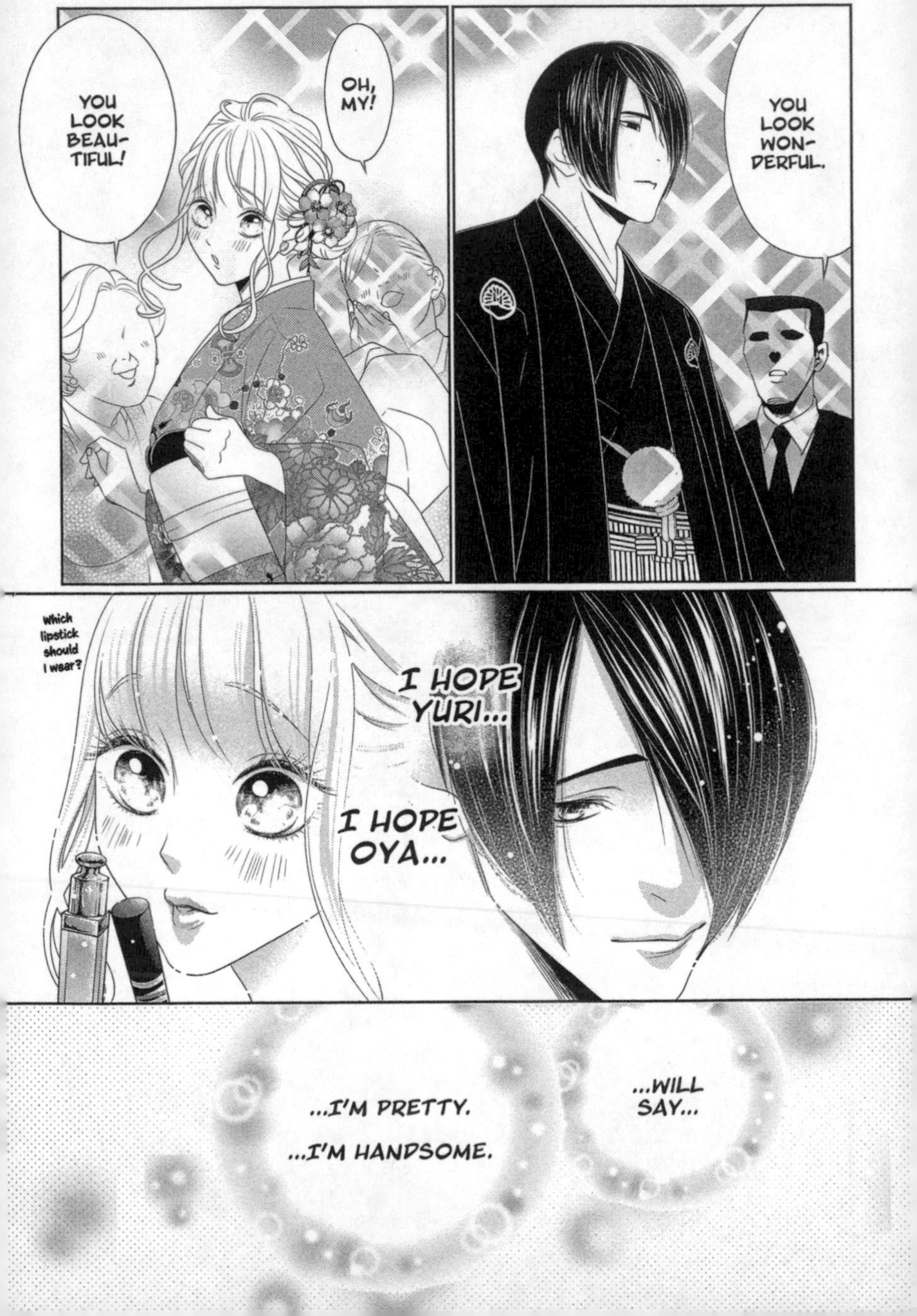

YOU LOOK WON-DERFUL.
OH, MY!
YOU LOOK BEAU-TIFUL!
I HOPE YURI...
I HOPE OYA...
Which lipstick should I wear?
...WILL SAY...
...I'M PRETTY.
...I'M HANDSOME.

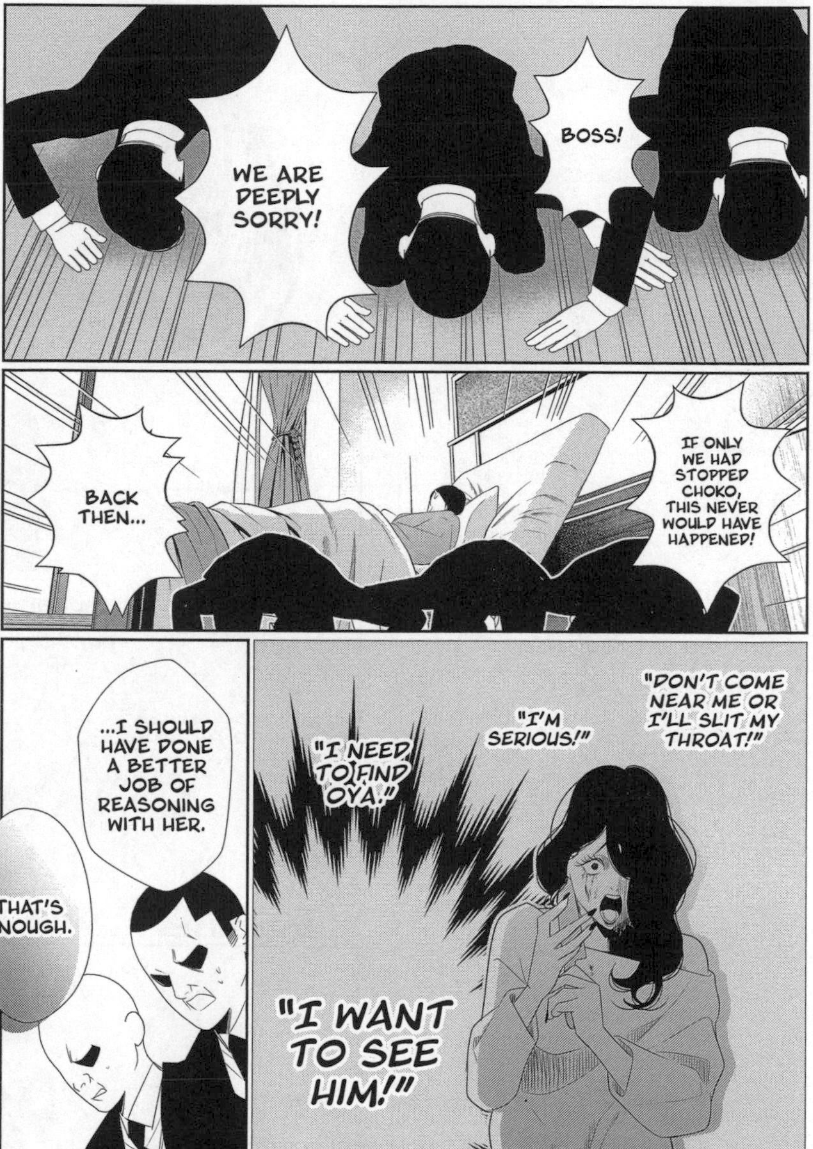
BOSS!
WE ARE DEEPLY SORRY!
IF ONLY WE HAD STOPPED CHOKO, THIS NEVER WOULD HAVE HAPPENED!
BACK THEN...
"DON'T COME NEAR ME OR I'LL SLIT MY THROAT!"
"I'M SERIOUS!"
"I NEED TO FIND OYA."
"I WANT TO SEE HIM!"
...I SHOULD HAVE DONE A BETTER JOB OF REASONING WITH HER.
THAT'S ENOUGH.

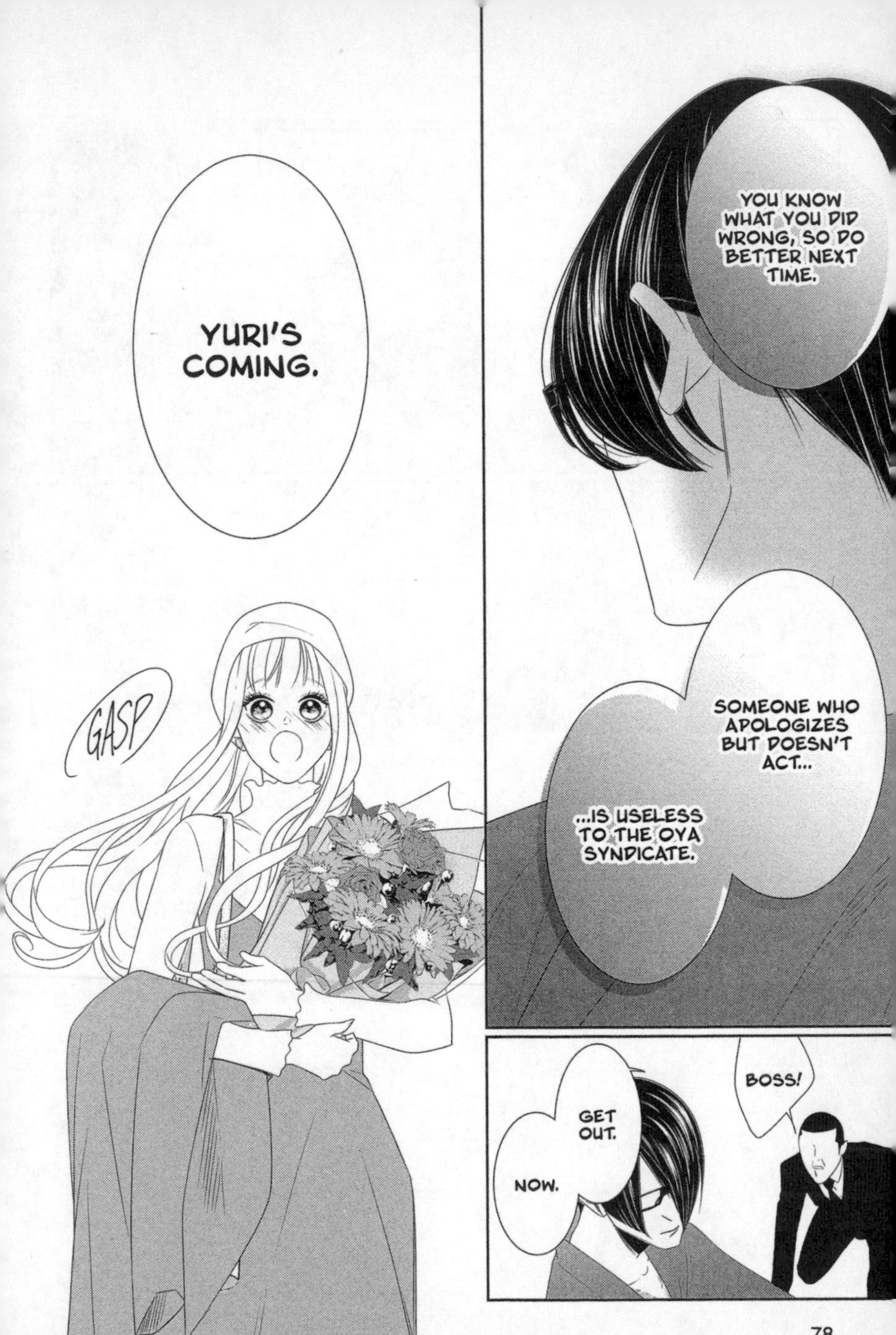
YOU KNOW WHAT YOU DID WRONG, SO DO BETTER NEXT TIME.
SOMEONE WHO APOLOGIZES BUT DOESN'T ACT...
...IS USELESS TO THE OYA SYNDICATE.
BOSS!
GET OUT.
NOW.
YURI'S COMING.
GASP

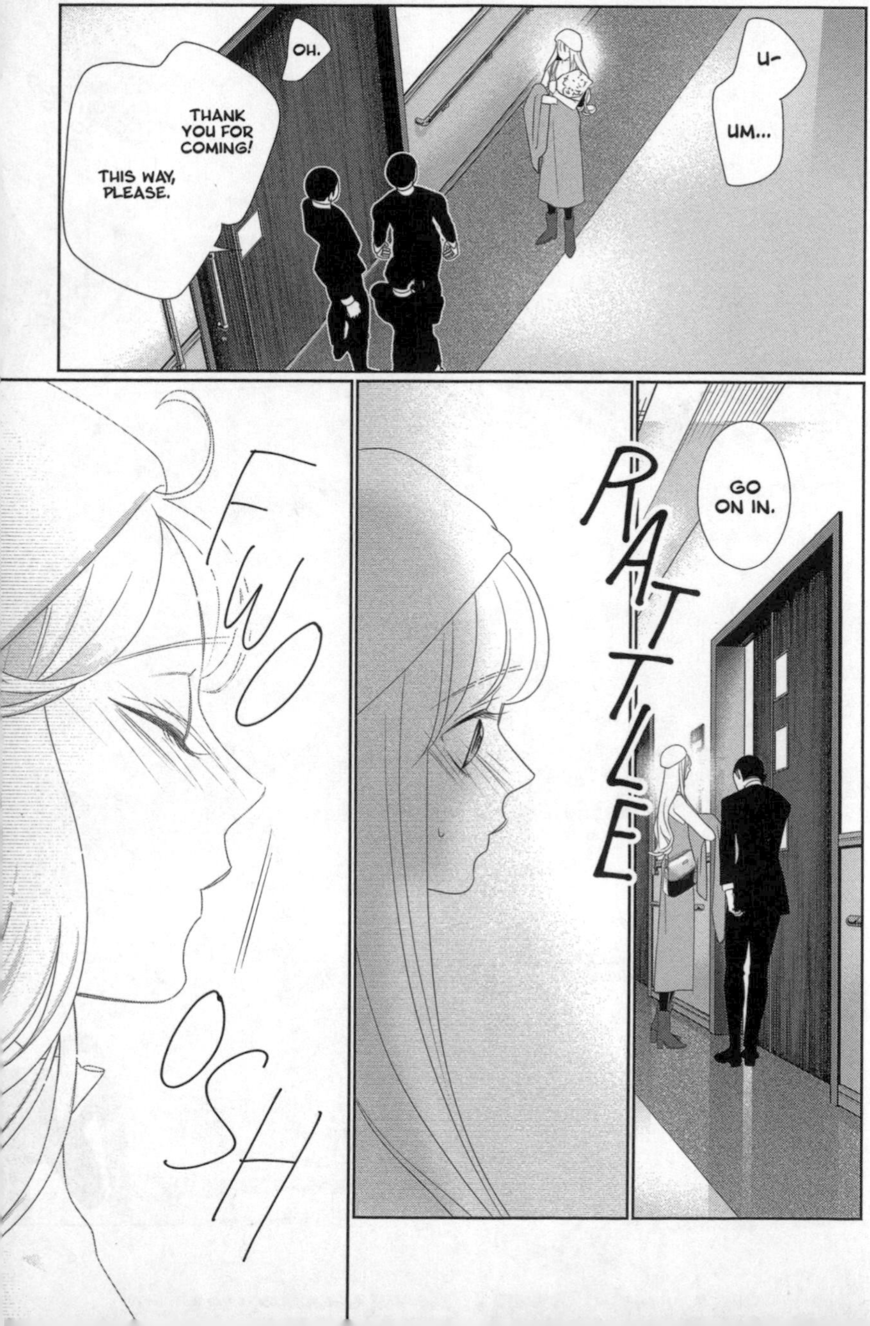
U-
UM...
OH.
THANK YOU FOR COMING!
THIS WAY, PLEASE.
RATTLE
GO ON IN.
FWOOSH

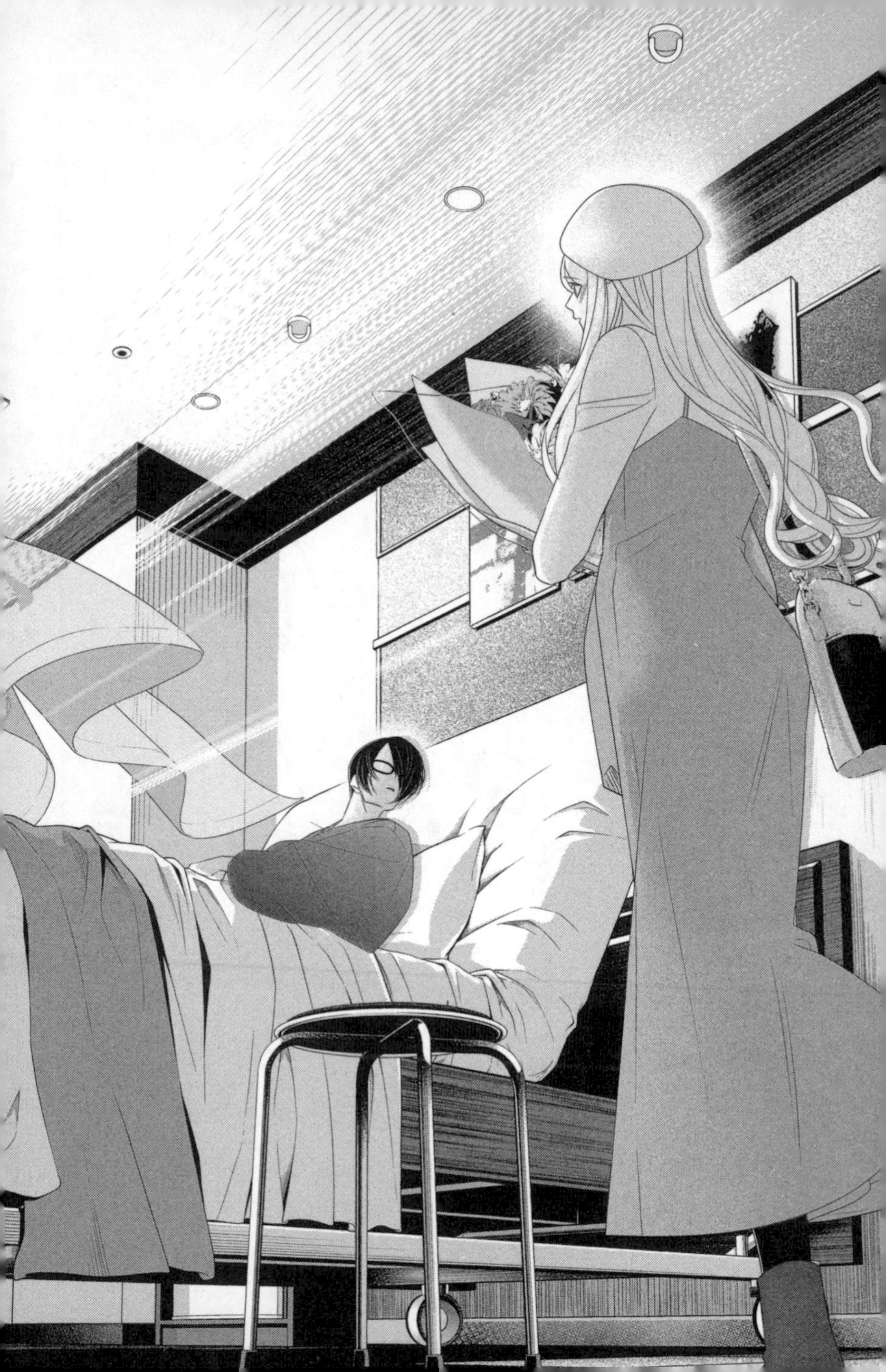

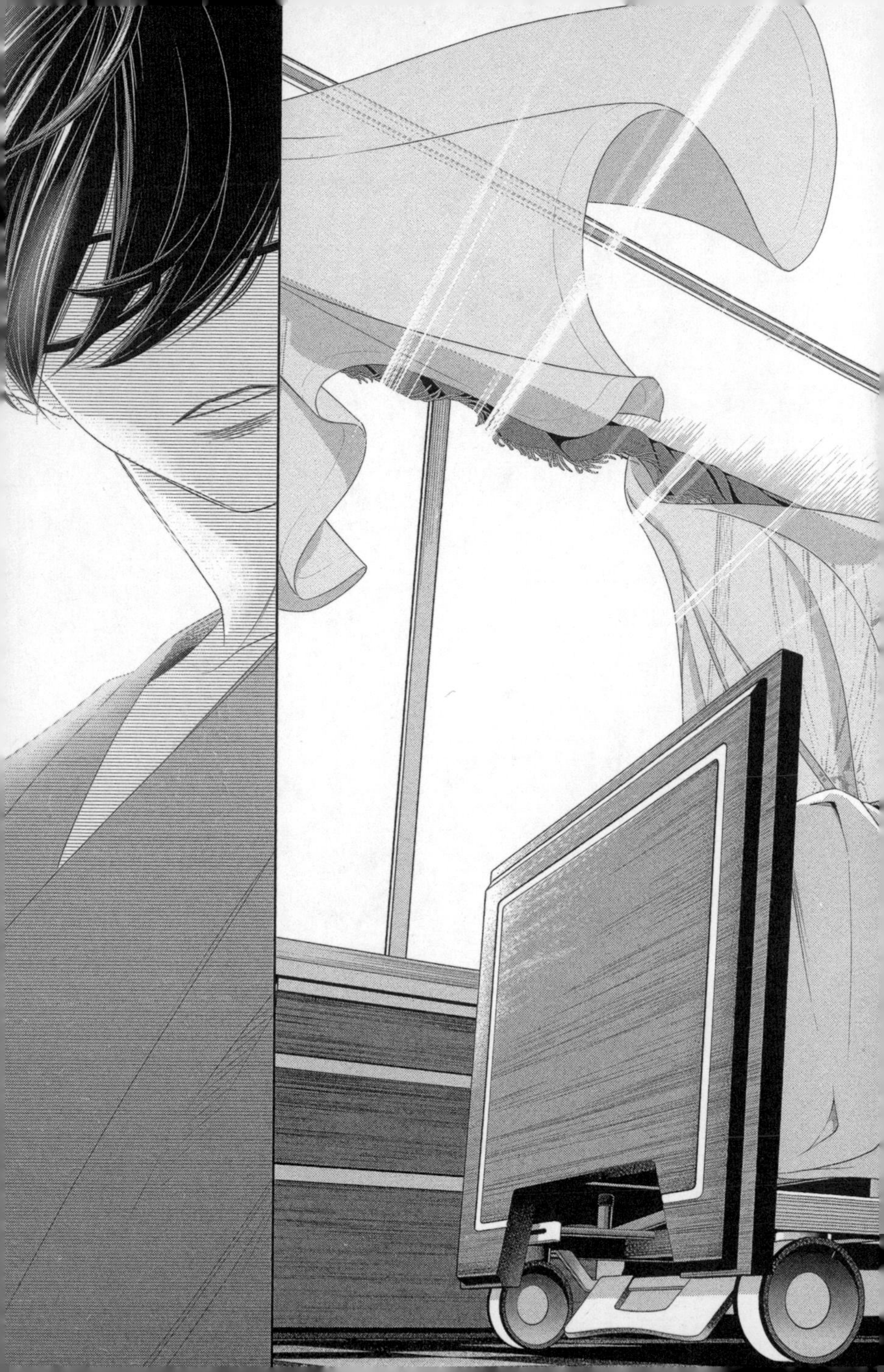

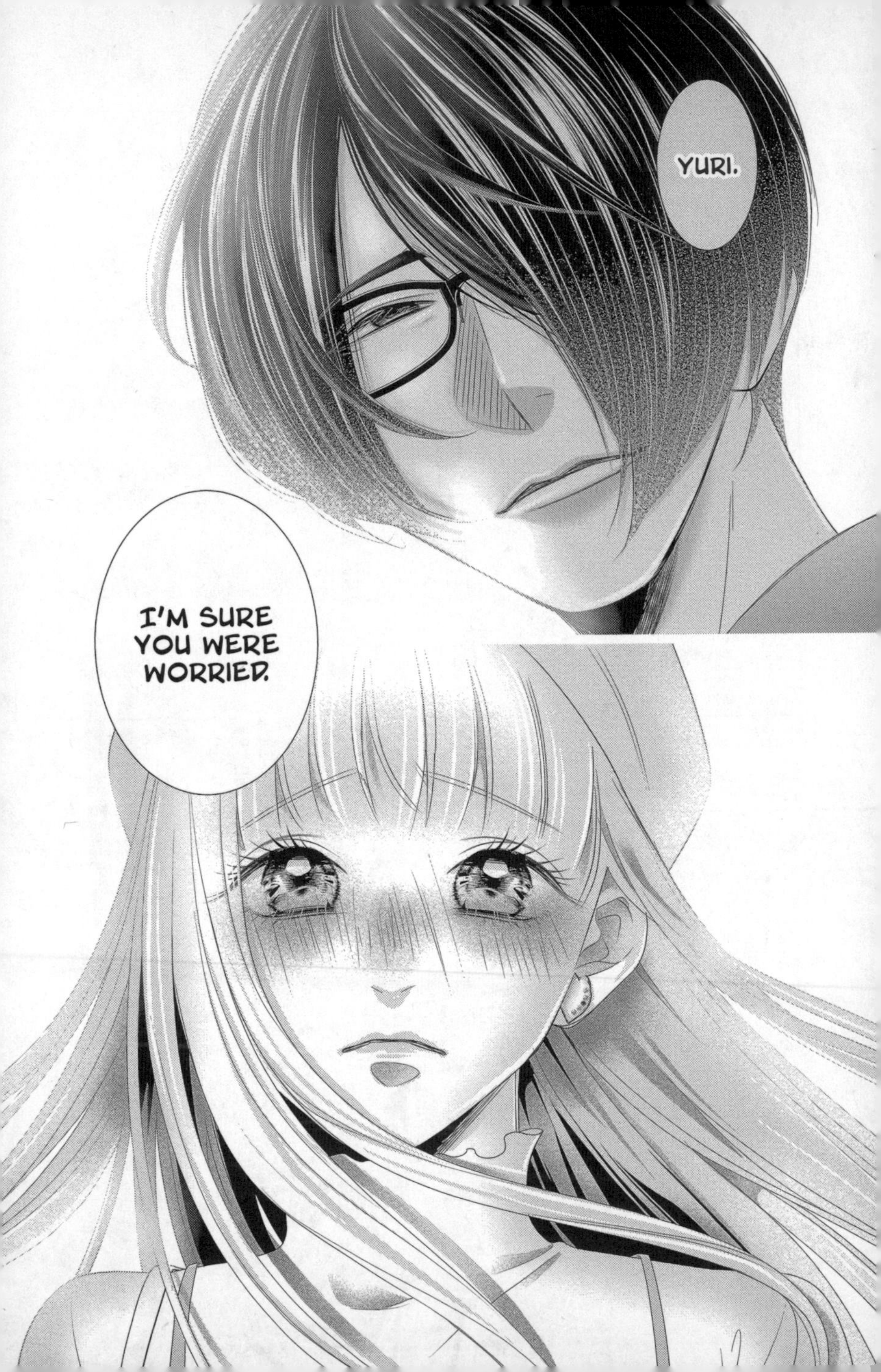
YURI.
I'M SURE YOU WERE WORRIED.

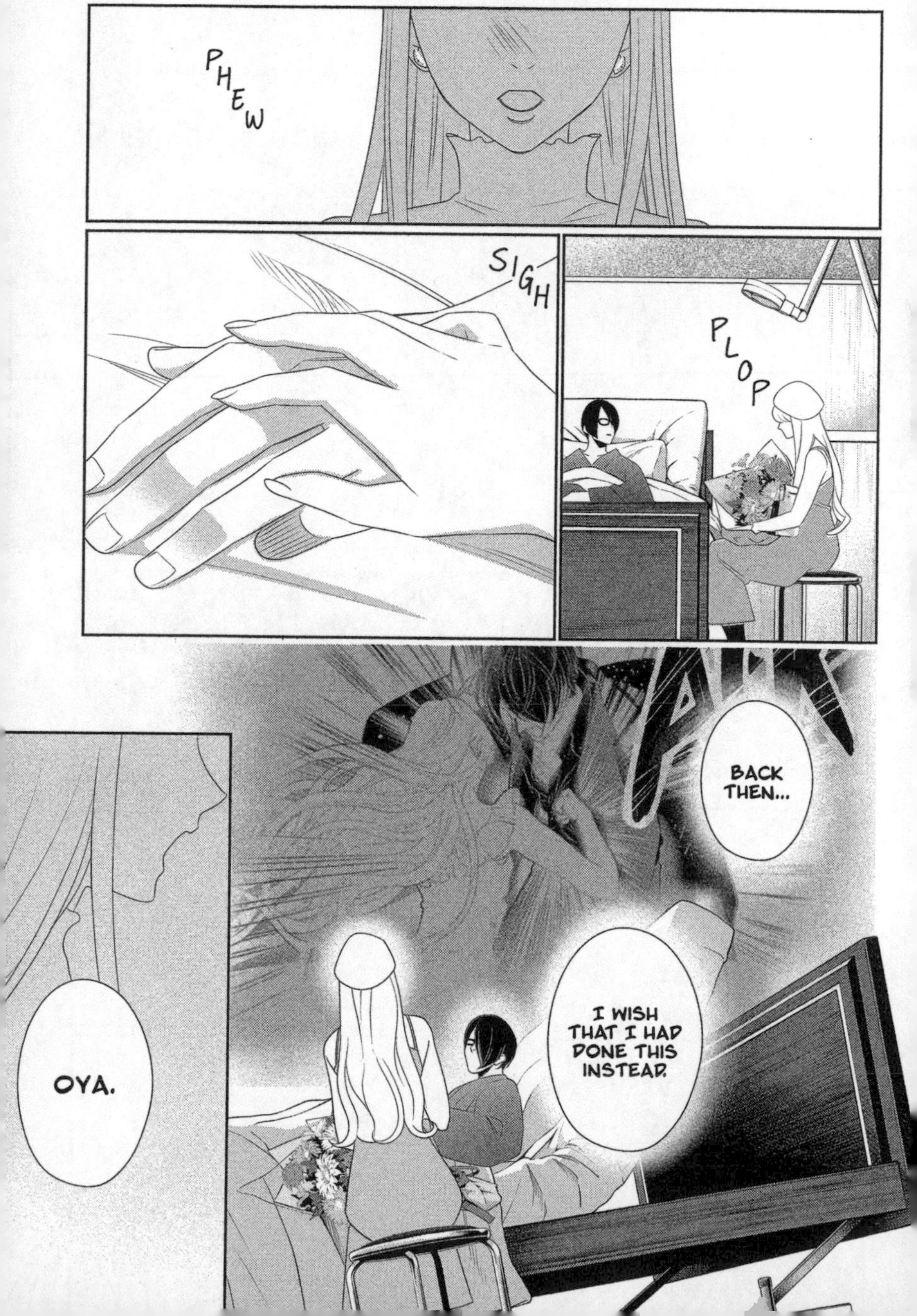
PHEW
PLOP
SIGH
BACK THEN...
I WISH THAT I HAD DONE THIS INSTEAD.
OYA.

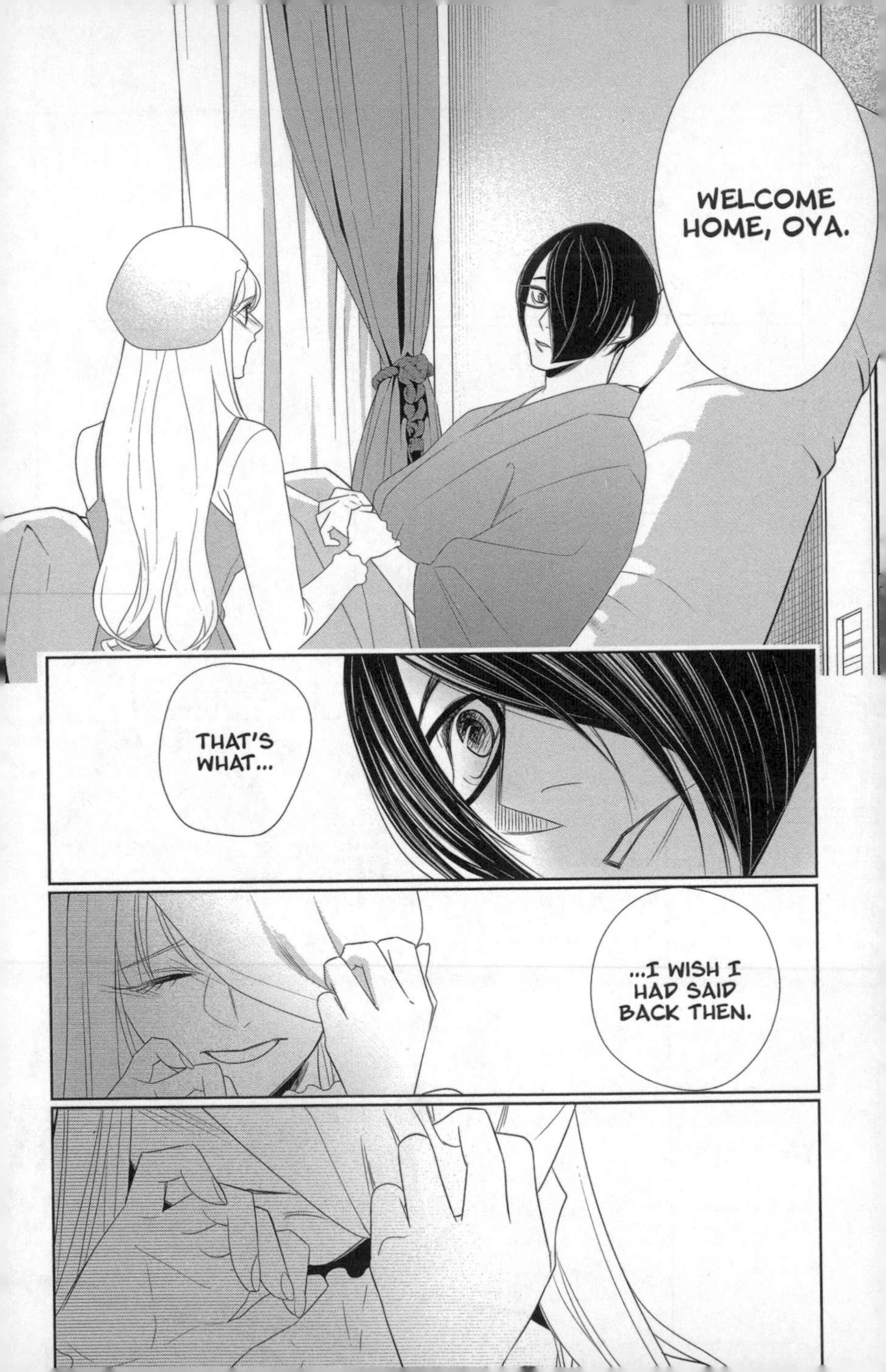
WELCOME HOME, OYA.
THAT'S WHAT...
...I WISH I HAD SAID BACK THEN.

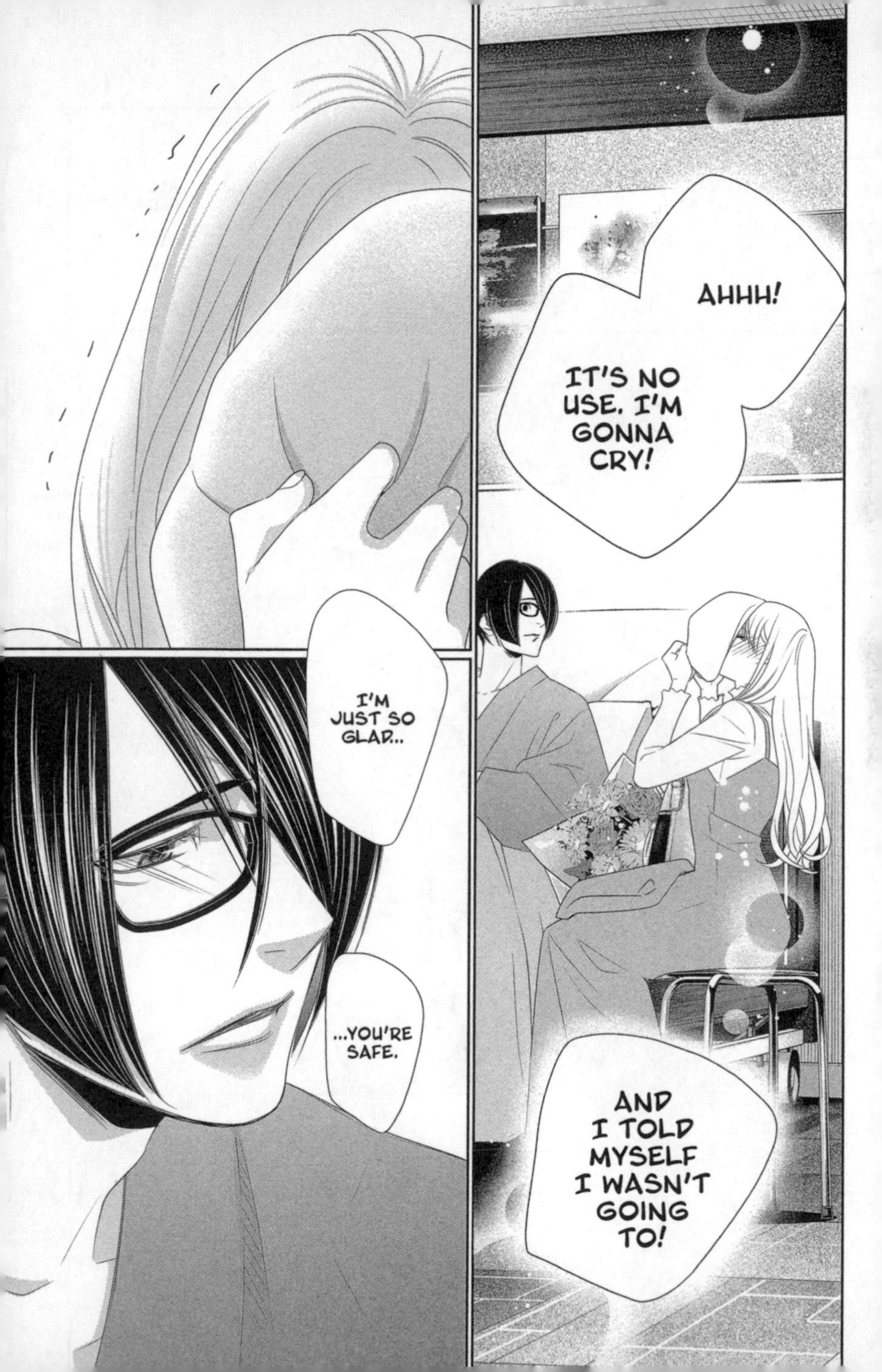
AHHH!
IT'S NO USE. I'M GONNA CRY!
AND I TOLD MYSELF I WASN'T GOING TO!
I'M JUST SO GLAD...
...YOU'RE SAFE.

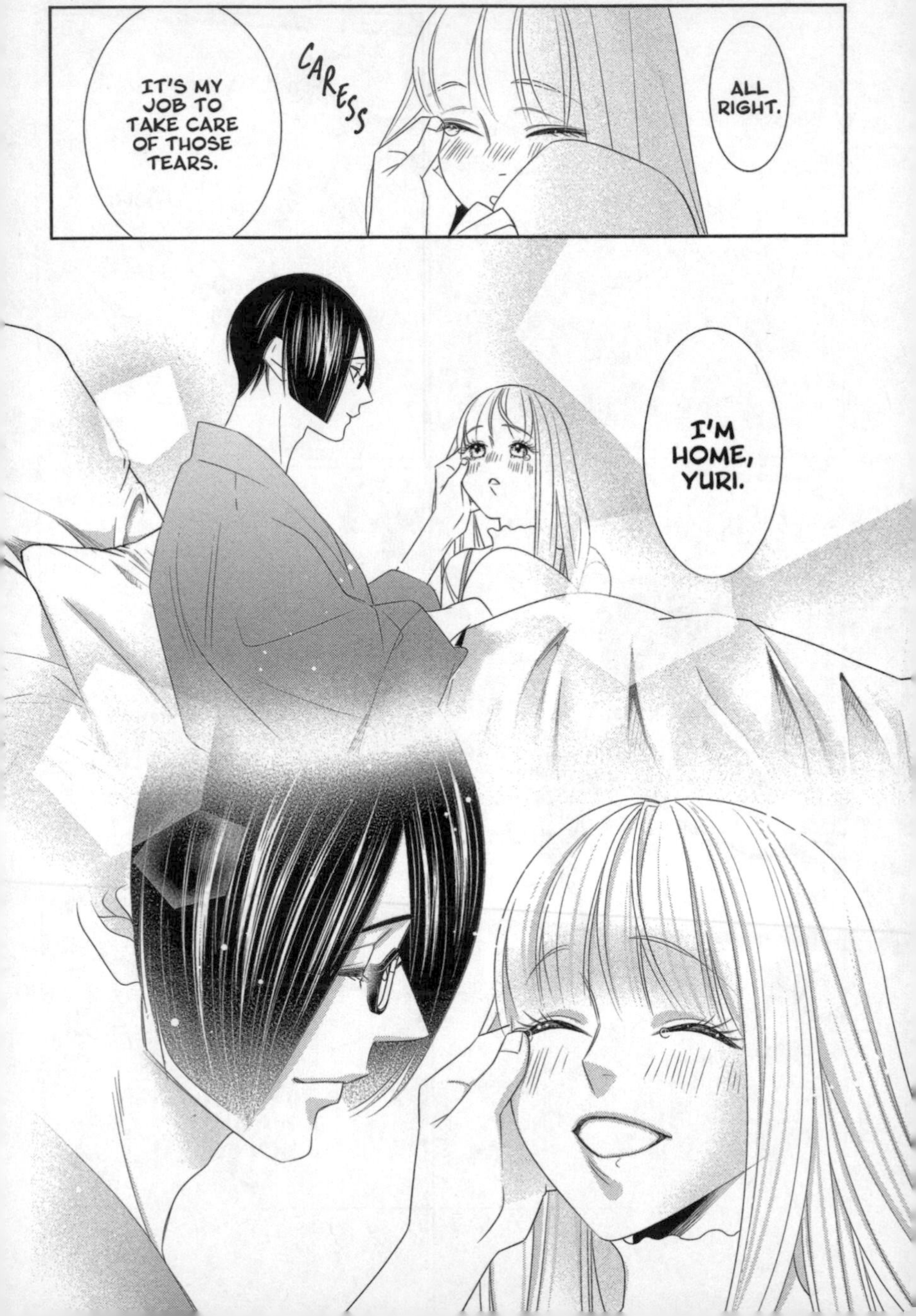
ALL RIGHT.
CARESS
IT'S MY JOB TO TAKE CARE OF THOSE TEARS.
I'M HOME, YURI.

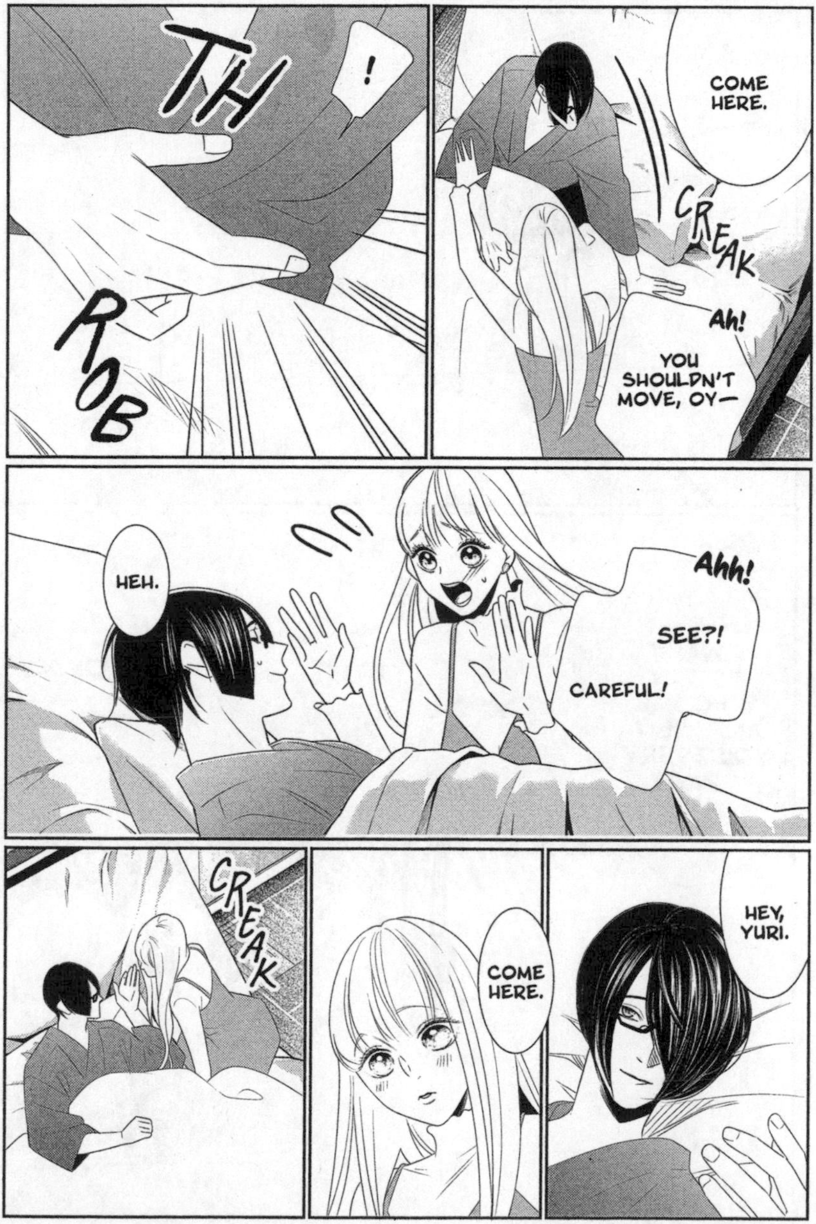
COME HERE.
CREAK
Ah!
YOU SHOULDN'T MOVE, OY—
TH
!
ROB
Ahh!
SEE?!
CAREFUL!
HEH.
HEY, YURI.
COME HERE.
CREAK

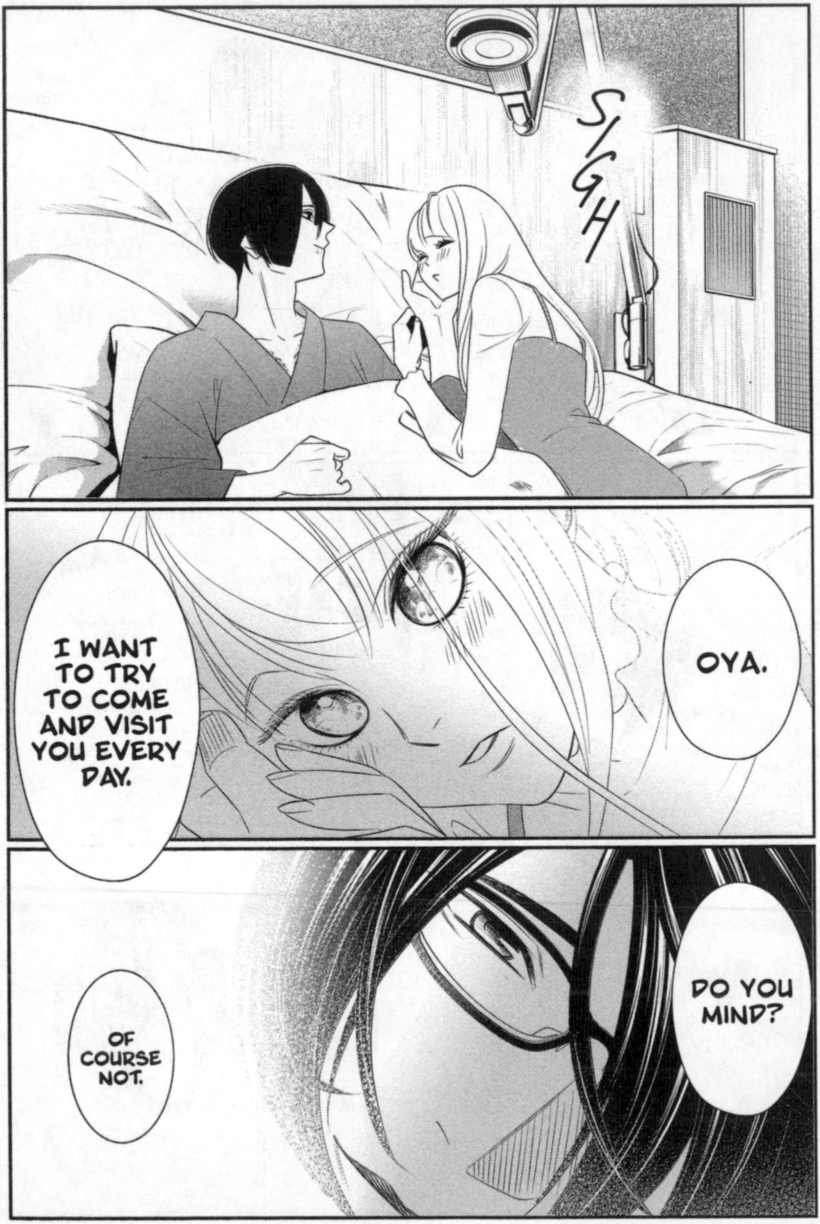
SIGH
OYA.
I WANT TO TRY TO COME AND VISIT YOU EVERY DAY.
DO YOU MIND?
OF COURSE NOT.

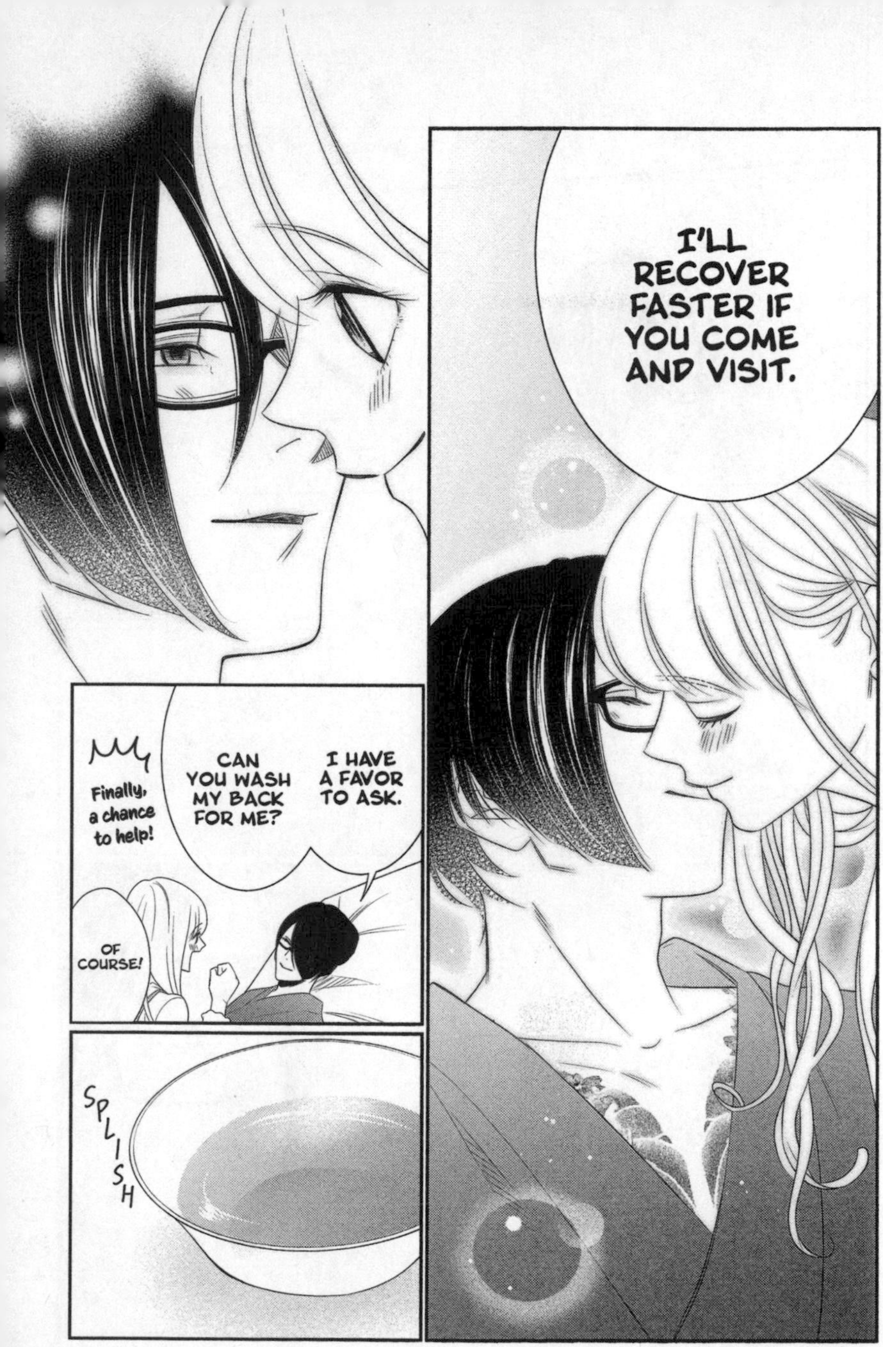
I'LL RECOVER FASTER IF YOU COME AND VISIT.
I HAVE A FAVOR TO ASK.
CAN YOU WASH MY BACK FOR ME?
Finally, a chance to help!
OF COURSE!
SPLISH

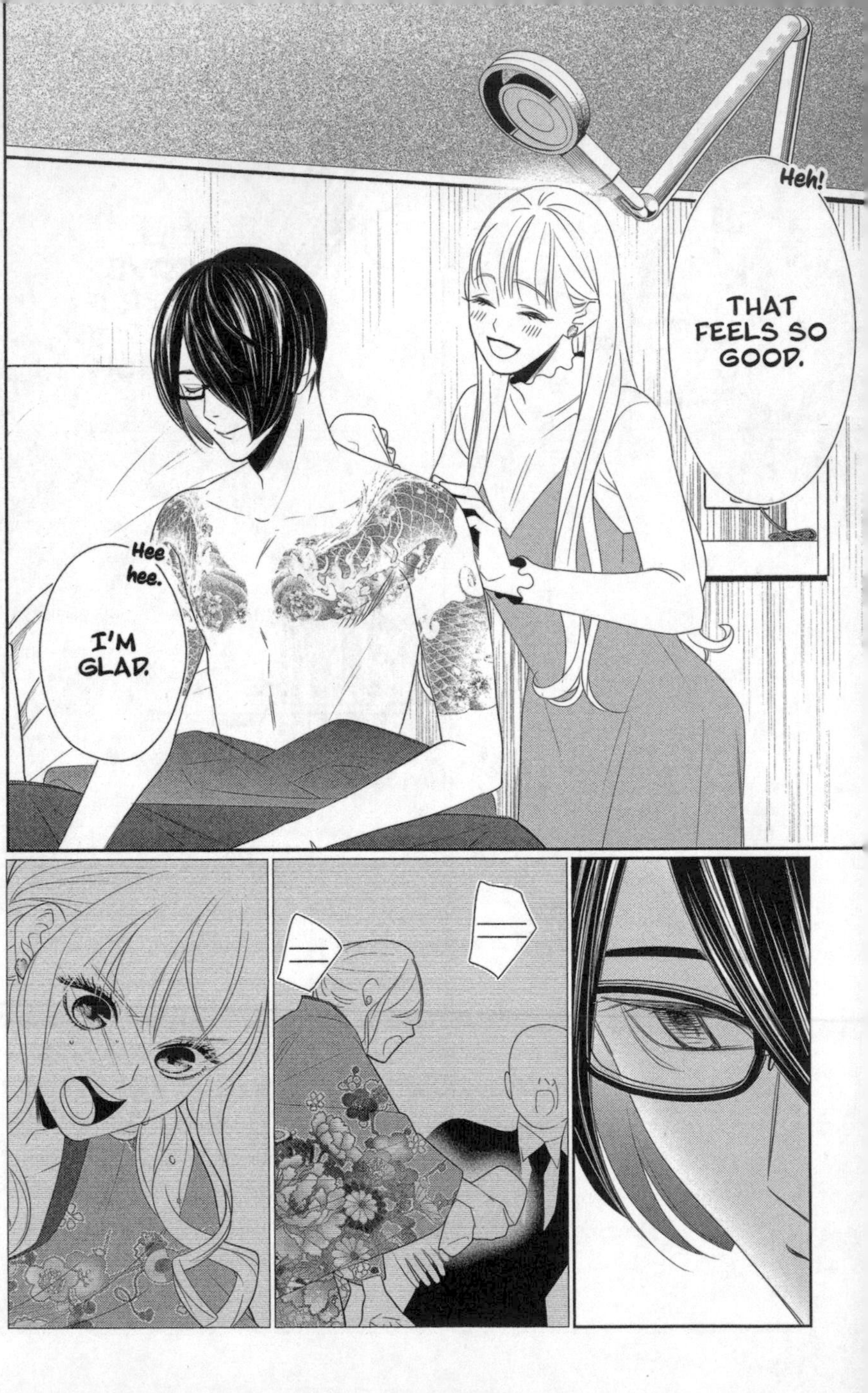
Heh!
THAT FEELS SO GOOD.
Hee hee.
I'M GLAD.

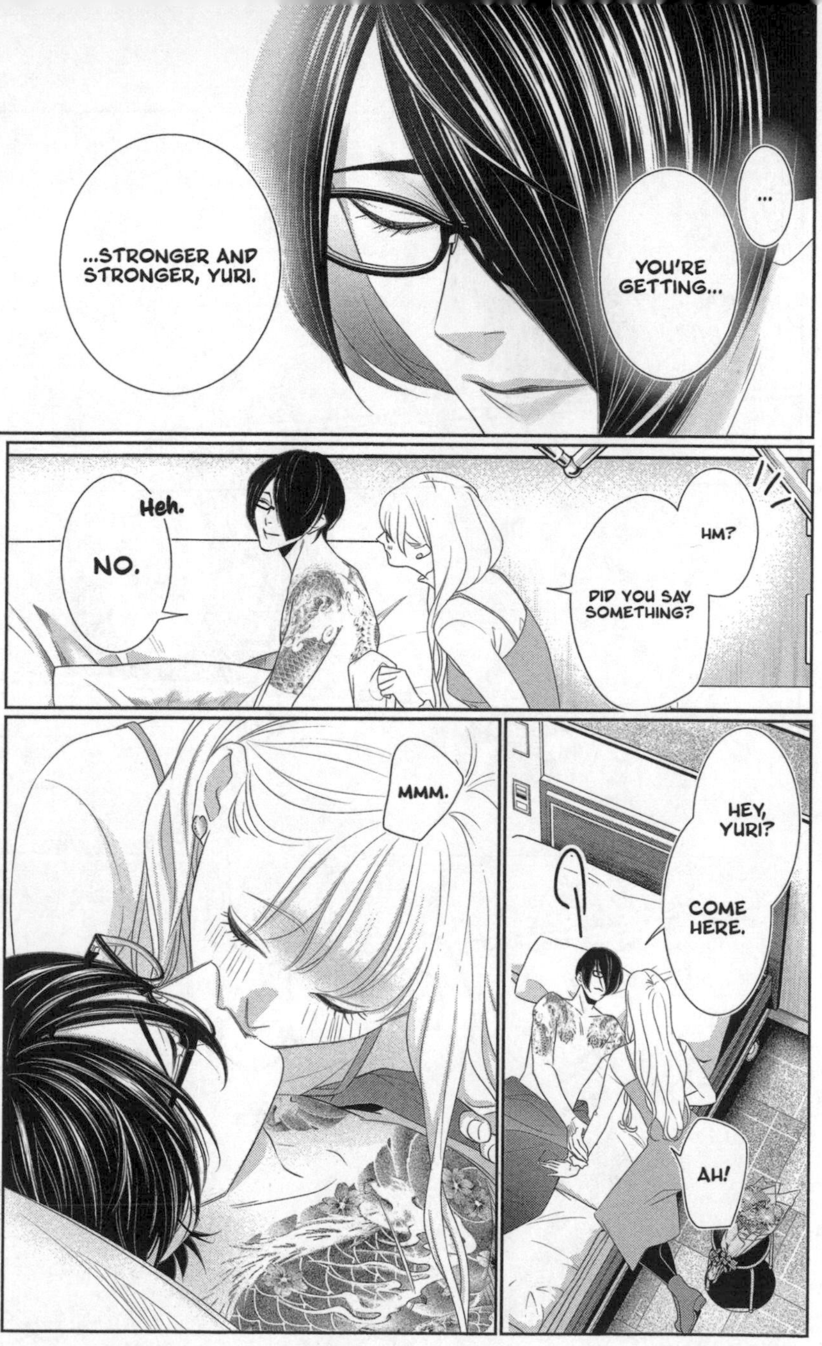
...
YOU'RE GETTING...
...STRONGER AND STRONGER, YURI.
HM?
DID YOU SAY SOMETHING?
Heh.
NO.
HEY, YURI?
COME HERE.
AH!
MMM.

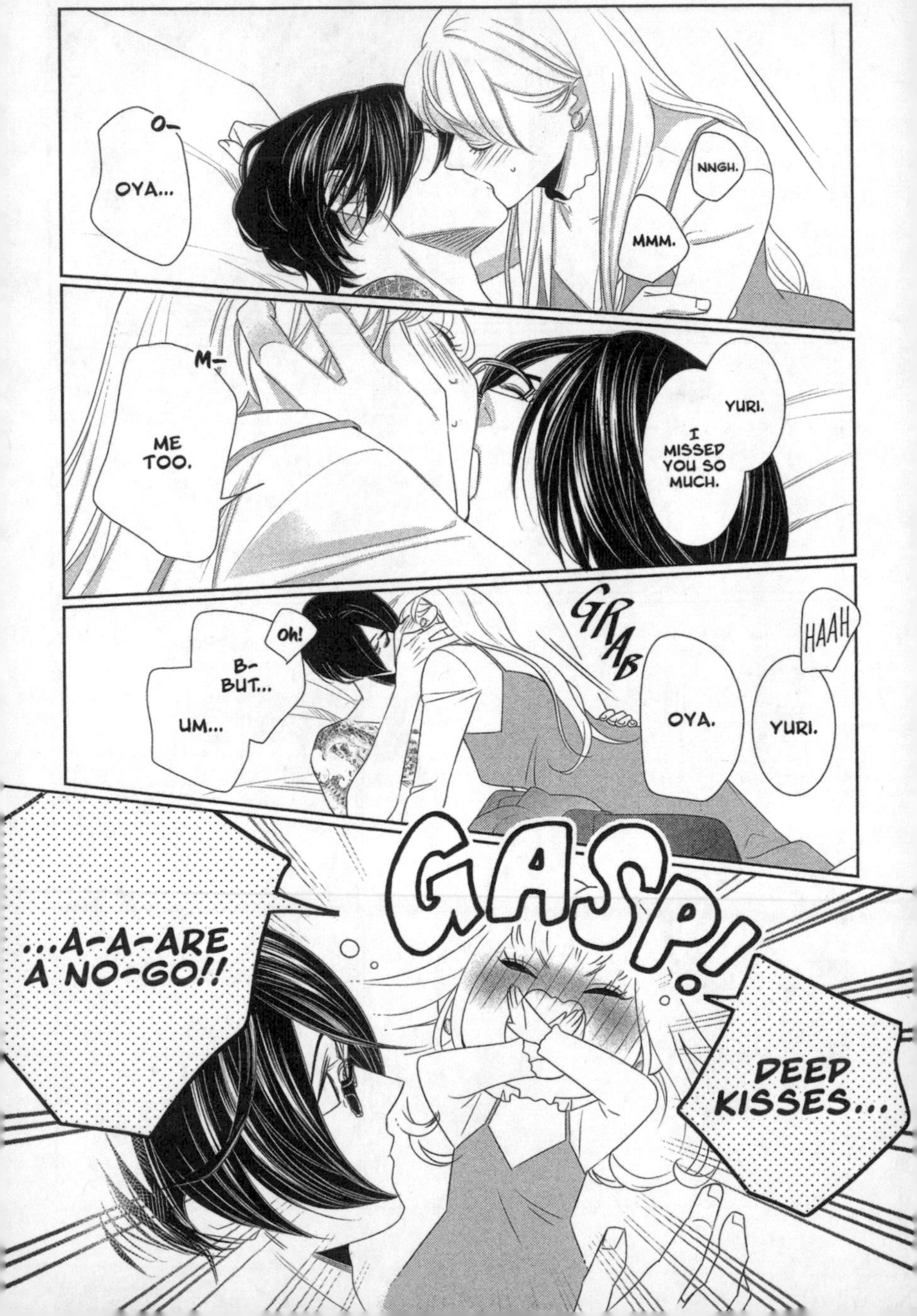
NNGH.
MMM.
O—
OYA...
YURI.
I MISSED YOU SO MUCH.
M—
ME TOO.
HAAH
YURI.
OYA.
GRAB
Oh!
B- BUT...
UM...
GASP!
DEEP KISSES...
...A-A-ARE A NO-GO!!

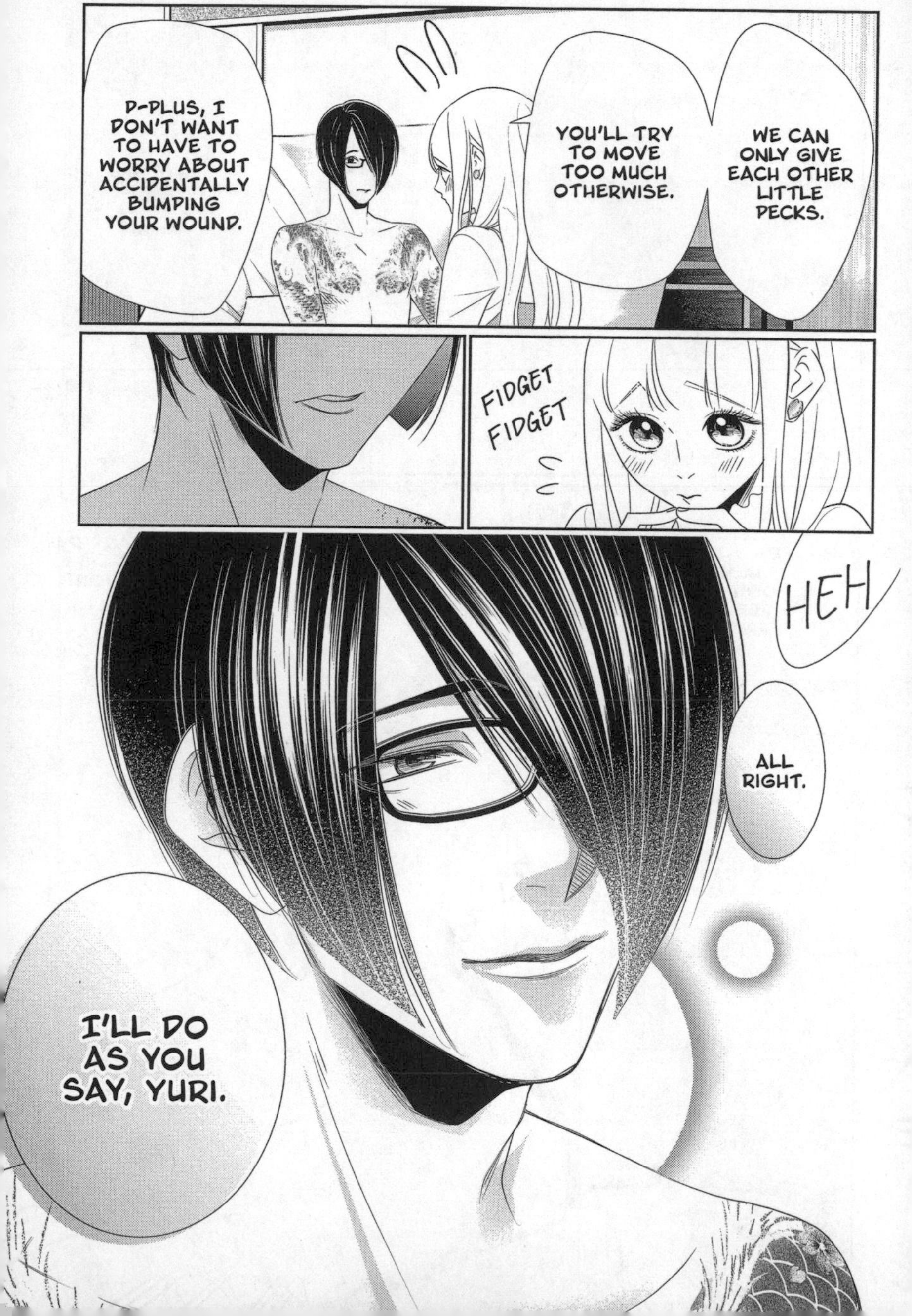
WE CAN ONLY GIVE EACH OTHER LITTLE PECKS.
YOU'LL TRY TO MOVE TOO MUCH OTHERWISE.
D-PLUS, I DON'T WANT TO HAVE TO WORRY ABOUT ACCIDENTALLY BUMPING YOUR WOUND.
FIDGET FIDGET
HEH
ALL RIGHT.
I'LL DO AS YOU SAY, YURI.

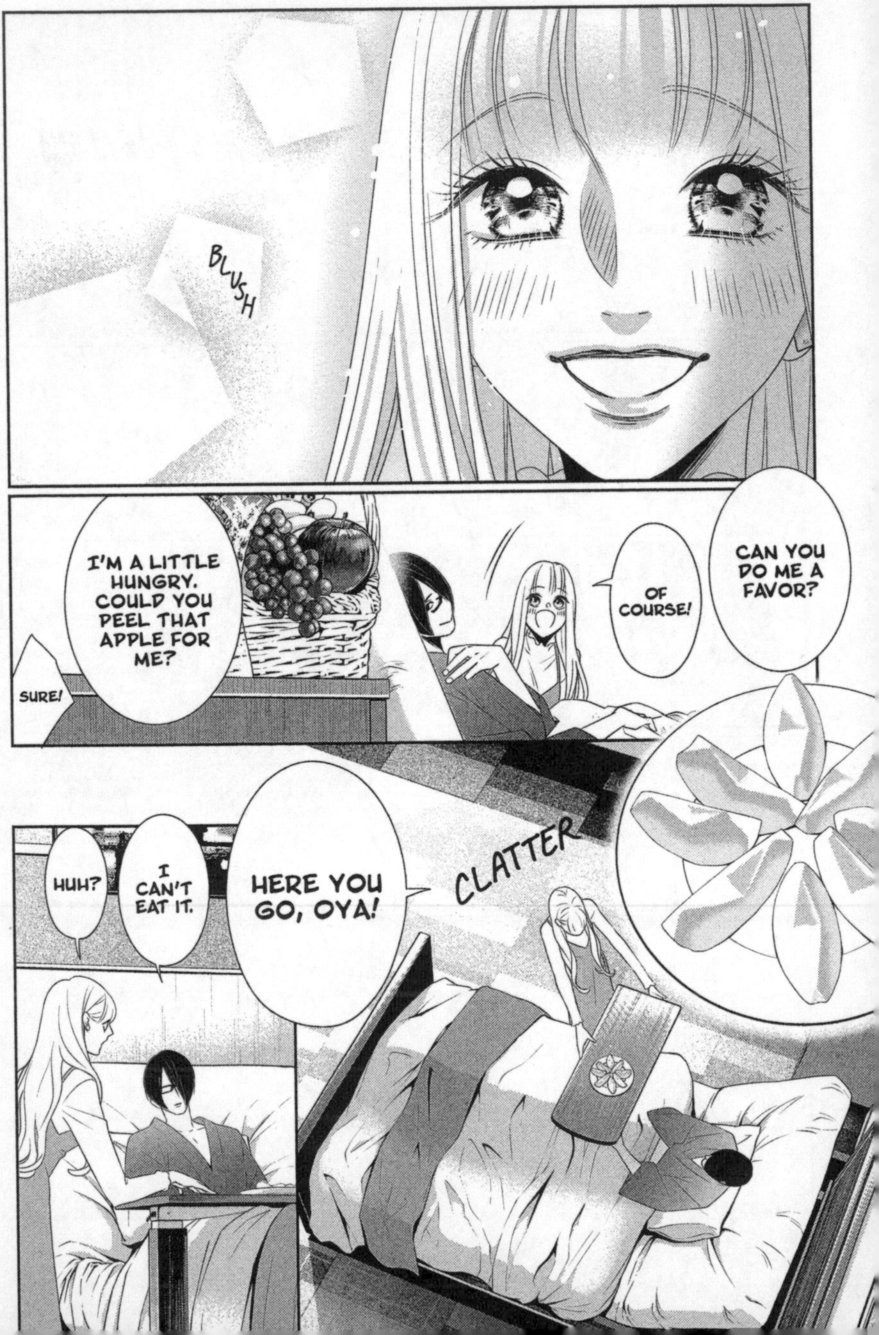
BLUSH
CAN YOU DO ME A FAVOR?
OF COURSE!
I'M A LITTLE HUNGRY. COULD YOU PEEL THAT APPLE FOR ME?
SURE!
CLATTER
HERE YOU GO, OYA!
I CAN'T EAT IT.
HUH?

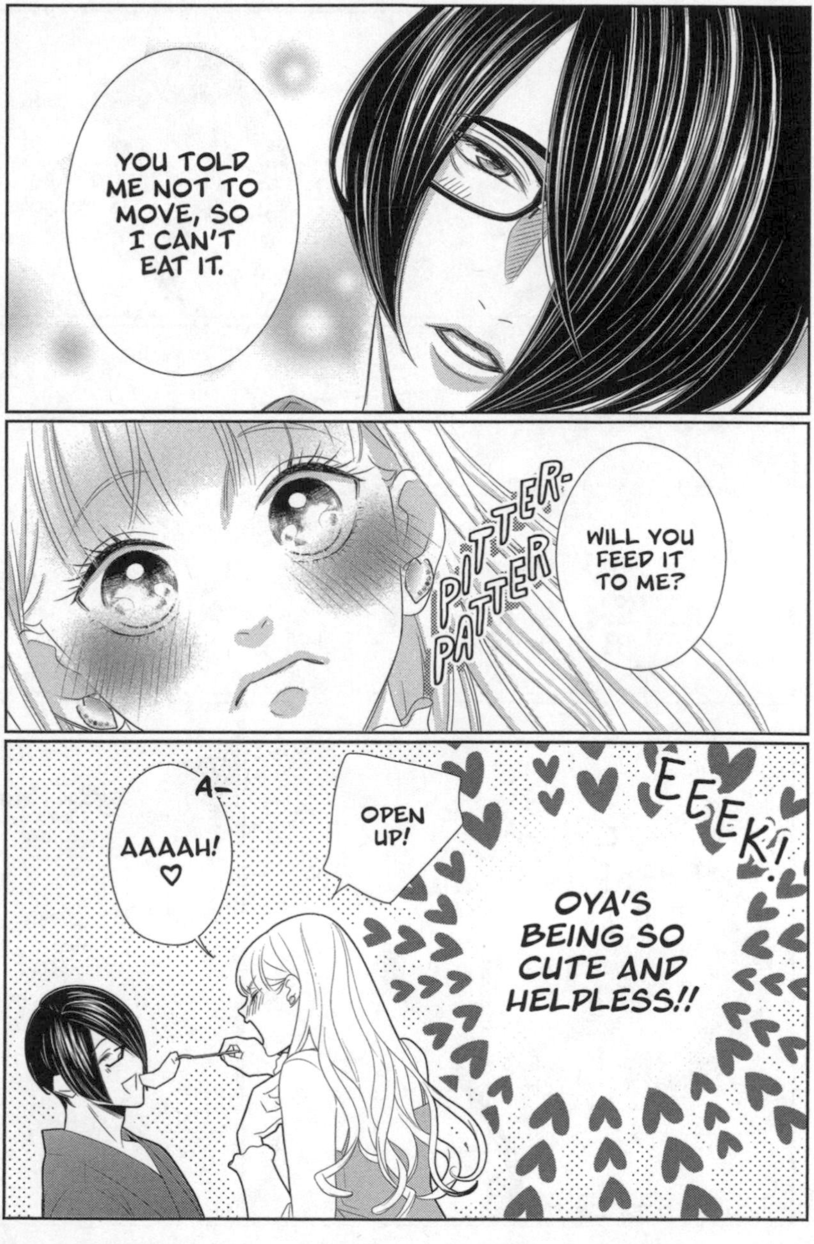
YOU TOLD ME NOT TO MOVE, SO I CAN'T EAT IT.
WILL YOU FEED IT TO ME?
PITTER-PATTER
EEEK!
OYA'S BEING SO CUTE AND HELPLESS!!
OPEN UP!
A- AAAAH! ♡

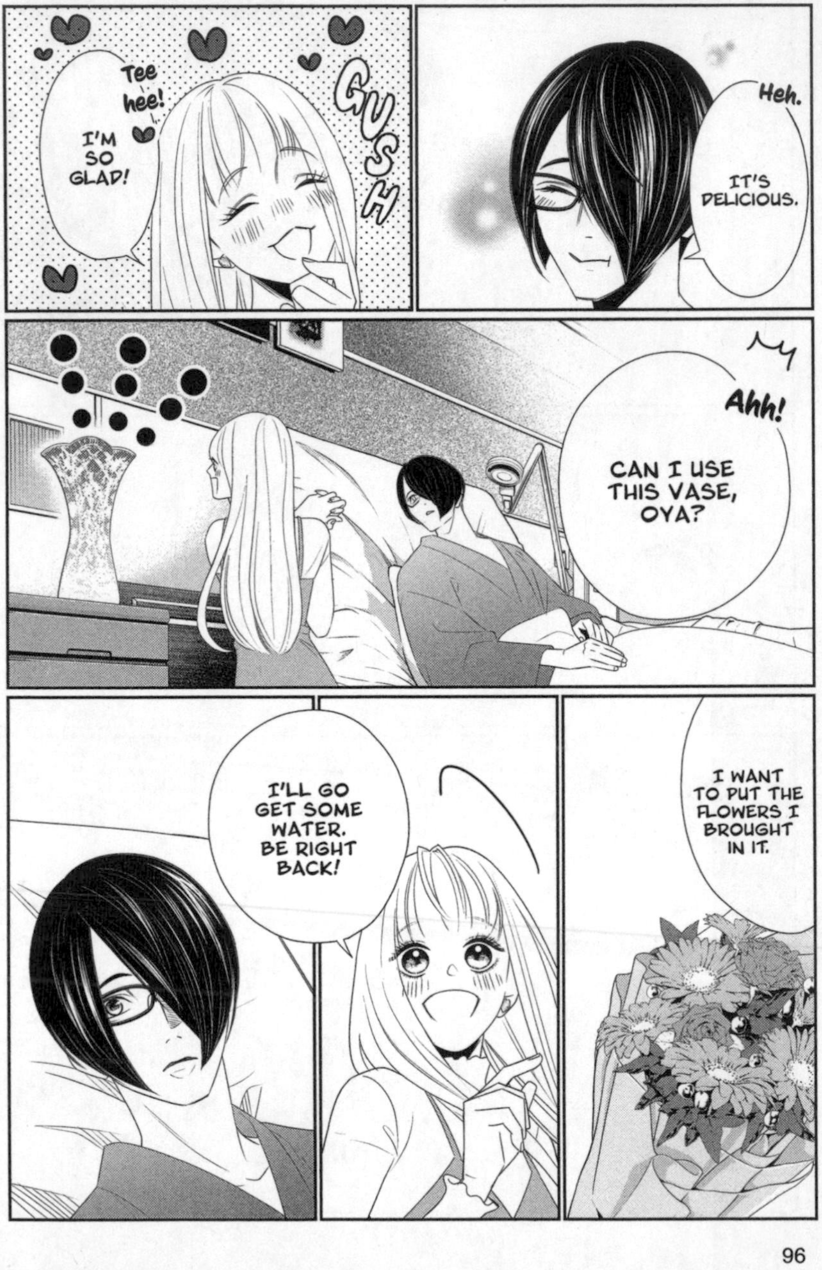
Heh.
IT'S DELICIOUS.
Tee hee!
I'M SO GLAD!
GUSH
Ahh!
CAN I USE THIS VASE, OYA?
I WANT TO PUT THE FLOWERS I BROUGHT IN IT.
I'LL GO GET SOME WATER. BE RIGHT BACK!

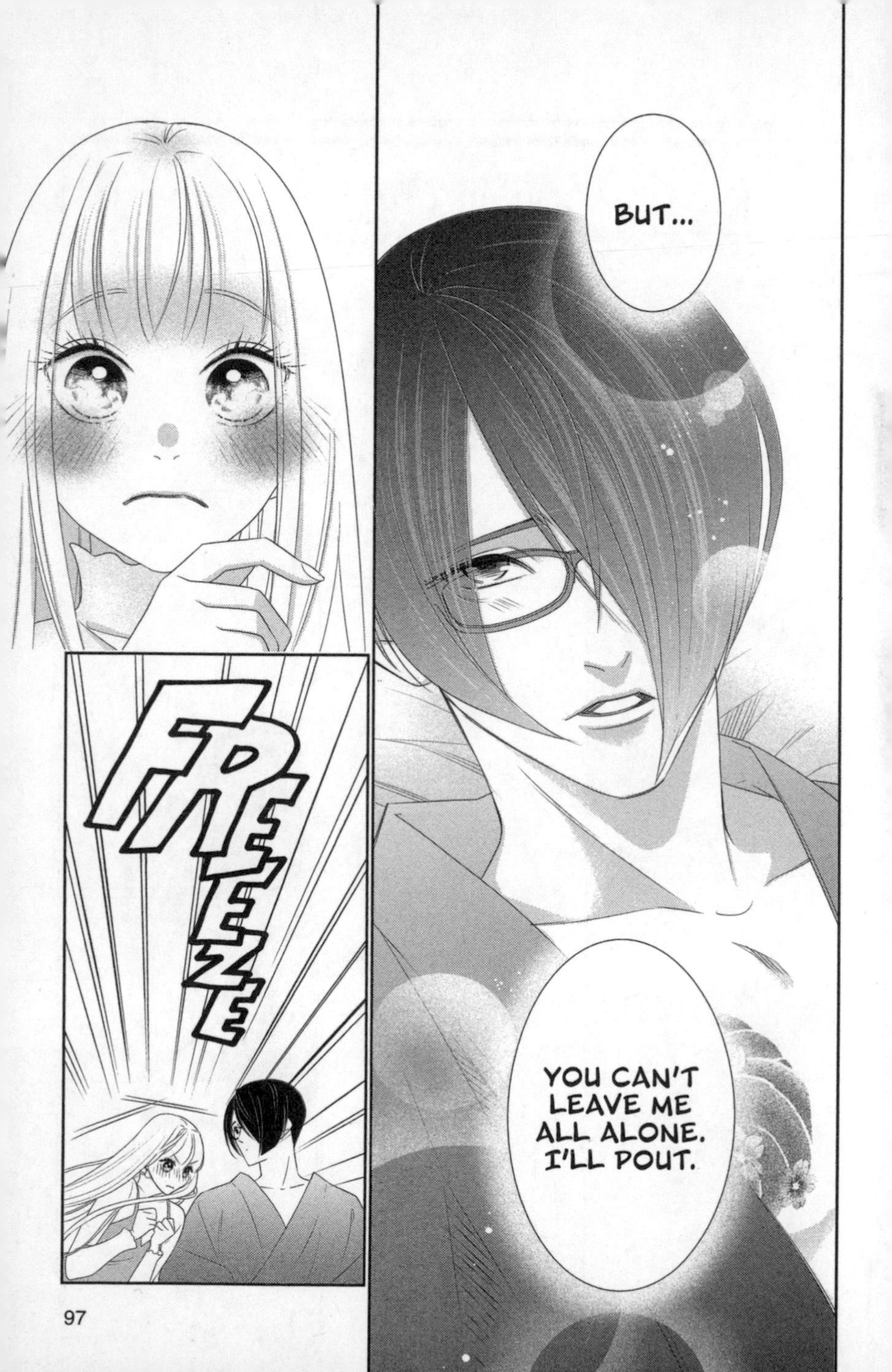
BUT...
YOU CAN'T LEAVE ME ALL ALONE. I'LL POUT.
FREEZE

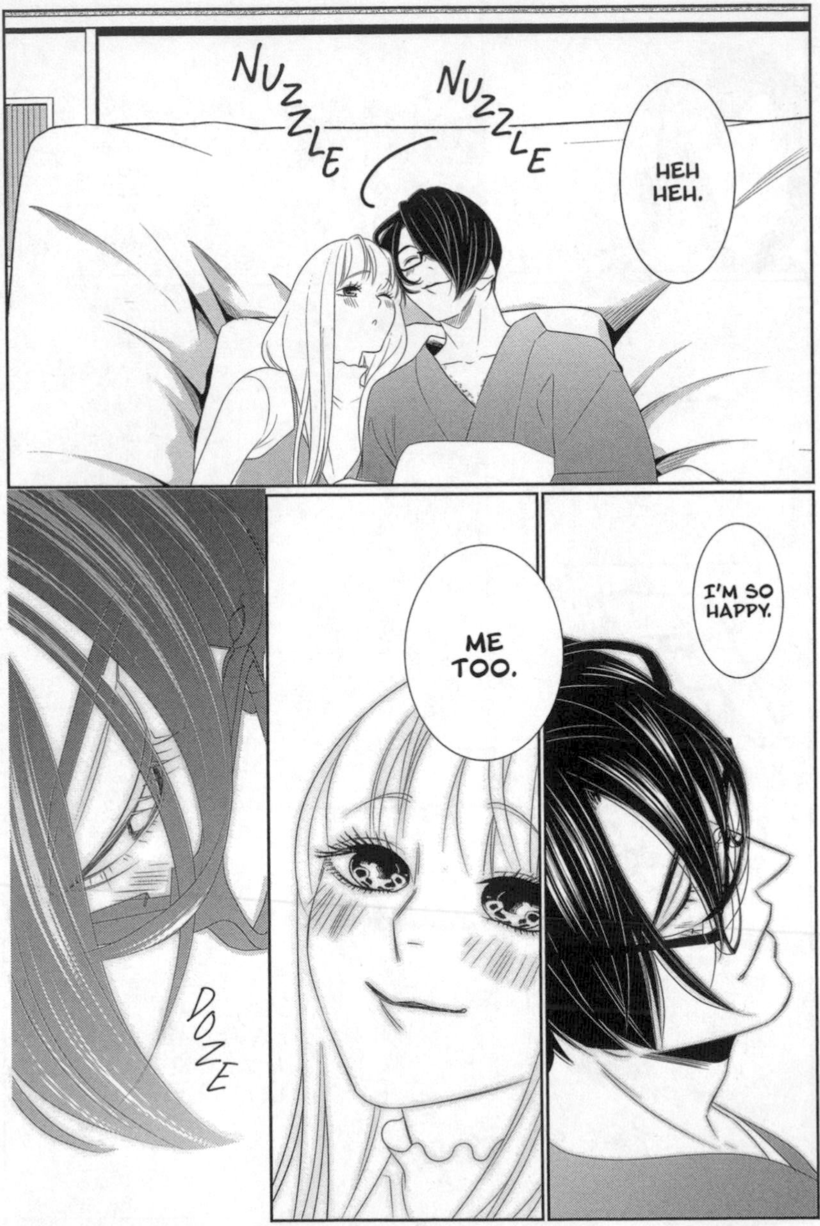
HEH HEH.
NUZZLE
NUZZLE
I'M SO HAPPY.
ME TOO.
DOZE

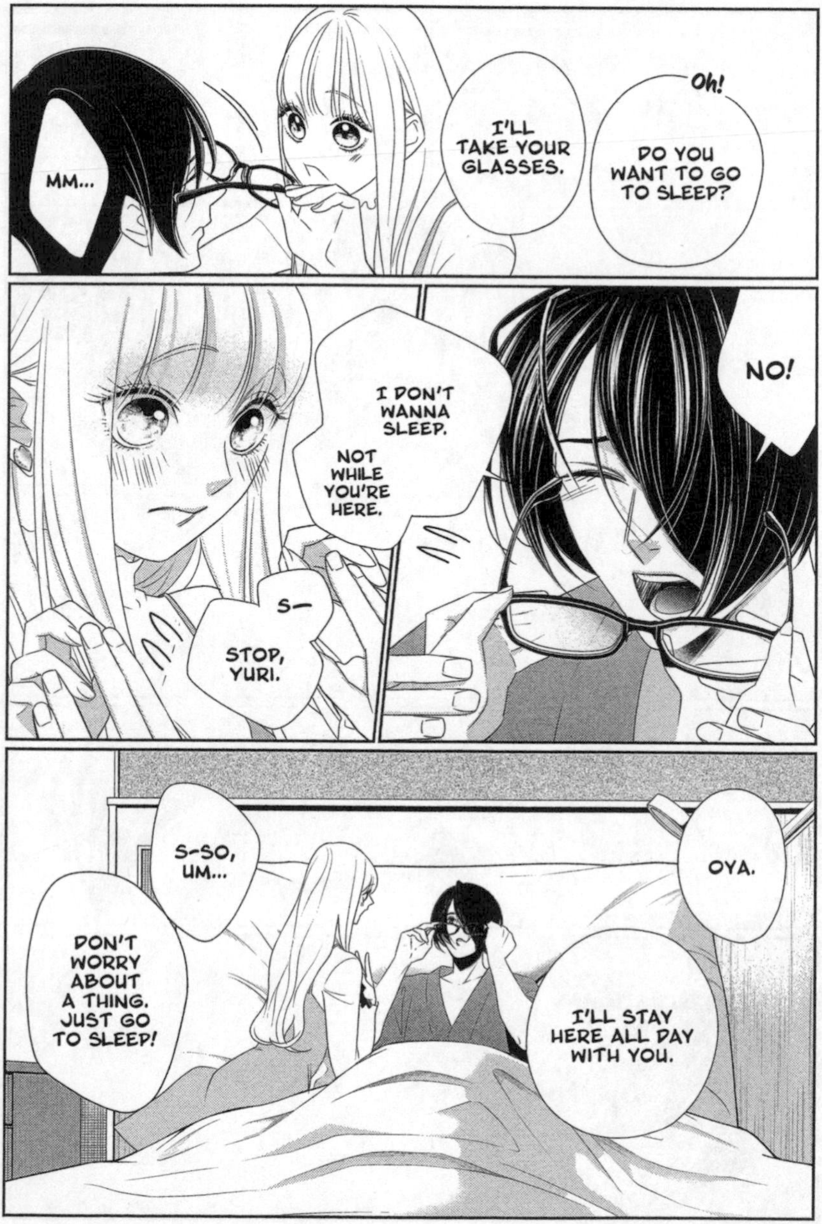
Oh!
DO YOU WANT TO GO TO SLEEP?
I'LL TAKE YOUR GLASSES.
MM...
NO!
I DON'T WANNA SLEEP.
NOT WHILE YOU'RE HERE.
S—
STOP, YURI.
OYA.
I'LL STAY HERE ALL DAY WITH YOU.
S-SO, UM...
DON'T WORRY ABOUT A THING. JUST GO TO SLEEP!

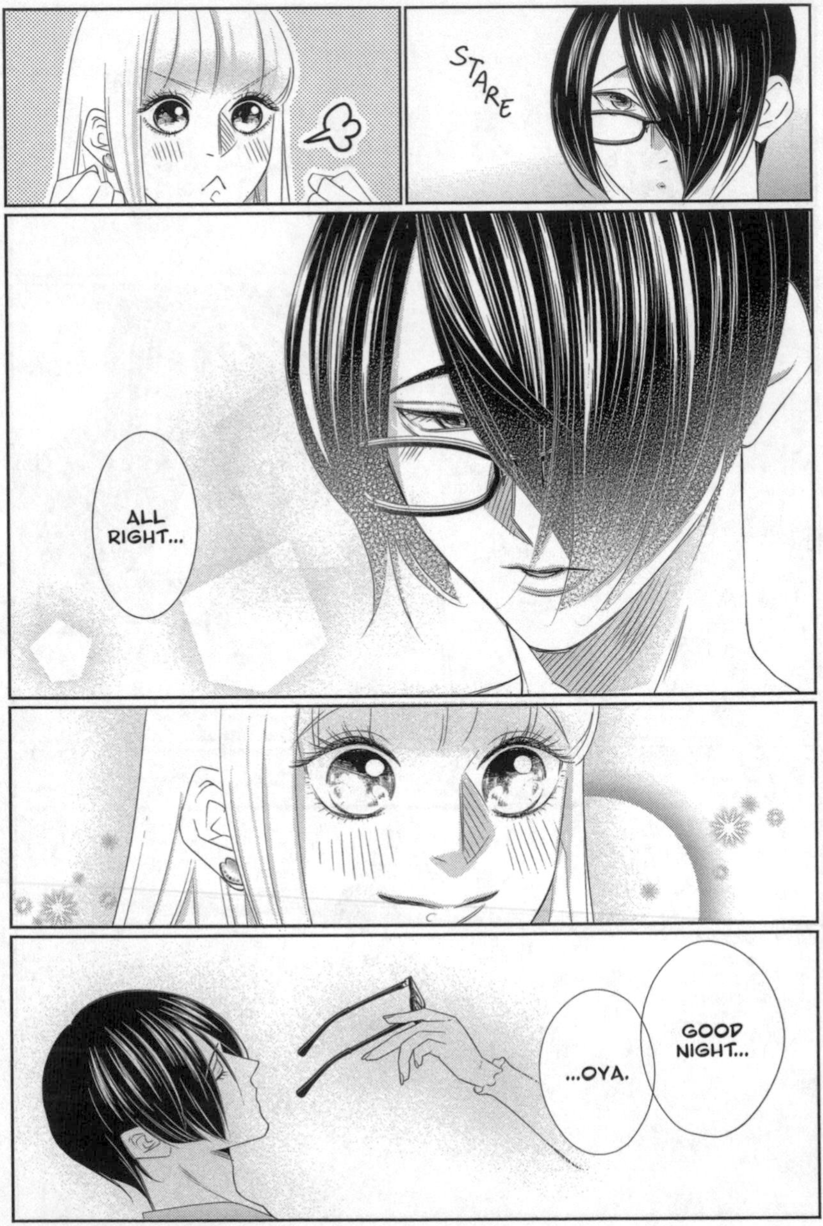
STARE
ALL RIGHT...
GOOD NIGHT...
...OYA.

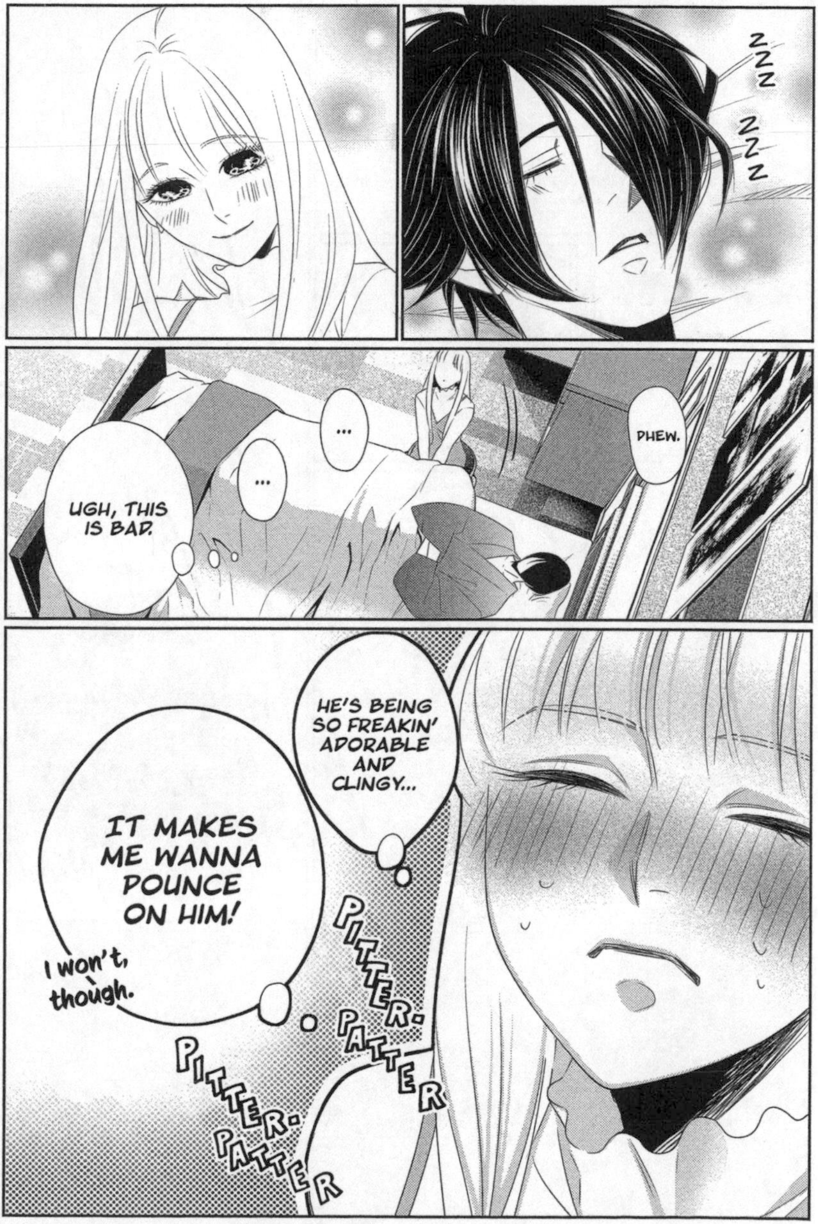
ZZZ
ZZZ
PHEW.
...
...
UGH, THIS IS BAD.
HE'S BEING SO FREAKIN' ADORABLE AND CLINGY...
IT MAKES ME WANNA POUNCE ON HIM!
I won't, though.
PITTER-PATTER
PITTER-PATTER

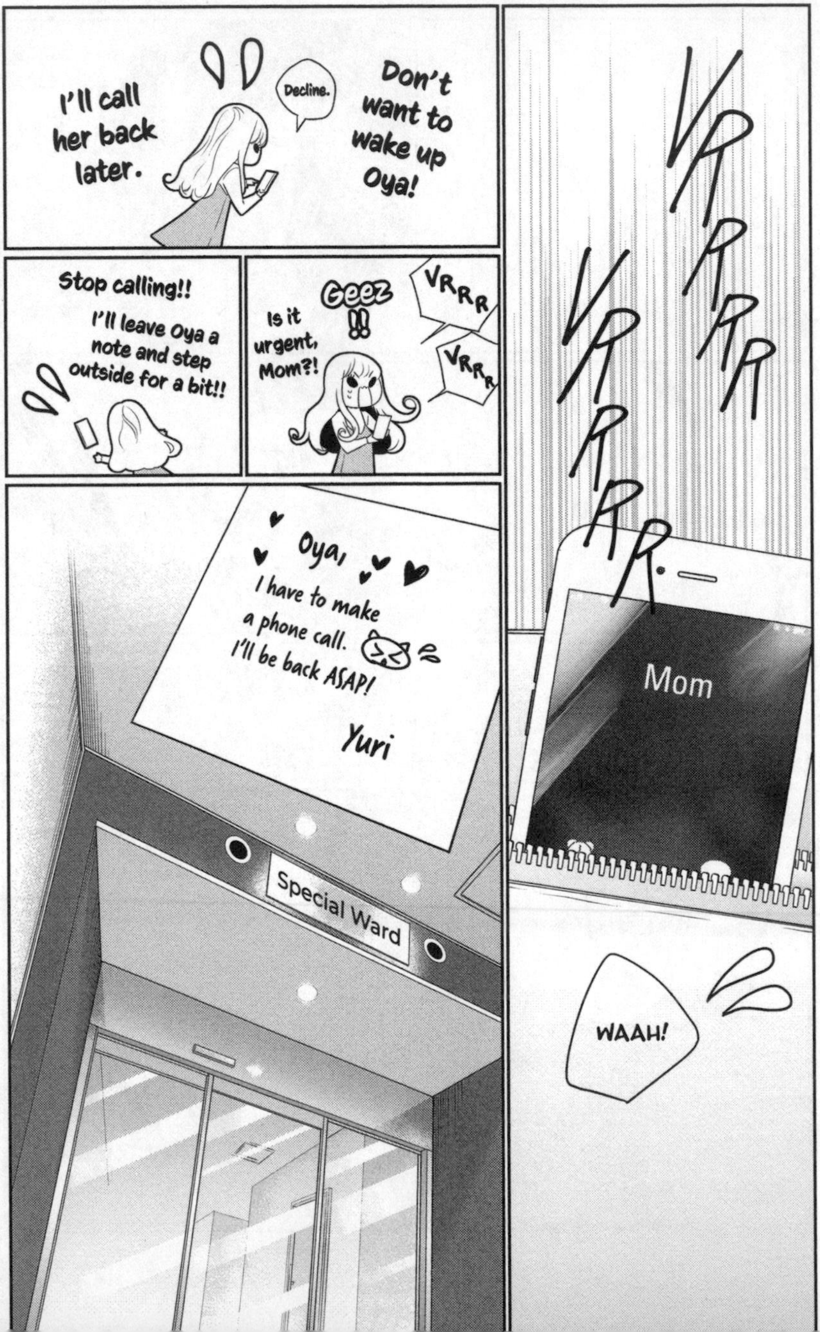
VRRRR
VRRRRR.
Mom
WAAH!
Don't want to wake up Oya!
Decline.
I'll call her back later.
VRRR
VRRR
Geez!!
Is it urgent, Mom?!
Stop calling!!
I'll leave Oya a note and step outside for a bit!!
Oya,
I have to make a phone call.
I'll be back ASAP!
Yuri
Special Ward

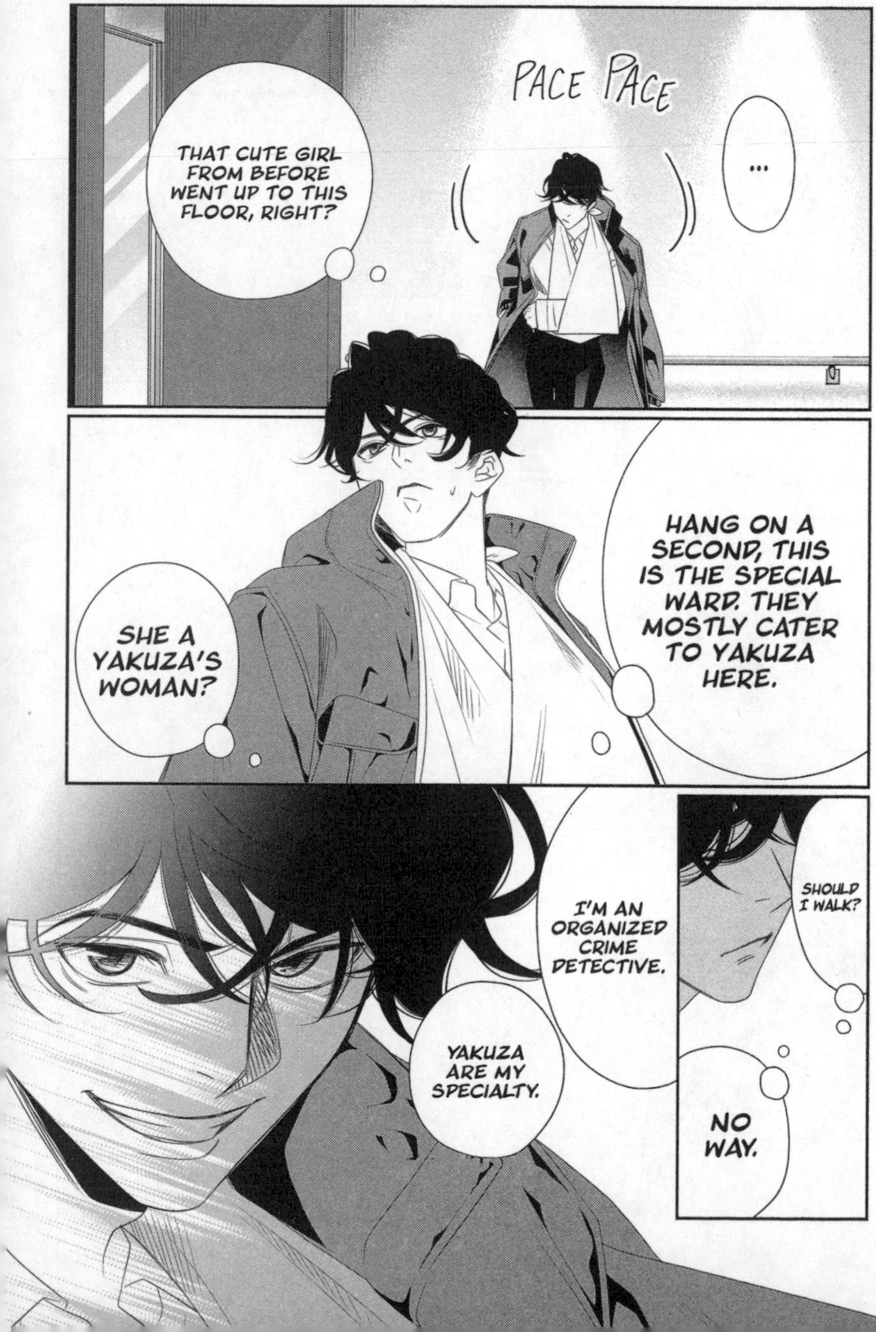
PACE PACE
...
THAT CUTE GIRL FROM BEFORE WENT UP TO THIS FLOOR, RIGHT?
HANG ON A SECOND, THIS IS THE SPECIAL WARD. THEY MOSTLY CATER TO YAKUZA HERE.
SHE A YAKUZA'S WOMAN?
SHOULD I WALK?
NO WAY.
I'M AN ORGANIZED CRIME DETECTIVE.
YAKUZA ARE MY SPECIALTY.

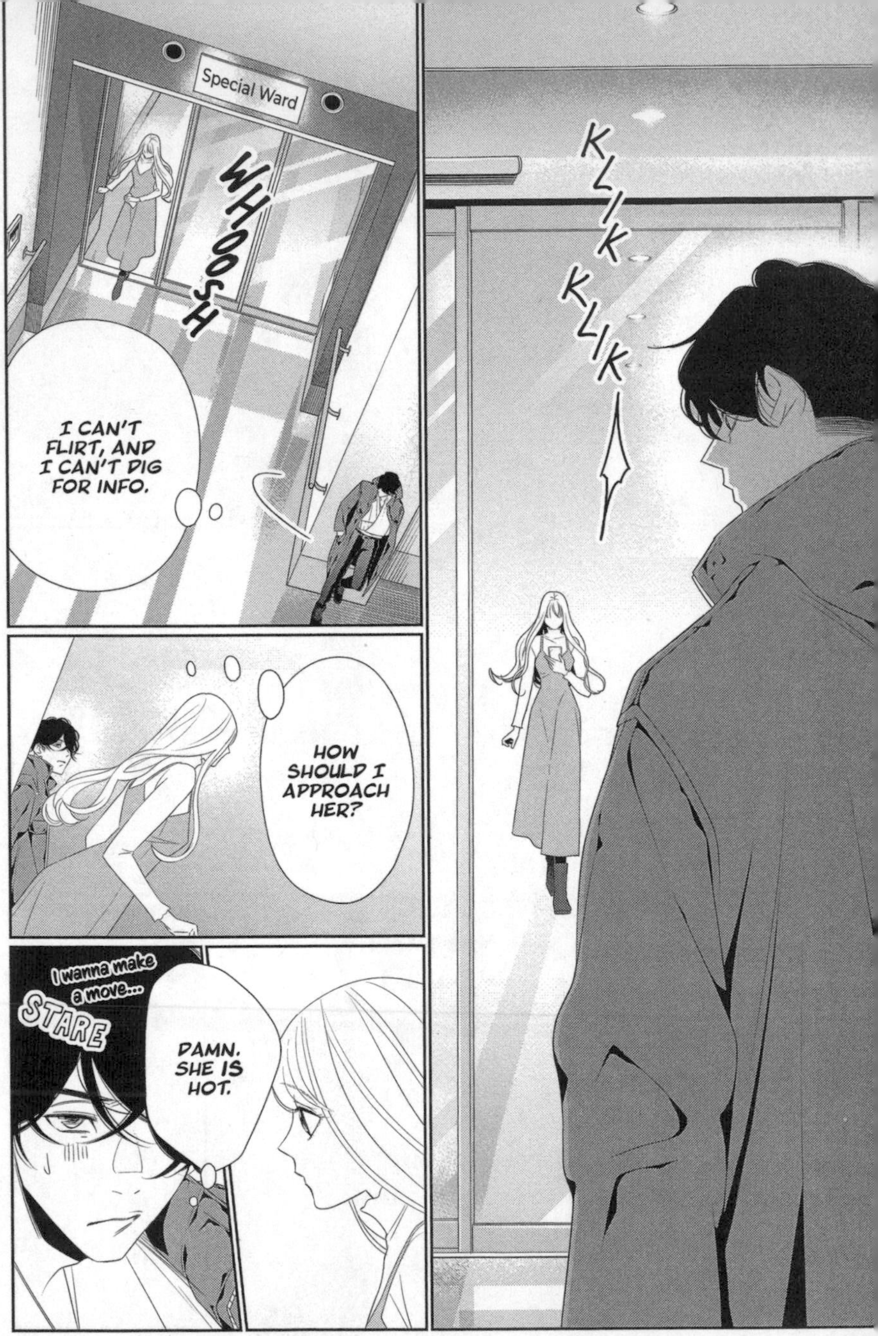
KLIK KLIK KLIK
Special Ward
WHOOSH
I CAN'T FLIRT, AND I CAN'T DIG FOR INFO.
HOW SHOULD I APPROACH HER?
DAMN. SHE IS HOT.
I wanna make a move...
STARE

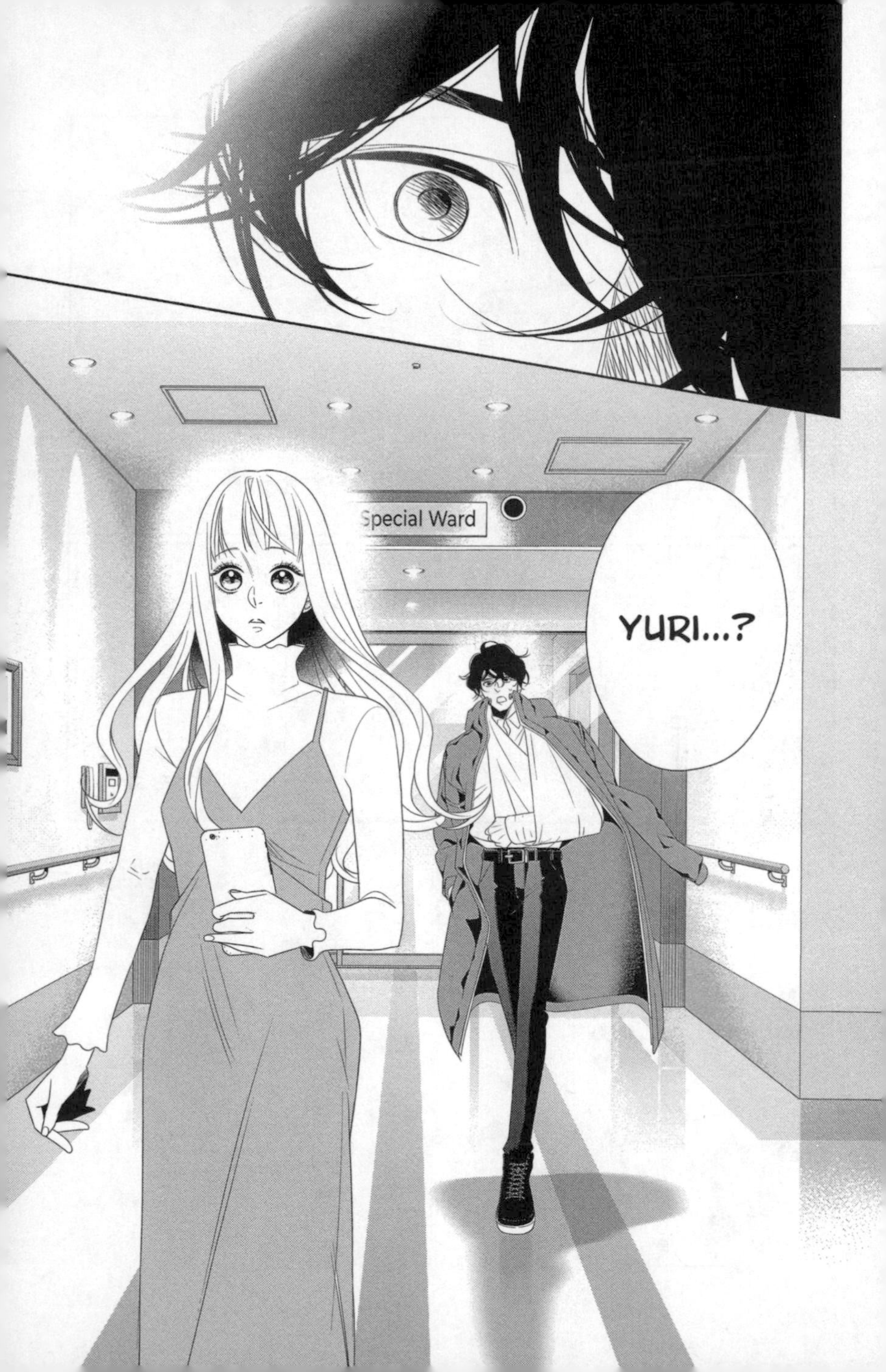
Special Ward
YURI...?

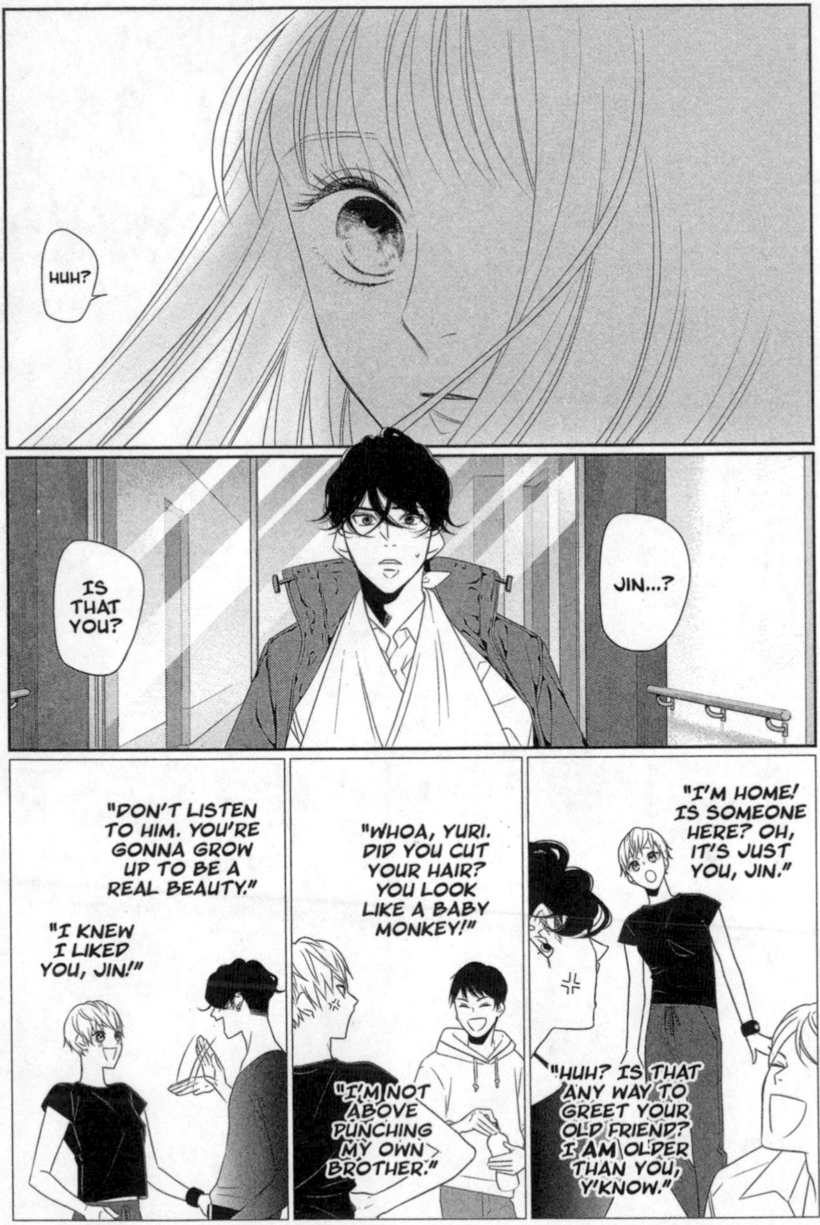
HUH?
JIN...?
IS THAT YOU?
"I'M HOME! IS SOMEONE HERE? OH, IT'S JUST YOU, JIN."
"HUH? IS THAT ANY WAY TO GREET YOUR OLD FRIEND? I AM OLDER THAN YOU, Y'KNOW."
"WHOA, YURI. DID YOU CUT YOUR HAIR? YOU LOOK LIKE A BABY MONKEY!"
"I'M NOT ABOVE PUNCHING MY OWN BROTHER."
"DON'T LISTEN TO HIM. YOU'RE GONNA GROW UP TO BE A REAL BEAUTY."
"I KNEW I LIKED YOU, JIN!"

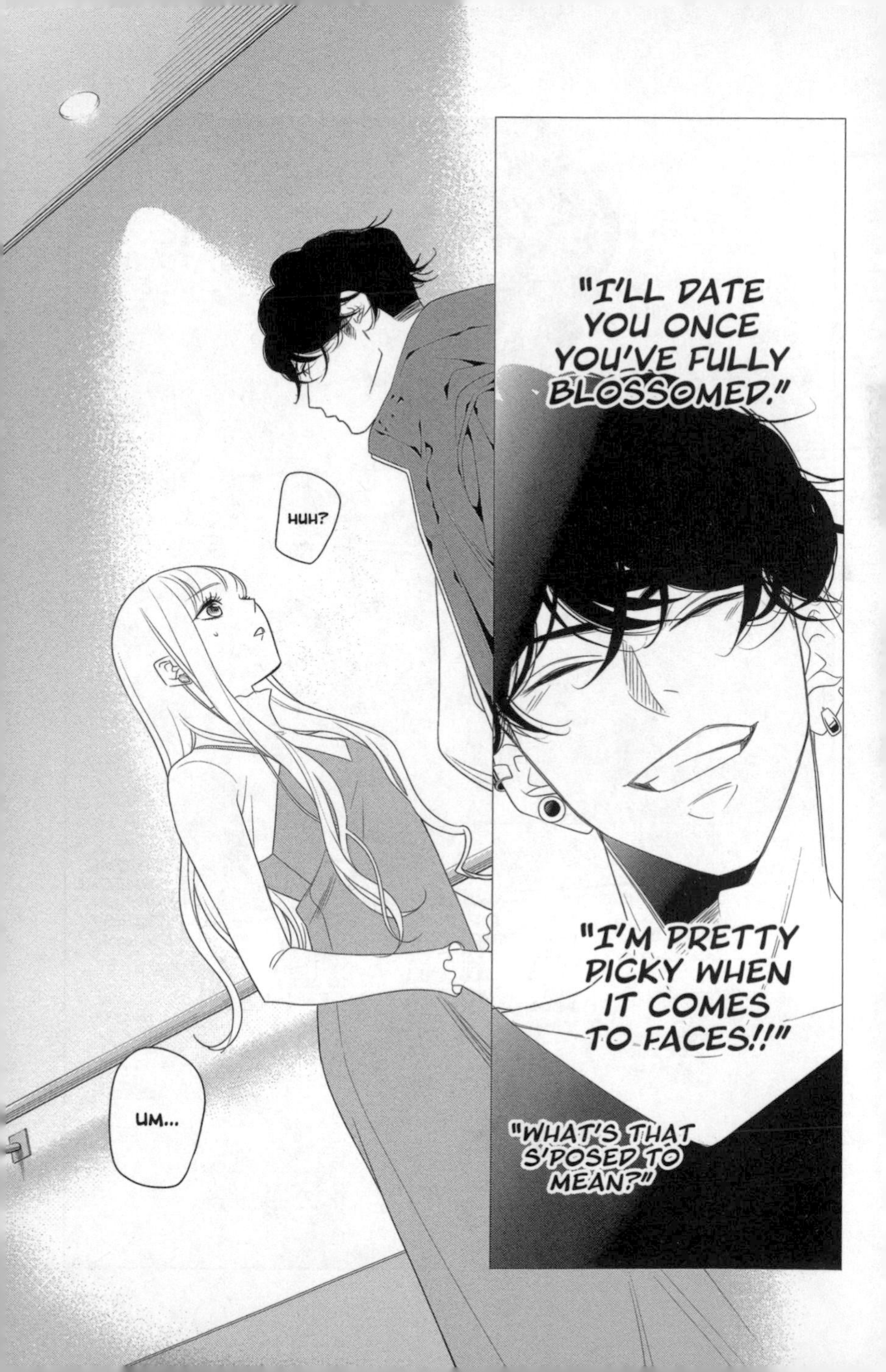
"I'LL DATE YOU ONCE YOU'VE FULLY BLOSSOMED."
"I'M PRETTY PICKY WHEN IT COMES TO FACES!!"
"WHAT'S THAT S'POSED TO MEAN?"
HUH?
UM...

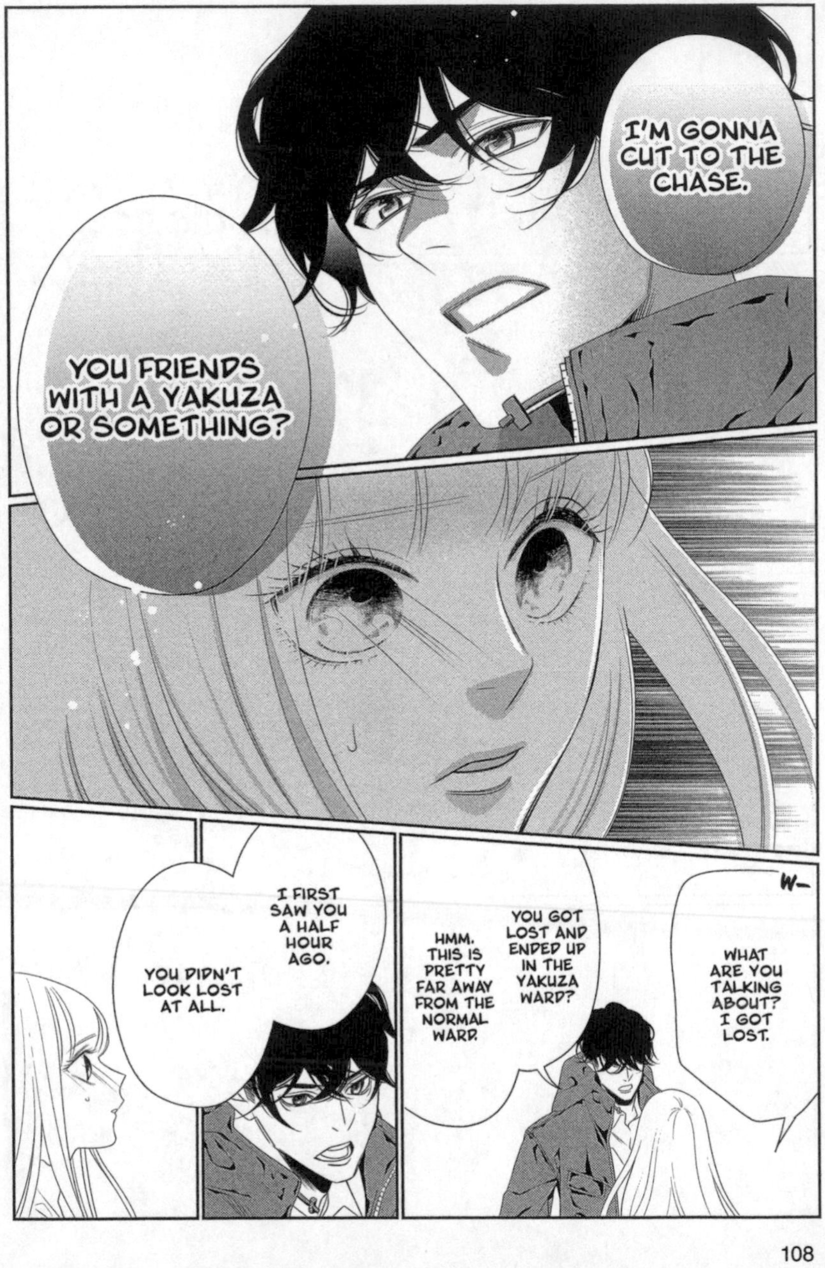
I'M GONNA CUT TO THE CHASE.
YOU FRIENDS WITH A YAKUZA OR SOMETHING?
W—
WHAT ARE YOU TALKING ABOUT? I GOT LOST.
YOU GOT LOST AND ENDED UP IN THE YAKUZA WARD?
HMM. THIS IS PRETTY FAR AWAY FROM THE NORMAL WARD.
I FIRST SAW YOU A HALF HOUR AGO.
YOU DIDN'T LOOK LOST AT ALL.

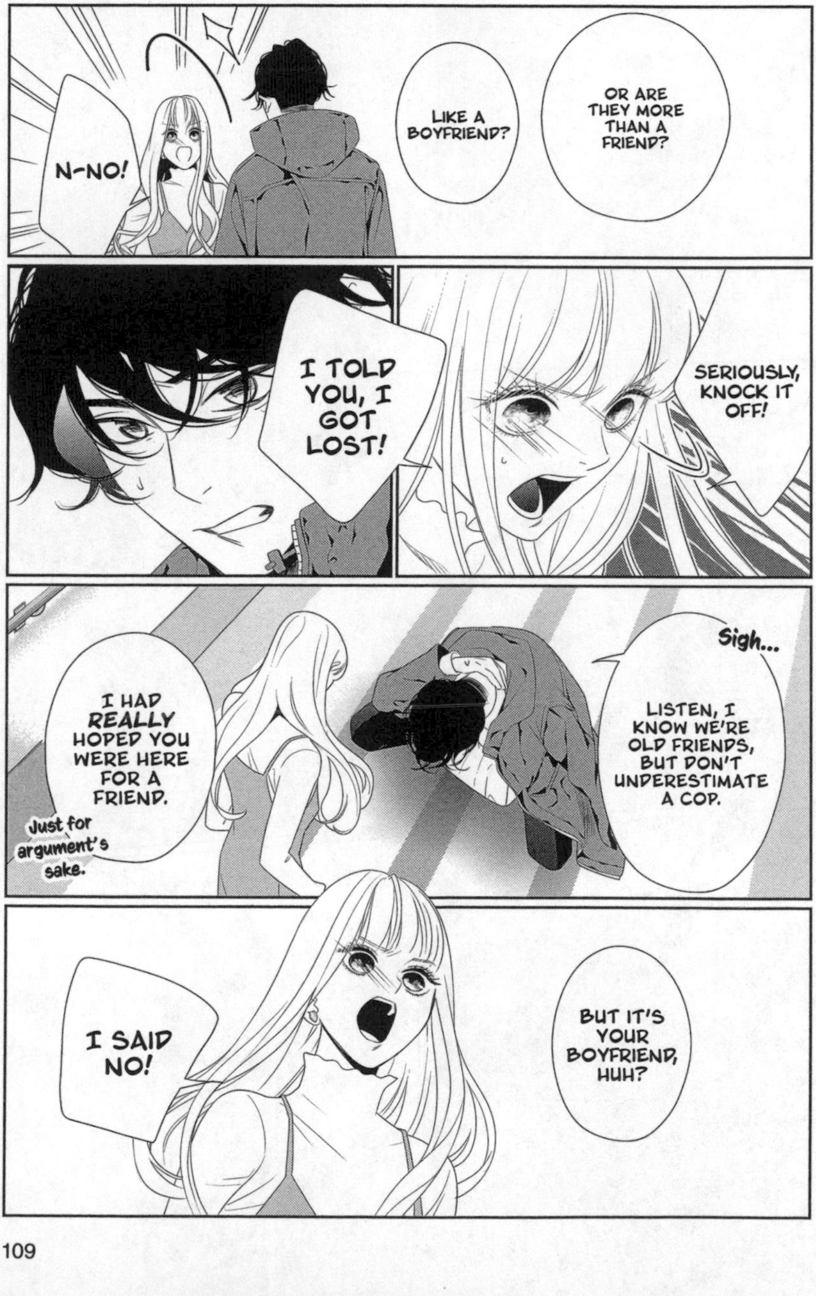
OR ARE THEY MORE THAN A FRIEND?
LIKE A BOYFRIEND?
N-NO!
SERIOUSLY, KNOCK IT OFF!
I TOLD YOU, I GOT LOST!
Sigh...
LISTEN, I KNOW WE'RE OLD FRIENDS, BUT DON'T UNDERESTIMATE A COP.
I HAD REALLY HOPED YOU WERE HERE FOR A FRIEND.
Just for argument's sake.
BUT IT'S YOUR BOYFRIEND, HUH?
I SAID NO!

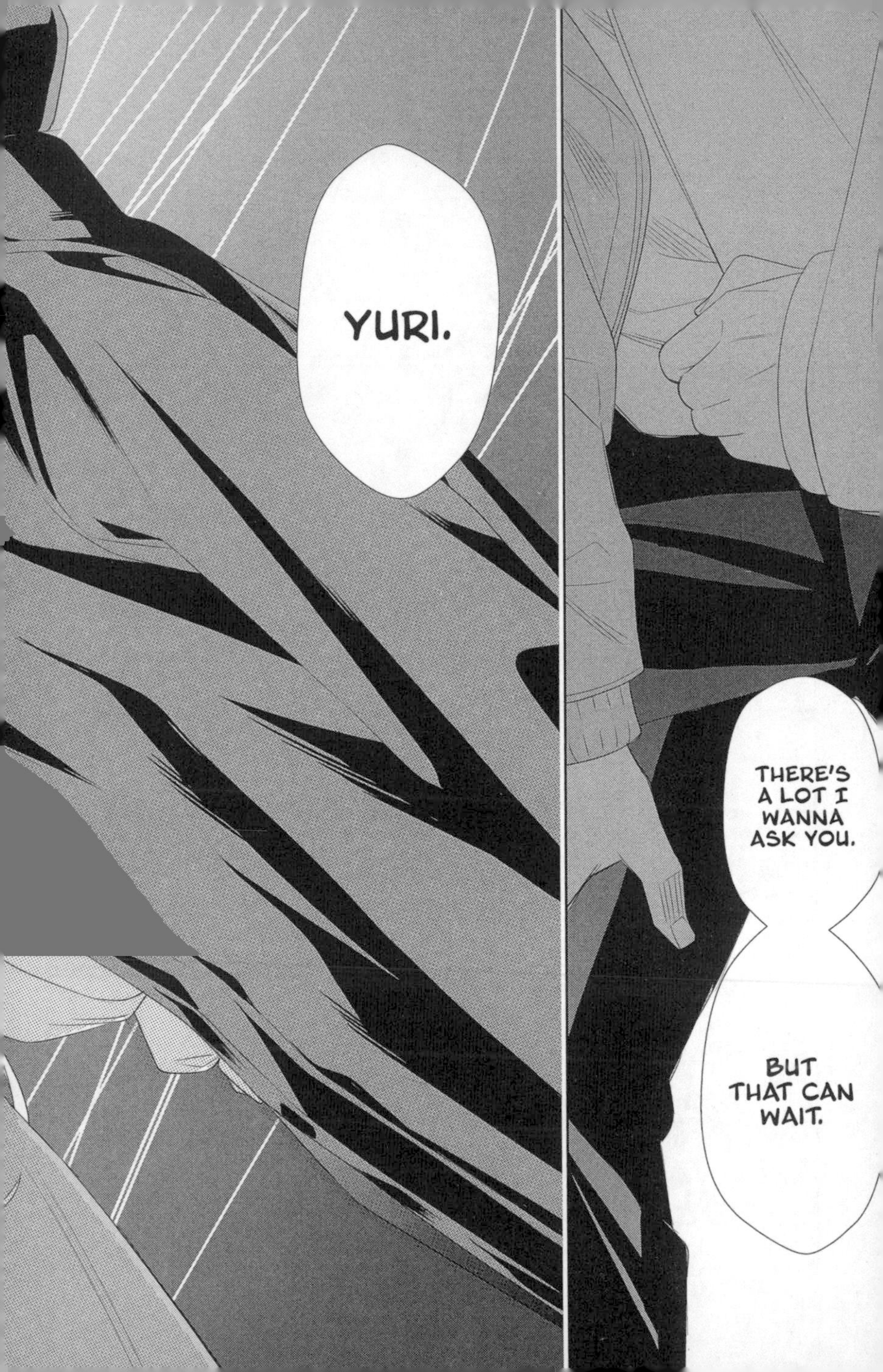
THERE'S A LOT I WANNA ASK YOU.
BUT THAT CAN WAIT.
YURI.

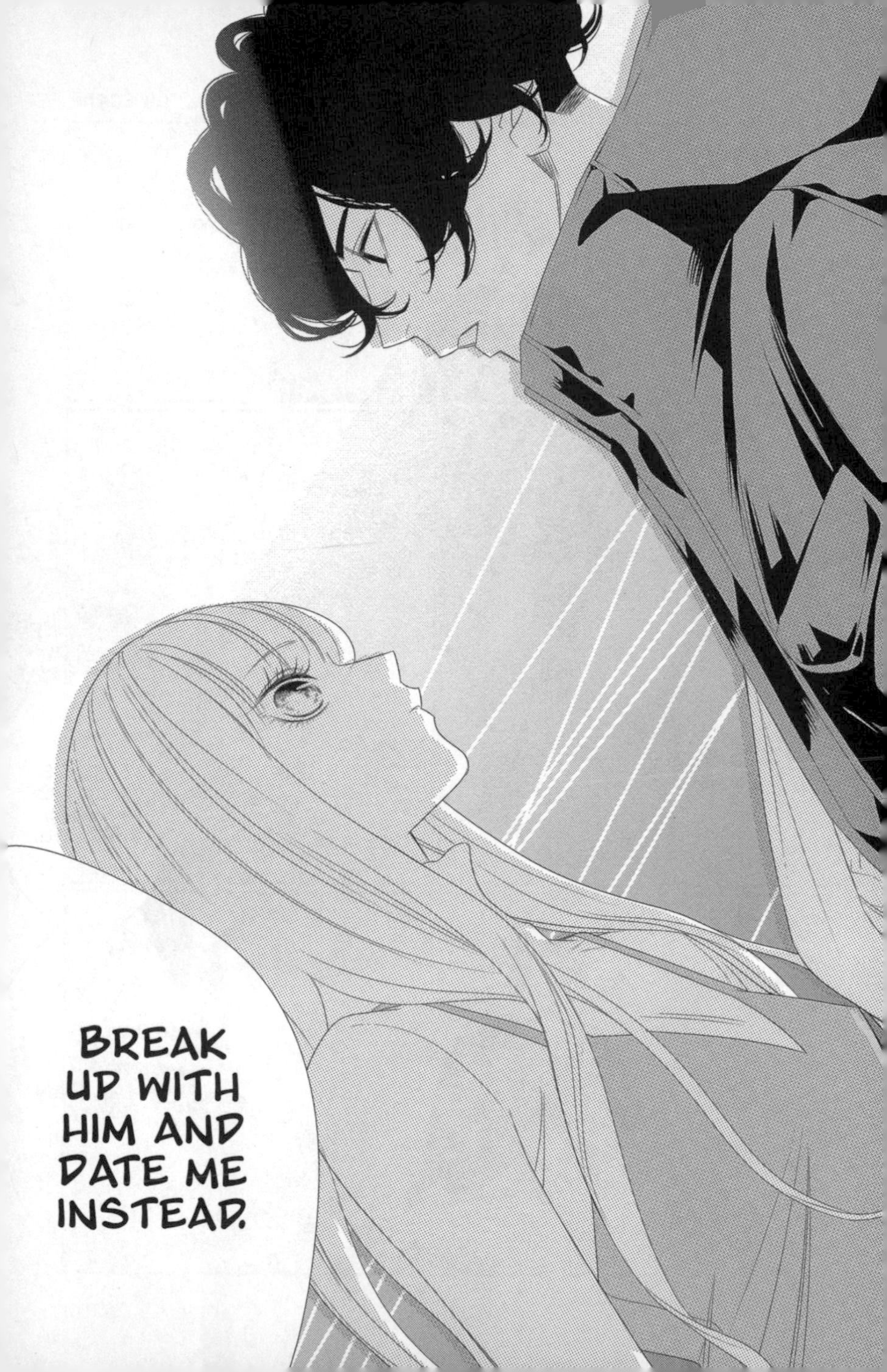
BREAK UP WITH HIM AND DATE ME INSTEAD.

bonus bullet 19 secret scene

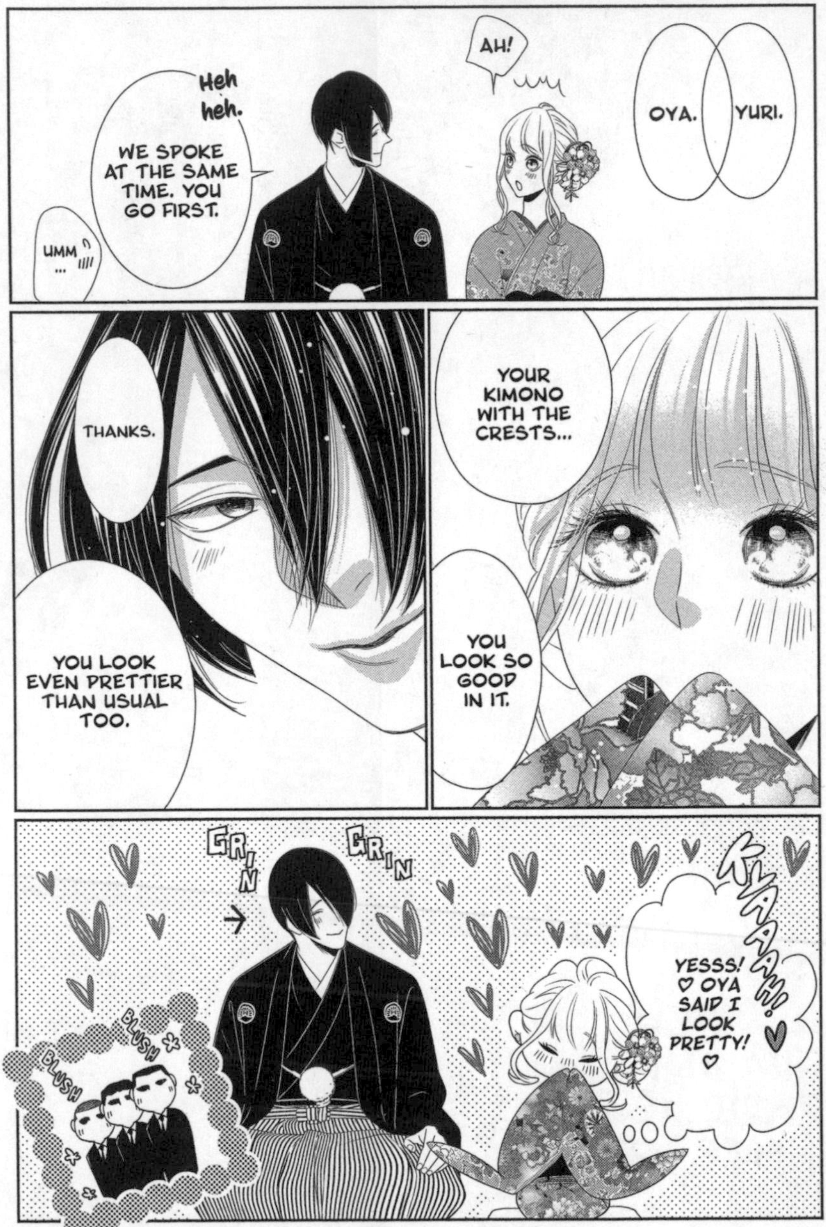
YURI.
OYA.
AH!
Heh heh.
WE SPOKE AT THE SAME TIME. YOU GO FIRST.
UMM...
YOUR KIMONO WITH THE CRESTS...
YOU LOOK SO GOOD IN IT.
THANKS.
YOU LOOK EVEN PRETTIER THAN USUAL TOO.
KYAAAH!
YESSS! ♡ OYA SAID I LOOK PRETTY! ♡
GRIN
GRIN
BLUSH
BLUSH

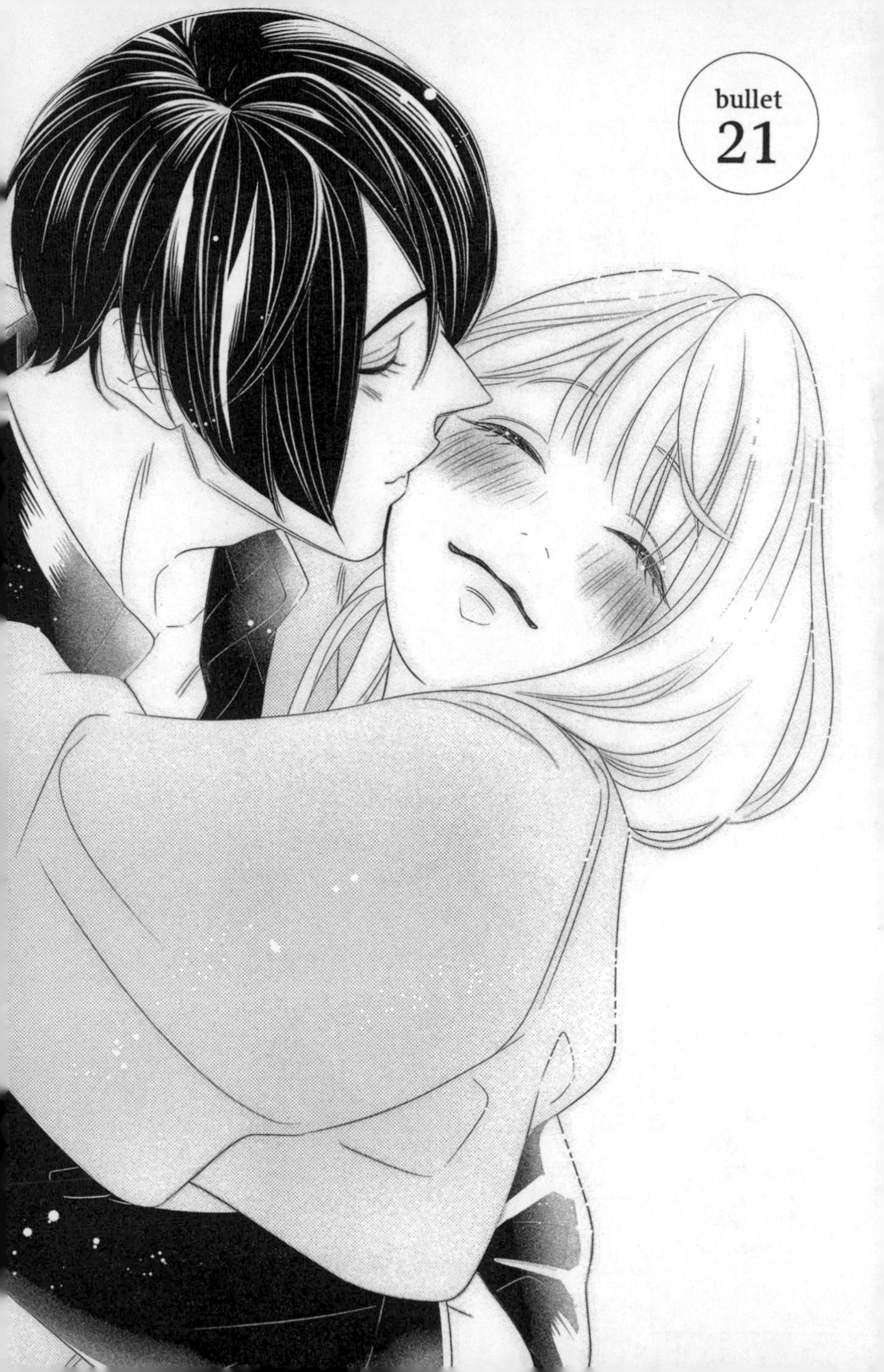
bullet
21

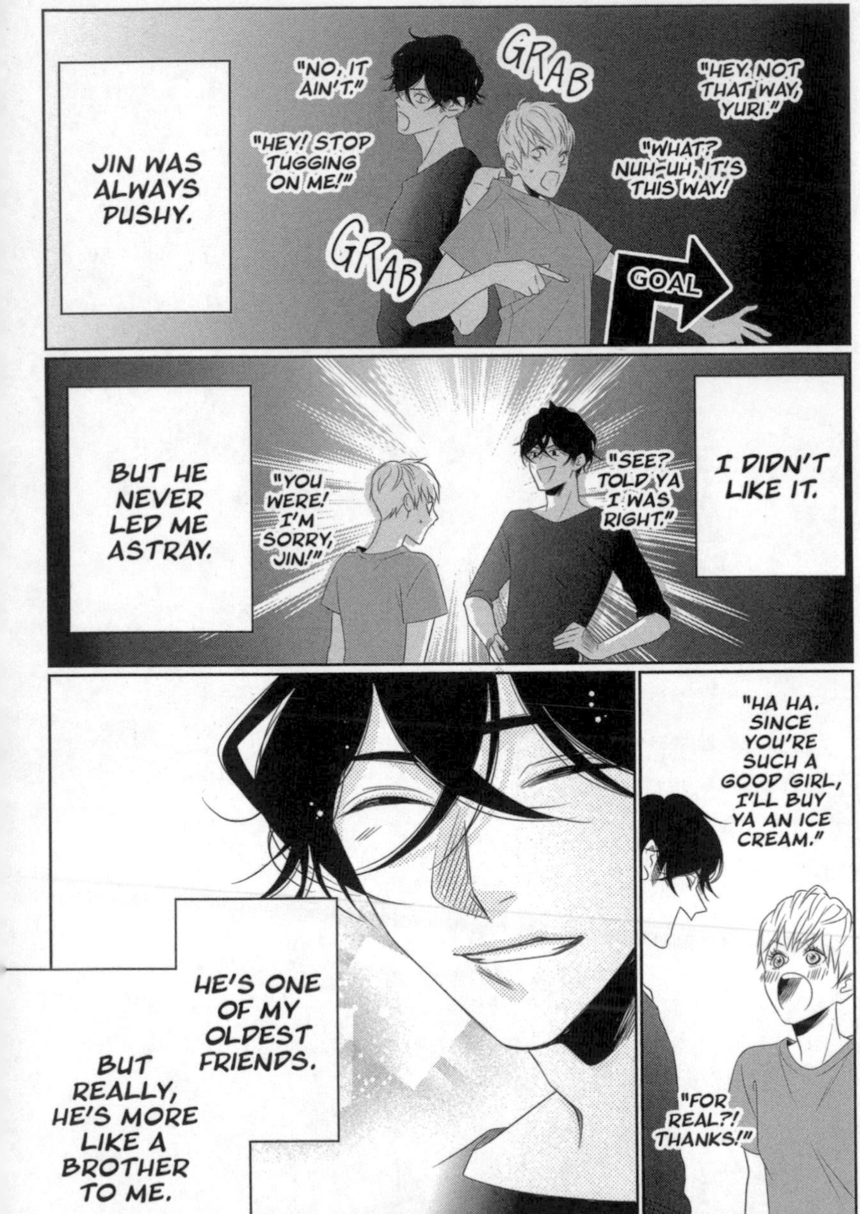
"HEY, NOT THAT WAY, YURI."
GRAB
"NO, IT AIN'T."
"WHAT? NUH-UH, IT'S THIS WAY!"
"HEY! STOP TUGGING ON ME!"
GOAL
GRAB
JIN WAS ALWAYS PUSHY.
I DIDN'T LIKE IT.
"SEE? TOLD YA I WAS RIGHT."
"YOU WERE! I'M SORRY, JIN!"
BUT HE NEVER LED ME ASTRAY.
"HA HA. SINCE YOU'RE SUCH A GOOD GIRL, I'LL BUY YA AN ICE CREAM."
"FOR REAL?! THANKS!"
HE'S ONE OF MY OLDEST FRIENDS.
BUT REALLY, HE'S MORE LIKE A BROTHER TO ME.

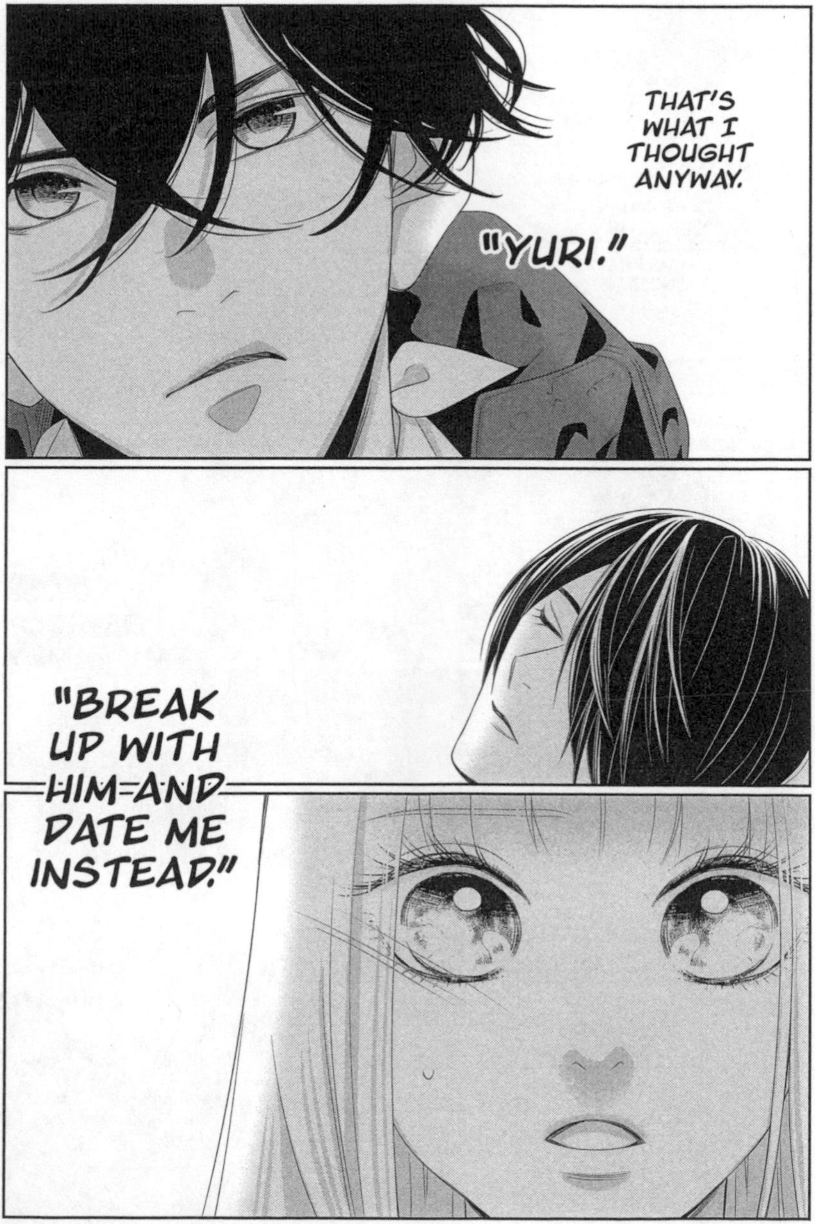
THAT'S WHAT I THOUGHT ANYWAY.
"YURI."
"BREAK UP WITH HIM AND DATE ME INSTEAD."

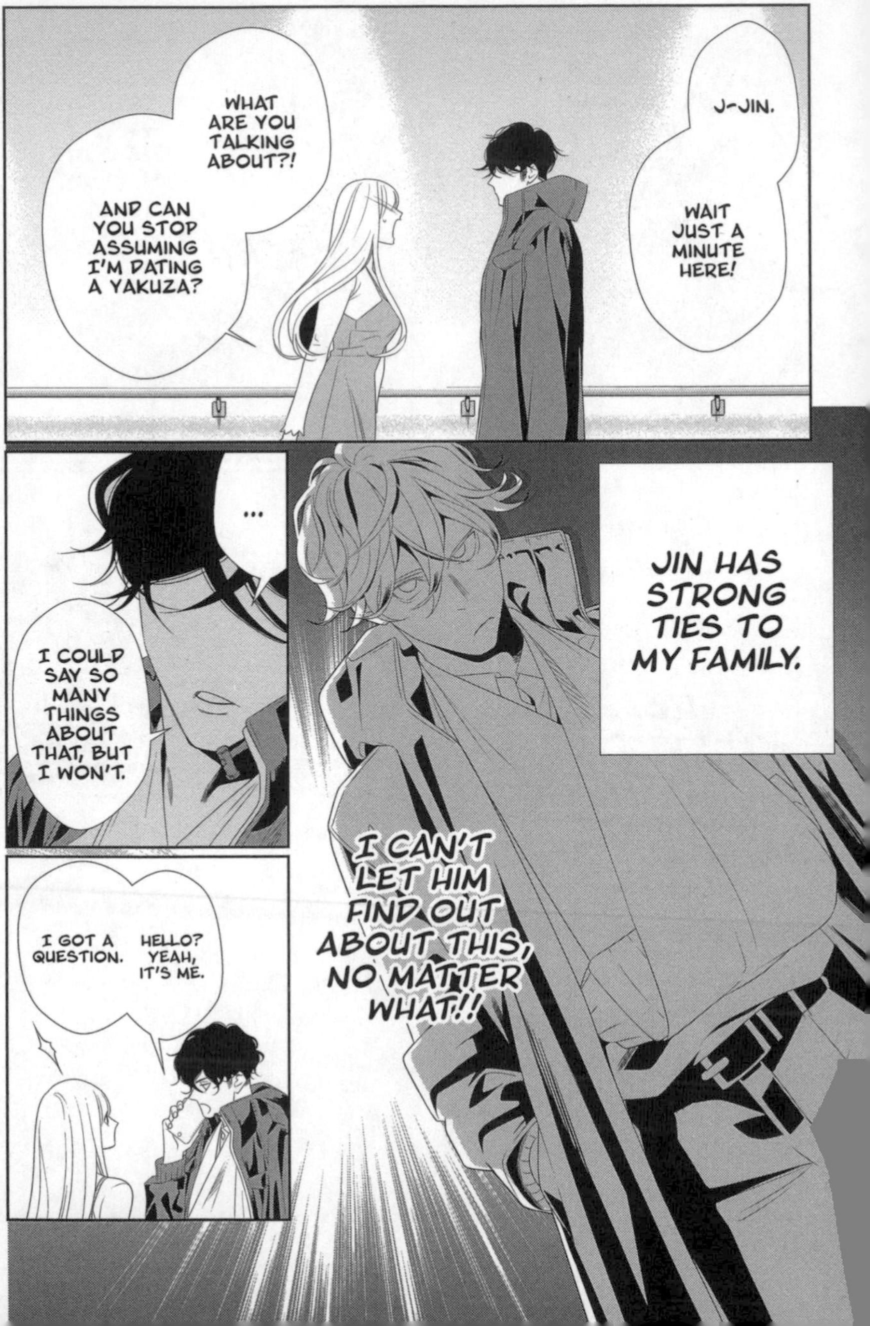
J-JIN.
WAIT JUST A MINUTE HERE!
WHAT ARE YOU TALKING ABOUT?!
AND CAN YOU STOP ASSUMING I'M DATING A YAKUZA?
JIN HAS STRONG TIES TO MY FAMILY.
I CAN'T LET HIM FIND OUT ABOUT THIS, NO MATTER WHAT!!
...
I COULD SAY SO MANY THINGS ABOUT THAT, BUT I WON'T.
HELLO? YEAH, IT'S ME.
I GOT A QUESTION.

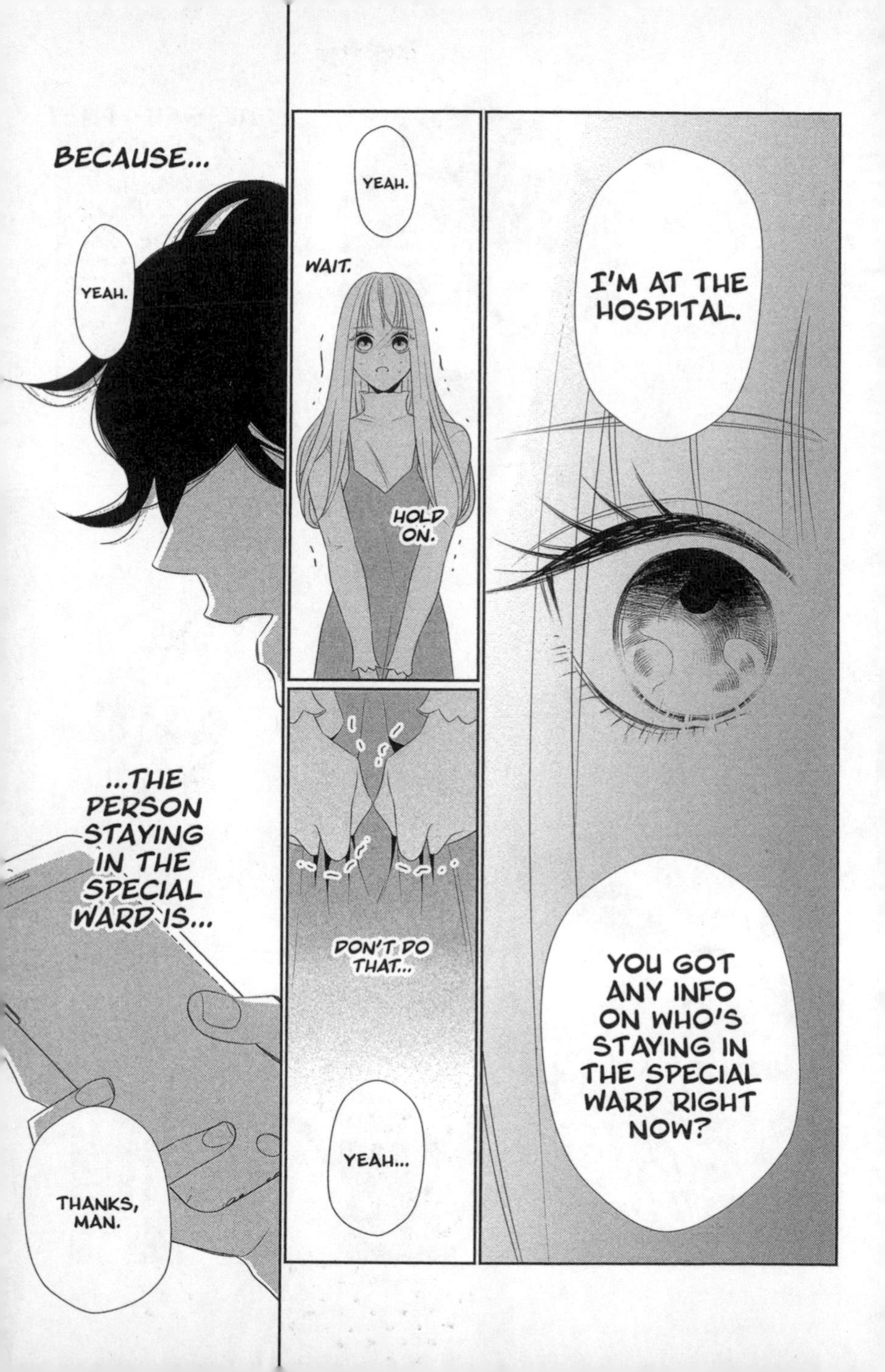
I'M AT THE HOSPITAL.
YOU GOT ANY INFO ON WHO'S STAYING IN THE SPECIAL WARD RIGHT NOW?
YEAH.
WAIT.
HOLD ON.
DON'T DO THAT...
YEAH...
BECAUSE...
YEAH.
...THE PERSON STAYING IN THE SPECIAL WARD IS...
THANKS, MAN.

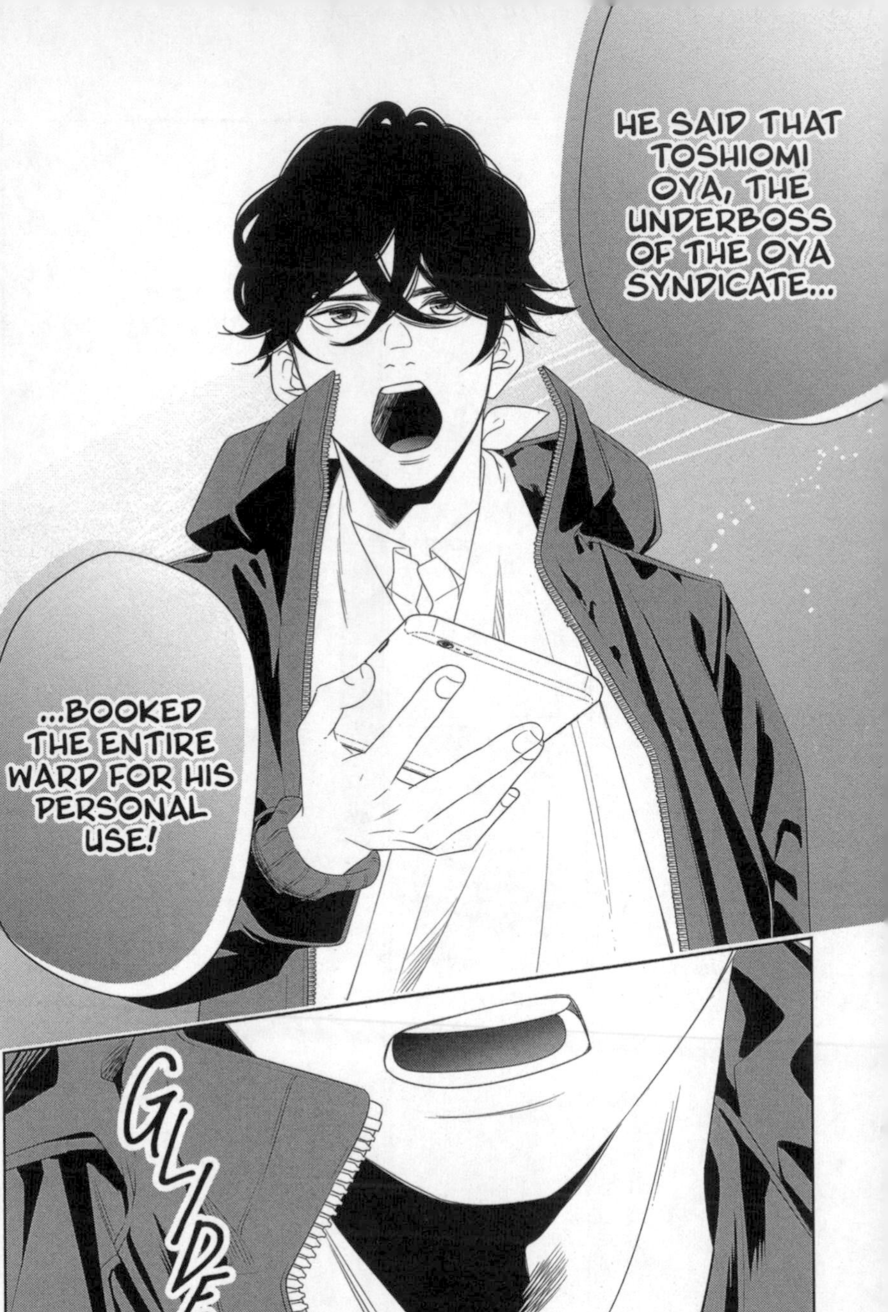
HE SAID THAT TOSHIOMI OYA, THE UNDERBOSS OF THE OYA SYNDICATE...
...BOOKED THE ENTIRE WARD FOR HIS PERSONAL USE!
GLIDE

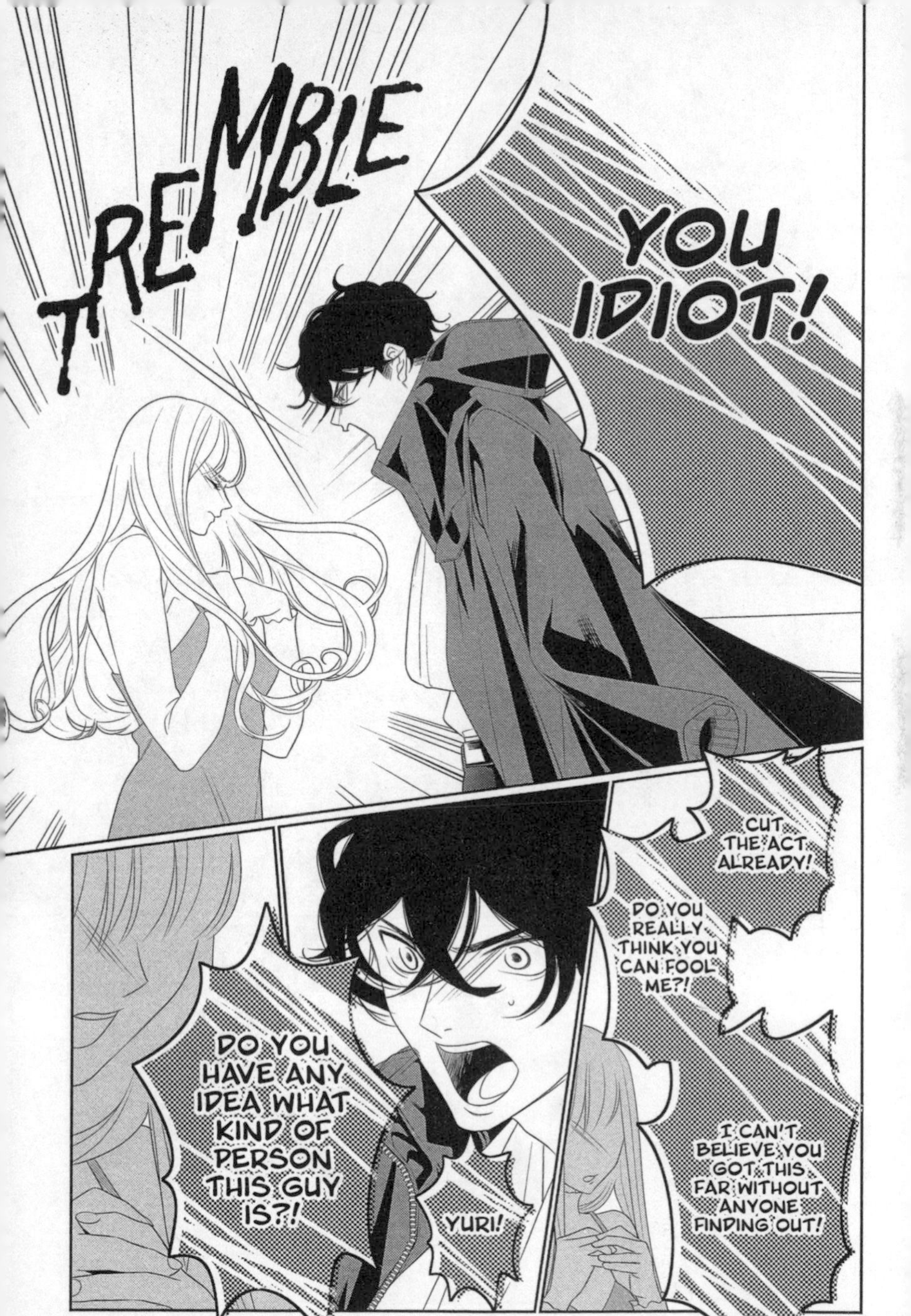
YOU IDIOT!
TREMBLE
CUT THE ACT ALREADY!
DO YOU REALLY THINK YOU CAN FOOL ME?!
I CAN'T BELIEVE YOU GOT THIS FAR WITHOUT ANYONE FINDING OUT!
YURI!
DO YOU HAVE ANY IDEA WHAT KIND OF PERSON THIS GUY IS?!

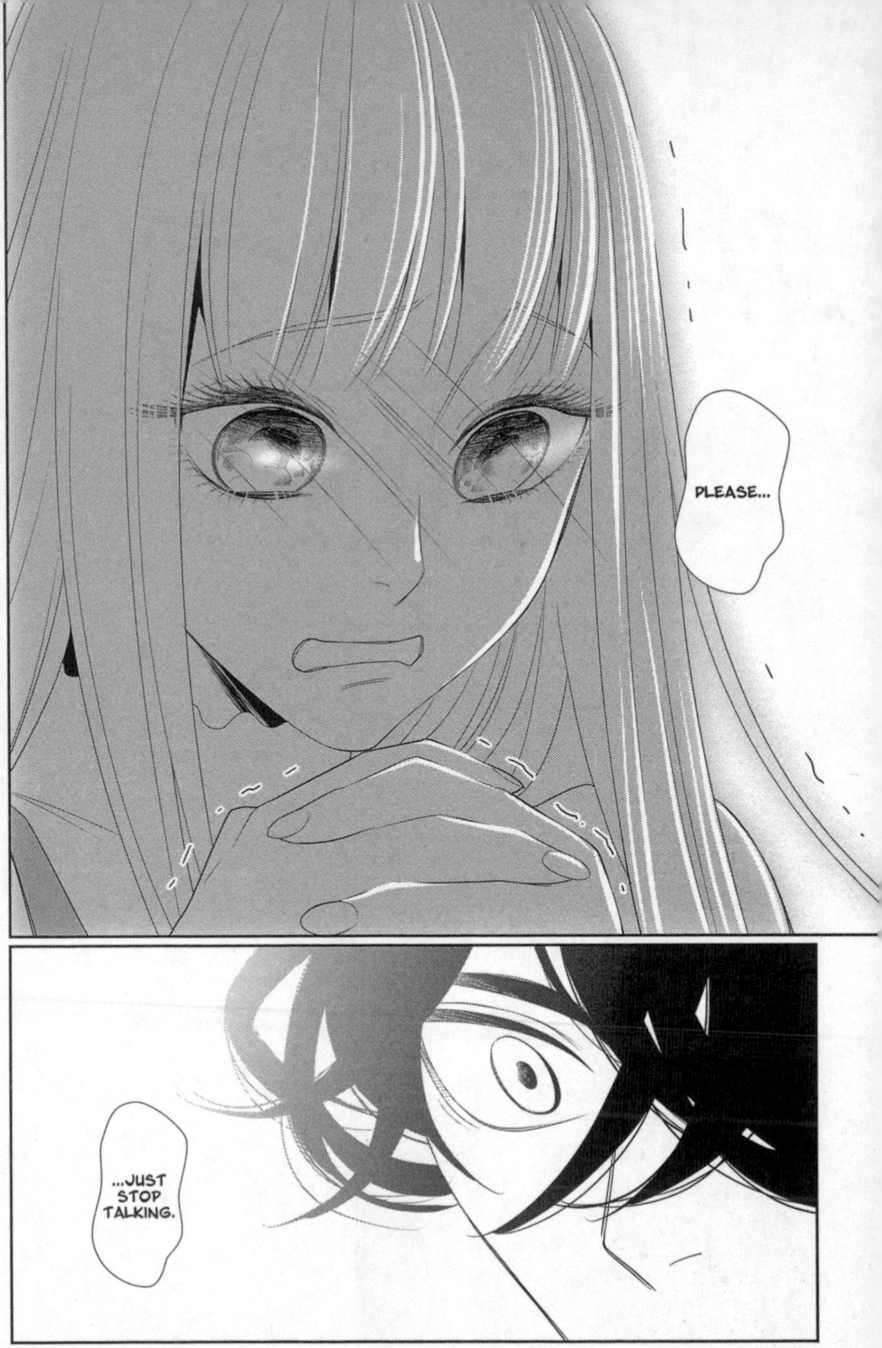
PLEASE...
...JUST STOP TALKING.

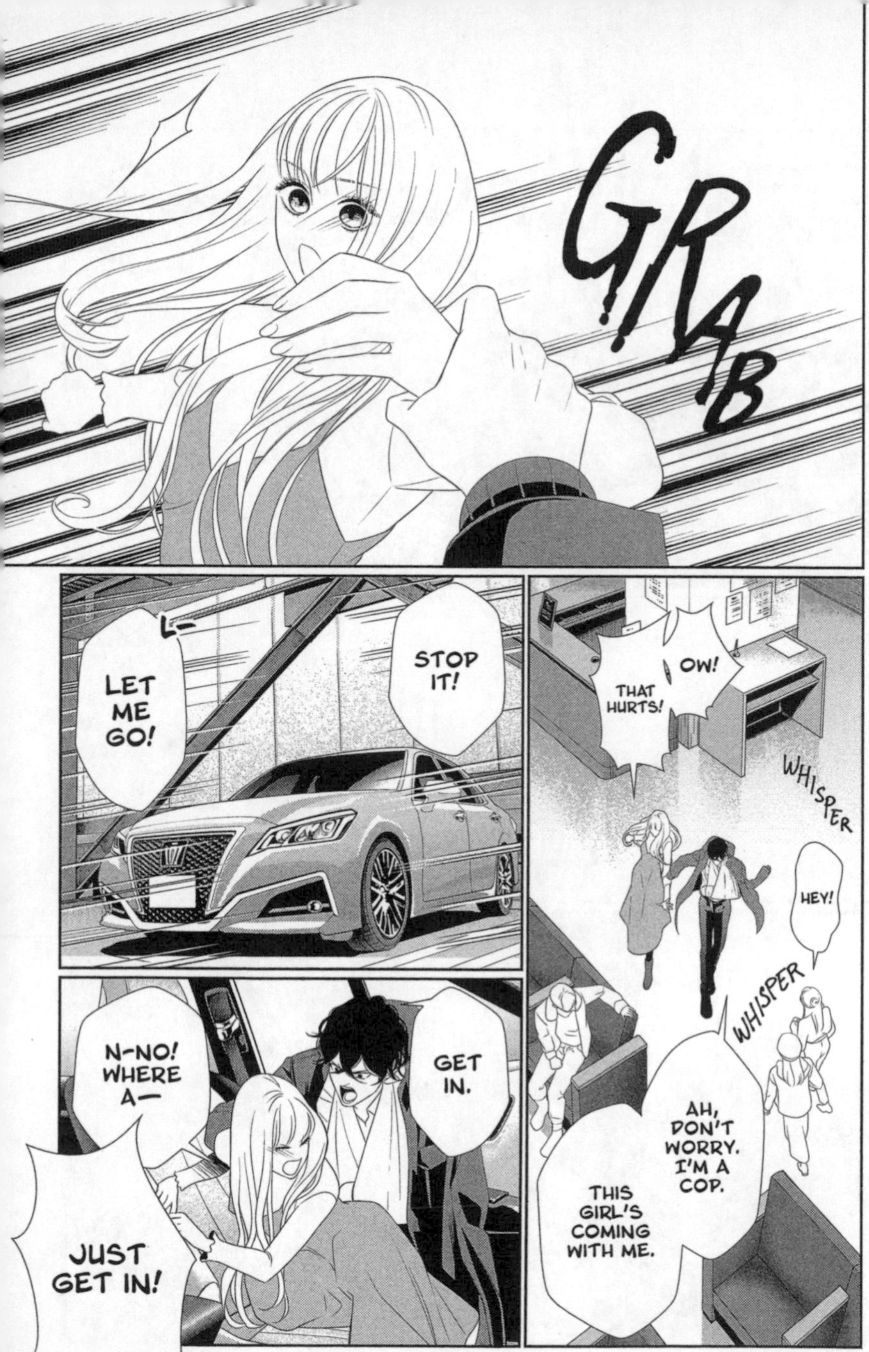
GRAB
OW!
THAT HURTS!
WHISPER
HEY!
WHISPER
AH, DON'T WORRY. I'M A COP.
THIS GIRL'S COMING WITH ME.
STOP IT!
L—
LET ME GO!
GET IN.
N-NO! WHERE A—
JUST GET IN!

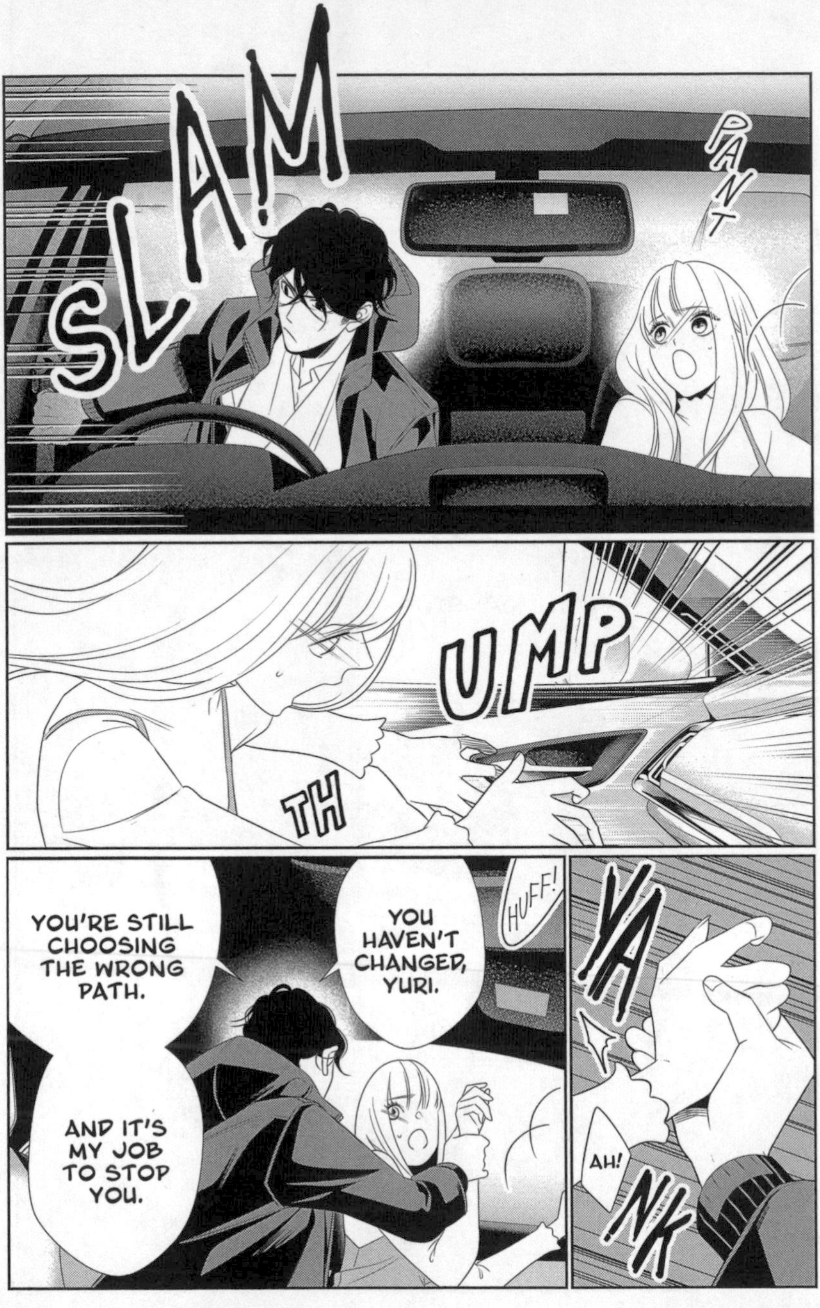

PANT
SLAM!
THUMP
YANK
AH!
HUFF!
YOU HAVEN'T CHANGED, YURI.
YOU'RE STILL CHOOSING THE WRONG PATH.
AND IT'S MY JOB TO STOP YOU.

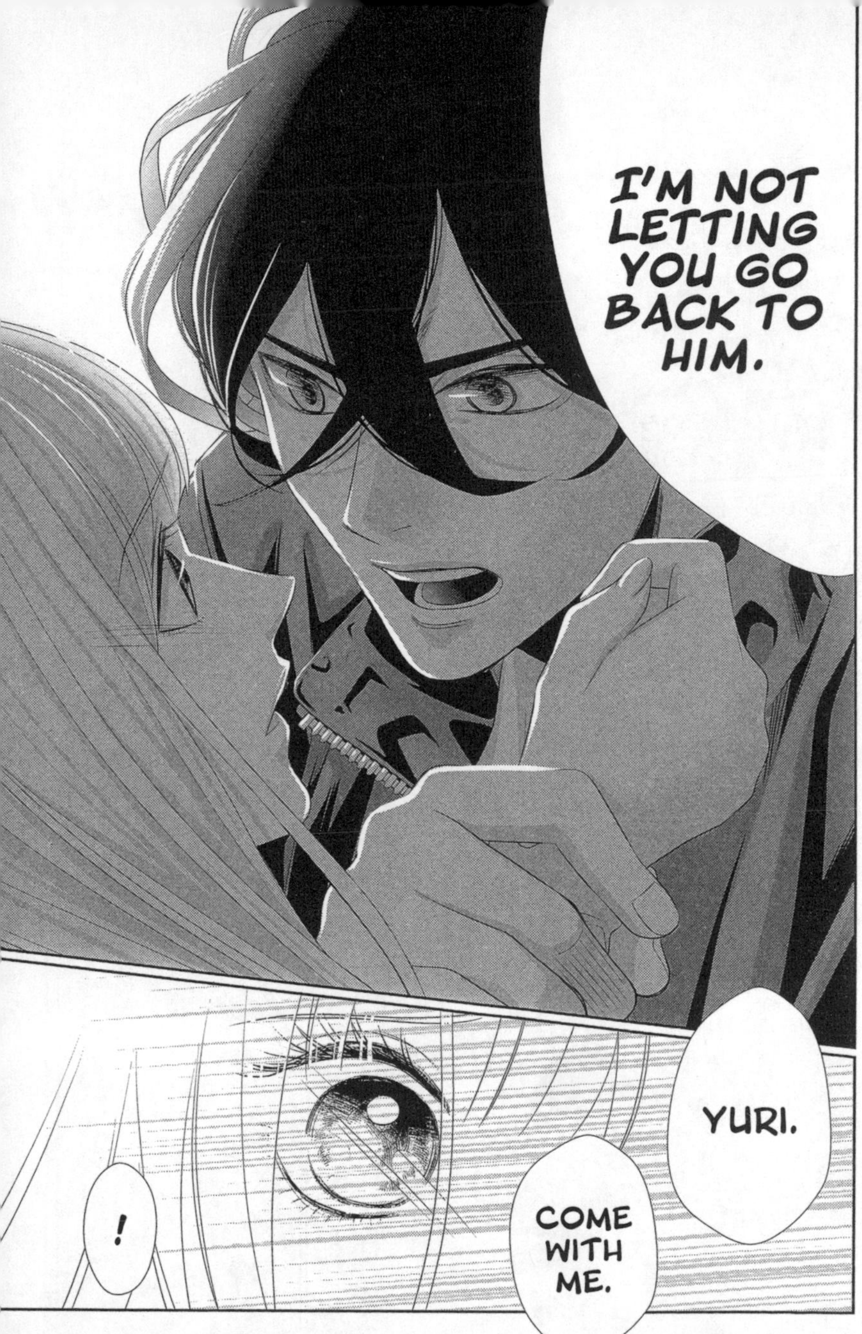
I'M NOT LETTING YOU GO BACK TO HIM.
YURI.
COME WITH ME.
!

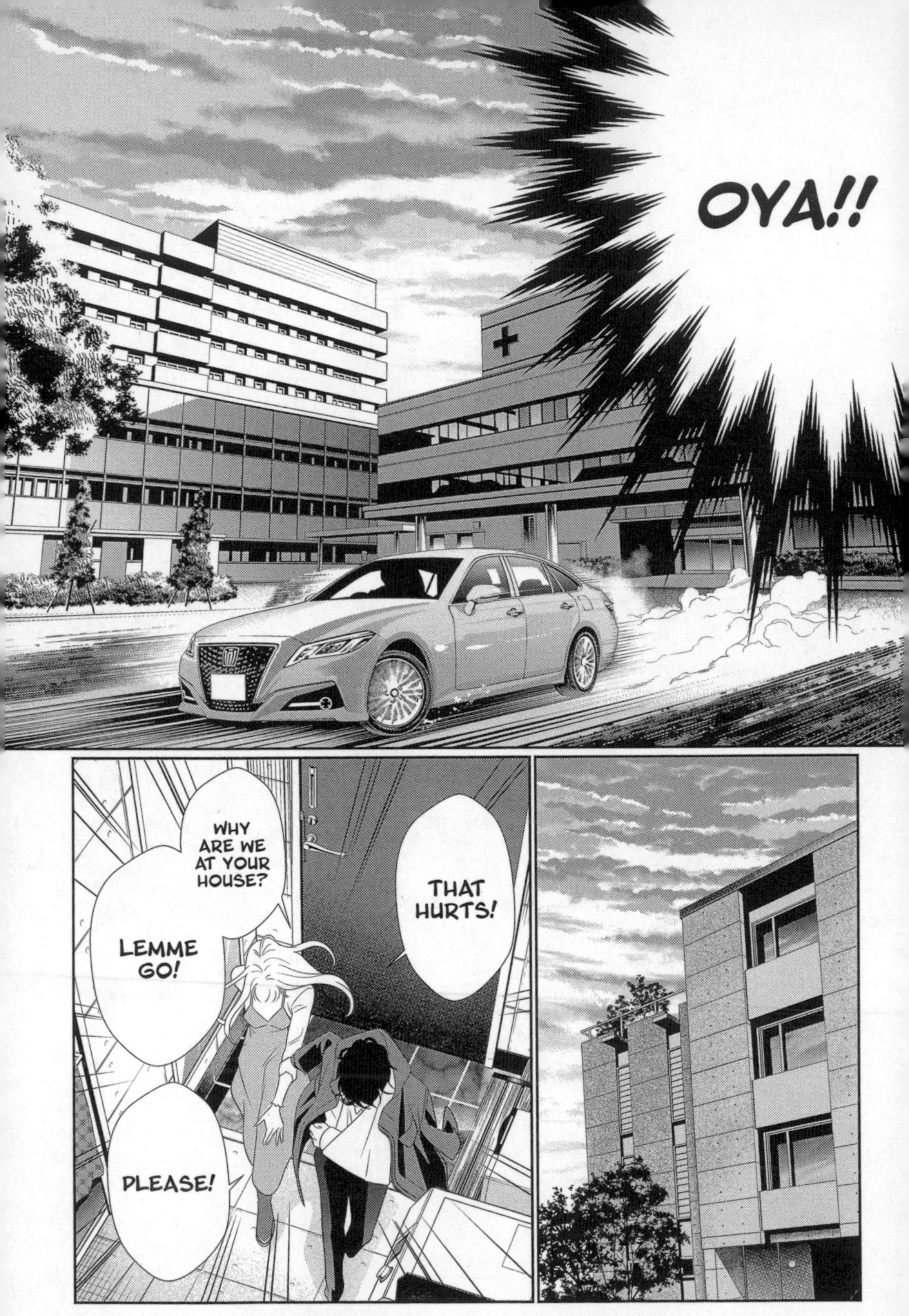
OYA!!
THAT HURTS!
WHY ARE WE AT YOUR HOUSE?
LEMME GO!
PLEASE!

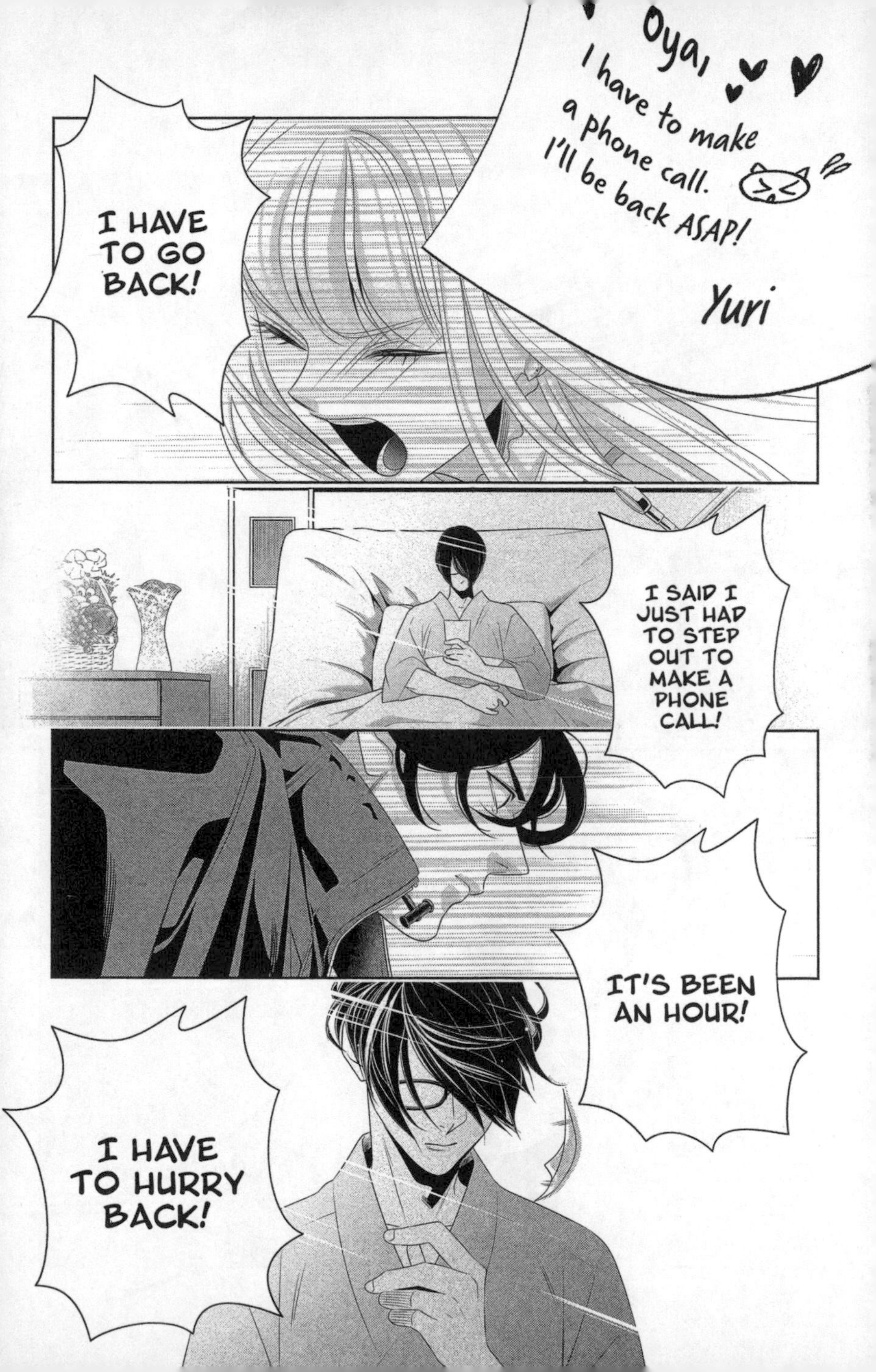
Oya,
I have to make a phone call. I'll be back ASAP!
Yuri
I HAVE TO GO BACK!
I SAID I JUST HAD TO STEP OUT TO MAKE A PHONE CALL!
IT'S BEEN AN HOUR!
I HAVE TO HURRY BACK!

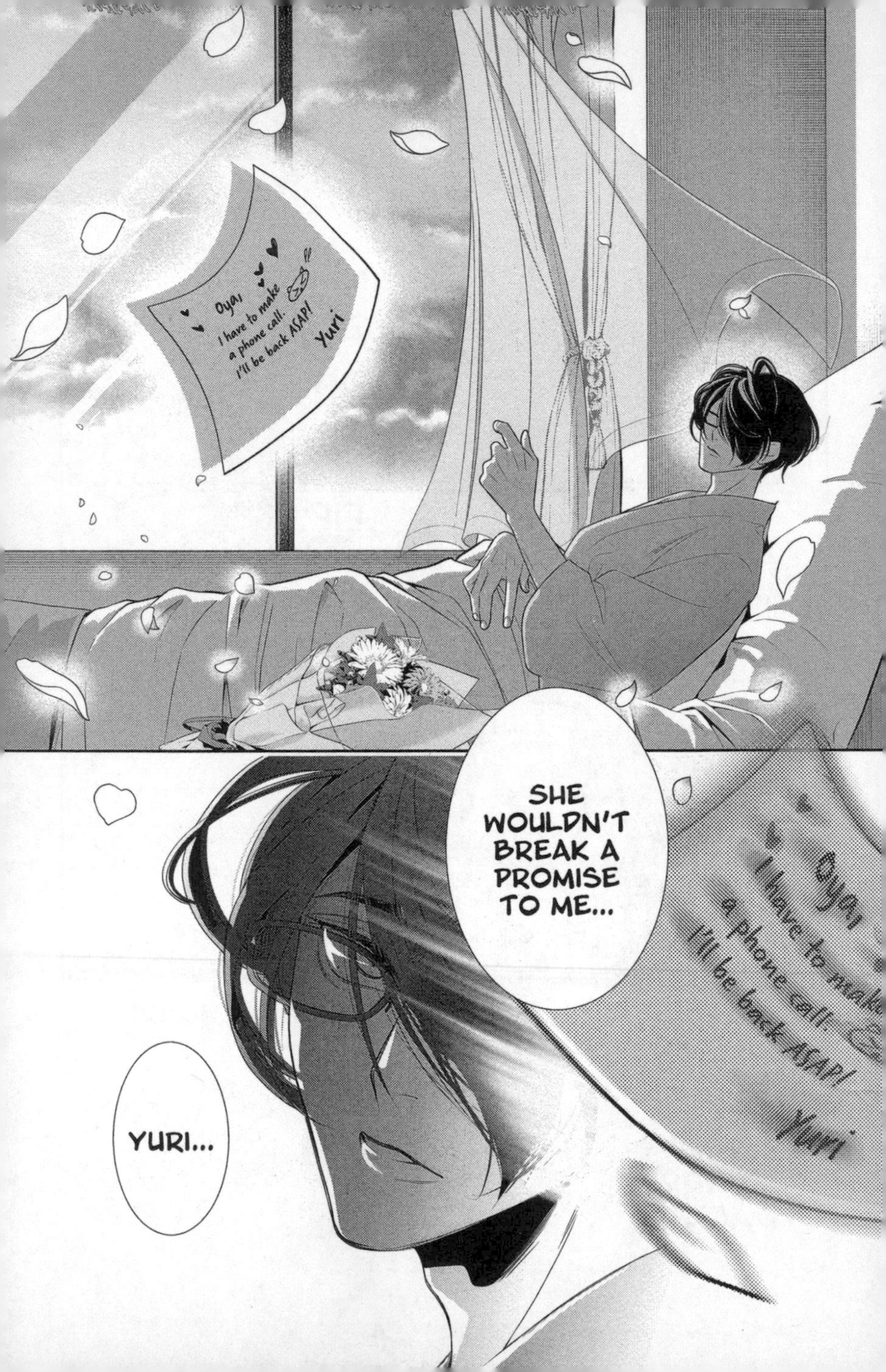
Oya,
I have to make a phone call. I'll be back ASAP!
Yuri
SHE WOULDN'T BREAK A PROMISE TO ME...
YURI...

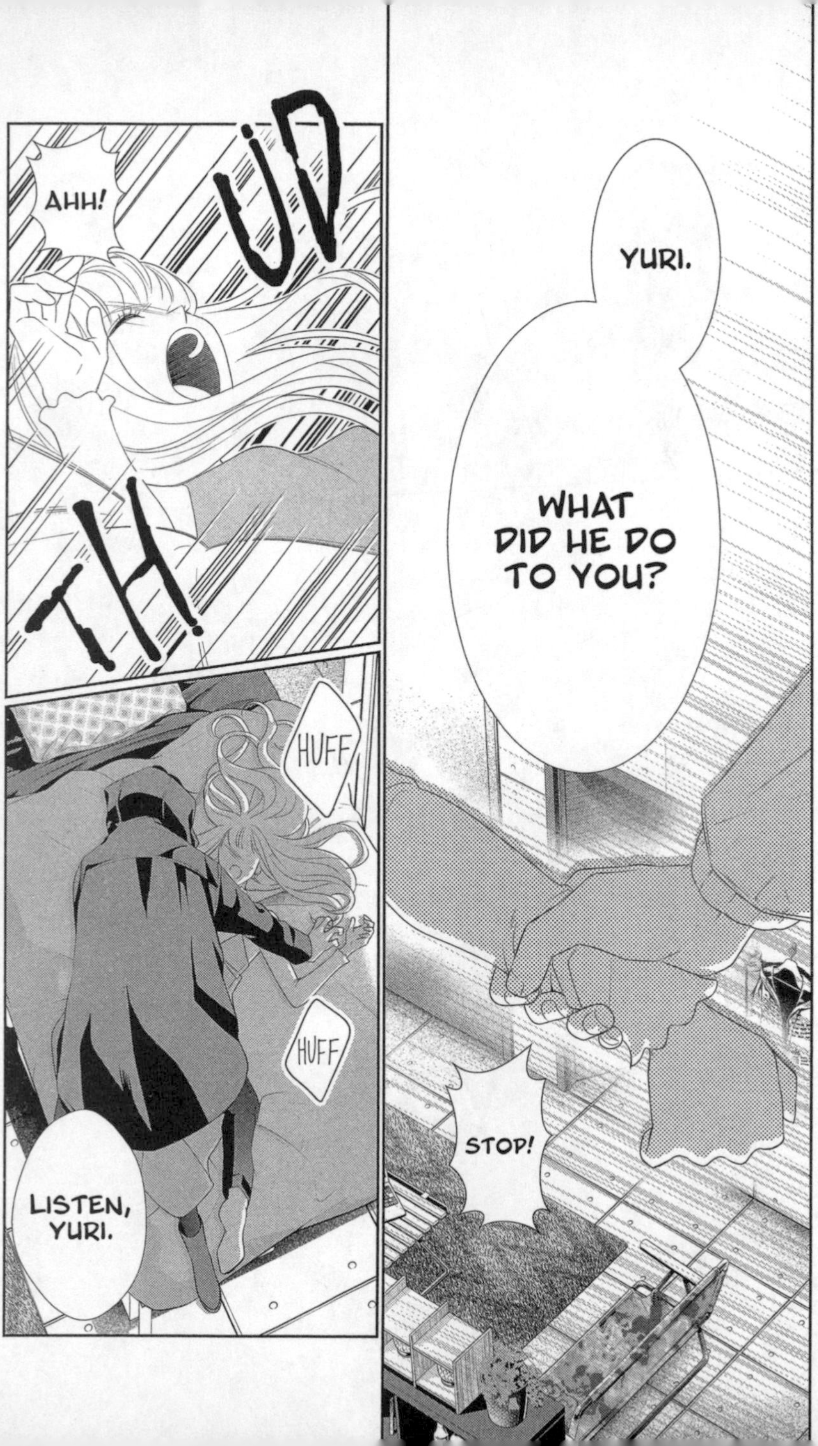
YURI.
WHAT DID HE DO TO YOU?
STOP!
AHH!
THUD
HUFF
HUFF
LISTEN, YURI.

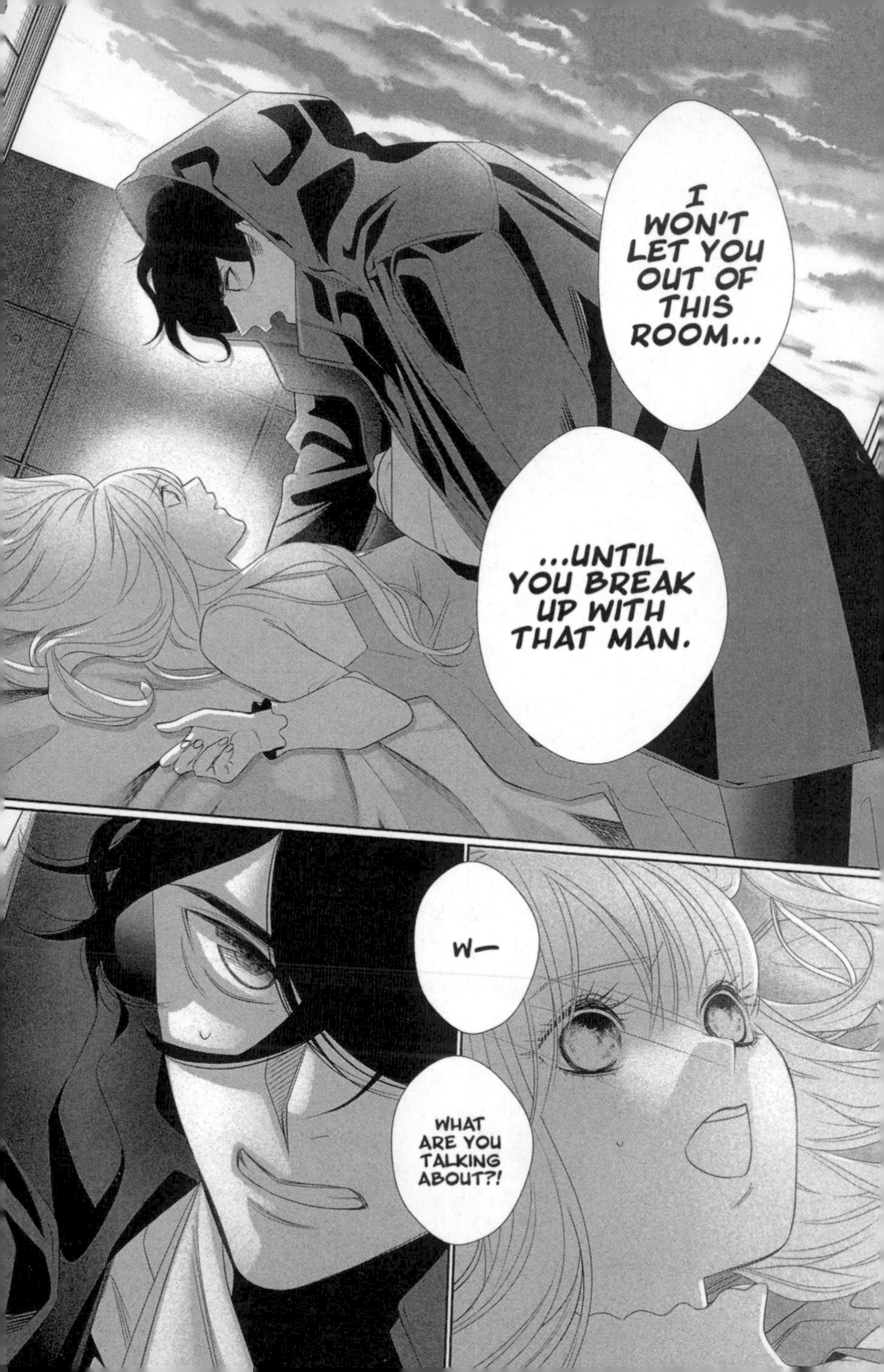
I WON'T LET YOU OUT OF THIS ROOM...
...UNTIL YOU BREAK UP WITH THAT MAN.
W—
WHAT ARE YOU TALKING ABOUT?!

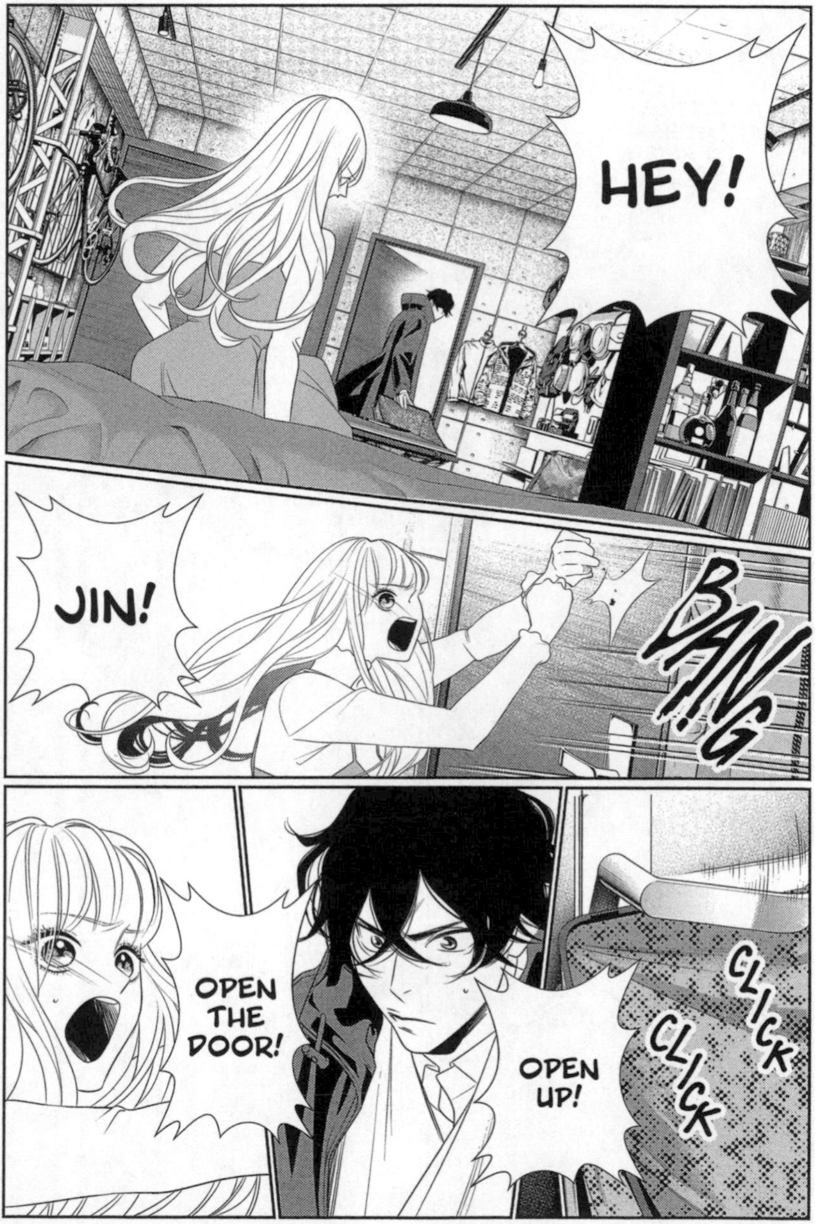
HEY!
BANG
JIN!
CLICK CLICK
OPEN UP!
OPEN THE DOOR!

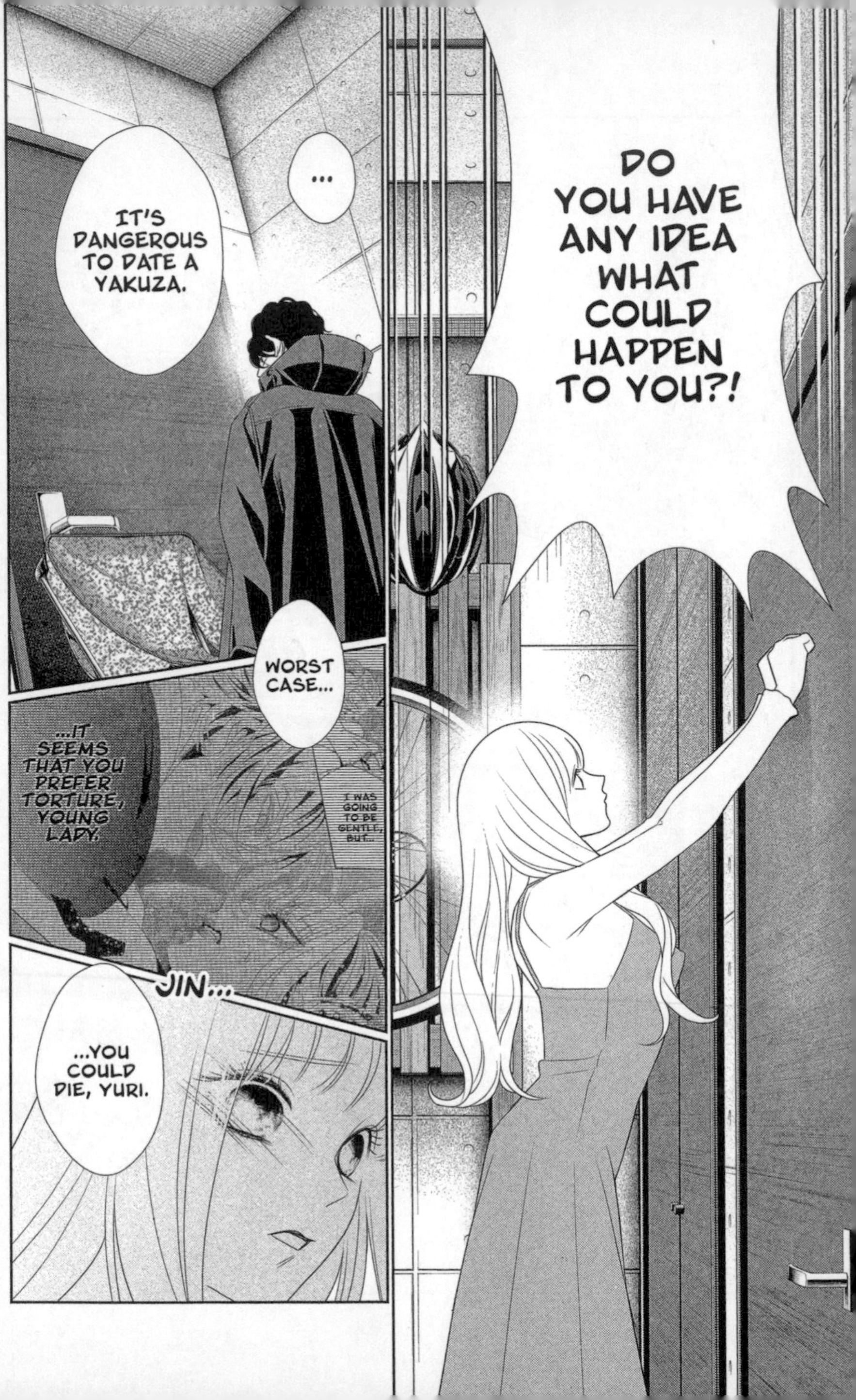
DO YOU HAVE ANY IDEA WHAT COULD HAPPEN TO YOU?!
...
IT'S DANGEROUS TO DATE A YAKUZA.
WORST CASE...
I WAS GOING TO BE GENTLE, BUT...
...IT SEEMS THAT YOU PREFER TORTURE, YOUNG LADY.
JIN...
...YOU COULD DIE, YURI.

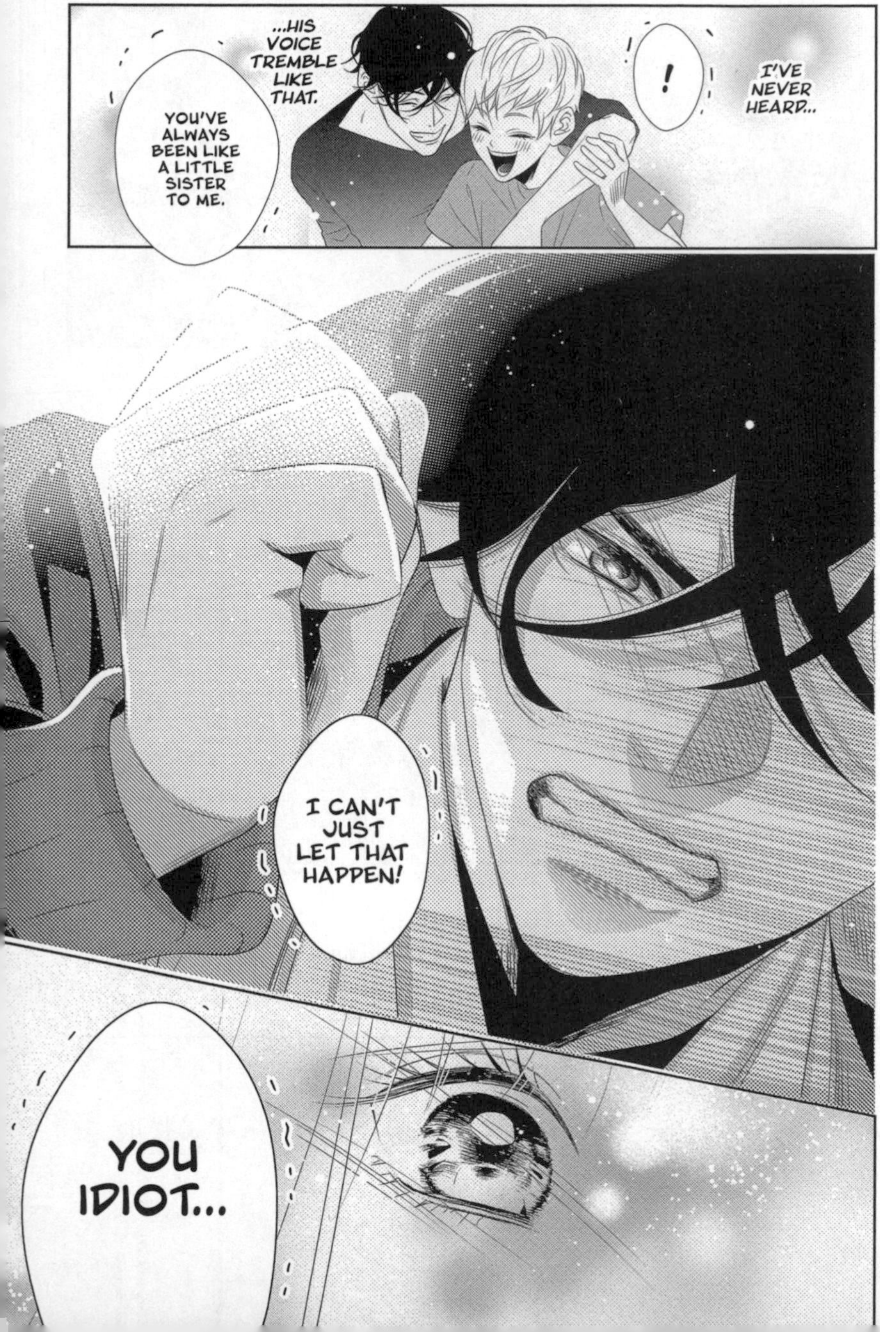
I'VE NEVER HEARD...
!
...HIS VOICE TREMBLE LIKE THAT.
YOU'VE ALWAYS BEEN LIKE A LITTLE SISTER TO ME.
I CAN'T JUST LET THAT HAPPEN!
YOU IDIOT...

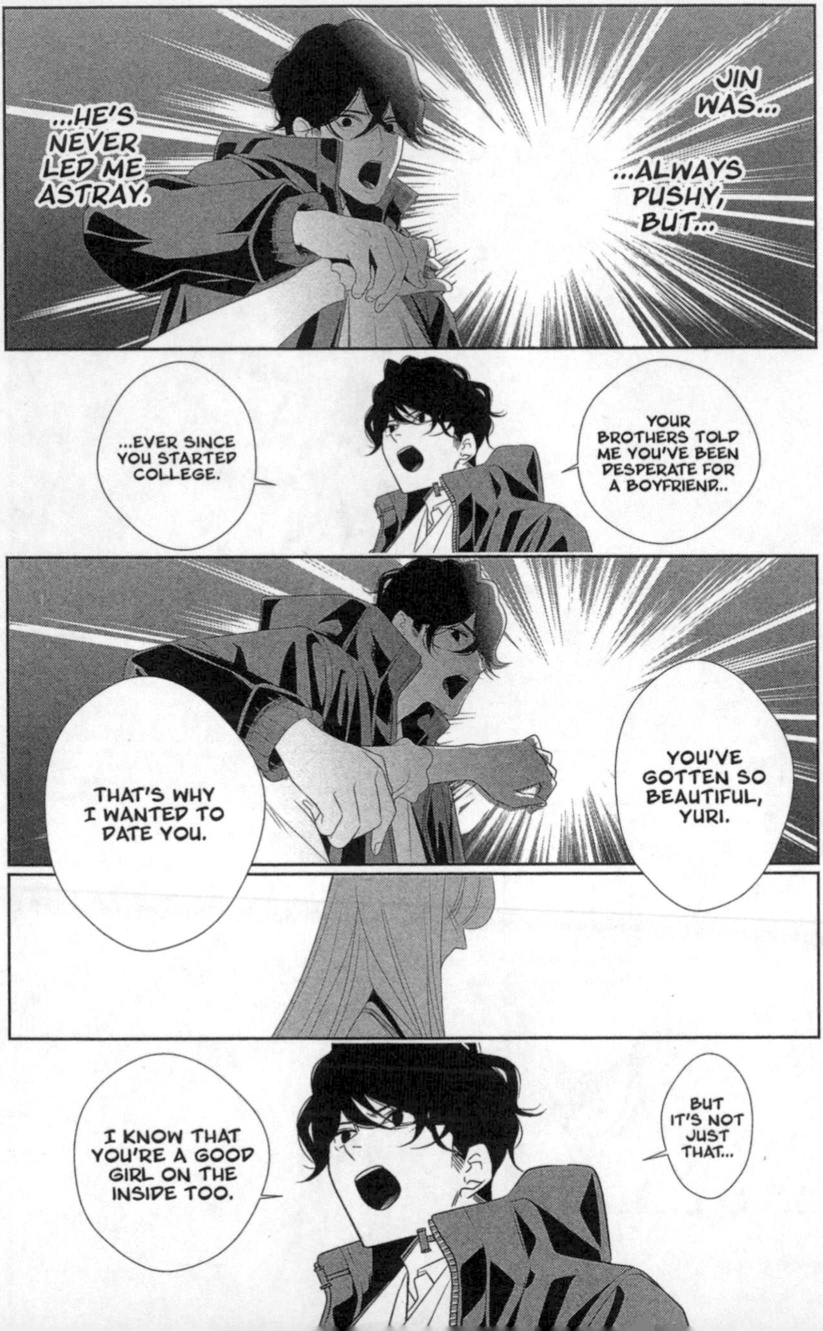
JIN WAS...
...ALWAYS PUSHY, BUT...
...HE'S NEVER LED ME ASTRAY.
YOUR BROTHERS TOLD ME YOU'VE BEEN DESPERATE FOR A BOYFRIEND...
...EVER SINCE YOU STARTED COLLEGE.
YOU'VE GOTTEN SO BEAUTIFUL, YURI.
THAT'S WHY I WANTED TO DATE YOU.
BUT IT'S NOT JUST THAT...
I KNOW THAT YOU'RE A GOOD GIRL ON THE INSIDE TOO.

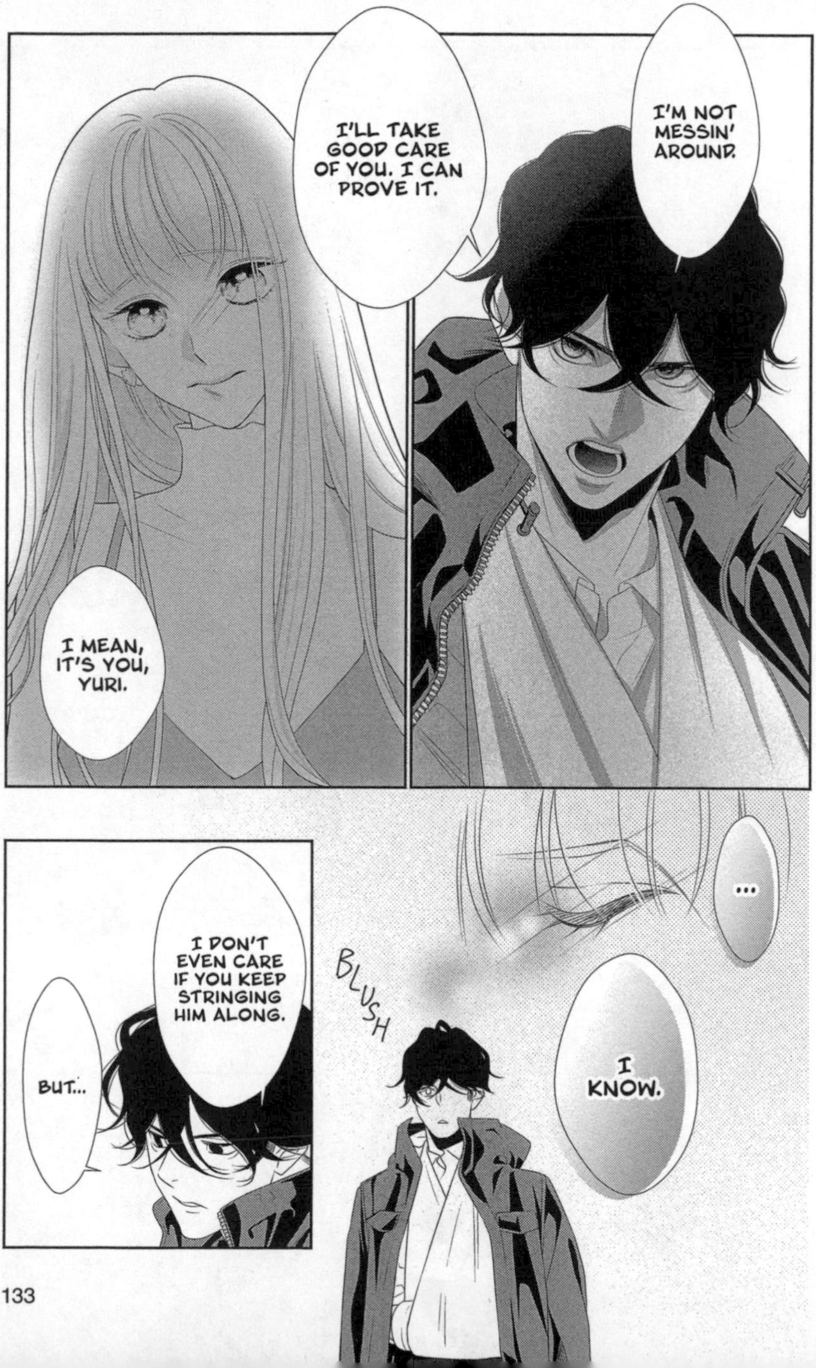
I'M NOT MESSIN' AROUND.
I'LL TAKE GOOD CARE OF YOU. I CAN PROVE IT.
I MEAN, IT'S YOU, YURI.
...
BLUSH
I KNOW.
I DON'T EVEN CARE IF YOU KEEP STRINGING HIM ALONG.
BUT...

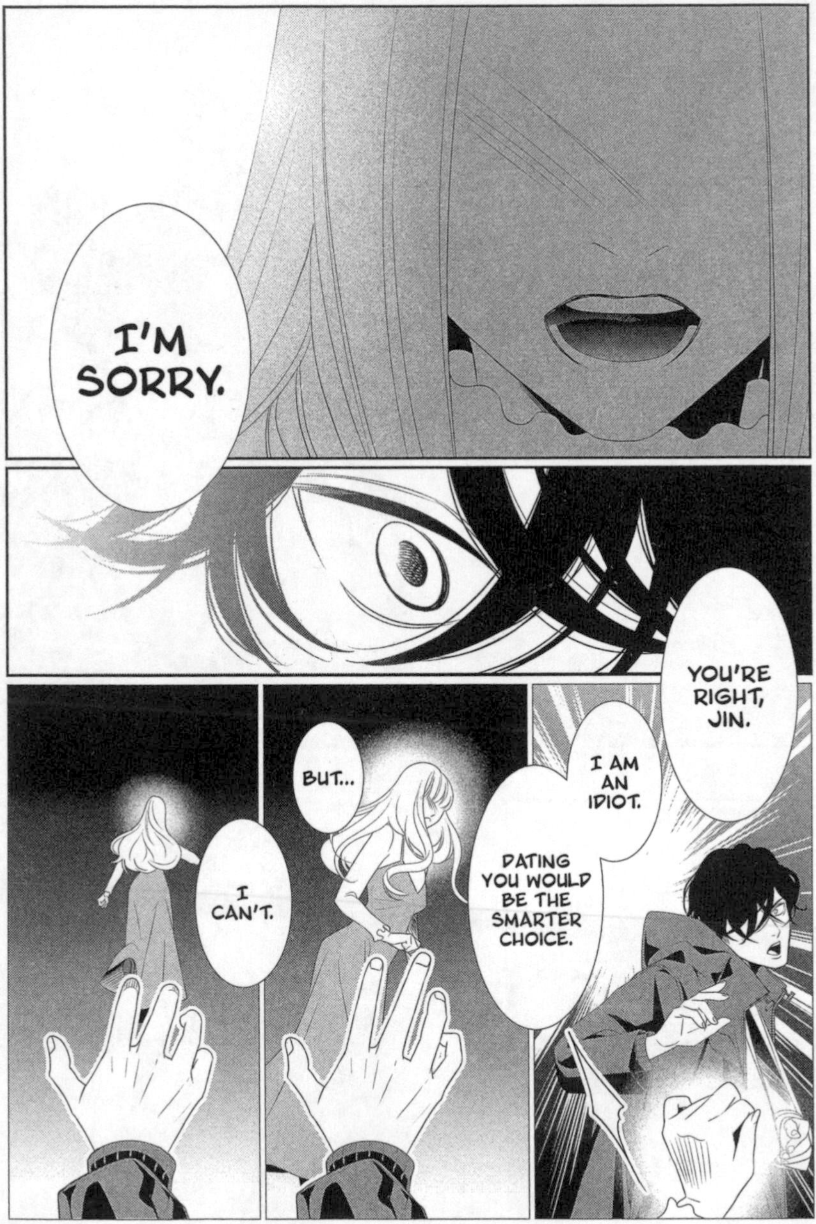
I'M SORRY.
YOU'RE RIGHT, JIN.
I AM AN IDIOT.
DATING YOU WOULD BE THE SMARTER CHOICE.
BUT...
I CAN'T.

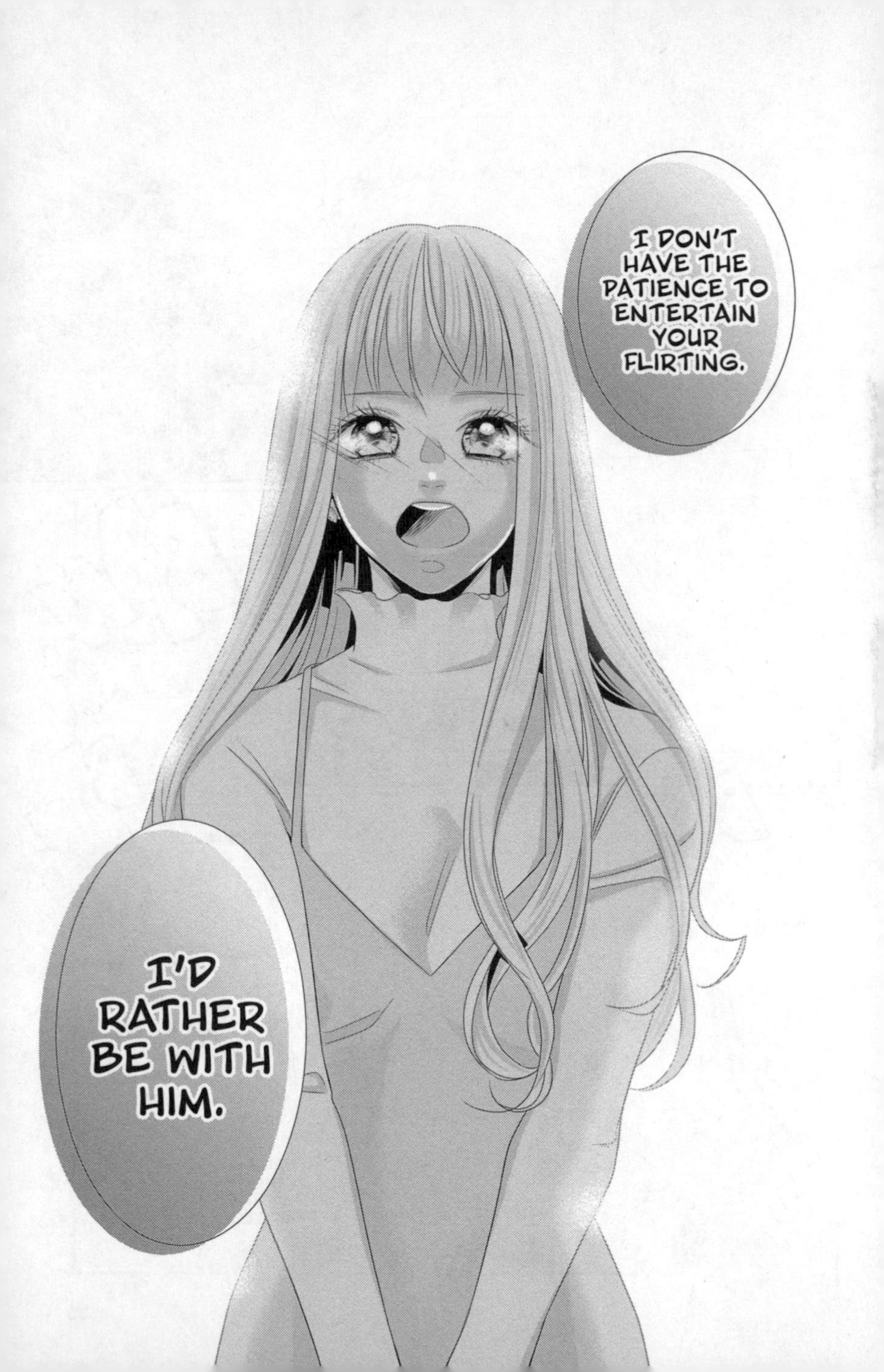
I DON'T HAVE THE PATIENCE TO ENTERTAIN YOUR FLIRTING.
I'D RATHER BE WITH HIM.

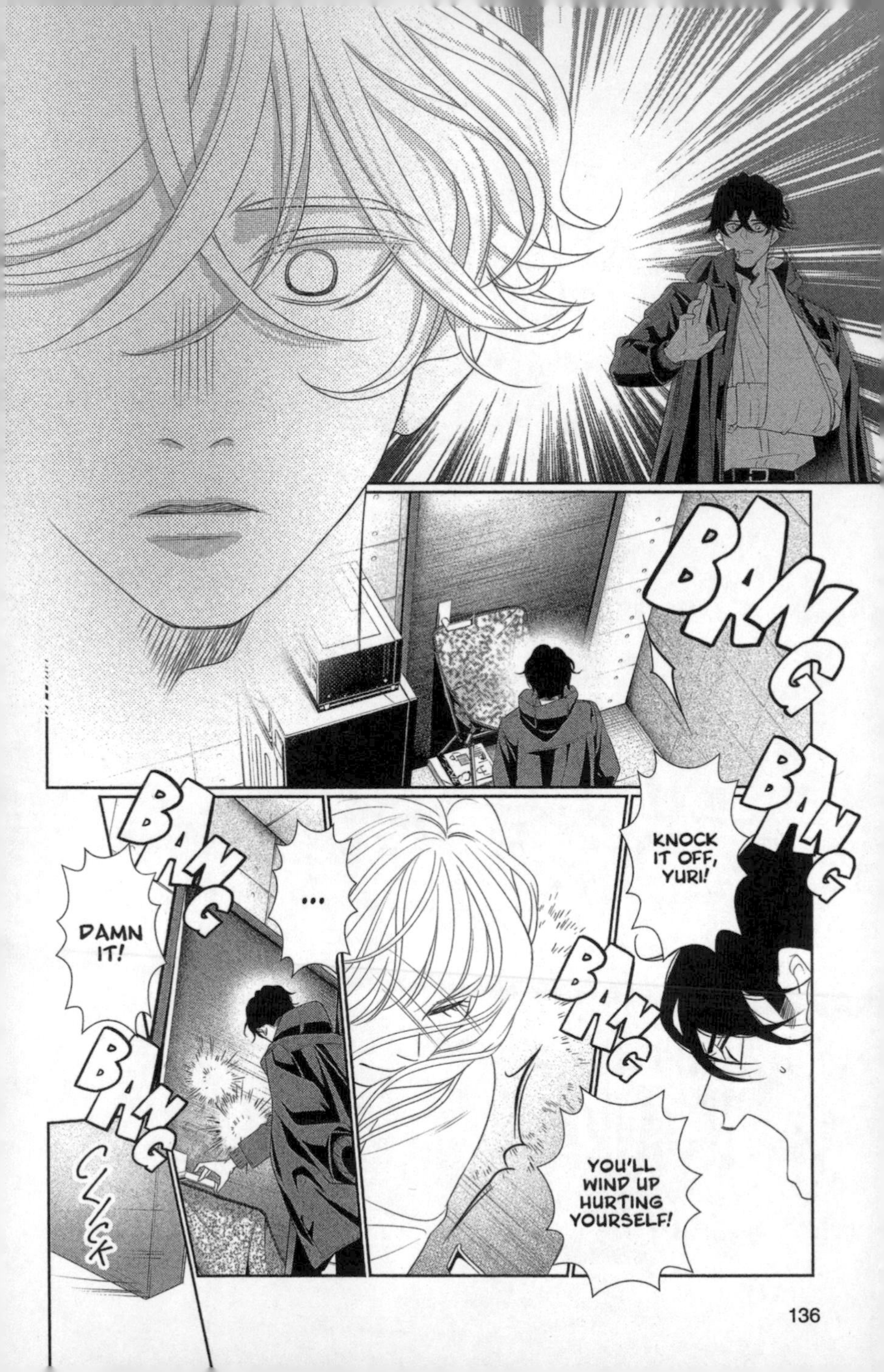
BANG
BANG
KNOCK IT OFF, YURI!
BANG
YOU'LL WIND UP HURTING YOURSELF!
...
BANG
DAMN IT!
BANG
CLICK

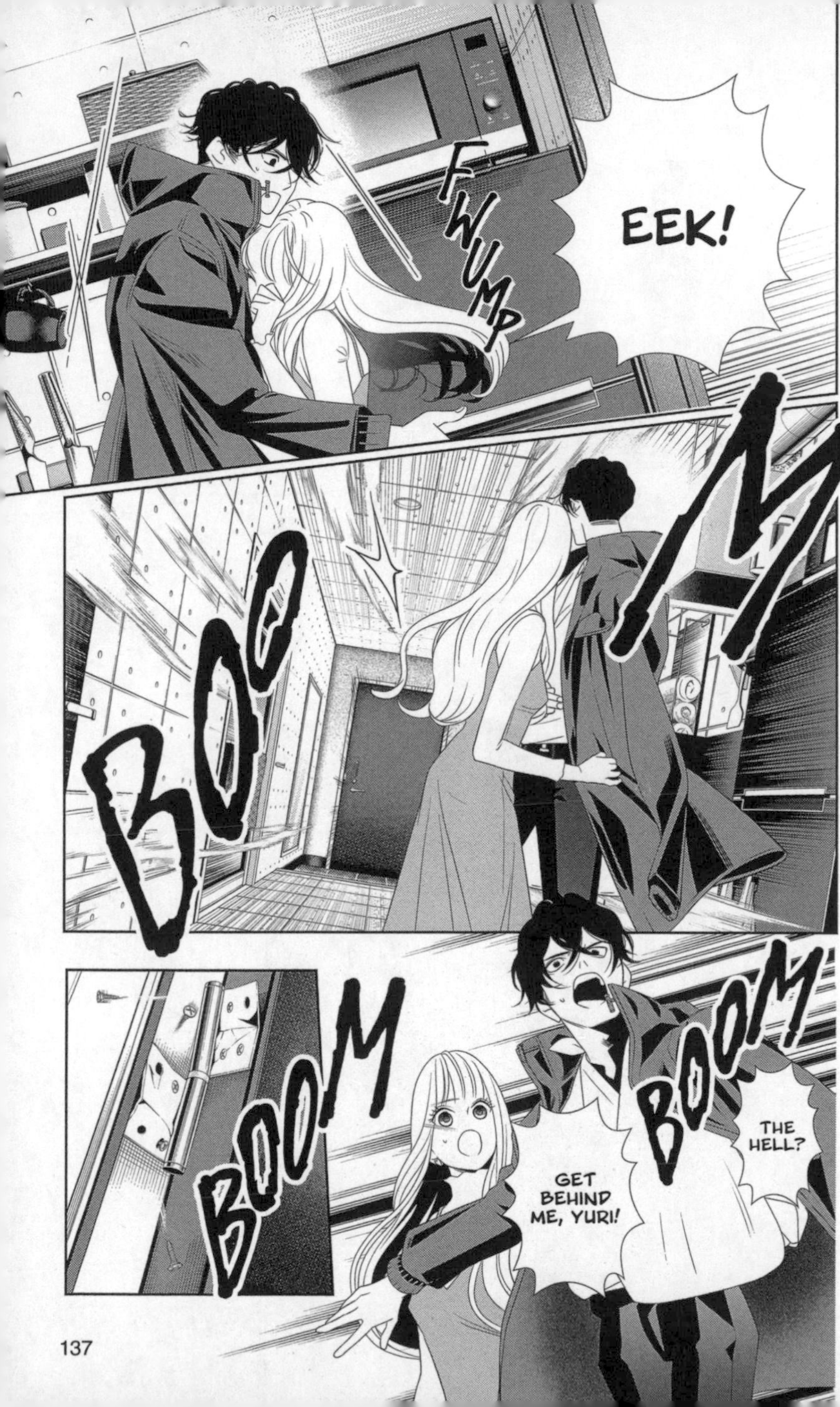
EEK!
FWUMP
BOOM
BOOM
THE HELL?
GET BEHIND ME, YURI!
BOOM

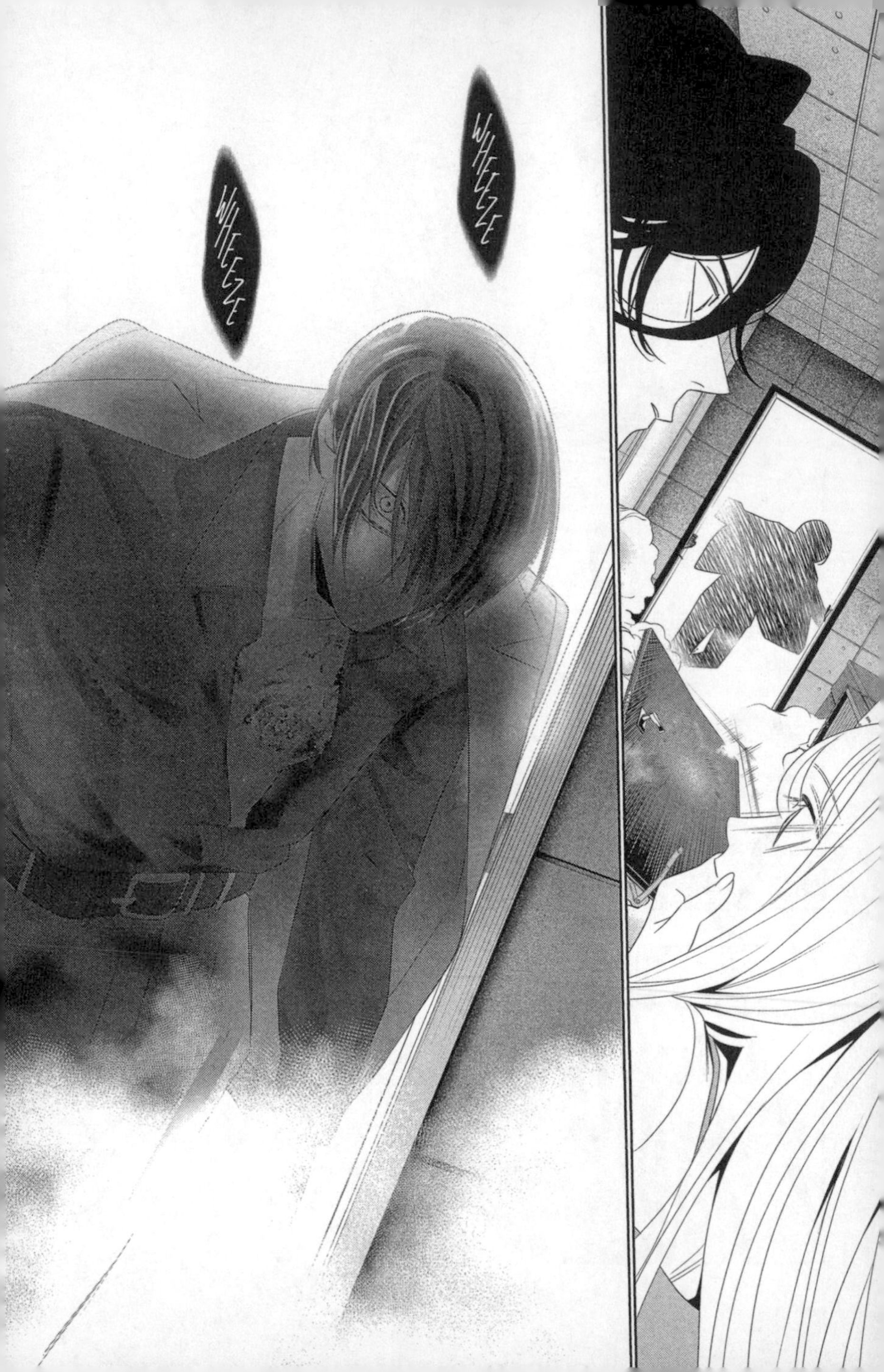
WHEEZE
WHEEZE

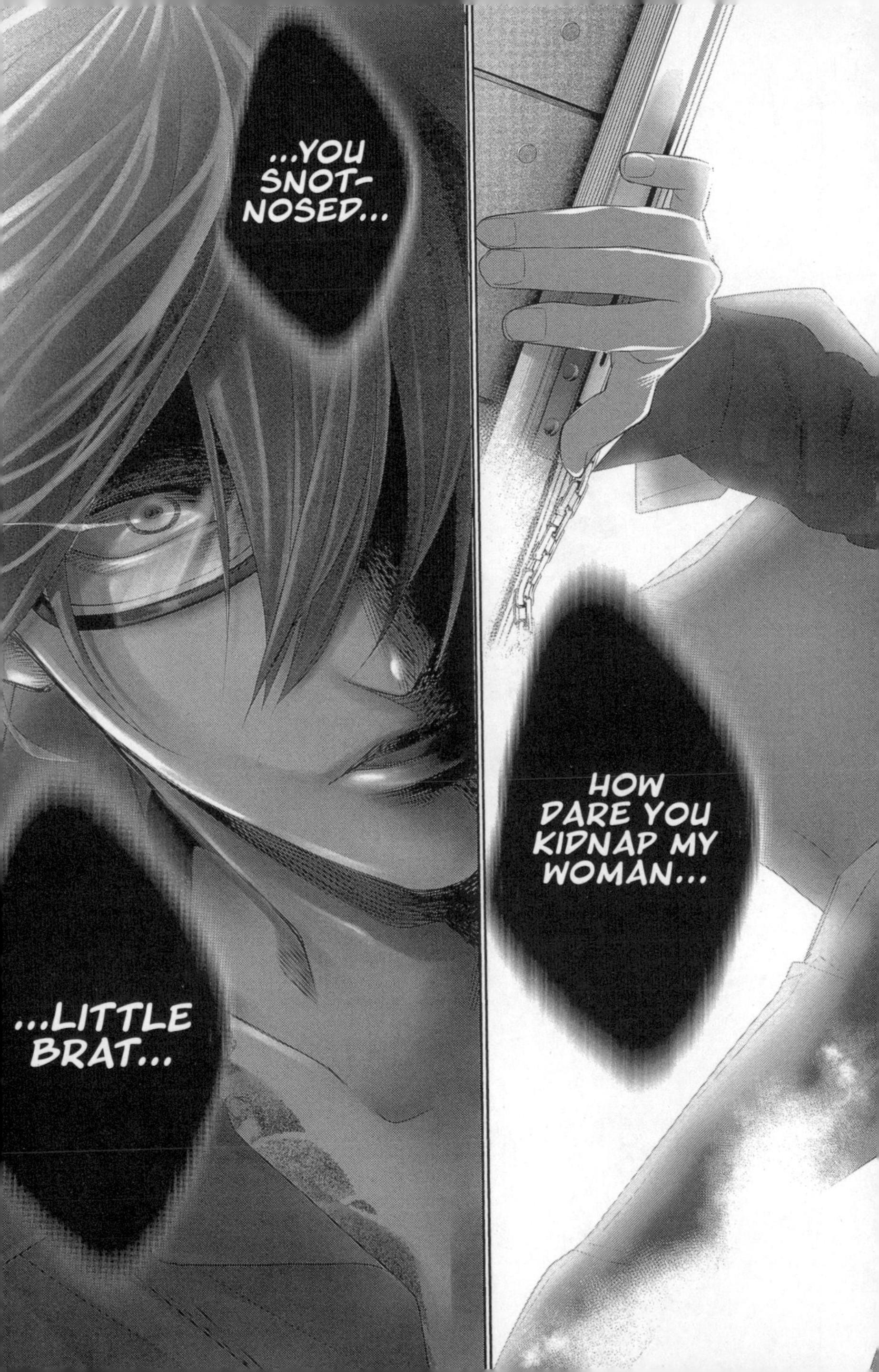
HOW DARE YOU KIDNAP MY WOMAN...
...YOU SNOT-NOSED...
...LITTLE BRAT...

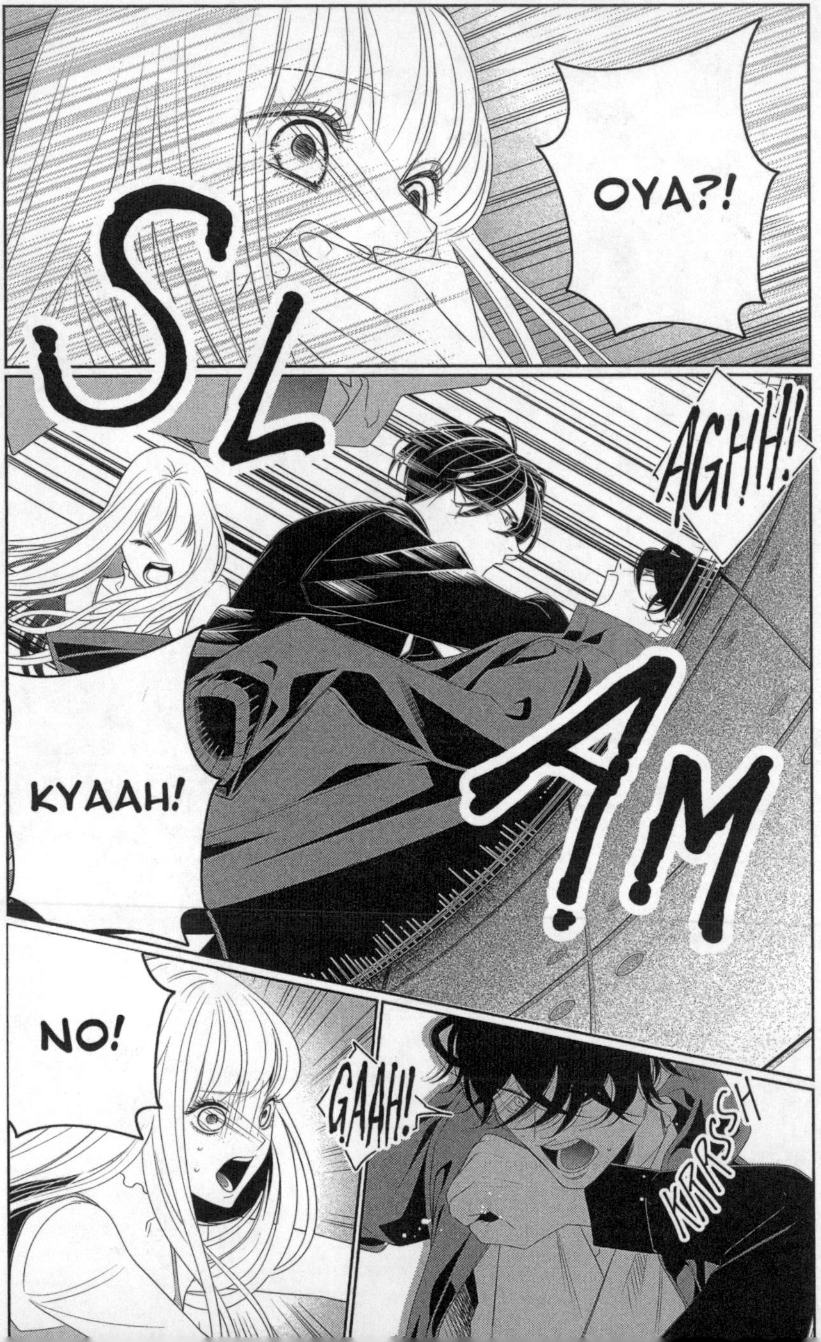
OYA?!
SLAM
AGHH!
KYAAH!
KRRSSH
GAAH!
NO!

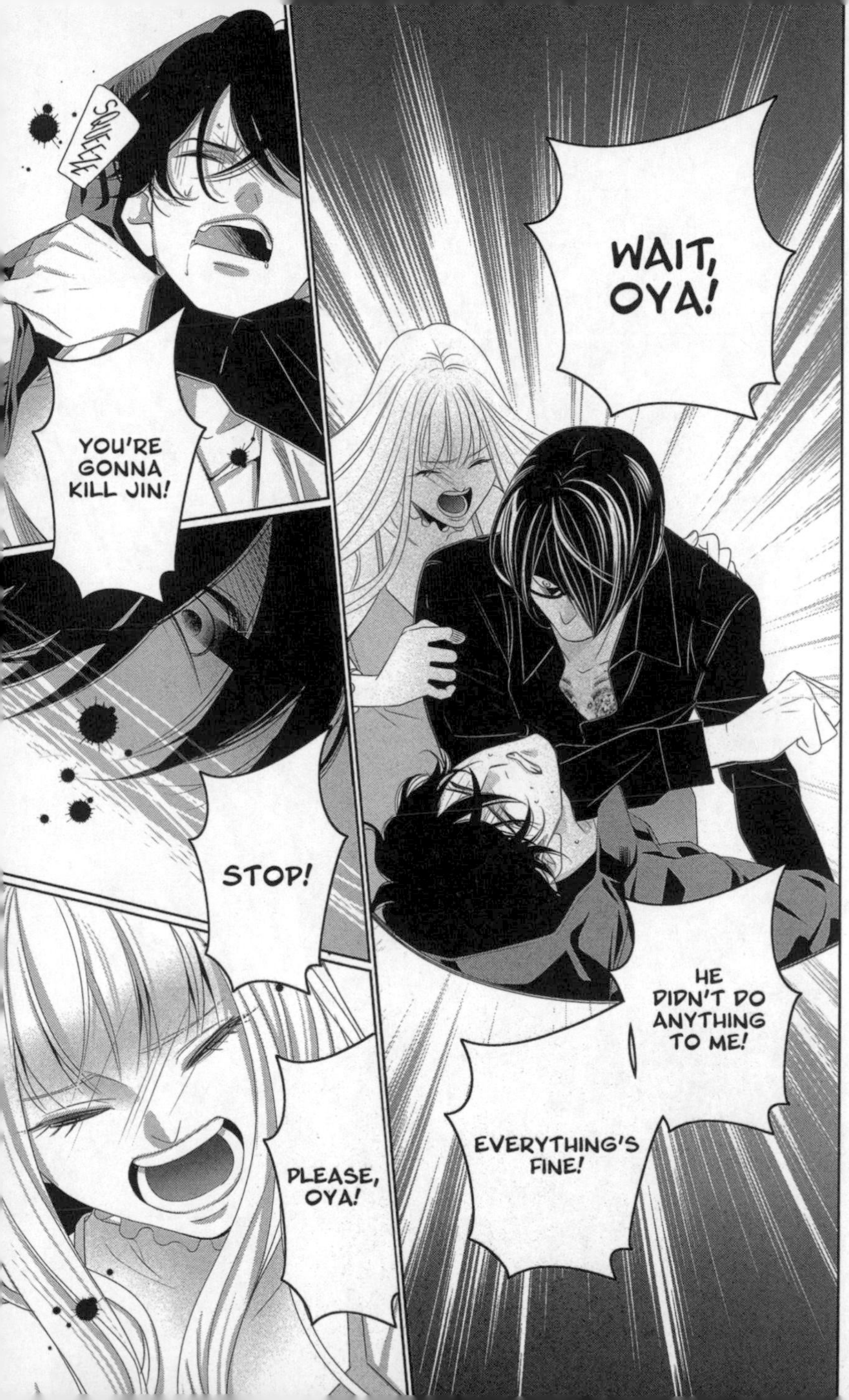
WAIT, OYA!
HE DIDN'T DO ANYTHING TO ME!
EVERYTHING'S FINE!
SQUEEZE
YOU'RE GONNA KILL JIN!
STOP!
PLEASE, OYA!

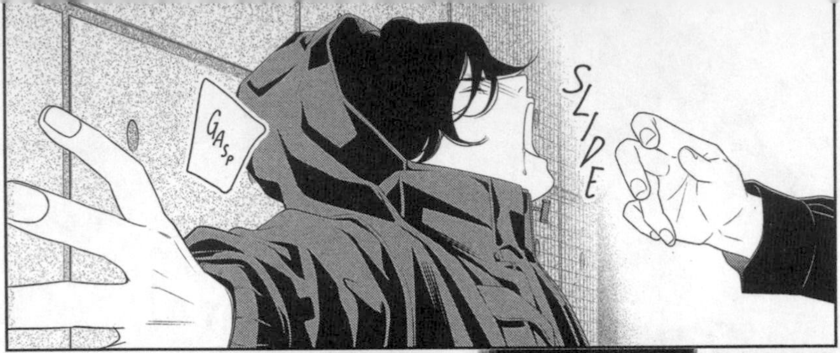
SLIDE
GASP

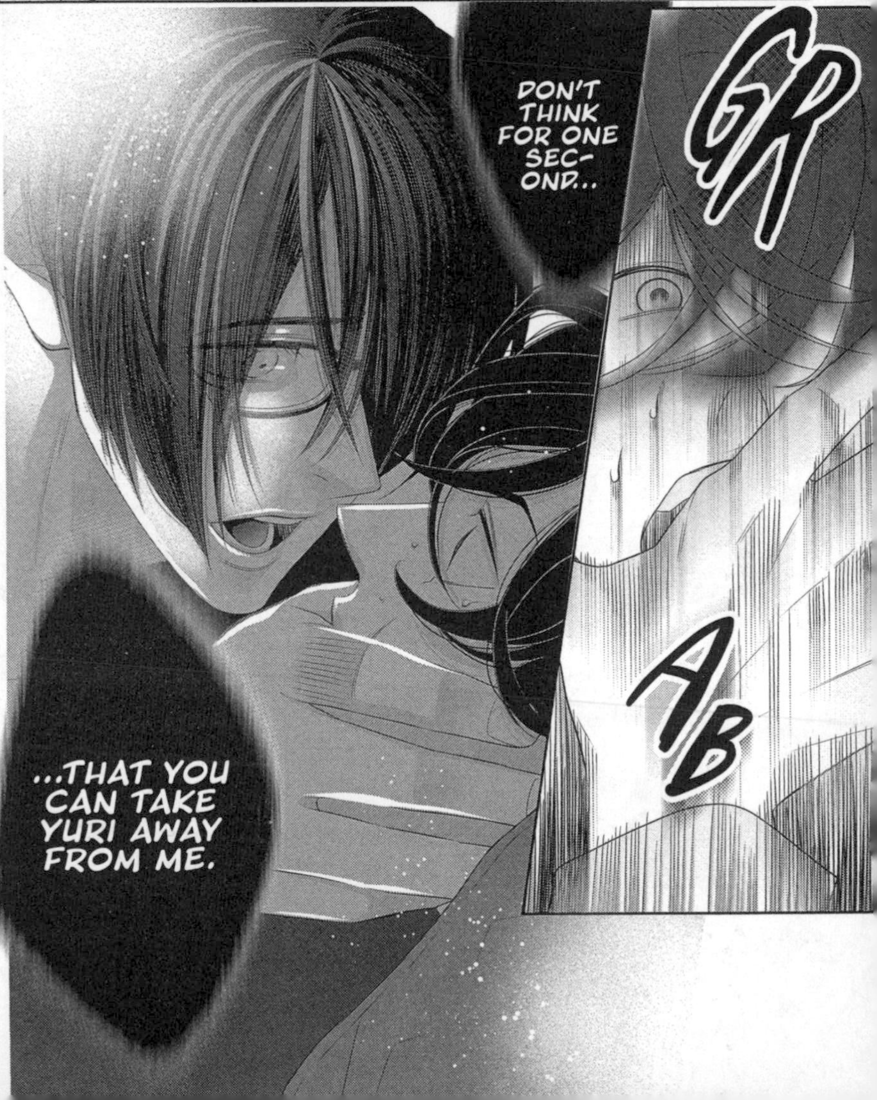
GR
DON'T THINK FOR ONE SEC-OND...
AB
...THAT YOU CAN TAKE YURI AWAY FROM ME.

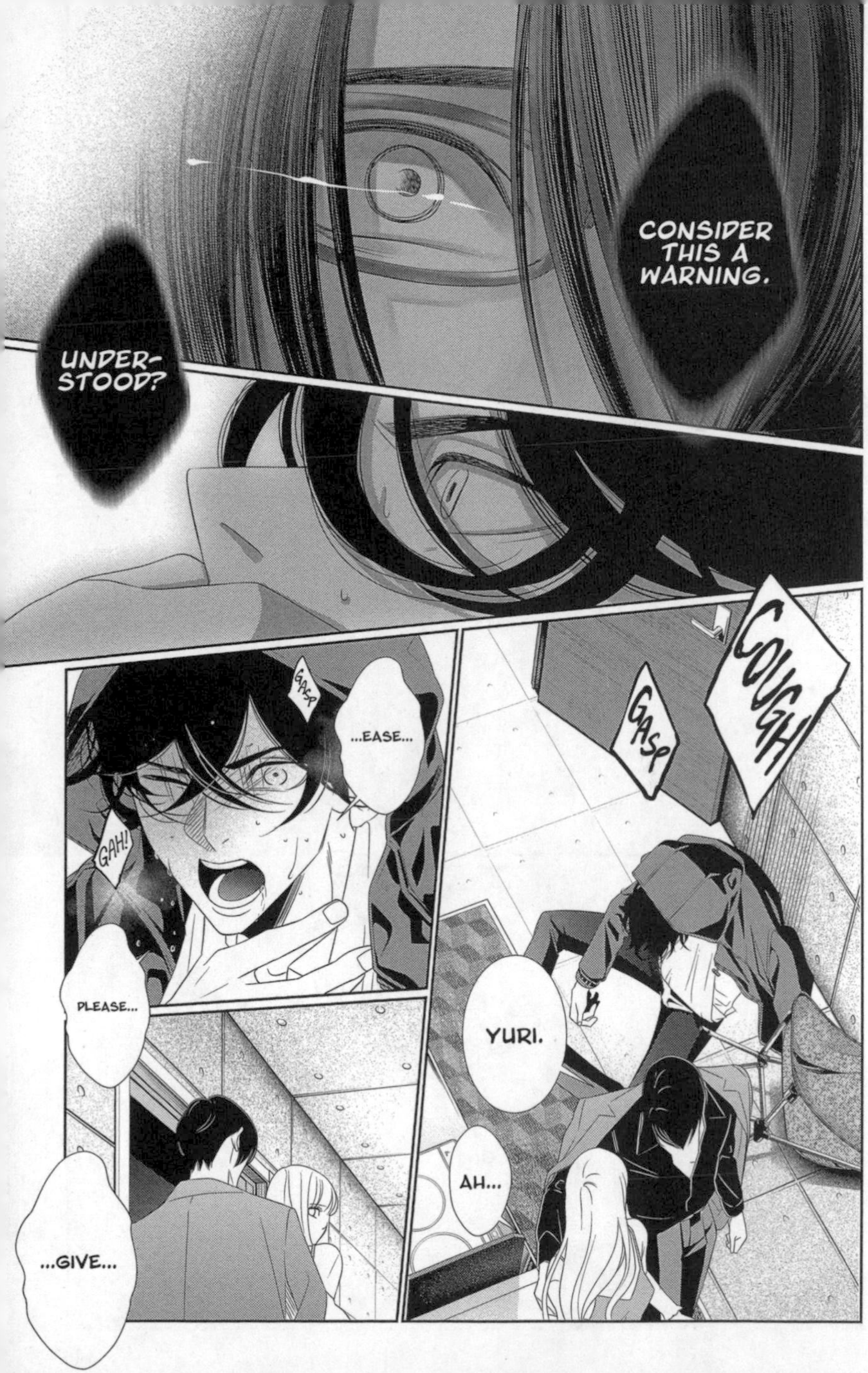
CONSIDER THIS A WARNING.
UNDER-STOOD?
COUGH
GASP
YURI.
AH...
GASP
...EASE...
GAH!
PLEASE...
...GIVE...

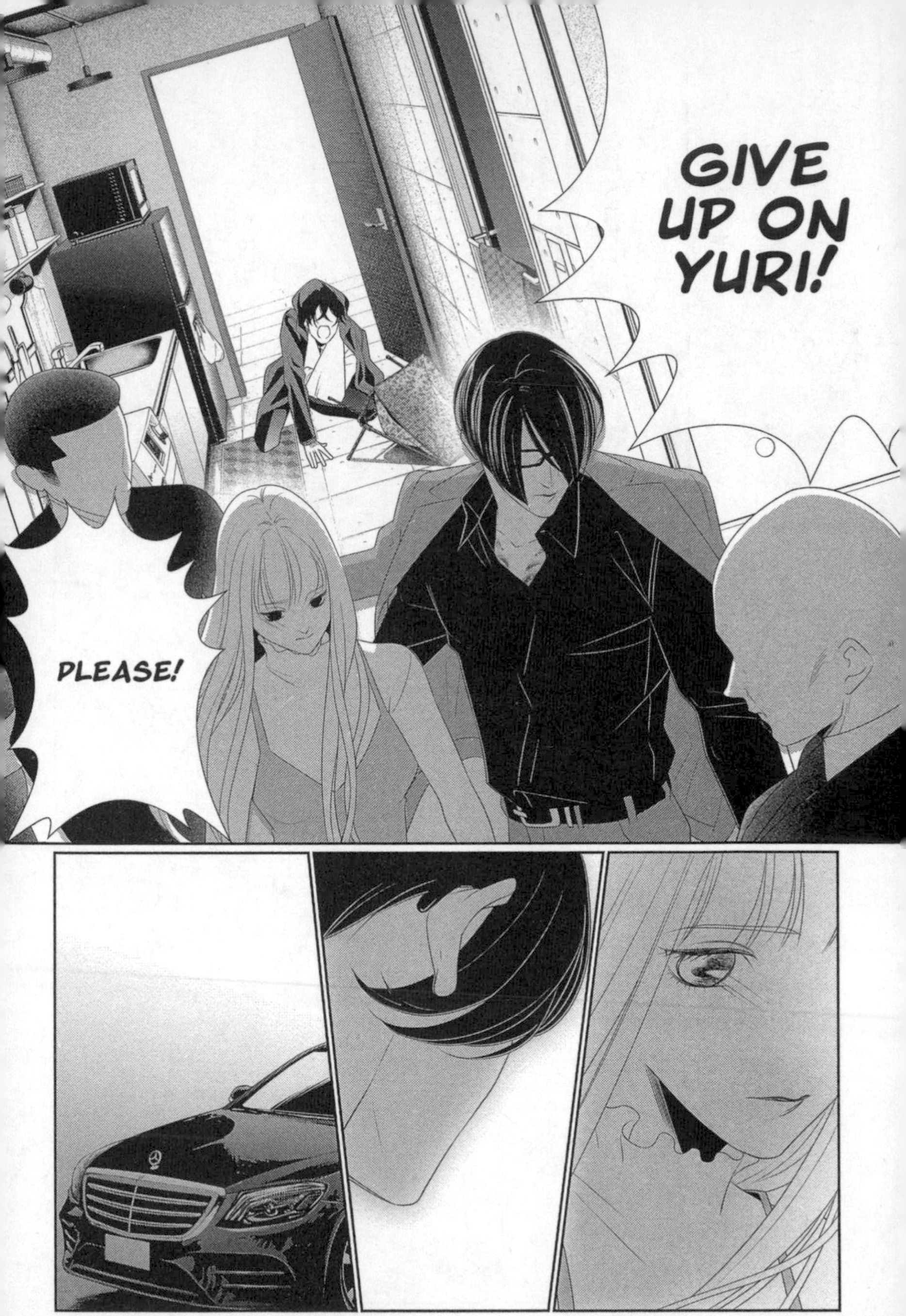
GIVE UP ON YURI!
PLEASE!

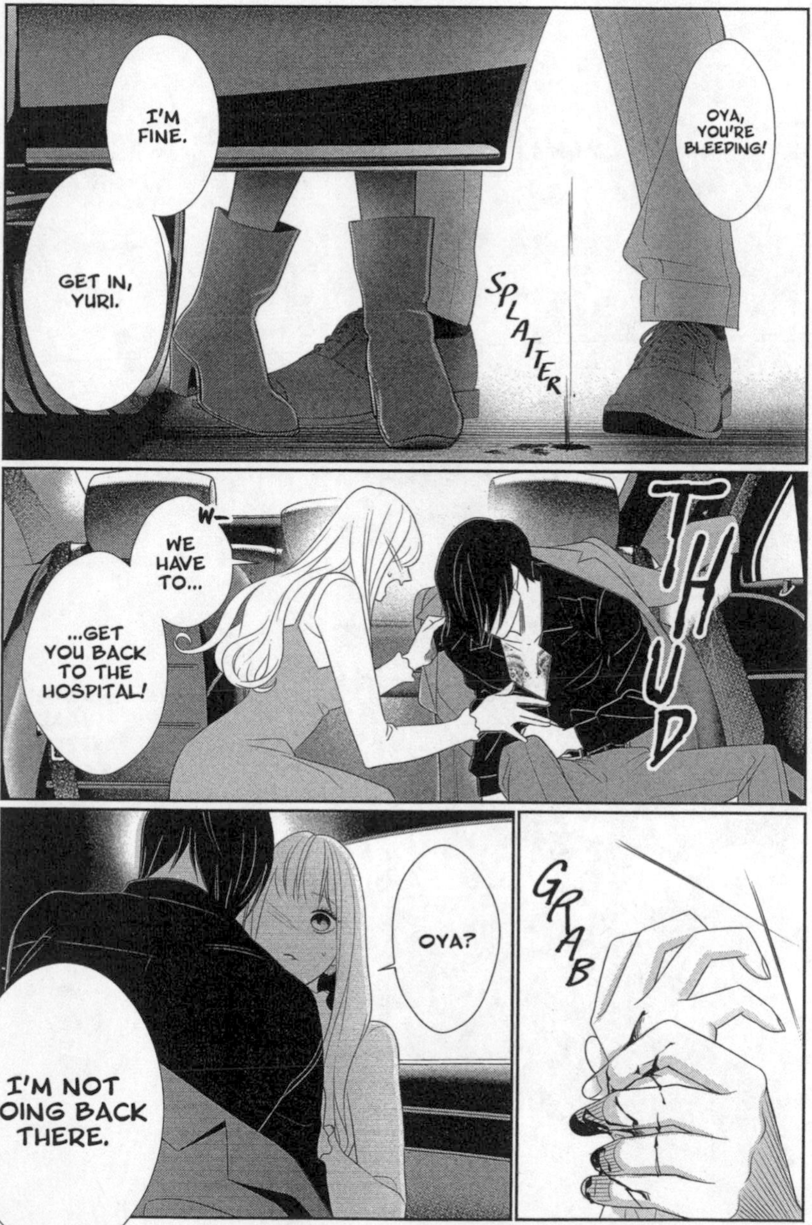
OYA, YOU'RE BLEEDING!
I'M FINE.
SPLATTER
GET IN, YURI.
THUD
W-
WE HAVE TO...
...GET YOU BACK TO THE HOSPITAL!
GRAB
OYA?
I'M NOT GOING BACK THERE.

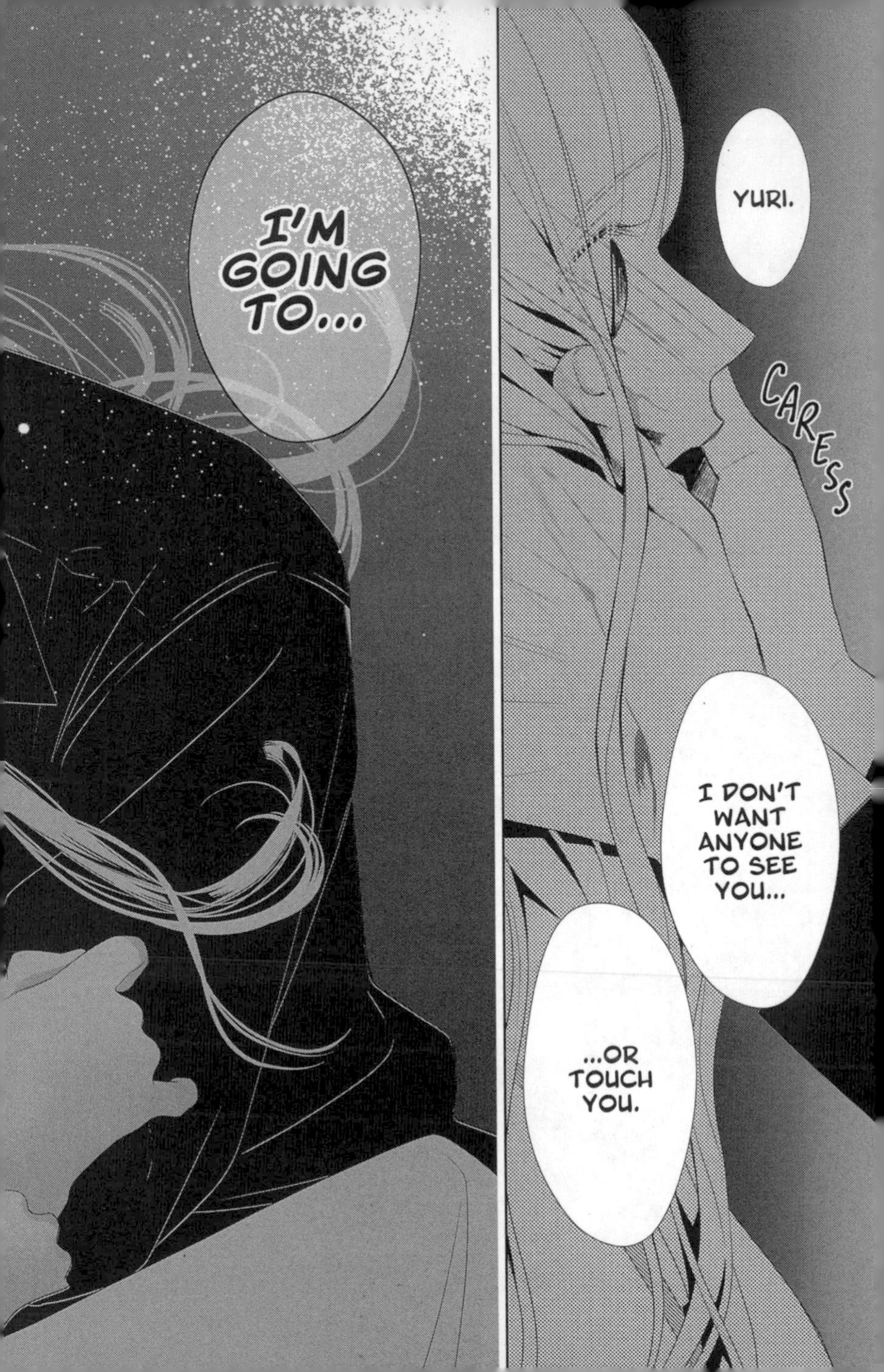
YURI.
CARESS
I DON'T WANT ANYONE TO SEE YOU...
...OR TOUCH YOU.
I'M GOING TO...

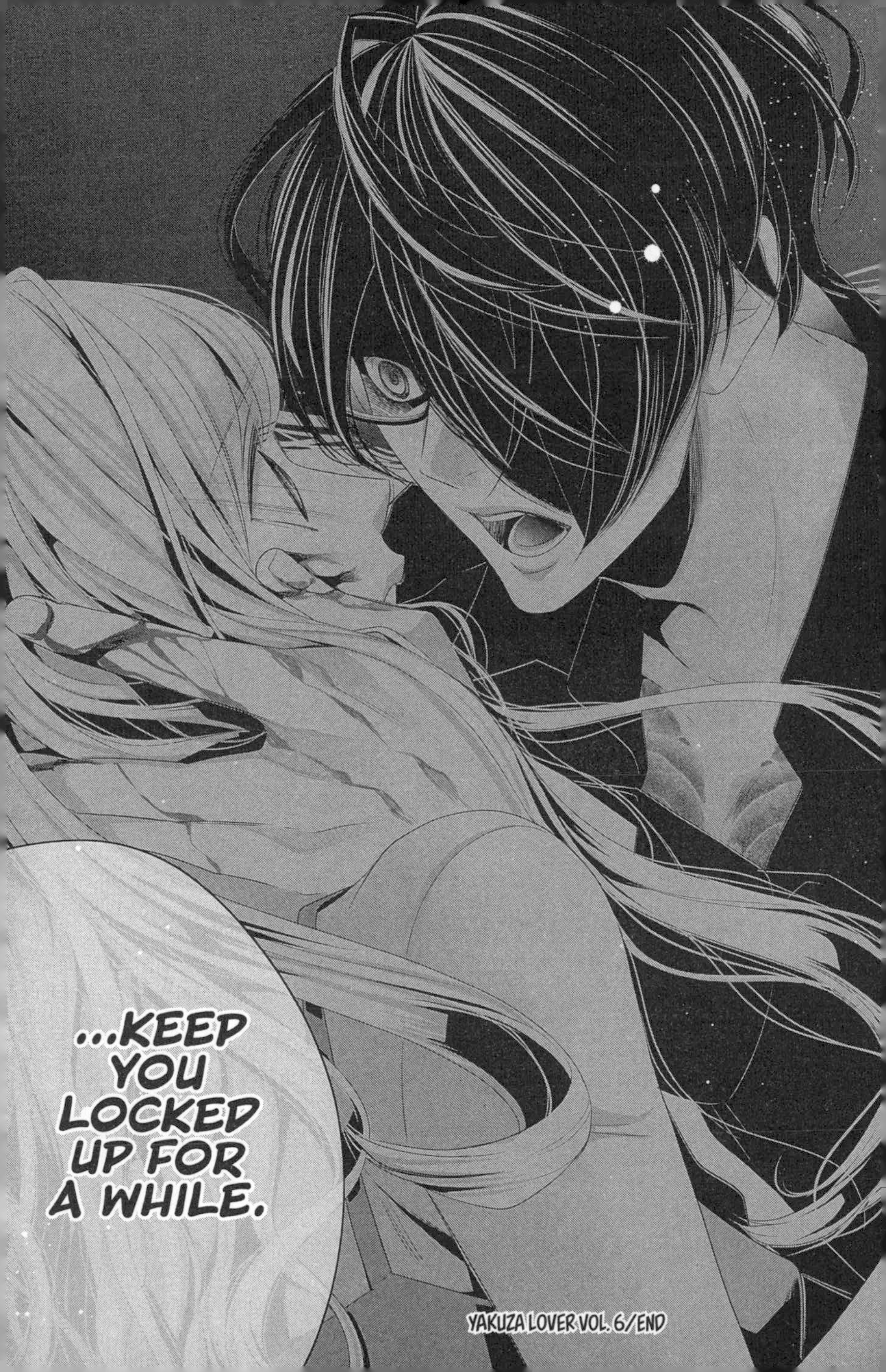
...KEEP YOU LOCKED UP FOR A WHILE.
YAKUZA LOVER VOL. 6/END

bonus bullet 21 secret scene

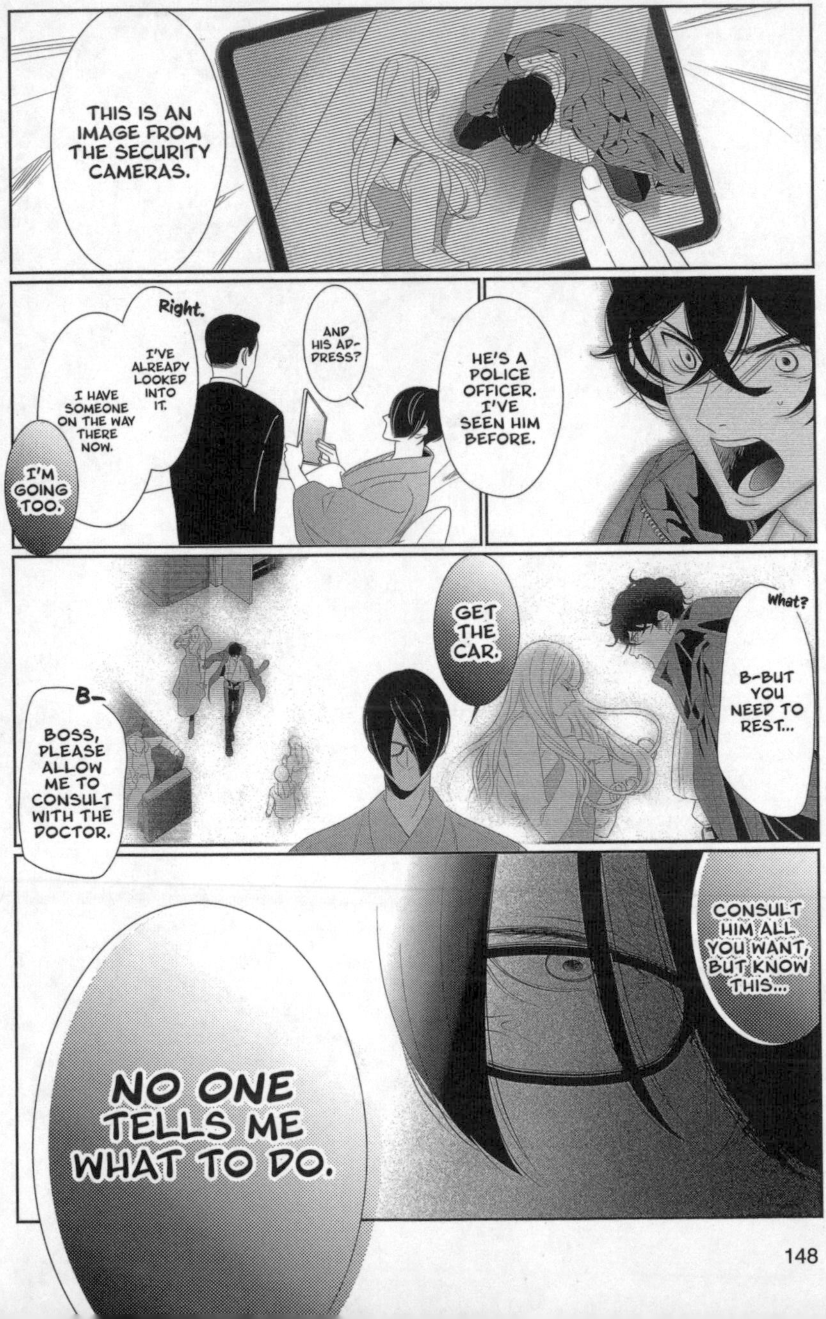
THIS IS AN IMAGE FROM THE SECURITY CAMERAS.
HE'S A POLICE OFFICER. I'VE SEEN HIM BEFORE.
AND HIS ADDRESS?
Right.
I'VE ALREADY LOOKED INTO IT.
I HAVE SOMEONE ON THE WAY THERE NOW.
I'M GOING TOO.
What?
B-BUT YOU NEED TO REST...
GET THE CAR.
B—
BOSS, PLEASE ALLOW ME TO CONSULT WITH THE DOCTOR.
CONSULT HIM ALL YOU WANT, BUT KNOW THIS...
NO ONE TELLS ME WHAT TO DO.

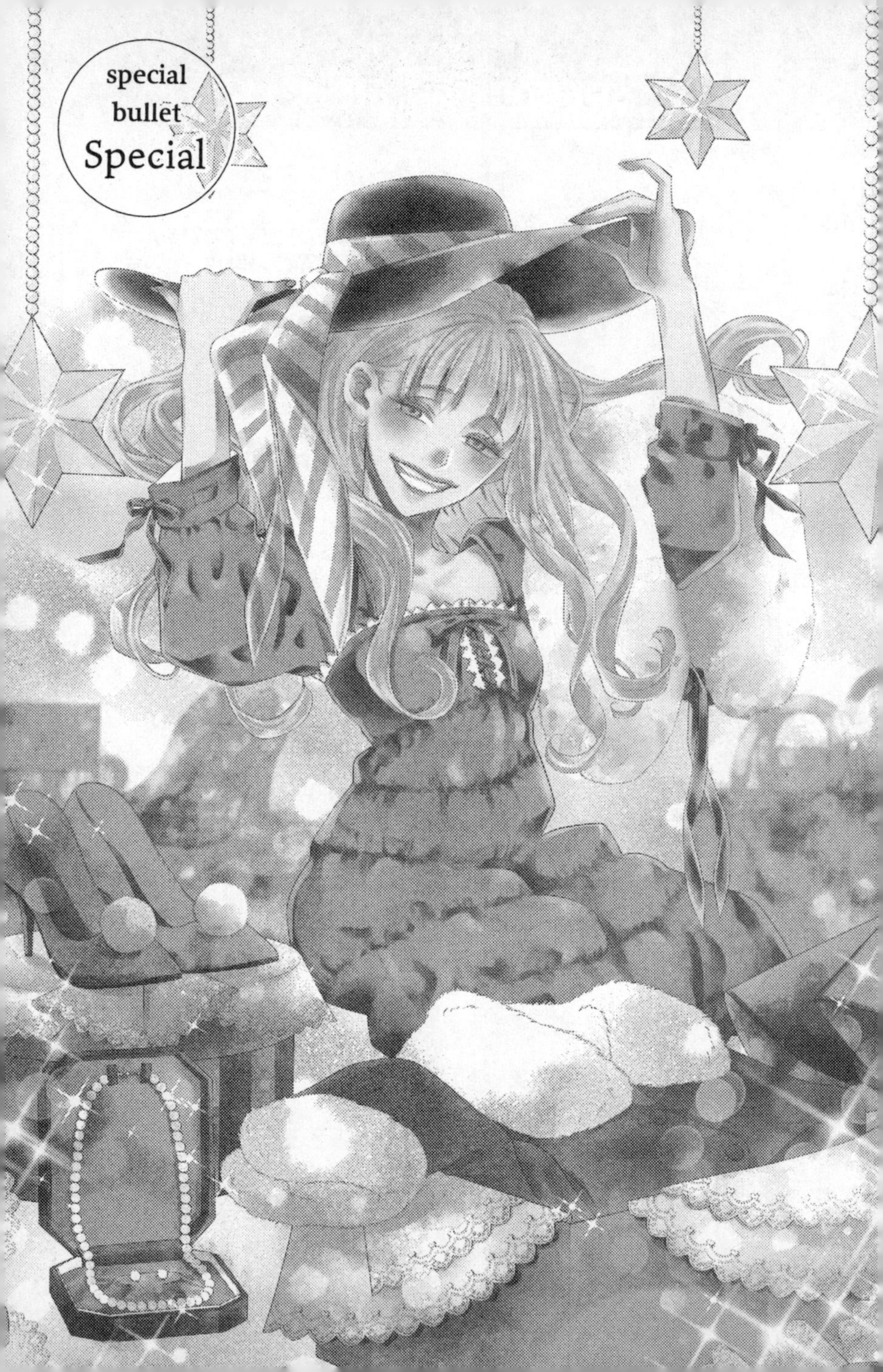
special bullet Special

Special Thanks

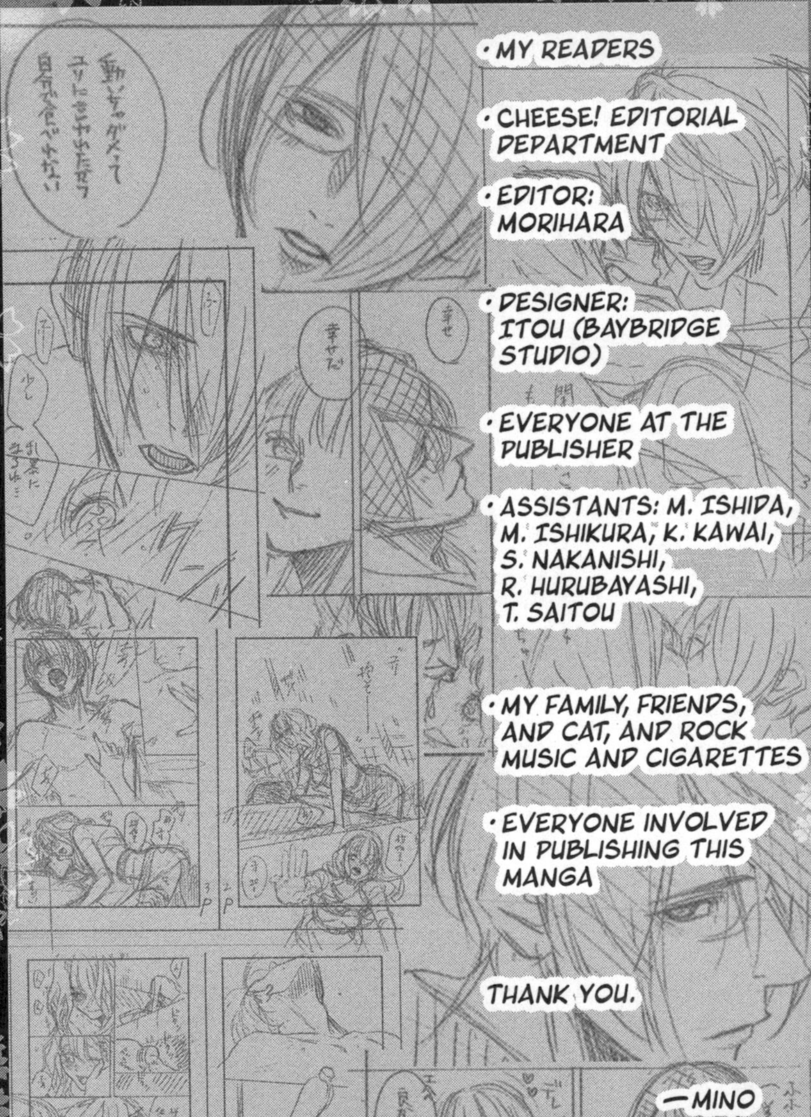

- MY READERS
- CHEESE! EDITORIAL DEPARTMENT
- EDITOR: MORIHARA
- DESIGNER: ITOU (BAYBRIDGE STUDIO)
- EVERYONE AT THE PUBLISHER
- ASSISTANTS: M. ISHIDA, M. ISHIKURA, K. KAWAI, S. NAKANISHI, R. HURUBAYASHI, T. SAITOU
- MY FAMILY, FRIENDS, AND CAT, AND ROCK MUSIC AND CIGARETTES
- EVERYONE INVOLVED IN PUBLISHING THIS MANGA

THANK YOU.

—MINO

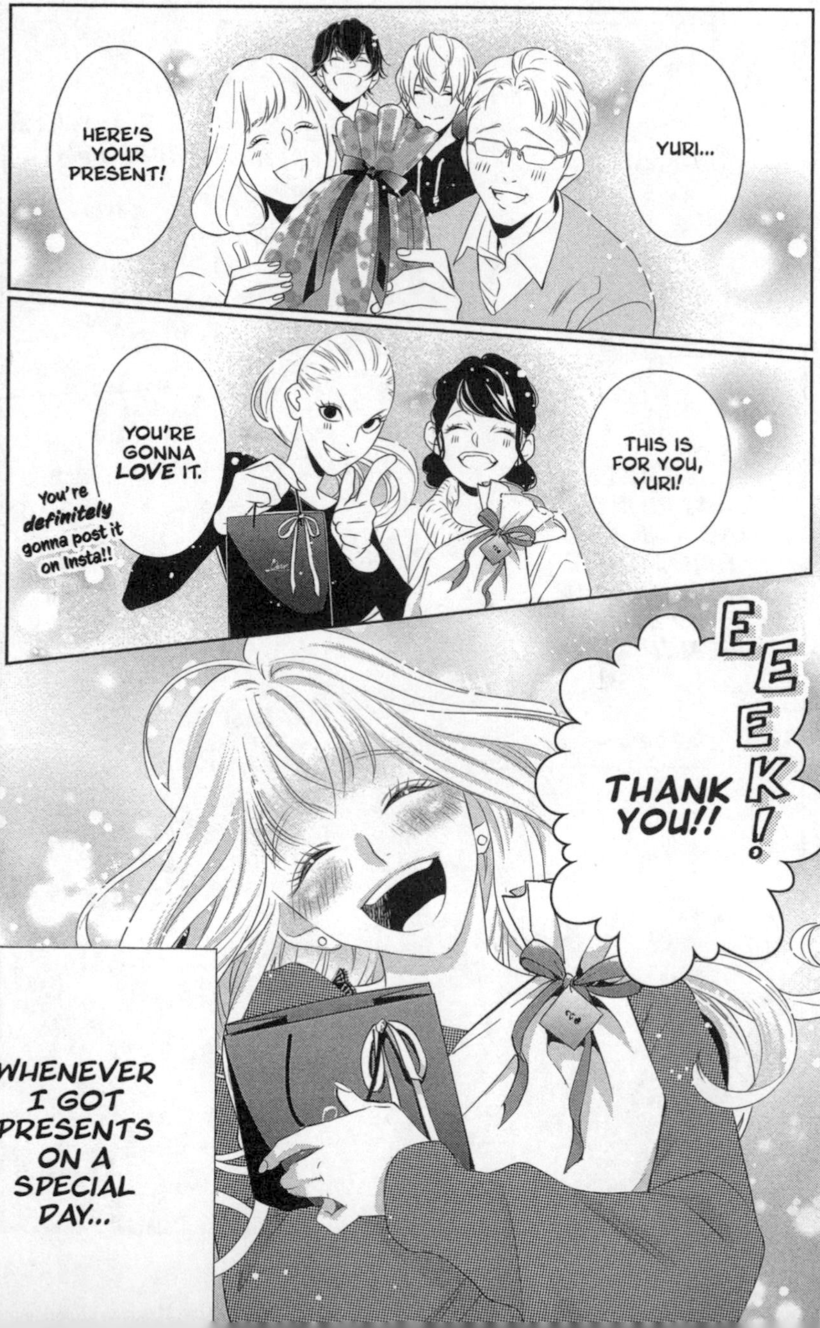
YURI...
HERE'S YOUR PRESENT!
THIS IS FOR YOU, YURI!
YOU'RE GONNA LOVE IT.
You're definitely gonna post it on Insta!!
EEEK!
THANK YOU!!
WHENEVER I GOT PRESENTS ON A SPECIAL DAY...

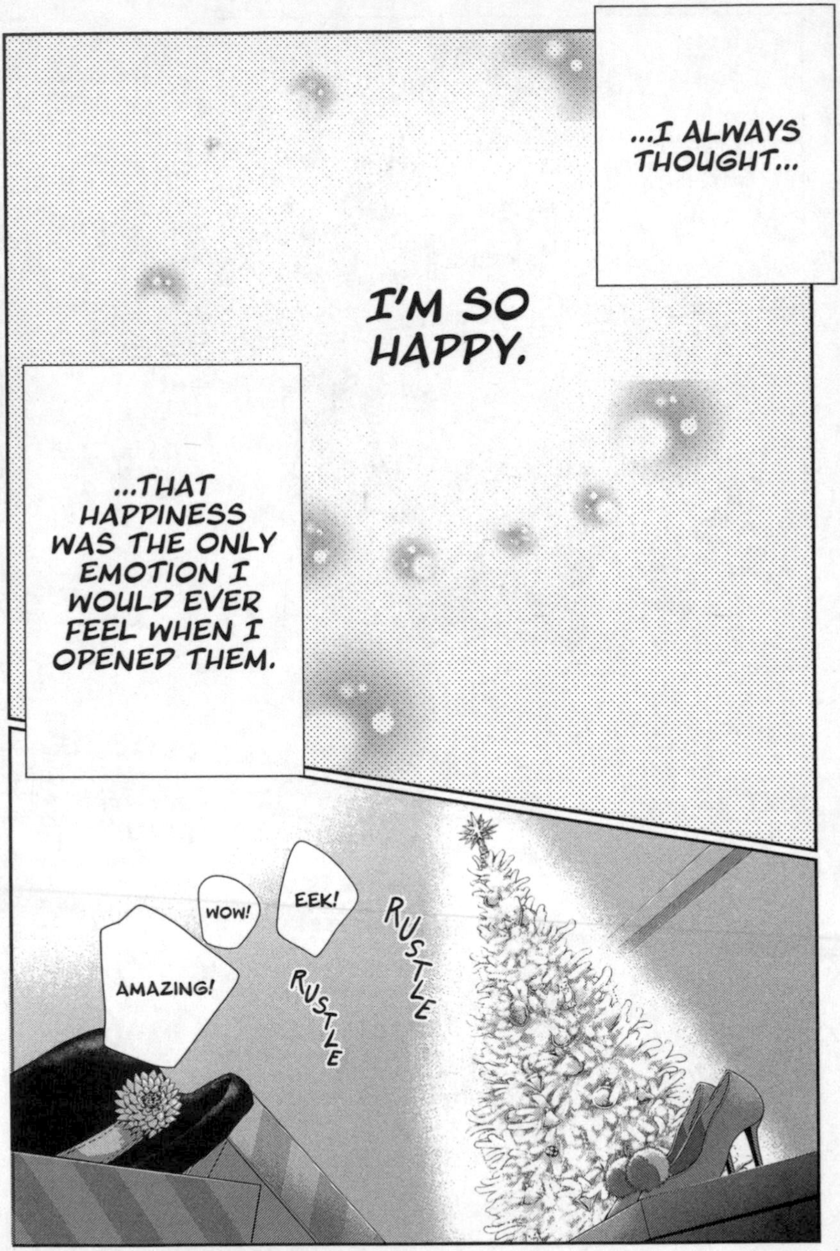
...I ALWAYS THOUGHT...
I'M SO HAPPY.
...THAT HAPPINESS WAS THE ONLY EMOTION I WOULD EVER FEEL WHEN I OPENED THEM.
RUSTLE
EEK!
RUSTLE
WOW!
AMAZING!

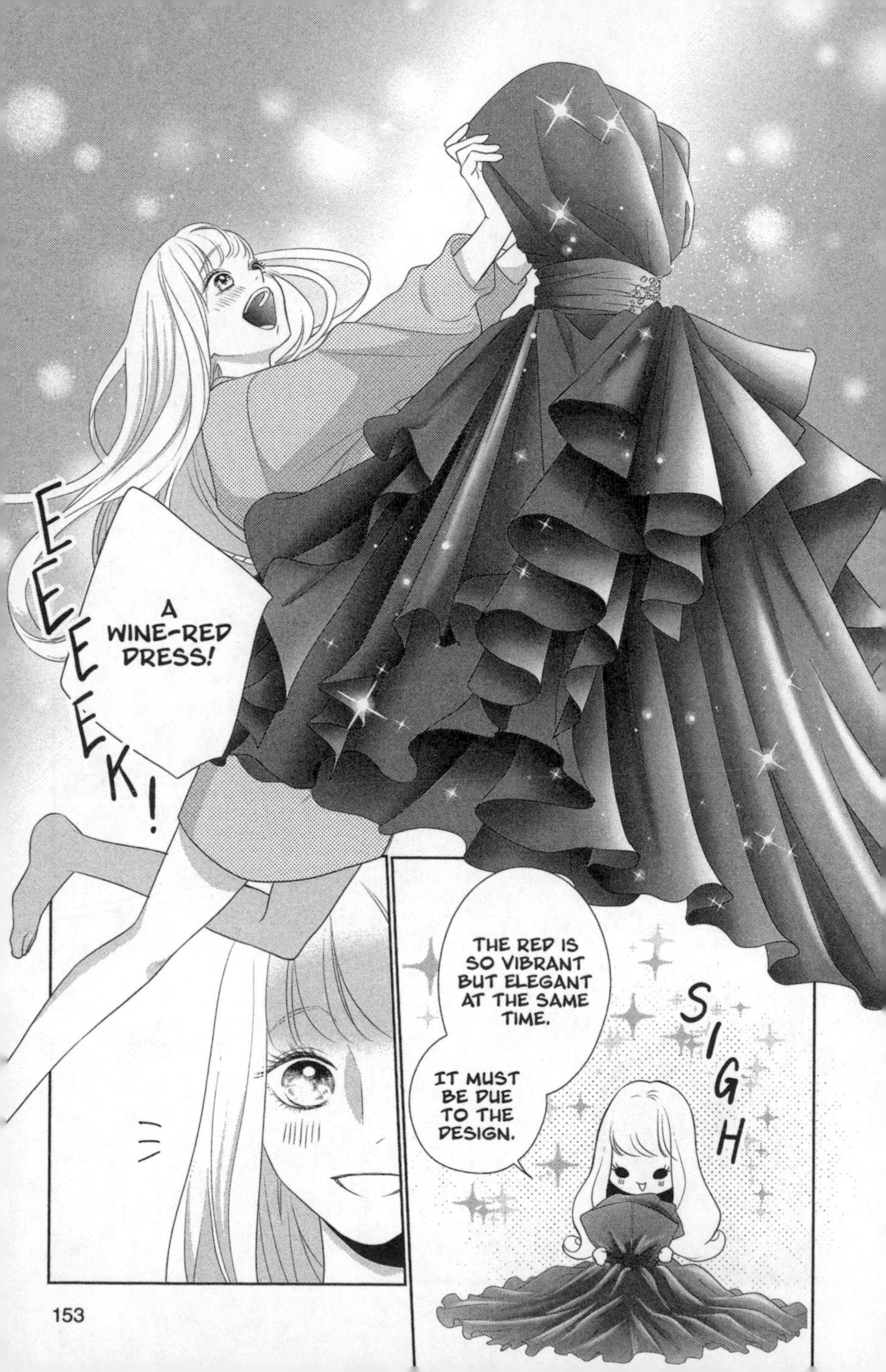
A WINE-RED DRESS!
EEEEK!
SIGH
THE RED IS SO VIBRANT BUT ELEGANT AT THE SAME TIME.
IT MUST BE DUE TO THE DESIGN.

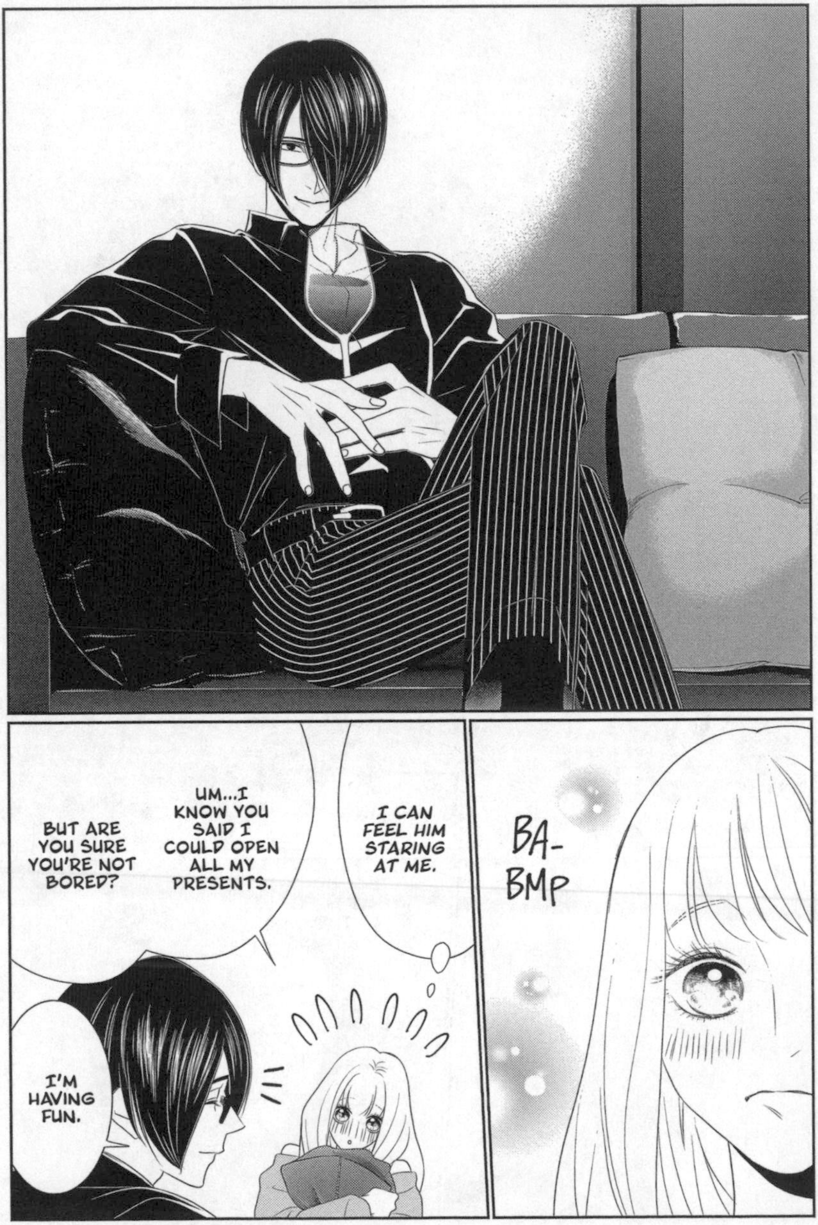
BA-BMP
I CAN FEEL HIM STARING AT ME.
UM...I KNOW YOU SAID I COULD OPEN ALL MY PRESENTS.
BUT ARE YOU SURE YOU'RE NOT BORED?
I'M HAVING FUN.

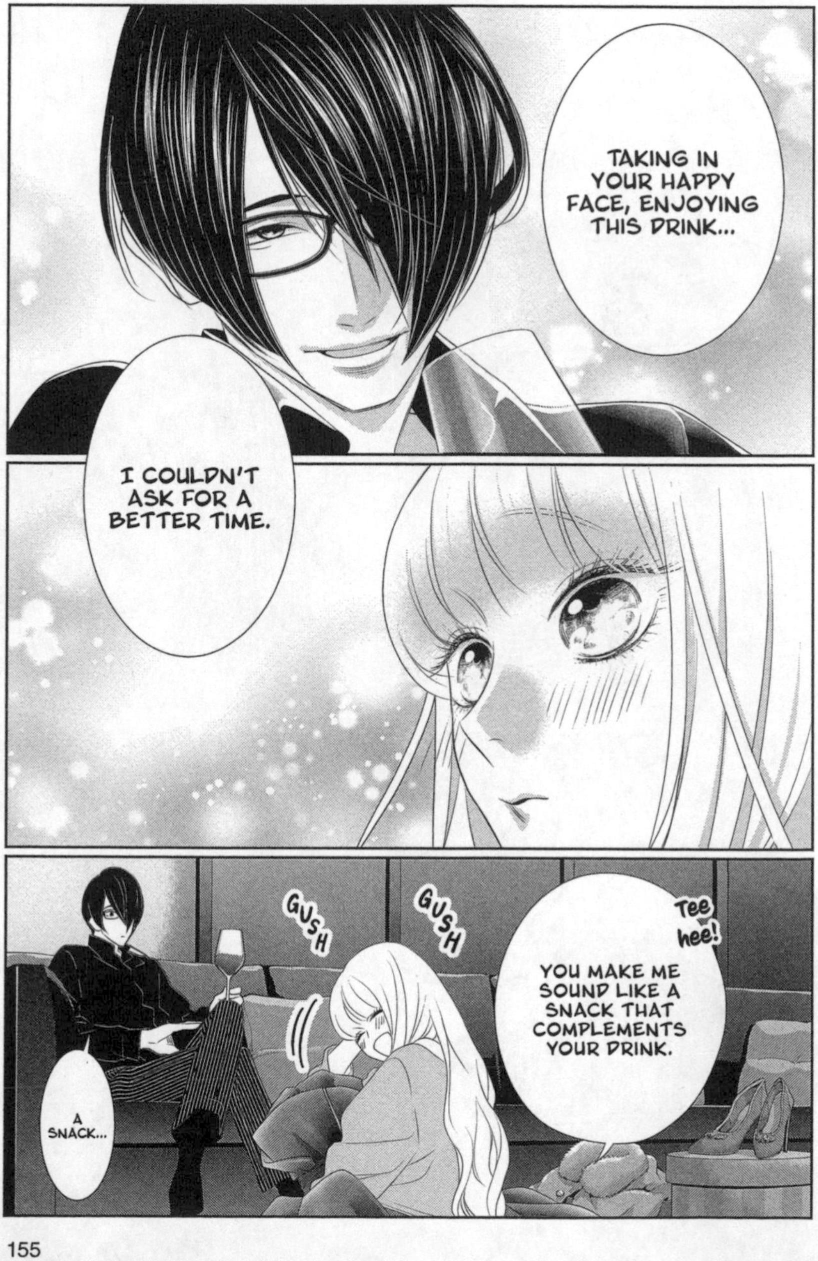
TAKING IN YOUR HAPPY FACE, ENJOYING THIS DRINK...
I COULDN'T ASK FOR A BETTER TIME.
Tee hee!
YOU MAKE ME SOUND LIKE A SNACK THAT COMPLEMENTS YOUR DRINK.
GUSH
GUSH
A SNACK...

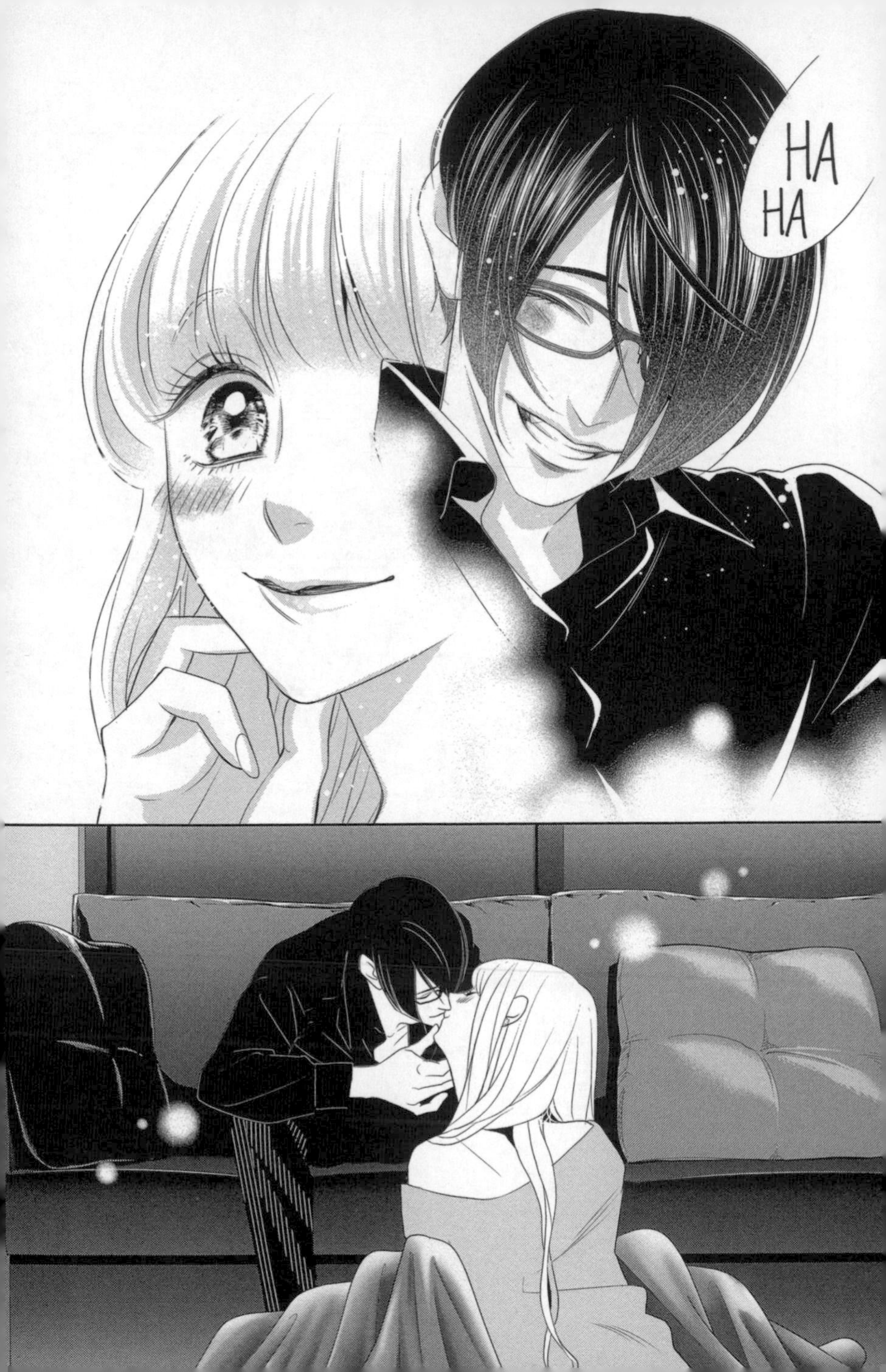
HA
HA

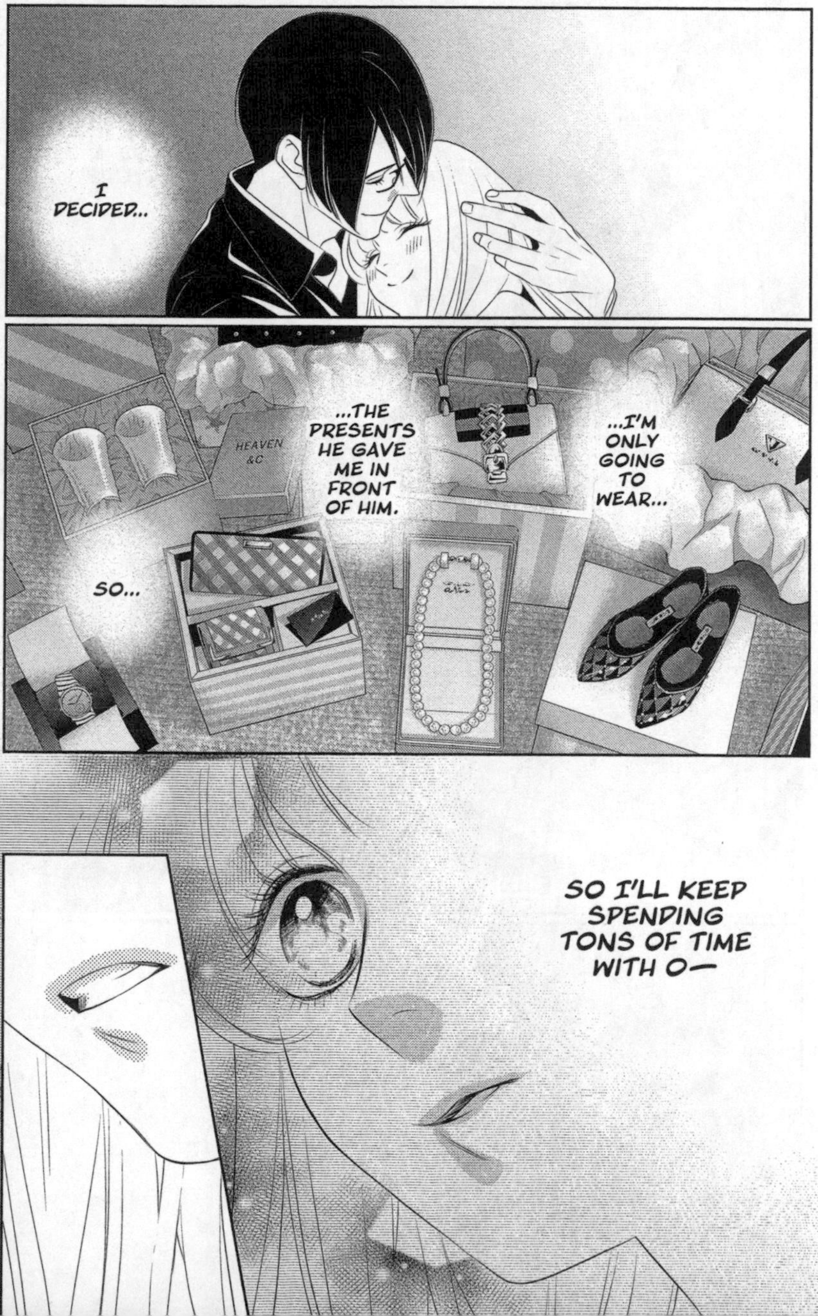
I DECIDED...
...I'M ONLY GOING TO WEAR...
...THE PRESENTS HE GAVE ME IN FRONT OF HIM.
HEAVEN &C
SO...
SO I'LL KEEP SPENDING TONS OF TIME WITH O—

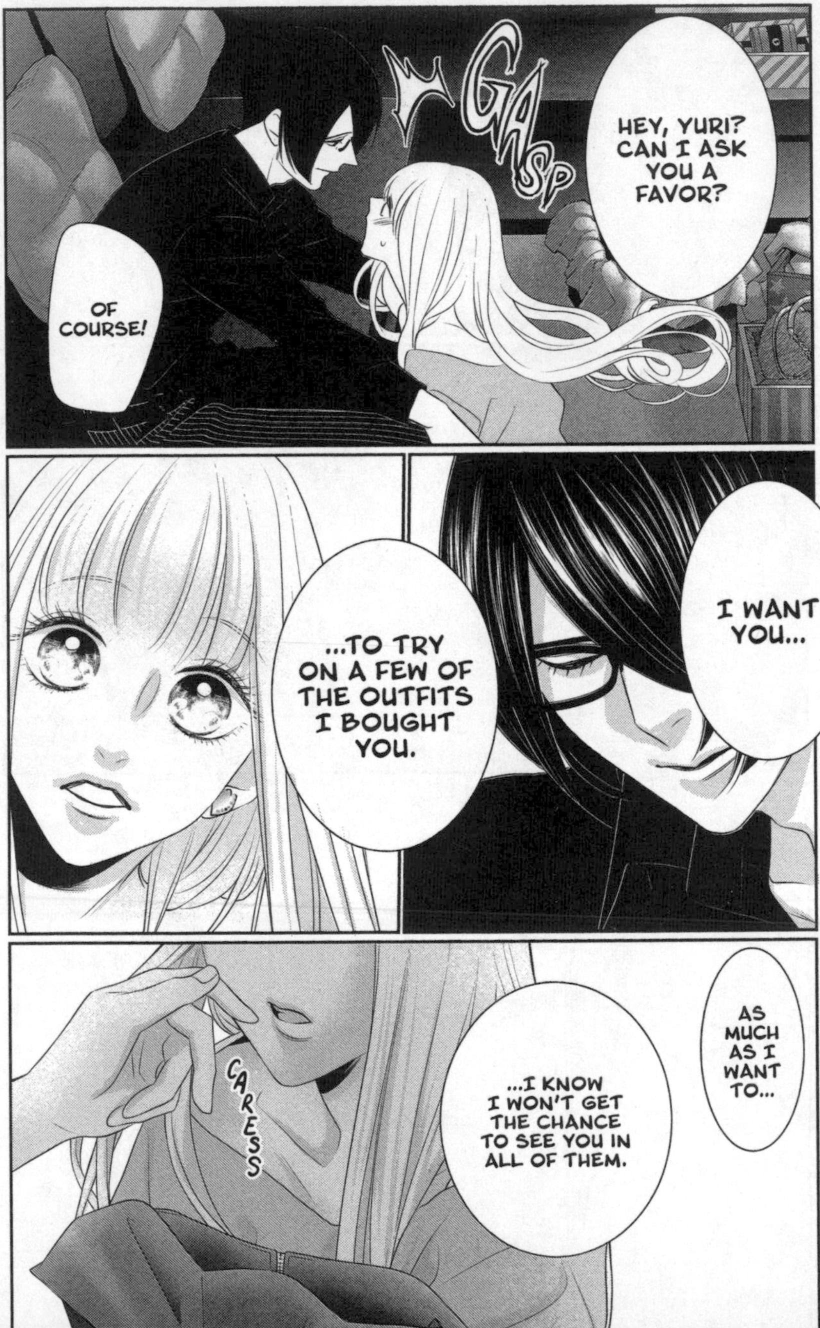
HEY, YURI? CAN I ASK YOU A FAVOR?
GASP
OF COURSE!
I WANT YOU...
...TO TRY ON A FEW OF THE OUTFITS I BOUGHT YOU.
AS MUCH AS I WANT TO...
...I KNOW I WON'T GET THE CHANCE TO SEE YOU IN ALL OF THEM.
CARESS

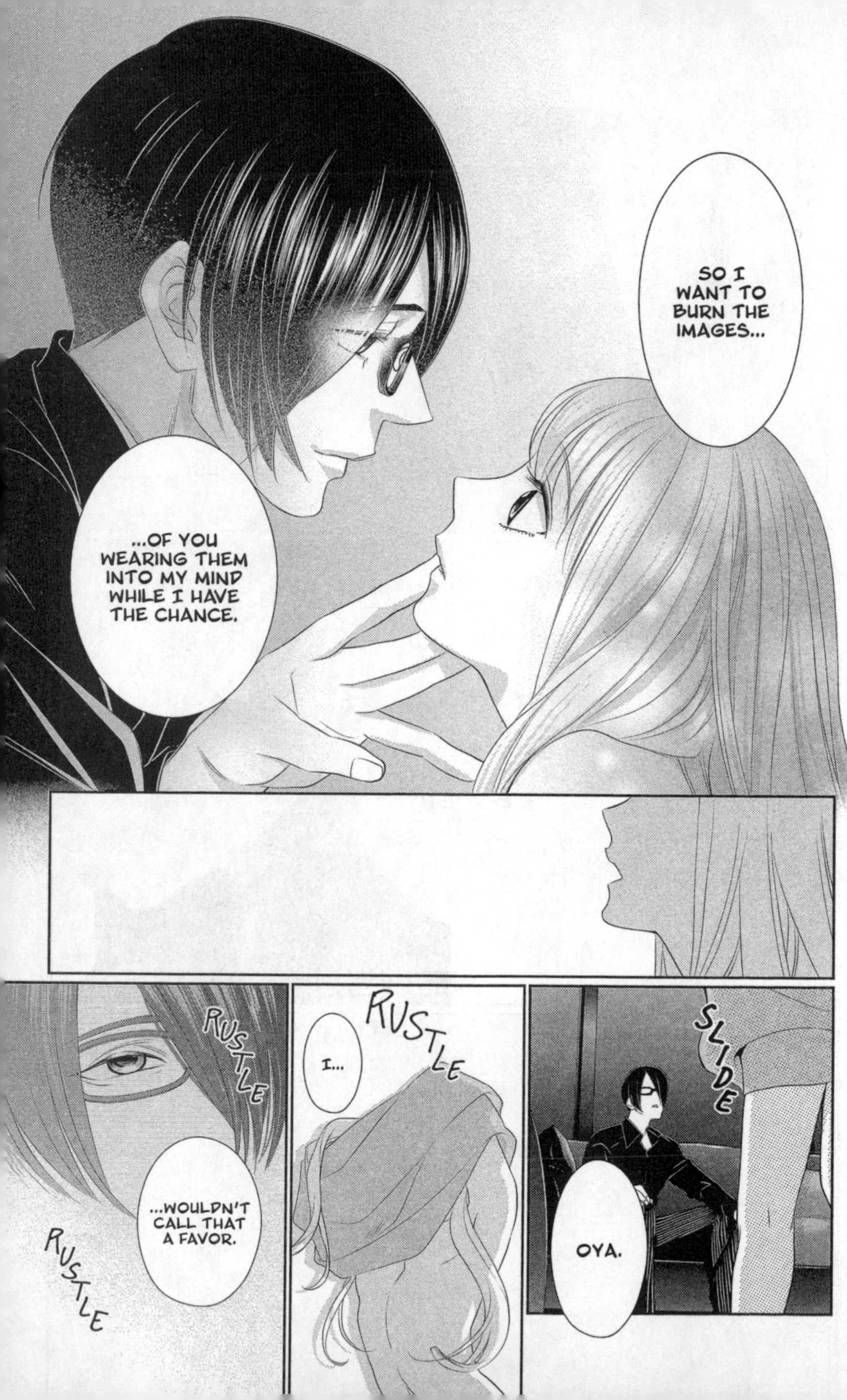
SO I WANT TO BURN THE IMAGES...
...OF YOU WEARING THEM INTO MY MIND WHILE I HAVE THE CHANCE.
SLIDE
OYA.
RUSTLE
I...
RUSTLE
...WOULDN'T CALL THAT A FAVOR.
RUSTLE

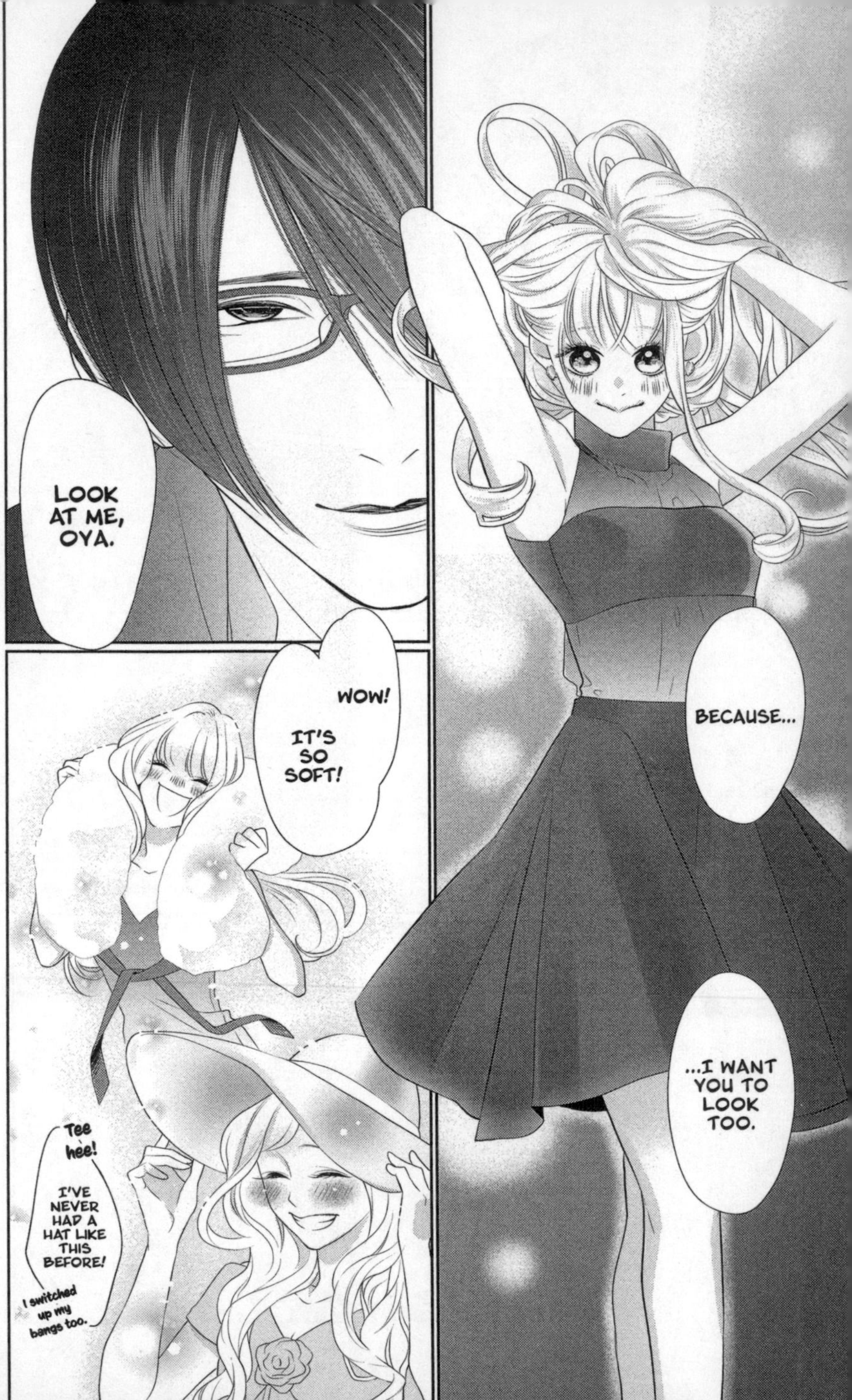
BECAUSE...
...I WANT YOU TO LOOK TOO.
LOOK AT ME, OYA.
WOW!
IT'S SO SOFT!
Tee hee!
I'VE NEVER HAD A HAT LIKE THIS BEFORE!
I switched up my bangs too.

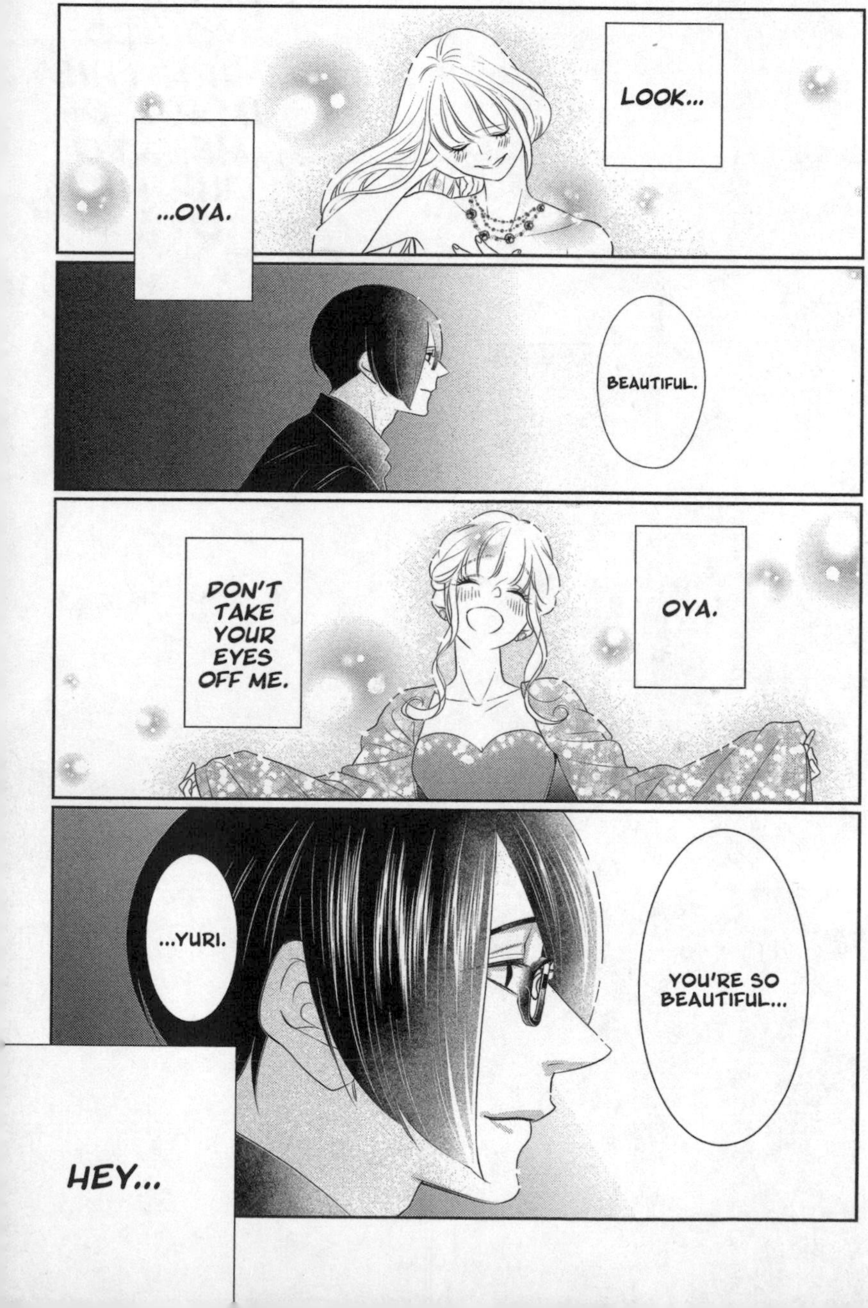
LOOK...
...OYA.
BEAUTIFUL.
OYA.
DON'T TAKE YOUR EYES OFF ME.
YOU'RE SO BEAUTIFUL...
...YURI.
HEY...

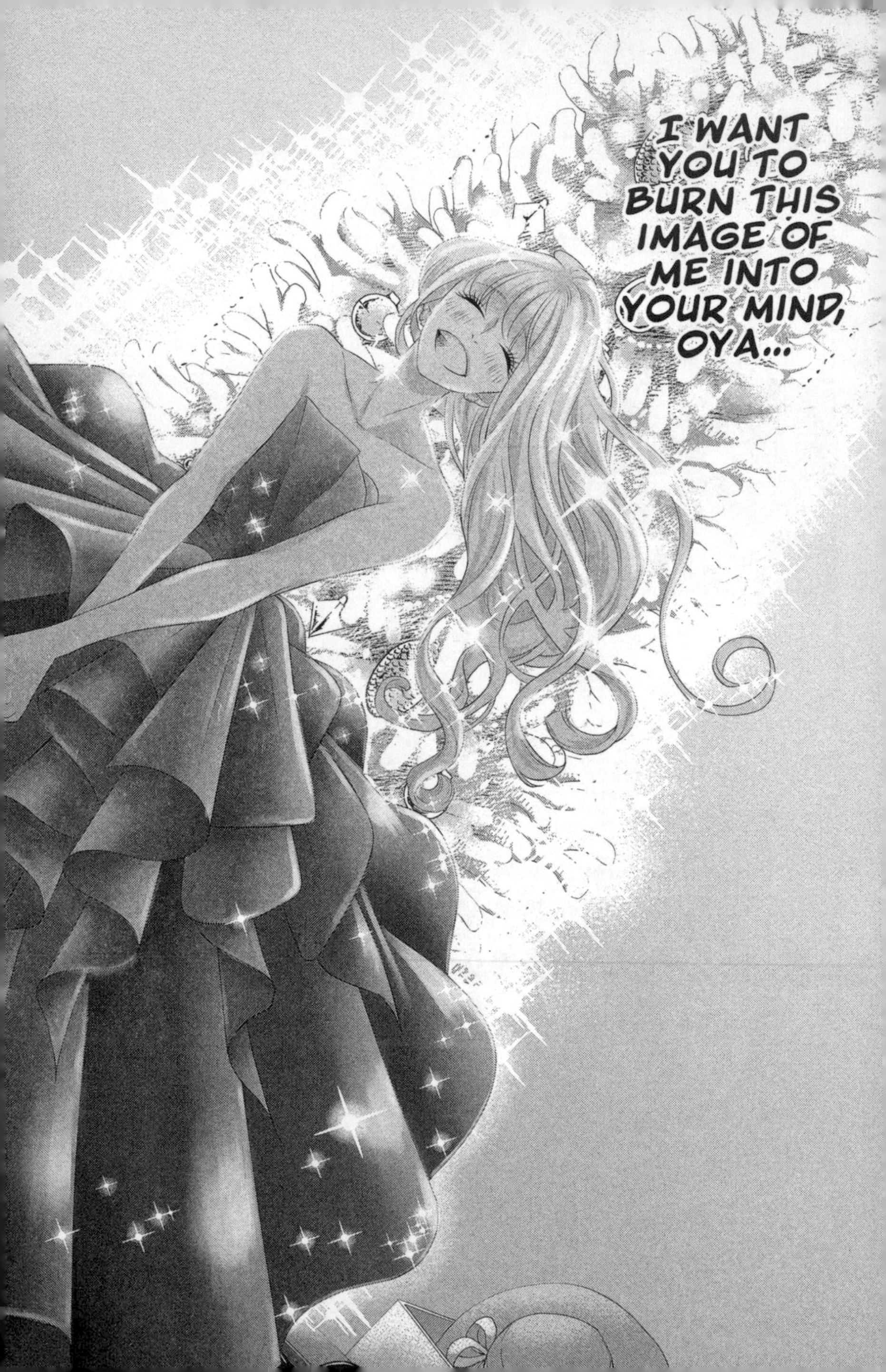
I WANT YOU TO BURN THIS IMAGE OF ME INTO YOUR MIND, OYA...

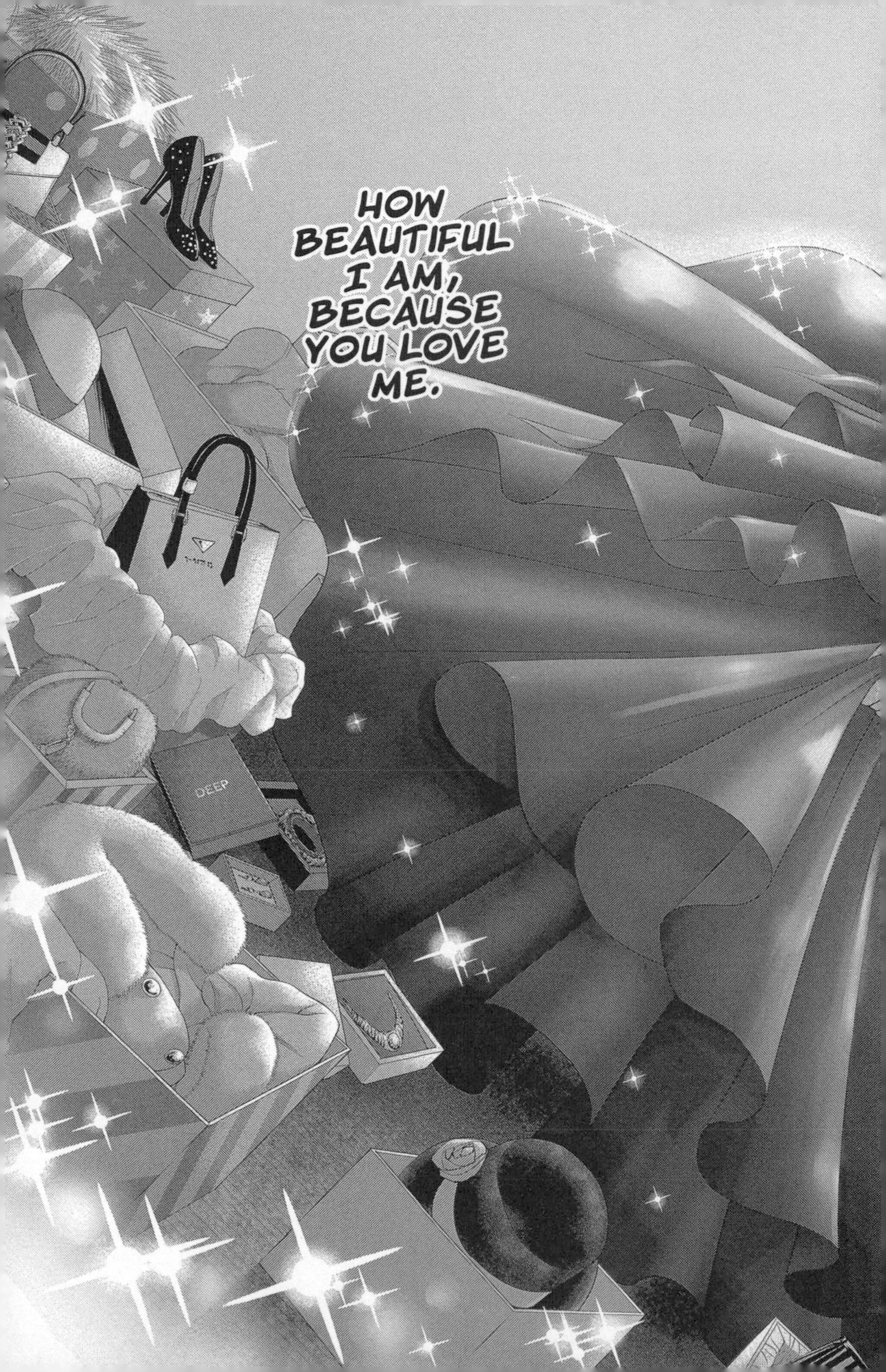
HOW BEAUTIFUL I AM, BECAUSE YOU LOVE ME.
DEEP

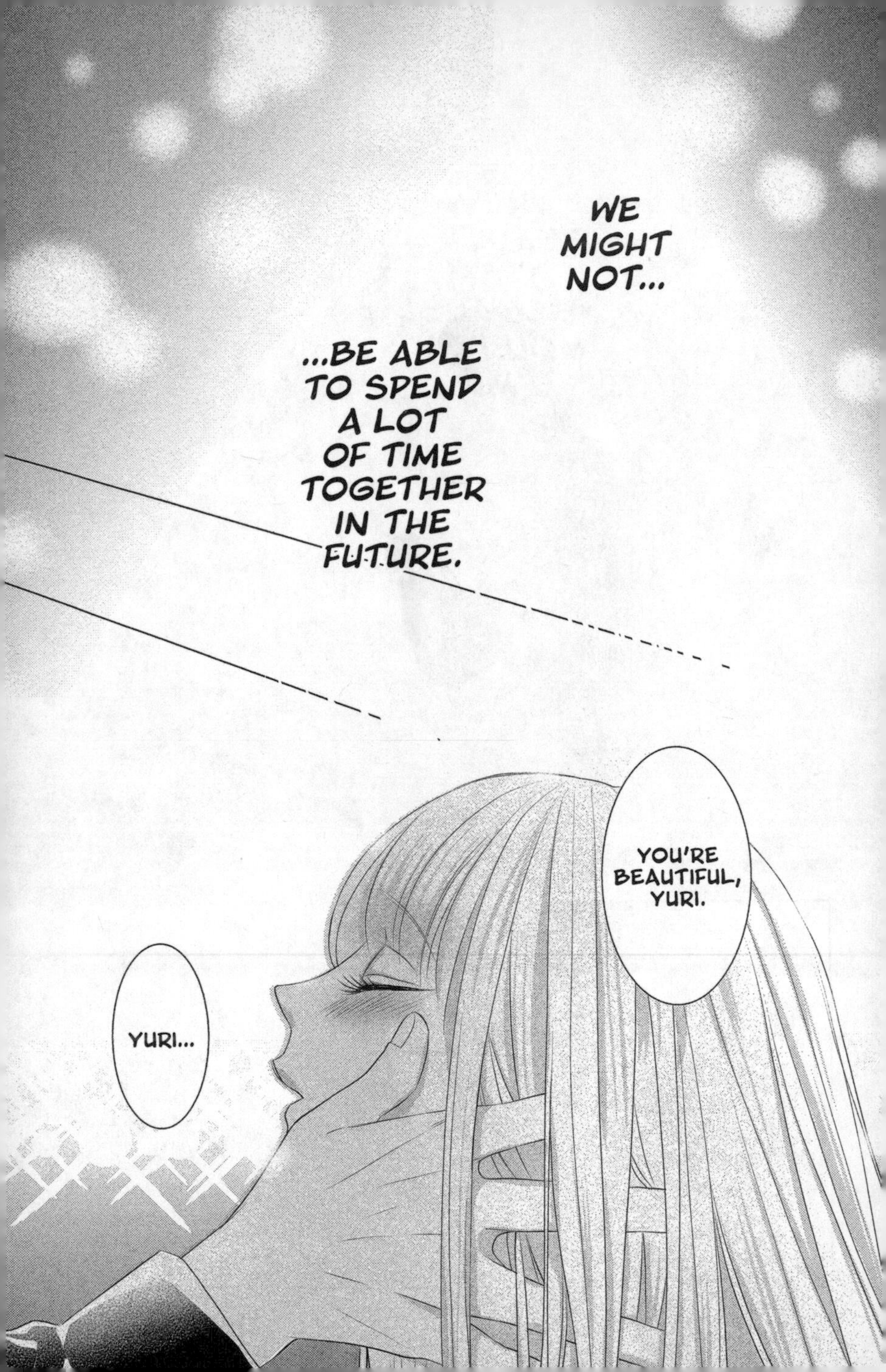
WE MIGHT NOT...
...BE ABLE TO SPEND A LOT OF TIME TOGETHER IN THE FUTURE.
YOU'RE BEAUTIFUL, YURI.
YURI...

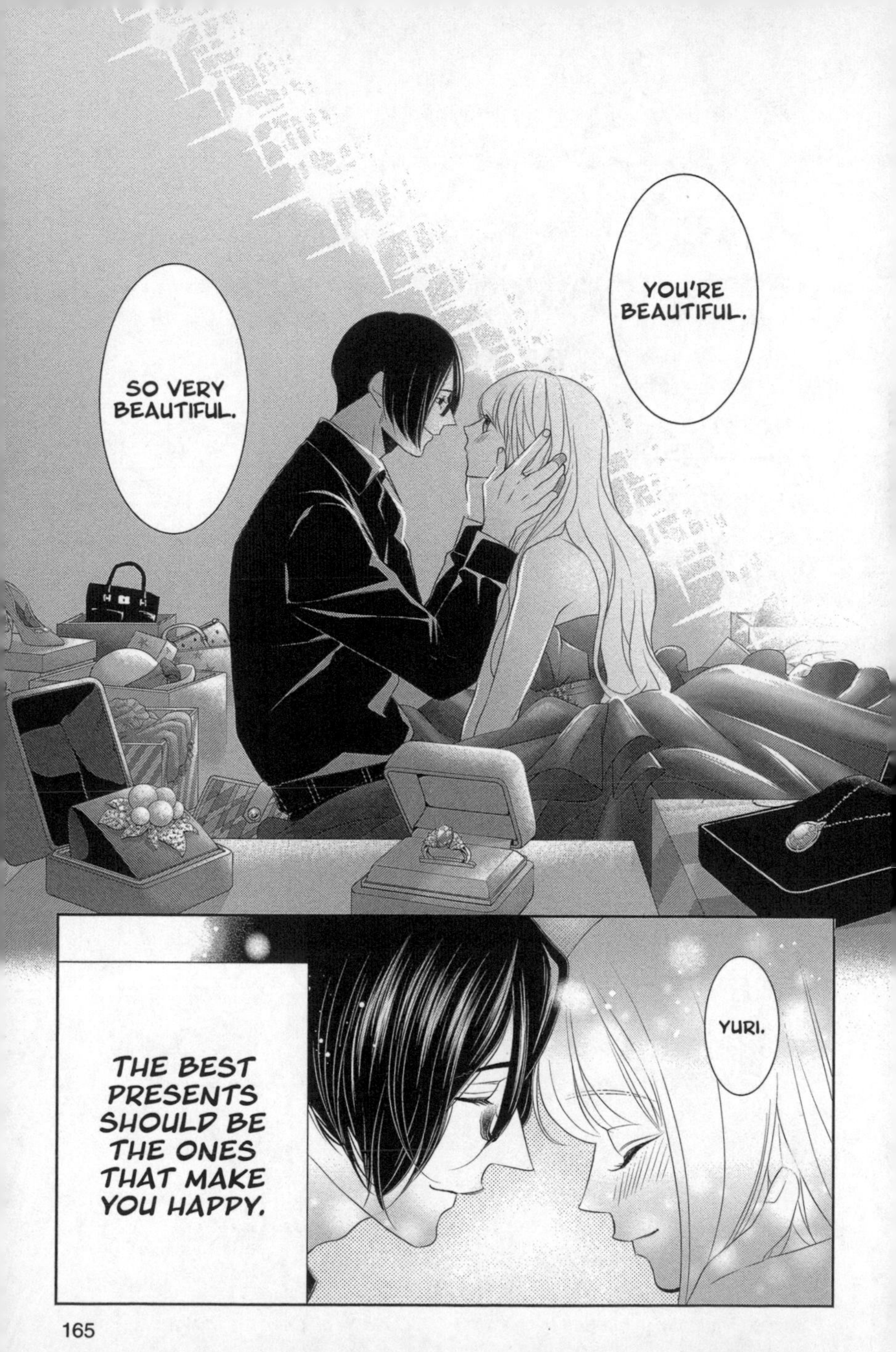
YOU'RE BEAUTIFUL.
SO VERY BEAUTIFUL.
YURI.
THE BEST PRESENTS SHOULD BE THE ONES THAT MAKE YOU HAPPY.

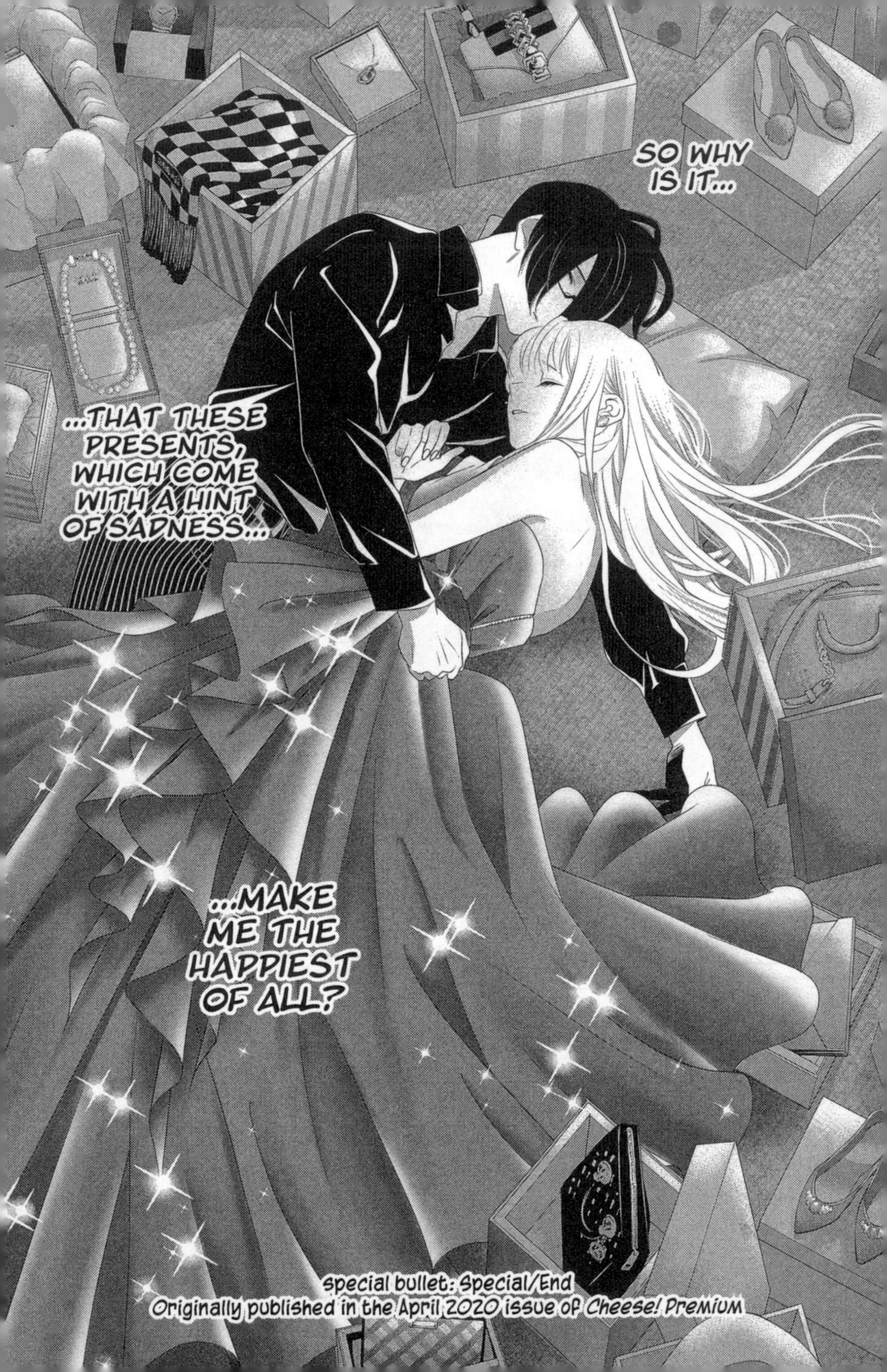
SO WHY IS IT...
...THAT THESE PRESENTS, WHICH COME WITH A HINT OF SADNESS...
...MAKE ME THE HAPPIEST OF ALL?
special bullet: Special/End
Originally published in the April 2020 issue of Cheese! Premium

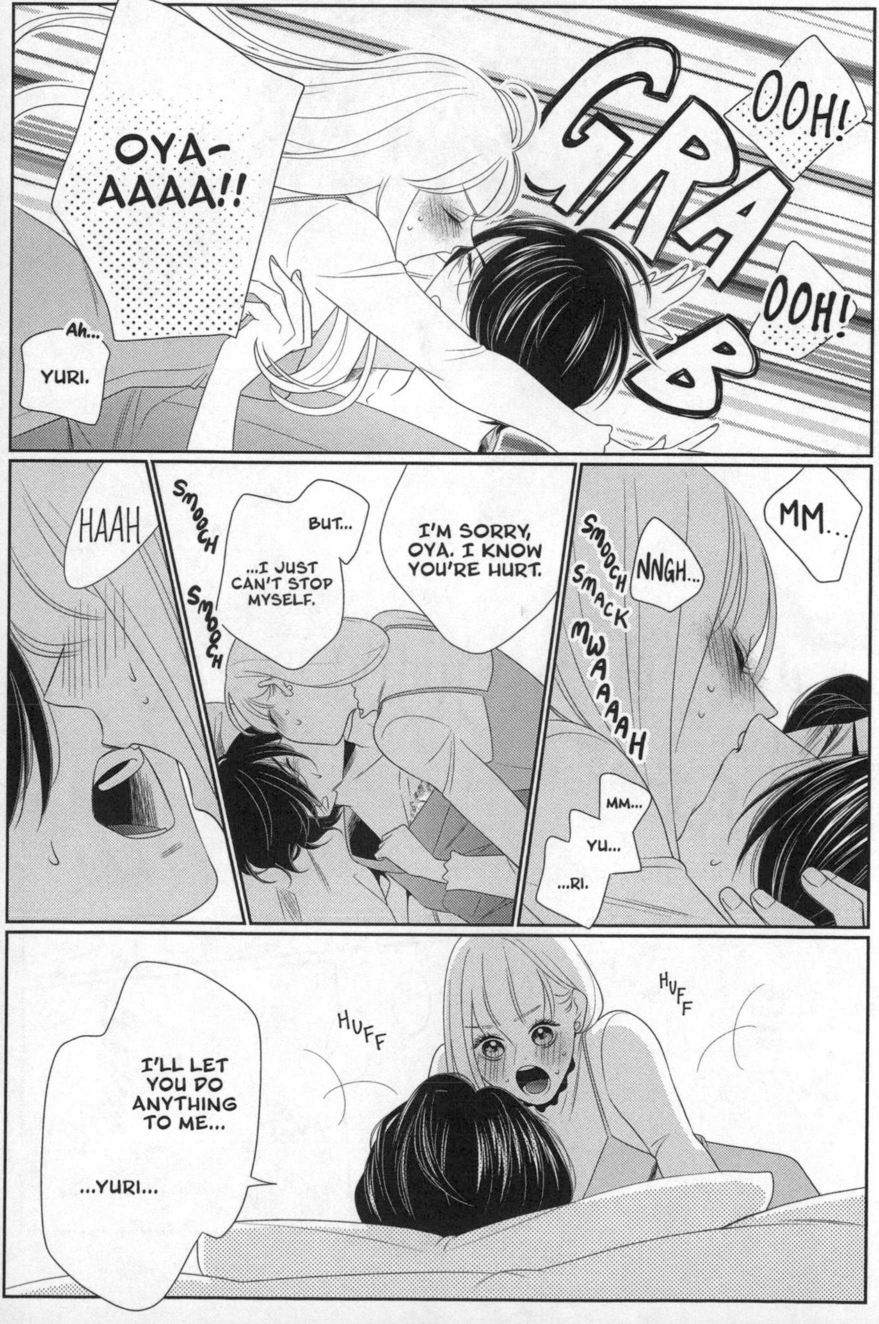
OOH!
GRAB
OOH!
OYA-AAAA!!
Ah... YURI.
MM...
NNGH...
SMOOCH SMACK MWAAAAAH
MM... YU... ...RI.
I'M SORRY, OYA. I KNOW YOU'RE HURT.
BUT... ...I JUST CAN'T STOP MYSELF.
SMOOCH SMOOCH
HAAH
HUFF
HUFF
I'LL LET YOU DO ANYTHING TO ME...
...YURI...

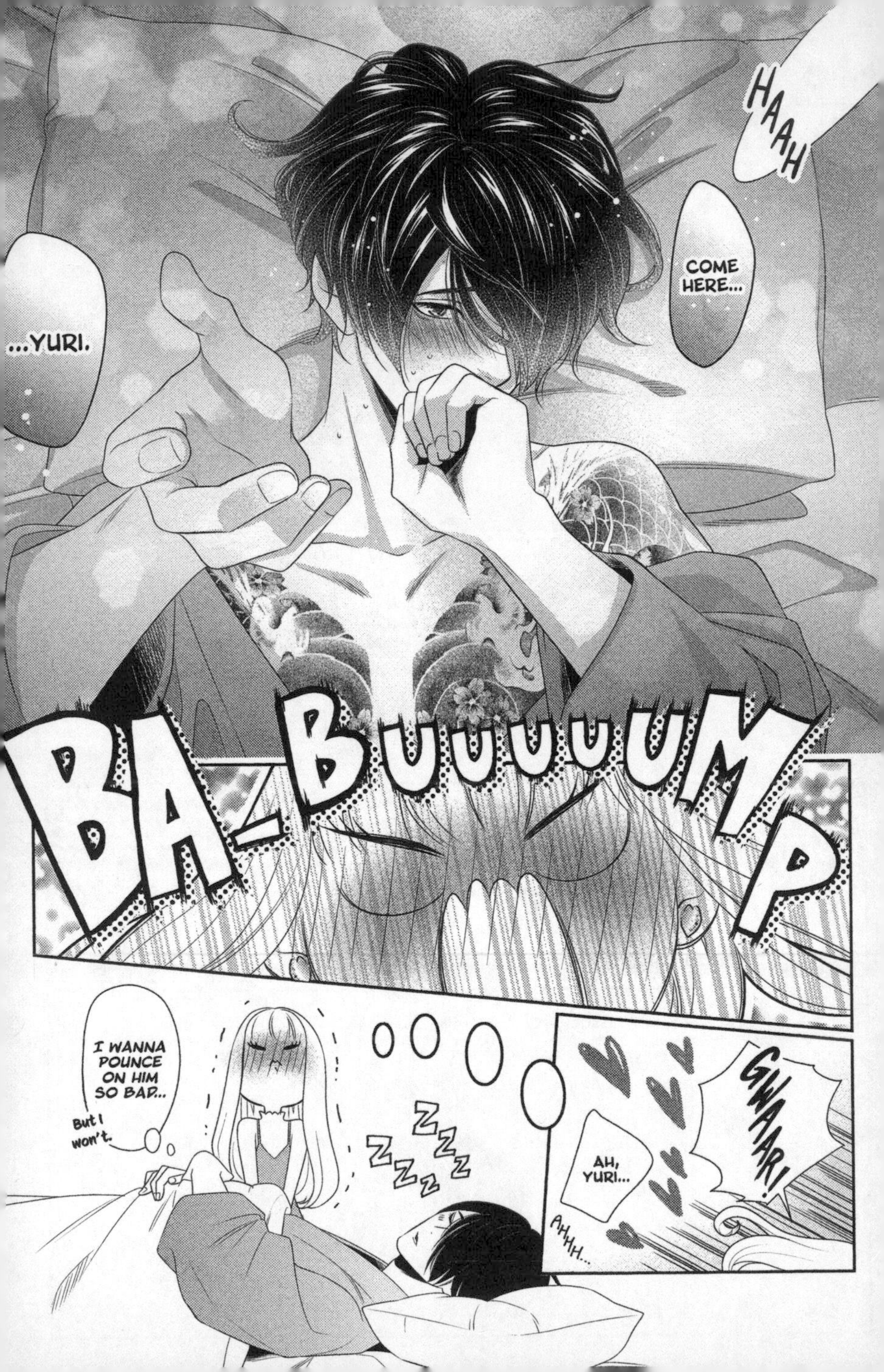
HAAAH
COME HERE...
...YURI.
BA-BUUUUUMP
GWAAAR!
AH, YURI...
AHHH...
I WANNA POUNCE ON HIM SO BAD...
But I won't.
ZZZZZZZ

Thank you so much for reading. I hope you enjoy the love triangle in this volume!

Follow *Yakuza Lover*'s official Twitter account @koidan_o_y

—Nozomi Mino

. . . .

Nozomi Mino was born on February 12 in Himeji, Hyogo Prefecture, in Japan, making her an Aquarius. She made her shojo manga debut in the May 2006 issue of *Cheese!* with "LOVE MANTEN" (Love Perfect Score). Since then, she has gone on to publish numerous works, including *Sweet Marriage*, *Wagamama Otoko wa Ichizu ni Koisuru* (Selfish Guys Love Hard), and *LOVE x PLACE.fam*. Her hobbies include going on drives and visiting cafes.

YAKUZA LOVER

Vol. 6
Shojo Beat Edition

STORY AND ART BY
Nozomi Mino

Translation: Andria Cheng
Touch-Up Art & Lettering: Michelle Pang
Design: Yukiko Whitley
Editor: Karla Clark

KOI TO DANGAN Vol. 6
by Nozomi MINO

Original Japanese edition published by SHOGAKUKAN.
English translation rights in the United States of America, Canada, the United Kingdom, Ireland, Australia and New Zealand arranged with SHOGAKUKAN.

Printed in the U.S.A.

Published by VIZ Media, LLC
P.O. Box 77010
San Francisco, CA 94107

10 9 8 7 6 5 4 3 2 1
First printing, September 2022

ratings.viz.com RATED M MATURE

PARENTAL ADVISORY
YAKUZA LOVER is rated M for Mature and is recommended for ages 18 and up. This volume contains sexually explicit content and realistic violence.

VIZ MEDIA
viz.com

Shojo Beat
shojobeat.com

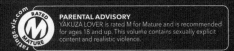

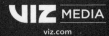

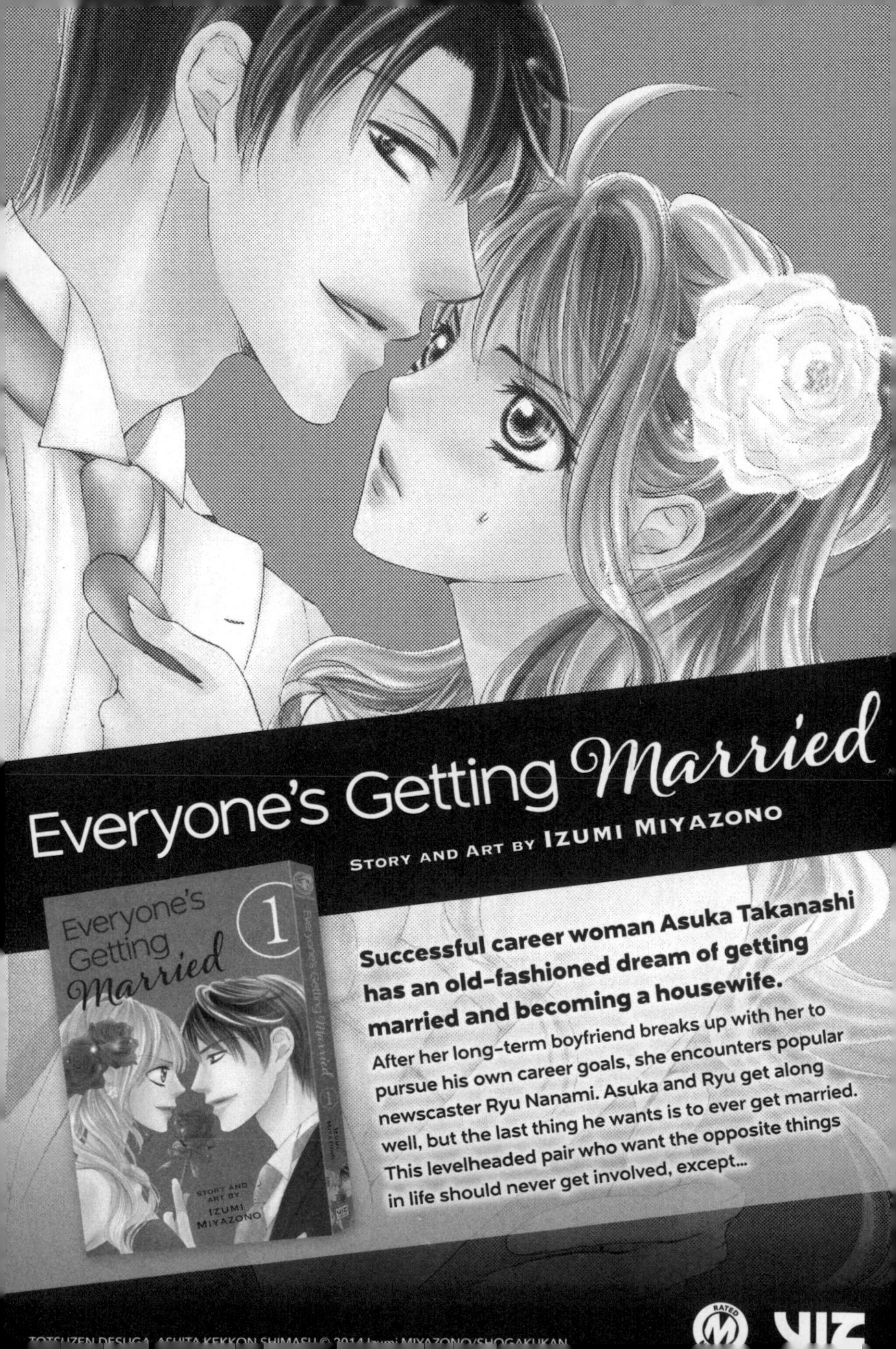
Everyone's Getting Married
Story and Art by Izumi Miyazono
Everyone's Getting Married 1
Story and Art by Izumi Miyazono
Successful career woman Asuka Takanashi has an old-fashioned dream of getting married and becoming a housewife.
After her long-term boyfriend breaks up with her to pursue his own career goals, she encounters popular newscaster Ryu Nanami. Asuka and Ryu get along well, but the last thing he wants is to ever get married. This levelheaded pair who want the opposite things in life should never get involved, except...
VIZ
TOTSUZEN DESUGA, ASHITA KEKKON SHIMASU © 2014 Izumi MIYAZONO/SHOGAKUKAN

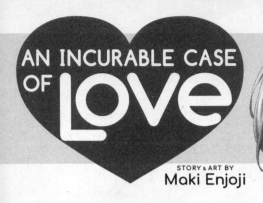

AN INCURABLE CASE OF LOVE

STORY & ART BY
Maki Enjoji

Nurse Nanase has striven to once again meet the prince of her dreams, so how is it he's become such an aggravating doctor?!

After witnessing a handsome and charming young doctor save a stranger's life five years ago, Nanase Sakura trained to become a nurse. But when she meets the doctor again and they start working together, she finds Kairi Tendo to be nothing like the man she imagined him to be!

VIZ

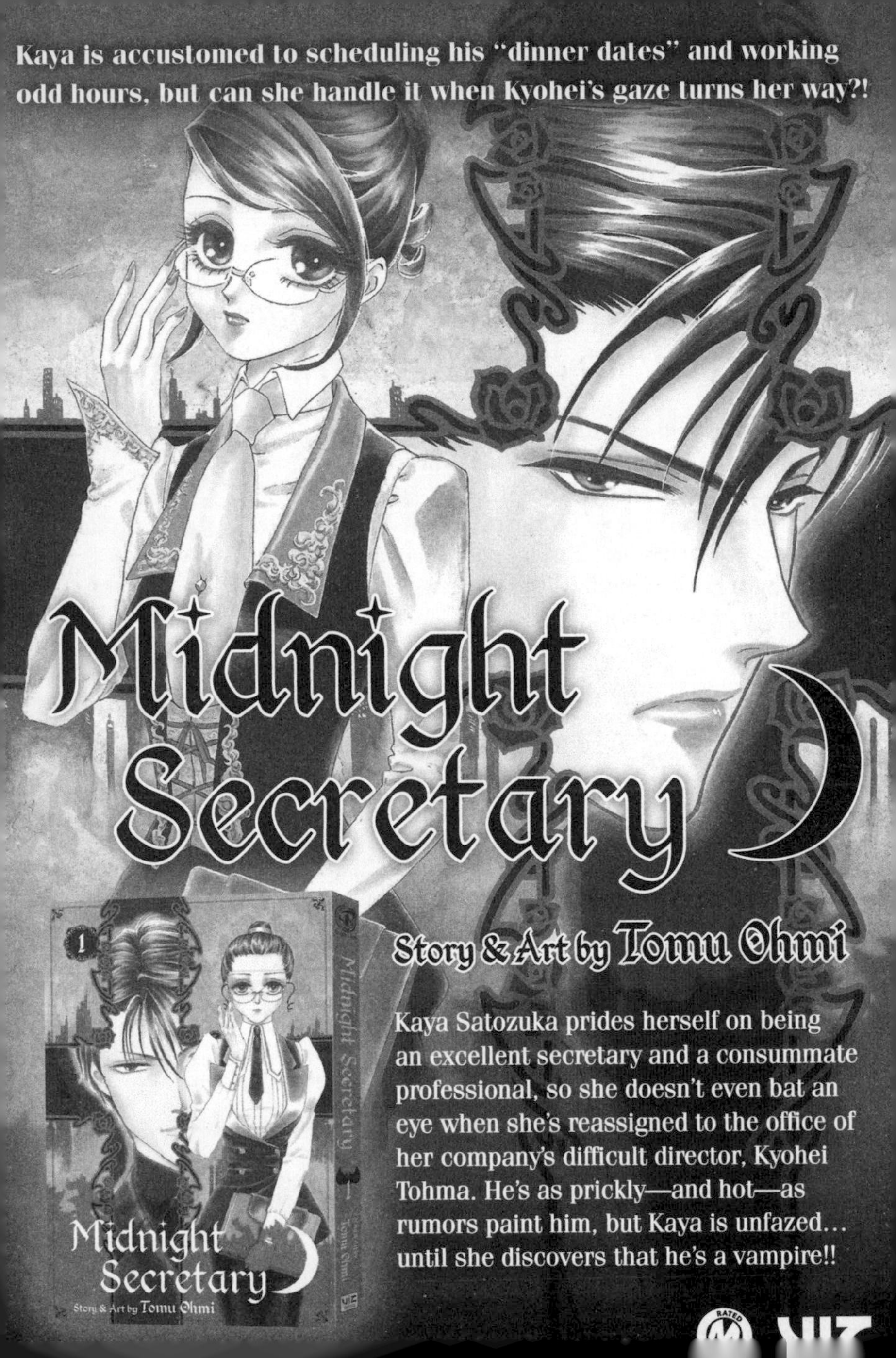
Kaya is accustomed to scheduling his "dinner dates" and working odd hours, but can she handle it when Kyohei's gaze turns her way?!
Midnight Secretary
Story & Art by Tomu Ohmi
1
Midnight Secretary
Story & Art by Tomu Ohmi
Kaya Satozuka prides herself on being an excellent secretary and a consummate professional, so she doesn't even bat an eye when she's reassigned to the office of her company's difficult director, Kyohei Tohma. He's as prickly—and hot—as rumors paint him, but Kaya is unfazed… until she discovers that he's a vampire!!

STOP RIGHT THERE!

You're reading the wrong way!

In keeping with the original Japanese comic format, *Yakuza Lover* reads from right to left, starting in the upper-right corner—so action, sound effects, and word-balloon order are completely reversed to preserve the orientation of the original artwork.

So go ahead and flip the book over. You wouldn't want to spoil the ending for yourself now, would you?

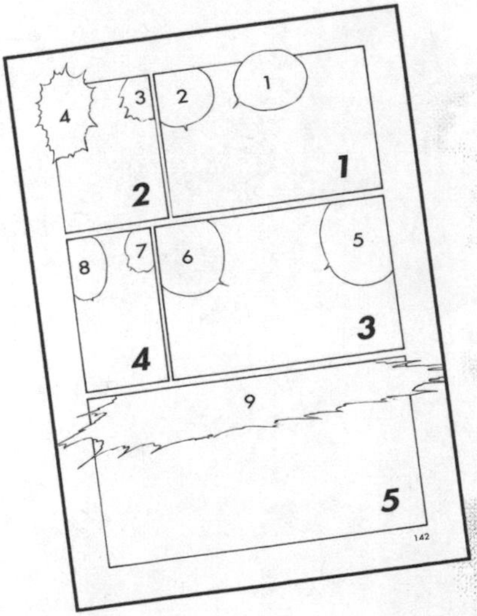
1
2
1
3
4
2
5
6
3
7
8
4
9
5
142

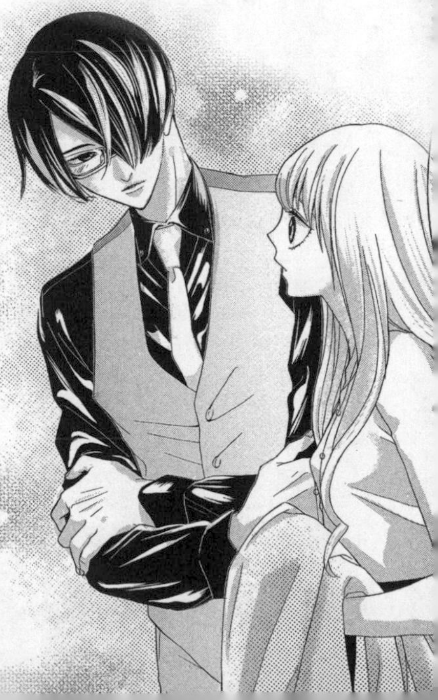

lolololol
So Cute It Hurts!! (>~<)

Story and Art by Go Ikeyamada

The Kobayashi twins, Megumu and Mitsuru, were named after historical figures, but only Megumu has grown up with a taste for history. So when Mitsuru is in danger of losing his weekends to extra history classes, he convinces his sister to swap clothes with him and ace his tests! After all, how hard can it be for them to play each other?

But Megumu can't rely on just her book smarts in Mitsuru's all-boys, delinquents' paradise of a high school. And Mitsuru finds life as a high school girl to be much more complicated than he expected!

VIZ **M** RATED MATURE

lolololol
So Cute It Hurts!! (>~<)
Story and Art by Go Ikeyamada